W9-CLM-199

INSIGHT GUIDE

GREAT BRITAIN

APA PUBLICATIONS

Part of the Langenscheidt Publishing Group

L

INSIGHT GUIDES
GREAT BRITAIN

ABOUT THIS BOOK

Editorial
Project Editor
Douglas Amrine
Editorial Director
Brian Bell

Distribution
UK & Ireland
GeoCenter International Ltd
The Viables Centre,
Harrow Way
Basingstoke, Hants,
RG22 4BJ
Fax: (44) 1256-817988

United States
Langenscheidt Publishers, Inc.
46–35 54th Road
Maspeth, NY 11378
Fax: (718) 784-0640

Worldwide
APA Publications GmbH & Co.
Verlag KG Singapore Branch, Singapore
38 Joo Koon Road
Singapore 628990
Tel: (65) 865-1600
Fax: (65) 861-6438

Printing
Insight Print Services (Pte) Ltd
38 Joo Koon Road
Singapore 628990
Tel: (65) 865-1600
Fax: (65) 861-6438

CONTACTING THE EDITORS
Although every effort is made to
provide accurate information in
this publication, we live in a
fast-changing world and would
appreciate it if readers would
call our attention to any errors or
outdated information that may
occur by writing to us at:
**Insight Guides, P.O. Box 7910,
London SE1 8ZB, England.
Fax: (44 171) 620-1074.**
e-mail:
insight@apaguide.demon.co.uk

The British remain ambivalent about tourism. They hate to think that their small offshore island, once the focus of the world's greatest empire, is in danger of becoming a museum, displaying its proud history as mere "heritage". But those tourist dollars are awfully useful.

This book sheds light on such attitudes with some authority since Insight Guides' editorial HQ is located in London, dubbed by *Newsweek* magazine as the world's coolest city. Having produced more than 30 Insight, Pocket and Compact Guides to various parts of Great Britain, the series' editors distilled their accumulated wisdom and knowledge into this introductory guide.

How to use this book
The book is carefully structured both to convey an understanding of the country and its culture, and to guide readers through its sights and activities:

◆ To understand Britain today, one needs to know something of its past. The first section covers its history and culture in lively essays.

◆ The main Places section provides a full run-down of all the attractions and destinations worth seeing. Places of major interest are coordinated by

Above: 17th-century embroidery of Charles II (left) and Charles I as martyr.

number with full-colour maps.

◆ The Travel Tips section provides essential information on travel, hotels, restaurants, shops and festivals. The relevant facts may be located quickly by using the index printed on the back cover flap, which can serve as a handy bookmark.

THE CONTRIBUTORS

This edition's project editor, **Douglas Amrine**, an American long resident in London, brought to bear wide experience of guidebook editing and was able to build on the work of two previous editors, **Merin Wexler** and **Roger Williams**. He was also able to call on the expertise of **Tony Halliday**, who has orchestrated 20 Insight Compact Guides to every part of the UK, and **Brian Bell**, the series' editorial director.

Pam Barrett, who squeezed several thousand years of British history into a manageable size, has a history degree from London University.

The A–Z section, designed to allow readers to dip into many aspects of British culture, enabled the editors to give full rein to their hobby-horses, and contributions also came from several experienced London-based freelance journalists, including **Richard Johnson**, **Angela Wilkes**, and **Daniela Soave**. The items on the Monarchy and on Pubs, updated from the first edition, were written by **Alan Hamilton** of *The Times*.

Contributors to the Places section include **Andrew Eames**, **Roland Collins**, **Joseph Yogerst**, **William Ruddick**, **Iain Crawford**, **Marcus Brooke** and **Gwyneth Lewis**.

Photographers include Insight Guide regulars **Glyn Genin**, **Bill Wassman**, **David Beatty** and the series' founder **Hans Höfer**.

Clare Griffiths updated sight opening times, while **Sue Platt** updated the Travel Tips and added many hotels and restaurants. The book was proofread and indexed by **Penny Phenix**, who also wrote on ancient monuments and stately homes.

Map Legend

‒‒ ‒‒	International Boundary
‒‒ ‒‒	National Boundary
‒ ‒ ‒	County Boundary
‒ • ‒	National Park
‒ ‒ ‒	Ferry Route
⊖	Underground
✈	Airport
🚐	Bus Station
Ⓟ	Parking
ⓘ	Tourist Information
✉	Post Office
✝	Church/Ruins
	Mosque
	Synagogue
	Castle/Ruins
∴	Archaeological Site
∩	Cave
★	Place of Interest

The main places of interest in the **Places** section are cross-referenced to a full-colour map by letter or number (e.g. ❶). A symbol at the top of each right-hand page tells you where to find the relevant map.

Contributors

Amrine   Bell

Barrett   Eames

Contents

A map of Great Britain
is on the inside front cover.

A map of Central London
is on the inside back cover.

A rural
post office
in the
heart of
England

Travel Tips

Insight on ...

Information panels

Places

THE BRITISH CHARACTER

If the English are ambiguous, the Welsh loquacious and the Scots cantankerous, how do they all manage to get along on the same overcrowded island?

Millions of people in Britain, wrote George Orwell in 1947, "willingly accept as their national emblem the bulldog, an animal noted for its obstinacy, ugliness, and impenetrable stupidity." A foreigner, he went on, would find the salient characteristics of the common people to be "artistic insensibility, gentleness, respect for legality, suspicion of foreigners, sentimentality about animals, hypocrisy, exaggerated class distinctions, and an obsession with sport."

The Welsh and the Scots would point out that Orwell was thinking primarily of the English who, to the fury of the Welsh and Scots, persistently equate the terms "British" and "English".

The contradictory English

But then the English have a gift for ambiguity. As a character in Alan Bennett's play *The Old Country* put it: "When we say we don't mean what we say, only then are we entirely serious." If that seems contradictory, there's worse to come. The British embrace marriage more frequently than any other European nation, yet their divorce rate is second only to Denmark's. On average, they work more hours per week than any other European Community country (43.9 hours for men), yet their productivity is lowest. They have 54,600 churches, but by far the lowest active church membership in Europe (14 percent of the total population). They laud family life, yet many prefer to send their children off to boarding school as soon as possible and park their aged parents in old people's homes. They pride themselves on their solidarity in war, yet cling to a divisive class system in peacetime.

They are also famed for their tolerance and sense of humour, yet, as the writer Paul Gallico observed: "No one can be as calculatedly rude as the British, which amazes Americans, who do not understand studied insult and can only offer abuse as a substitute." Britain's nearest neighbours can be just as amazed as Americans. André Maurois advised his fellow countrymen: "In France it is rude to let a conversation drop; in England it is rash to keep it up. No one there will blame you for silence. When you have not

opened your mouth for three years, they will think, 'This Frenchman is a nice quiet fellow'."

The truth, as always, is more complicated. If Maurois had been in Liverpool or in Leeds, in Glasgow or in Cardiff, he might not have got a word in. The Englishman who has "all the qualities of a poker except its occasional warmth" probably lives in the overcrowded southeast, where standoffishness is a way of protecting precious privacy.

But certain generalisations can be made. Because Britain is an island its people have retained their bachelor outlook despite marrying into the European Union. Because it has not been successfully invaded for nearly 1,000

PRECEDING PAGES: Knights of the Most Noble Order of the Garter parade at Windsor Castle; following the fillies at Ascot; on the river at Eton; punts at St John's College, Cambridge. **LEFT:** patriotism at the summer Promenade Concerts. **ABOVE:** dressed to shop.

years, Britain remains deeply individualistic. On the one hand, its people perhaps overvalue tradition – a substitute for thought, critics say; on the other hand, they tend not to kill one another in civil conflict and they have absorbed, with relatively little civic pain, large numbers of their former imperial subjects.

The voluble Welsh

To the English, the Welsh appear a much more homogeneous group than themselves: ebullient, warm-hearted and emotional but also rather sly and extremely garrulous. A certain amount of antipathy exists. Evelyn Waugh, for instance,

but homogeneous. Many in North Wales, where Welsh is still widely spoken, look down on people from South Wales whose blood is much more mixed and whose habits are thought too anglicised. Naturally, South Walians return the compliment by regarding North Walians as less progressive and less sociable.

Whether their preferred tongue is English or Welsh, however, there is no point in denying that most of the Welsh are extremely voluble. "It is not so long ago," remembers the poet Dannie Abse, "that the trains leaving from London for South Wales consisted of separate carriages – that is, they were not open-planned. Then, half

claimed in his novel *Decline and Fall*: "We can trace almost all the disasters of English history to the influence of Wales." And Shakespeare poked fun at Welsh hyperbole by having the Welsh hero Owain Glyndwr boast, in *Henry V*, "I can call spirits from the vasty deep" – only to be put down by Hotspur, who replies, "So can any man; but will they come?" The Welsh, for their part, have had to work hard, like many minority nations, to protect their self-esteem and culture from a strong neighbour, but have been wary of independence.

Within Wales itself, the people seem anything

SKILL WITH WORDS

The gift of the gab was nourished in the 19th century, when Wales was fertile ground for preachers and trade union leaders.

a dozen strangers would look out of the window, or suck their mints, or read their newspapers, but they would not speak to each other. It was not the 'done' English thing. The English are happy with few words and like to keep strangers at a comfortable distance from themselves. And in a train leaving England for Wales, who knows who is not English? Only when the train had passed through the Severn Tunnel, only when the passengers felt themselves to be safely in Wales, only then would the carriage suddenly hum with conversation."

The uncompromising Scots

In contrast, the Scots are seen by the English as "dour", though they'd be hard put to justify the claim in a noisy Glasgow pub. English literature is peppered with anti-Scots aphorisms, such as P.G. Wodehouse's observation that "it is never difficult to distinguish between a Scotsman with a grievance and a ray of sunshine."

The Scots' principal grievance is that the London-based parliament treats them as second-class citizens, especially when imple-

THE INSCRUTABLE ISLE

To understand Great Britain, its people will tell you, will take many visits. This, bearing in mind their inability to say exactly what they mean, translates as: "Although we regard tourism as terribly vulgar, we do rather need the repeat business."

the differences in character are long-established. Unlike the English and Welsh, the Scots were never conquered by the Romans, and they also avoided Norman centralisation after the Conquest in 1066. Their religious experience also set them apart: while England absorbed the Reformation with a series of cunning compromises, Scotland underwent a revolution, replacing the panoply of Roman Catholicism with an aus-

menting its economic policies. This is far from being a new complaint, having been echoed long before the two nations united in 1707 in what most Scots still regard as a shotgun marriage. Indeed, when the future Pope Pius II visited the country in the 15th century, he concluded: "Nothing pleases the Scots more than abuse of the English."

That's not to say that the Scots can't cooperate with the English when it suits them: the work ethic and ingenuity of Scots played a major role in creating the British Empire. But

tere Presbyterianism designed to put the people directly in touch with their God. No man was deemed inherently better than the next.

In many ways, the Scots character baffles the English. It combines sourness and humour, meanness and generosity, arrogance and tolerance, cantankerousness and chivalry, sentimentality and hard-headedness. A *Punch* cartoon caught some of these contradictions by showing a hitchhiker trying to entice passing motorists with a sign reading "Glasgow – or else!"

In 1997 the Scots voted to set up their own parliament in Edinburgh. This will give them a degree of independence – but a divorce from England, most insist, is highly unlikely. ❑

LEFT: Welsh couple at the Eisteddfod, Llangollen.
ABOVE: spectators at a Highland games in Scotland.

1   2   3   4   5   6   7

8   9   10   11   12   13   14   15

16   17   18   19   20   21   22   23

DECISIVE DATES

Britain has history like the Sahara has sand. Here are the main milestones...

PREHISTORY

250,000 BC: First evidence of human life.
5000 BC: Britain becomes an island.
3000 BC: Stone-age people arrive, probably from the Iberian peninsula.
2000 BC: Stonehenge built.
700 BC: Celts arrive from central Europe.

ROMAN OCCUPATION (55 BC–AD 410)

55 BC: Julius Caesar heads first Roman invasion.
AD 43: Conquest begins under emperor Claudius.
AD 61: Rebellion of Boudicca, Queen of Iceini in East Anglia, crushed.
AD 119: Hadrian's Wall built to keep back Picts and Scots.

ANGLO-SAXON & DANISH KINGS (449–1066)

449–550: Arrival of Jutes from Jutland, Angles from south of Denmark and Saxons from Germany, around Hanover.
563: St Columba establishes monastery on island of Iona, Scotland.
597: St Augustine arrives to convert English and becomes first Archbishop of Canterbury.
779: King Offa builds dyke to keep out Welsh.
843: Kenneth MacAlpine unites Picts and Scots.
897: Danish Vikings are defeated at sea by Alfred the Great, generally regarded as being the founder of the British navy.
980–1016: Viking invasions renewed.
1017: Canute, first Danish king, chosen by the Witan (council).

THE NORMANS (1066–1154)

1066: Conquest of England by William, Duke of Normandy. Authority and parcels of land are given to French-speaking Norman barons.
1080–1100: Great monastery and cathedral building begins.
1086: Domesday Book, a complete inventory of Britain, is completed.
1124: David I succeeds to Scottish throne.
1167: Oxford University founded.

PRECEDING PAGES: Stonehenge. **LEFT:** costumes from medieval Britain. **RIGHT:** William the Conqueror.

THE PLANTAGENETS (1154–1399)

1154: Henry II, descendent of Geoffrey of Anjou, inherits the throne, thus starting the line of Angevin kings. He owned more land in France than he did in Britain.
1170: Archbishop Thomas Becket murdered.
1215: Barons force King John to sign Magna Carta.
1265: The first House of Commons.

1277–88: English conquest of Wales. Llewellyn ab Gruffydd, the country's last prince, is killed.
1306: Robert Bruce crowned King of the Scots.
1348–49: The Black Death plague kills nearly half the population.
1337–1453: Hundred Years' War with France.
1350–1550: Gothic perpendicular flourished.
1381: Peasants' Revolt.
1387: Chaucer's *Canterbury Tales* published.

HOUSES OF LANCASTER AND YORK (1399–1485)

1415: Owain Glyndwr, Welsh hero, dies.
1455–85: Wars of the Roses between the competing Houses of York and Lancaster.
1412: St Andrew's University founded.

1476: William Caxton sets up Britain's first printing press.

THE TUDORS (1485–1558)

1485: Henry VII, grandson of the Welsh Owain Tudor, crowned king.
1509: Henry VIII succeeds to the throne.
1534: Papal authority in England abolished.
1535: Henry VIII becomes Supreme Head of the Church of England.
1536–39: Destruction or closure of 560 monasteries and religious houses.
1536: Act of Union joins England and Wales.
1558: Under Queen Mary, England's last posses-

sion on the Continent, Calais, falls to France.
1558: Elizabeth I begins her 45-year reign.
1558: John Knox, Scottish disciple of Calvin, launches First Blast of the Trumpet against the Monstrous Regiment of Women.
1580: Sir Francis Drake (pictured below) completes circumnavigation of the world.
1585: William Shakespeare begins his dramatic career in London.
1587: Mary, Queen of Scots is executed.
1588: The Spanish Armada is defeated.

THE STUARTS (1603–1714)

1603: James VI of Scotland, son of Mary, Queen of Scots, is crowned James I of England, uniting the two kingdoms.
1605: Guy Fawkes tries to blow up parliament.
1620: Pilgrim Fathers set sail for America.
1642–49: Civil War between Royalists and republican Roundheads. Many castles and fortified houses razed. Defeated, Charles I is beheaded.
1660: Monarchy reinstated with Charles II.
1665: The Great Plague of London.
1666: The Great Fire of London.
1672–1700: St Paul's Cathedral, in London, is built.
1694: Bank of England established.

THE HOUSE OF HANOVER (1714–1936)

1714: George I of Hanover, Germany, is invited to take the throne. He speaks no English and shows very little interest in his new subjects.
1721: Sir Robert Walpole becomes Britain's first prime minister, a new parliamentary concept.
1739: Wesley begins to preach Methodism.
1775: James Watt makes the first steam engine.

ENGLISH MONARCHS SINCE THE NORMAN CONQUEST

NORMAN	LANCASTER	STUART	HANOVER
William 1066-87	Henry IV 1399-1413	James I 1603-25	George I 1714-27
William II 1087-1100	Henry V 1413-22	Charles I 1625-49	George II 1727-60
Henry I 1100-35	Henry VI 1422-61	[Commonwealth	George III 1760-1820
Stephen 1135-54	**YORK**	1649-53	George IV 1820-30
PLANTAGENET	Edward IV 1461-83	Protectorate 1653-60]	William IV 1830-37
Henry II 1154-89	Edward V 1483	Charles II 1660-85	**SAXE-COBURG-GOTHA**
Richard I 1189-99	Richard III 1483-85	James II 1685-89	Victoria 1837-1901
John 1199-1216	**TUDOR**	William and Mary	Edward VII 1901-10
Henry III 1216-72	Henry VII 1485-1509	1689-1702	**WINDSOR** (from 1917)
Edward I 1272-1307	Henry VIII 1509-47	Anne 1702-1714	George V 1910-36
Edward II 1307-27	Edward VI 1547-53		Edward VIII 1936
Edward III 1327-77	Mary 1553-58		George VI 1936-52
Richard II 1377-99	Elizabeth I 1558-1603		Elizabeth II from 1952

1786: Robert Burns dazzles Edinburgh society.
1802: J.M.W. Turner elected to Royal Academy aged 27, the same year John Constable first exhibits at the Academy.
1805: Death of Admiral Lord Nelson at the crucial Battle of Trafalgar.
1807: Abolition of the slave trade.
1815: Duke of Wellington defeats Napoleon Bonaparte at Battle of Waterloo in modern Belgium.
1830: Liverpool to Manchester railway opened.

THE VICTORIAN AGE (1837–1901)

1837: Victoria becomes Queen, aged 18. She marries Albert of Saxe-Coburg three years later.
1851: The Great Exhibition held in London.
1853–56: Crimean War against Russia, the first major war to be photographed.
1857: Indian Mutiny results in Britain taking over administration of the East India Company.
1876: The Queen becomes Empress of India.
1890–96: Cecil Rhodes, founder of Rhodesia, becomes prime minister of Cape Colony, South Africa. His ambition is to see British territory extend across the whole continent.
1898–1902 Boer War to settle South Africa between British and Dutch.

THE EDWARDIAN ERA (1901–14)

1909: Charles Rennie Mackintosh completes Glasgow School of Art.
1909: Old age pensions introduced.
1909: Bleriot flies the English Channel.
1914–18: World War I. More than 1 million Britons and Allies die, mainly in northern France.

HOUSE OF WINDSOR (*so named from 1917*)

1918: Universal suffrage (except women under 30).
1926: General Strike paralyses the nation.
1927: The BBC is founded.
1936: Edward VIII abdicates so that he can marry a divorcée, Mrs Wallis Simpson.
1939–45: World War II. Fewer military casualties than World War I, but many civilians die in heavy bombing of ports and cities.
1946: National Health Service established.
1947: Edinburgh Festival begun, Welsh Eisteddfod re-established.
1947: India and Pakistan gain independence.
1951: Festival of Britain.
1953: Coronation of Queen Elizabeth II.

LEFT: Sir Francis Drake, Elizabethan adventurer. **RIGHT:** Queen Victoria, who ruled the world's largest empire.

1961: South Africa leaves Commonwealth because of apartheid policy.
1962: The Beatles enter the pop charts with their first hit, Love Me Do.
1965: Capital punishment is abolished.
1969: Sectarian strife breaks out in Northern Ireland; troops sent in.
1972: Northern Ireland government removed and replaced with direct rule from Westminster.
1973: Britain joins the European Community.
1979: Margaret Thatcher becomes Britain's first woman prime minister.
1981: Prince of Wales weds Lady Diana Spencer.
1982: Argentinian troops beaten off the Crown

Colony of the Falkland Islands.
1984: IRA bomb aimed at the Conservative government in conference at Brighton kills five people.
1990: Tory party sacks Margaret Thatcher.
1994: Britain rejoins the Continent as the first trains start running through the Channel Tunnel.
1996: Shakespeare's Globe, a replica of the theatre burnt down in 1599, opens in London.
1997: The Labour Party, led by Tony Blair, wins its first general election since 1974. In referenda, the Scots and the Welsh vote for limited devolution of power from Westminster. New talks on Northern Ireland's future get under way. Diana, Princess of Wales, dies in a car crash in Paris.
1998: A controversial, costly Millennium Dome at Greenwich, London, gets government backing. ❑

PICT

FEMALE PICT

ANCIENT DRUID

ANCIENT BRITON

THE CELTIC DAWN

One wave of immigrants followed another, creating a truly mongrel breed.

Then came the conquerors: the Romans, Saxons, Angles and Normans

When French and British construction workers met beneath the English Channel in 1990, Britain became linked to Continental Europe for the first time in 7,000 years. For it was then, when the last Ice Age ended, that melting ice flooded the low-lying lands, creating the English Channel and the North Sea, and turning Britain into an island. This fact of being "set apart" from Europe was one of two seemingly contradictory factors which would affect every aspect of the country's subsequent history. The other was a genius for absorbing every invader and immigrant, creating a mongrel breed whose energies would establish an empire incorporating a quarter of the population of the planet.

Early settlers

A race of nomadic hunter-gatherers were the earliest inhabitants. By about 3000 BC tribes of Neolithic people had crossed the water from Europe, probably from the Iberian peninsula, now Spain. They were farming folk who kept animals and grew crops. The barrows which can still be found, mostly in the chalky lands of Wiltshire and Dorset, were their huge communal burial mounds.

More dramatic monuments were the henges, the most important of which was Stonehenge in Wiltshire, constructed before 2000 BC. Exactly why it was built is unknown, but it must have had religious and political significance; the massive undertaking involved in bringing bluestones all the way from Wales for part of its construction suggests that its builders had a substantial power base. Although in popular mythology Druids are associated with Stonehenge, they were Celtic priests who arrived much later. They met in sacred groves, usually near water, the symbol of fertility, and there is evidence that they made human sacrifices.

At about the time Stonehenge was built another race arrived from Europe. With them they brought the art of pottery making, the abil-

ity to fashion bronze tools and the custom of individual burial. Because decorated pottery beakers have been found in their graves, they are known as Beaker people. They appear to have accepted the existing culture and many were buried at Stonehenge. But they developed their own farming society and built hill forts

which took over the role of henges. These forts, of which Maiden Castle in Dorset is one of the finest examples, became small fortified towns.

As far as can be known – and, by definition, very little can be known about pre-history except through archaeological finds and modern dating methods – the next wave of immigrants were the Celts. They began to arrive about 700 BC and kept coming until the arrival of the Romans. They may originally have come from eastern and central Europe and they probably became dominant because, being iron-workers, their weapons were superior. They seem to have been a more sophisticated people altogether. They drained much of the marsh-

LEFT: early Britons. **RIGHT:** early map.

lands and built houses of wood and wickerwork with a weatherproof coating of mud. The Celtic tribes are ancestors of the Highland Scots, the Irish and the Welsh, and their languages are the basis of both Welsh and Gaelic.

We have been left with a rich legacy of intricate and beautiful Celtic metalwork, some purely decorative, some with religious significance and many fine examples can be seen in London's British Museum.

The Celts have given history an undeniably famous figure: Boadicea (or Boudicca) queen of the Iceni in what is now East Anglia. She is said to have been tall, red-haired and fearsome,

and she attempted to drive the Romans from Britain in AD 61. She succeeded in destroying their capital, Londinium, before being defeated. Her bravery and that of other female warriors was reported by her Roman enemies.

The Romans

British recorded history begins with the Roman invasion. Julius Caesar first crossed the English Channel and arrived in Britain in 55 BC but, meeting resistance and bad weather, he returned to Gaul. The successful invasion did not take place until nearly a century later, in AD 43, headed by the Emperor Claudius. This time, the land they knew by its Greco-Roman name, Pre-

tani, was subdued with relative ease, apart from the country in the far north they called Caledonia (now Scotland). To repel persistent raids by the warlike Picts, or "painted ones", the Emperor Hadrian had a wall built right across the north of England. Much of the wall still remains, running from Carlisle to Newcastle, but the border with Scotland is now further north. When raids continued, a second wall was built by the Emperor Antoninus Pius, linking the firths (estuaries) of the Forth and the Clyde, but this also failed to contain the Picts.

The Romans remained in control of Pretani, renamed Britannia, for nearly 400 years. Then, with barbarians at the gates of Rome, under repeated attacks from Picts and also from the Scots (the "tattoed ones" who invaded from the north of Ireland) and needing to set up a new military front on the east coast to repel the Germanic Saxon tribes invading from Europe, they pulled out.

Behind them they left a network of towns, mostly walled, many on the sites of Celtic settlements or their own military camps. The suffix *-caster* or *-chester* in English place names – Lancaster, Winchester and Chester itself – derives from *castra*, the Latin word for camp. The Roman capital was London (Londinium), York had been created as a northern stronghold and Bath (Aquae Sulis) rapidly developed because of its medicinal waters. Many of these centres were linked by a network of roads, so well constructed that they survived for centuries and became the routes of other, much later, highways. Their main purpose was military, but they also encouraged trade by enabling goods to be moved rapidly about the country. The most famous, Watling Street, stretched from Dover to Chester, and passed through London.

The Romans also utilised Britain's natural resources, mining lead, iron and tin and manufacturing pottery. They constructed baths, temples, amphitheatres and ornate and beautiful villas, some with rudimentary under-floor central heating, the remains of which can still be seen today. They also brought literacy to the country, the use of the Latin language and the new religion, Christianity. This came at first by indirect means, probably brought by traders and soldiers, and was quite well-established before the first Christian Emperor, Constantine, was proclaimed in AD 306.

But the majority of the indigenous people

continued to live much as they had before Roman rule and, when the conquerors left, their influence faded surprisingly fast. Buildings crumbled through lack of repair and language, literacy and religion soon disappeared.

Anglo-Saxon assault

The new wave of invaders from central Europe, Saxons, Angles and Jutes, gradually pushed the native Celts westward into Wales and north into Scotland. The Saxons established their kingdoms in Essex, Sussex and Wessex (which covered most of the West Country), the Jutes were confined to Kent, and the Angles settled in East

Picts and Scots were finally united into a kingdom under King Kenneth MacAlpine.

In the mid-9th century the Danes or Norsemen, popularly known as Vikings, who had been raiding the country for almost a century and taking their booty home, decided it was time to settle. Of the local leaders, Alfred of Wessex (AD 871–901) was the only one strong enough to defeat them and come to a relatively amicable agreement. The Danes, who established a large settlement in York, were to control the north and east of the country, ("the Danelaw"), while Alfred would rule the rest. Alfred is known as "the father of the British

Anglia, Mercia (the Midlands and the Welsh borders) and Northumbria, which reached to the Scottish border. This border was still well-defended and a Northumbrian attack on Scotland in the 7th century was swiftly repulsed.

For the next four centuries the Anglo-Saxons battled it out among themselves. Offa, the King of Mercia (AD 757–797), emerged as a strong leader and built Offa's Dyke along the border with Wales to contain the Celts in this mountainous region. But, after his death, Wessex became the dominant kingdom. In Scotland, the

LEFT: Victorian depiction of Caesar's arrival in Britain.
ABOVE: Roman mosaic found in Dorset.

navy" as he founded a strong fleet which first beat the Danes at sea, then protected the coasts and encouraged trade.

Although the Anglo-Saxons were a ferocious bunch, constantly squabbling, they laid the foundations of the English state. They divided the country into shires (which the Normans later called counties) and devised the narrow-strip, three-field farming system which continued until the agricultural revolution in the 18th century. They also established the manorial system, whereby the lord of the manor collected taxes, and organised the local army. And they created the Witan, or council, to advise the king, the basis of the Privy Council, which still exists.

Religious change

The Anglo-Saxons brought their own Teutonic religion. Among their gods were Woden, king of heaven, Thor, the god of storms, and Freya, goddess of peace. The names Wednesday, Thursday and Friday derive from these gods.

Christianity soon disappeared, except among the Celts of Cornwall, Wales, Scotland and Ireland. In AD 563 on the island of Iona, off the west coast of Scotland, a monk called Columba established a monastery which was to be responsible for much of the Christian conversion of the people of the north. Under its influence a monastery was founded at Lindisfarne in archbishop. He was remarkably successful in converting the king and the nobility, and the monks in the north converted the commoners.

Monasteries sprang up around the country and became places of learning. In Jarrow-on-Tyne a monk called Bede (AD 673–735) wrote the *Ecclesiastical History of the English People*. Bede's work, and the *Anglo-Saxon Chronicle*, compiled under the King Alfred's direction the following century, are the principal sources of knowledge for this period. An 8th-century epic poem, *Beowulf*, captures the essence of courtly life of the time and is the first poem written in a European vernacular language.

Northumberland and another at Kells in Ireland, and many smaller ones sprang up throughout the Celtic areas. The earlier decorative traditions of the Celts were continued, under Christian auspices. Lindisfarne produced its beautifully illustrated *Gospels*, now in the British Museum; the Irish abbey created the exquisite *Book of Kells*, much of it executed at Lindisfarne; it is now on display in Dublin, in the Irish Republic. Even so, Christianity remained a fringe belief.

At the end of the 6th century the monk Augustine (who was once heard to remark "O Lord make me chaste, but not yet") was sent from Rome to convert the Anglo-Saxons. He went to Canterbury, in Kent, and became its first

Alfred, said to have taught himself Latin at the age of 40, translated Bede's work into English. A learned man himself, he encouraged learning in others, established schools and formulated a legal system and built up the army and navy, earning his title "Alfred the Great".

After the great king's death, trouble broke out again. His successors reconquered the Danelaw, but in 980 Viking invasions recommenced. King Ethelred tried paying them to stay away by imposing a tax, called the *danegeld*, on his people. But Ethelred, whose title "The Unready" was as well earned as Alfred's, was a poor psychologist. The Danes merely grew more predatory while he grew more confused.

When his death left no strong Saxon successor, the Witan chose Canute, the Danish leader, as king. Canute proved to be a wise ruler. He divided power between Danes and Saxons and, to protect his northern border, compelled Malcolm II, king of the Scots, to recognise him as overlord. Some 20 years later, Malcolm's grandson, Duncan, would be murdered by Macbeth, Lord of Moray, who was greedy for power. Macbeth, in his turn, was killed and the throne restored to Duncan's son, who became King Malcolm III. Thus the bones of Shakespeare's plot for *Macbeth* are true, although his scheming Lady and Banquo's ghost are less well authenticated. Had

man than Saxon and soon upset his father-in-law, Earl Godwin, by filling his court with "foreign" favourites and appointing a Norman priest Archbishop of Canterbury. He is also said to have promised the English throne to William, Duke of Normandy. But, when Edward died, the Witan chose Harold, son of Godwin, as king.

Harold's reign lasted less than a year. In October 1066 William of Normandy came to claim the throne. He landed at Pevensey on the Sussex coast, near the great Roman fort of Anderida, and defeated Harold in battle on Senlac Field, near Hastings. The Norman Conquest of 1066 is perhaps the best-known event in Eng-

Canute's sons, Harold and Hardicanute, not died within a few years of him, the whole history of Britain might have been very different. As it was, the succession passed to Edward, son of Ethelred, who had spent most of his life in Normandy, the part of France settled by the Vikings.

The Norman Conquest

Edward (1042–66), known as the Confessor, was a pious man who built Westminster Abbey to the glory of God. He was also far more Nor-

lish history and probably remains so important because England has never been invaded since.

William was crowned king in Westminster Abbey on Christmas Day and set out to consolidate his kingdom. Many Saxon nobles had died in battle while others fled to Scotland. Their coming intensified the anglicisation of Scotland which had begun with the marriage of King Malcolm III to Margaret, an English princess. William filled the vacuum with Norman barons and strengthened and formalised the feudal system which had begun before his arrival.

His barons received their land in return for a promise of military service and a proportion of the land's produce. The barons then parcelled

LEFT: Canute counters his courtiers' flattery by showing that he can't keep back the sea. **ABOVE:** William the Conqueror sails to England (from the Bayeux Tapestry).

out land to the lesser nobles, knights and free-men, also in return for goods and services. At the bottom of the heap were the villeins or serfs, unfree peasants who were virtually slaves.

William's influence was strongest in the south. Faced with combined Saxon-Danish rebellion in the north, he took swift and brutal action in what has been called the "harrying of the north", devastating the countryside and destroying much of the Roman city of York.

He then built a string of defensive castles, and replaced the Witan with a Great Council consisting of his new tenants-in-chief, which met three times a year in the southern cities of Win-

chester, Westminster and Gloucester.

William needed to know exactly who owned what in his new kingdom, the amount of produce he could expect and the taxes he could demand. So he sent his clerks to compile a property record. This collection, called the Domesday Book because it seemed to the English not unlike the Book of Doom to be used by the greatest feudal lord of all on Judgment Day, was completed in 1086. Today, it is kept in the Public Records Office in London, and is a fascinating document of early social history.

The early Norman kings had trouble keeping peace on their borders. William's son, Henry I, tried a pacific approach to Scotland: he married King Malcolm III's daughter, Matilda. He died in 1135, leaving no male heir. His daughter, also called Matilda, had married Henry Plantagenet, Count of Anjou, and became embroiled in a civil war against the followers of her cousin, Stephen. This war ended in 1153 with Stephen in control of the Crown but forced to accept Matilda's son, Henry, as joint ruler. When Stephen died the following year, Henry, founder of the Angevin dynasty (the dynasty of Anjou), usually known as the Plantagenet dynasty, became king and went on to rule for 35 years.

The great monasteries

While battles raged and kings connived, there was another side to life in this period, which has been described as "the flowering of Norman culture on English soil". The monasteries, both Benedictine and Cistercian, formed the new cultural centres; Canterbury, Westminster and Winchester were among the most active in the south, as were Fountains Abbey and Rievaulx in the north and Strata Florida in mid-Wales.

In Scotland the great monasteries at Melrose, Dryburgh, Jedburgh and Kelso were all built in the reign of Malcolm III's son, David I (1124–53), who also established a capital at Edinburgh.

These great houses produced erudite historians and scholars, some of whom went in search of other branches of learning in European monasteries, but they made no attempt to educate those outside the Orders.

Benedictine monasteries were a vital part of the feudal system, some gradually becoming almost indistinguishable from the great landed estates. Their abbots lived very well indeed, eating and drinking with great abandon. The Cistercian orders were not feudalised and their members were far less self-indulgent. Located in remote spots, many in the Yorkshire dales and Welsh valleys, they lived a far more spiritual life and supported their communities through sheep farming.

The Cistercians were the founders of the wool trade, which was to become the country's main source of wealth. The Benedictines would also become involved in this profitable business a century later.

Both Black and White monks, as the Benedictines and Cistercians were called, after the colours of their habits, offered hospitality to travellers and charity to the poor, although the

Abbot of Evesham may have been unusual in "washing their feet, giving clothes to some and money to others". A constant stream of pilgrims also had to be provided for, because pilgrimages were a feature of the age. Two pilgrimages to St David's in Wales were deemed the equivalent of one to Rome.

Chaucer's *Canterbury Tales* was not written until the 14th century; but his characters, a group of pilgrims travelling towards Canterbury, would have been a common enough sight at any time in the Middle Ages. They might not all have had such bawdy tales to tell but the popularity of Chaucer's book shows that a ribald

of the Crusades. From this tradition sprang the Arthurian myth.

Arthur probably existed and may well have been a Celtic leader of the 6th or 7th century. But it was Geoffrey of Monmouth, a 12th-century historian, who invented many Arthurian legends: his magical sword, Excalibur, and the wizard Merlin. Tintagel Castle in Cornwall, supposedly Arthur's birthplace, was not built until the 12th century – but there is no need to let historical facts spoil a good story.

As more people learned to read, curiosity about the history of Britain grew and writers were tempted to embellish, romanticise and

sense of humour was appreciated and that women, if his Wife of Bath is anything to go by, were expected to be just as lascivious as men.

King Arthur and Albion

But Chaucer's knight, his "verray parfit gentil knight", shows another side of medieval life: the courtly tradition and the code of chivalry. The highly exaggerated, romantic ideals of knights who would fight and die to win a smile from their pure and unblemished ladies first gained popularity in the 12th century at the time

quite simply invent. Geoffrey attributed one of Britain's early names, Albion, to the fact that the country had first been ruled by Albina, daughter of a Roman Emperor, Diocletian. More sober writers believe the name comes from the Latin for white, *alba*, and refers to the cliffs at Dover, the Romans' first sight of Britain.

In the 15th century William Caxton, the printing pioneer, blended historical fact and fantasy, myth and legend, in a fascinating account called *The Description of Britain*. A century later, Raphael Holinshed compiled his *Chronicles*; this work featured the story of King Lear, later dramatised by Shakespeare, who relied heavily on Holinshed's work for several plays.   ❏

LEFT: illuminated 12th-century psalter from York.
ABOVE: pilgrims on their way to Canterbury.

PREHISTORIC BRITAIN

Of all Britain's historic places, it is the prehistoric sites that are the most evocative – the legacy of ancient cultures whose lifestyle remains a mystery

It is impossible to travel far in Britain without seeing some evidence of the peoples who settled the land in the far-off centuries before history was recorded. These sites are not always immediately apparent – only a grassy bank between two fields may remain, perhaps, or a series of ridges around the summit of a prominent hill. These ridges were the banks and ditches which defended the hill-top forts of Iron-Age tribes, who could watch over the lower ground from behind the encircling wooden pallisades. Maiden Castle in Dorset is a particularly fine example, and Cadbury Castle, just off the busy A303 in Somerset, has been linked to Arthurian legend as the possible site of Camelot.

CIRCLES OF STONE

While the hill-forts were obviously places of habitation, the enigmatic stone circles that loom on many a remote hillside still lack a definitive explanation. Were they temples of ancient religions, places for pagan sacrificial rituals, meeting places, monuments celebrating some wonder of nature...?

Stonehenge is the most famous site, and remains a remarkable place in spite of the many visitors who are drawn to it at the height of the season. Many maintain that Castlerigg Stone Circle, high up on remote moorland in the Lake District, has the most picturesque setting, while the standing stones and ancient burial cairns of Orkney have a very special atmosphere. Cornwall and Wales, last strongholds of the Celtic tribes of Britain, are littered with cairns and standing stones.

△ **HEBRIDEAN STONES**
The 4,000-year-old standing stones at Callanish, on Lewis, in Scotland's Outer Hebrides, are laid out like a Celtic cross, a burial cairn at their centre.

◁ **SECRET OF THE SAND**
A violent storm in 1897 cleared a covering of sand from Jarlshof, a supposedly Norse site in the Shetland Islands, to the north of Scotland. It revealed a great variety of dwellings, from the Bronze Age to medieval times.

◁ THE CHALK GIANT

Even without his obvious charms, the Cerne Abbas Giant is an impressive sight. Standing 180ft (55 metres) tall, he was carved into the turf of Dorset's chalk downland, probably during the Roman occupation or earlier. No-one can be certain of his significance, though legend has understandably endowed him with powers of fertility.

▽ PICTISH HOMES

The lack of industrial development in the far north left many ancient sites relatively unspoiled. The substantial remains of a late Neolithic settlement at Skara Brae on Mainland Orkney, to the north of Scotland, give some impression of Stone Age life. Because of a lack of wood, for instance, the furniture had to be made from stone.

▽ STONEHENGE

This mysterious monument in Wiltshire doesn't impress from a distance because the stones are diminished by the surrounding plain. Close up, they are awesome. The stones were assembled between 2200 and 1300 BC – but how, why and by whom? The axis of Stonehenge is aligned with the sunrise on 21 June, the longest day of the year, so it may have been used to calculate the passing of time. Efforts are being made to provide the monument with more dignified surroundings.

HISTORY OF DRUIDS

The original Druids, spiritual leaders of the Celts, were a far cry from the present-day variety, who don flowing robes and gather at Stonehenge to celebrate dawn on midsummer's day. Now largely based in Wales, these Druids appear principally to be a society for promoting Celtic culture.

Druidism was a pre-Christian religion which formed the cornerstone of Celtic society and its priesthood held tremendous power and influence. The Celts were volatile and warlike, but they were also hospitable, extremely artistic and very spiritual. They worshipped gods who controlled nature and the seasons, having a direct bearing on their day-to-day lives, and the Druids were the fount of all knowledge.

Well versed in magic, the Druids revered the oak tree and mistletoe, and held their rituals in oak forests. They probably used dolmens (stone monuments) as temples and altars, though Stonehenge itself predates them by many centuries.

The Druids, who acted not only as priests but also as religious teachers and judges, maintained their power by creating an aura of mystery. They committed their knowledge to memory. Thus it was literacy as much as the conversion of many of them to Christianity that ultimately eroded the influence of the Druids in the 2nd to 4th centuries AD.

SHAKESPEARE'S KINGS

Threatened at home by powerful barons and abroad by fragile alliances and the power of the Pope, England's monarchs were a dramatist's dream

For his Histories, William Shakespeare drew on the lives of the Plantagenet and Tudor kings who ruled from 1154 to 1547. These were the King Henrys, the Richards and King John, around whom he wove fanciful plots, bloody deeds and heroic tales. He did not tackle the first of the Plantagenet kings, Henry II: that was left for T.S. Eliot, in the 20th century, who made a classic drama out of the king and his archbishop in *Murder in the Cathedral*.

Henry cemented the Anglo-Norman state. Through his mother's line he was the rightful king of England and through his father he inherited the title Count of Anjou. With his marriage to Eleanor of Aquitaine he also gained control of her lands, which stretched to the Pyrenees. Scotland, Ireland and Wales, however, formed no part of his kingdom. In order to consolidate his power, he introduced administrative reforms and instigated the system of common law which still operates today, distinguishing English from Continental and Scottish legal systems.

Church versus State

Relations between Church and State became increasingly strained during Henry's reign. He tried to end the Church's monopoly of jurisdiction over members of the clergy who committed secular crimes, and to bring clerics under the law of the land. Thomas Becket, his strong-willed Archbishop and erstwhile friend, resisted this and was berated by the king. In 1170, four knights of the royal household took literally Henry's wish that someone would "rid me of this meddlesome priest" and murdered Becket on the altar steps of Canterbury Cathedral.

When Henry II died in 1189, his son Richard came to the throne. Richard has always been one of England's most popular kings even though – or maybe because – he spent most of his time in the Holy Land fighting Crusades against the Infidel. Known as Coeur de Lion (Lionheart) for his bravery, he was deeply mourned when killed in France, despite the

domestic mess into which his prolonged absence and expensive exploits had plunged the country. It was the injustice at home, presided over in part by Richard's brother and successor John, that produced the legendary Nottingham outlaw, Robin Hood, who, with his Merry Men, preyed on the rich to give to the poor.

Magna Carta

Every English schoolchild knows that King John was a Bad King. He quarrelled with the Pope over his practice of siphoning off the revenues of ecclesiastical estates and over the Papal appointment of Stephen Langton as Archbishop of Canterbury. This resulted in another Interdict and John's excommunication.

He also caused a rising tide of resentment among the barons, chiefly because he failed to protect their Norman lands from the advances of the French king, Philip Augustus. Another important grievance was that John had imposed high taxes, undermined the power of the feudal courts and taken for himself the fines of offend-

LEFT: brave King Henry V. **RIGHT:** bad King John.

ers which had previously been part of the barons' income.

Angered by the king's contempt of them, the barons threatened to take up arms against John unless he agreed to a series of demands on behalf of the people. These became the basis of the Magna Carta (Great Charter) signed at Runnymede near Windsor in 1215. Under its terms, the Church was given back its former rights. The Charter also limited royal power over arrests and imprisonments and prevented the king from expropriating fines. For the barons the main interest was to stop him encroaching on their feudal rights and privileges.

Although history sees the Charter as a milestone, the document on which British freedoms are based, it brought no immediate solution. The Pope condemned it and John defied it and his barons; as soon as he could, he raised troops and ravaged the north. The barons retaliated by turning to Louis of France for help, but John died in 1216 before he could cause any more trouble.

Battles with the barons

John's son, who became Henry III, proved little better. He gave most of the top jobs to foreign favourites who flocked to England after his marriage to Eleanor of Provence and, in 1242 he embarked on a disastrous war with France which ended with the loss of the valuable lands of Poitou. The barons, under Simon de Montfort, rebelled and the king was defeated at the Battle of Lewes (now the county town of East Sussex). In 1265 de Montfort summoned a parliament, which represented the chief towns and boroughs and has been called the first House of Commons, although anything like a fair system of representation was still centuries away. But de Montfort's lust for power soon lost him the support of the barons. In 1266 Henry was restored to the throne where he reigned peacefully, if not very well, until his death in 1272.

Under Edward I, Henry's son, Wales was conquered. Llewellyn, Prince of Wales, was killed in the Battle of Builth on the River Wye and his brother David was captured and executed. The Statute of Wales in 1284 placed the country under English law and Edward presented his newborn son to the Welsh as Prince of Wales, a title held by the heir to the throne ever since.

THE STRUGGLE WITH SCOTLAND

Scotland became a united country in the 12th century – apart from the islands, still controlled by the Danes. Gaelic was still the language of the Highlands, but elsewhere most people spoke English and trade links with England had been established. But this didn't mean that the Scots had to like the English.

When Alexander II died in 1286, rivals claimed the throne. The first, John Balliol, son of the founder of Balliol College, Oxford, was persuaded to accept the throne as England's vassal. But he resented owing allegiance to England and made a treaty with King Edward I's enemy, the king of France, then crossed the border and

ravaged Cumberland. Edward fought back, Balliol was captured and imprisoned and the sacred kingmaking Stone of Scone was taken to Westminster Abbey.

The struggle against English domination was later renewed by Robert Bruce (1274–1329), one of Scotland's greatest heroes. Defeated by the Earl of Pembroke, he became a fugitive but re-emerged to be crowned at Scone, and in 1314 defeated the English at Bannockburn in Stirlingshire. Scottish independence was recognised. Robert's daughter Margery married Walter Stewart and their son Robert II came to the throne in 1371, the first Stuart King.

The Hundred Years' War

In England, the reign of Edward II had little to commend it. His defeat by Bruce paved the way for a Scottish invasion of Ireland. He lost Gascony and thoroughly upset his own barons by appointing his unsuitable friends to high office. Even his wife eventually deserted him and joined his enemy, Roger Mortimer. The pair assumed power and in 1327 Edward was deposed by Parliament, who named his young son king. Edward was later murdered, unmourned, in Berkeley Castle in Gloucestershire.

As soon as he was old enough, young Edward III, showing little filial loyalty, had his mother

3,000 dead. But by 1371 the English had lost most of their French possessions.

After a long peaceful lull, Edward's claim was revived by his great-grandson, Henry V, immortalised by Shakespeare (and memorably portrayed on film in our own time by Laurence Olivier and Kenneth Branagh) as the heroic Prince Hal. With miraculously few English casualties – although rather more than Shakespeare claimed – Henry defeated the French at Agincourt, starved Rouen into submission four years later, and made a strategic marriage to a French princess. By the time of his death in 1422 he controlled all of northern France.

incarcerated for life in Castle Rising, Norfolk, and Mortimer executed. Much of his long reign was spent fighting the Hundred Years' War with France, which actually lasted from 1337 to 1453 with several periods of peace.

These protracted hostilities began when Edward, whose maternal grandfather was Philip IV of France, claimed the French throne. The fortunes of war shifted from one side to the other. At the Battle of Crécy more than 30,000 French troops were killed and the Massacre of Limoges, led by England's Black Prince, left

Left: a knight's coat of arms. **Above:** the Battle of Agincourt, where Henry V defeated the French in 1415.

Plague and Poll Tax

On the domestic front, times were also hard. The Black Death, which reached England in 1348, killed nearly half the population. Followed by lesser epidemics during the next 50 years, it had reduced Britain's population from 4 million to 2 million by the end of the century. This had far-reaching effects. By leaving so much land untended and making labour scarce, it gave surviving peasants, and those who came after them, a better bargaining position. But it also meant that some landlords, unable or unwilling to pay higher wages, tried to force peasants back into serfdom. The more affluent peasants of Kent and East Anglia began to flex their economic muscles and when a Poll Tax was introduced in 1381 they rose in rebellion, both against the tax and against the landlords' oppressive treatment.

Wat Tyler and Jack Straw were the most prominent leaders of the Peasants' Revolt, which gained the support of the urban poor and briefly took control of London. Soon the rebellion was brutally suppressed and Richard II reneged on his promise to abolish serfdom. But this manifestation of the power of the people had made their

WHAT'S IN A NAME?

A pub, Jack Straw's Castle, commemorates the leader of the Peasants' Revolt and does a thriving trade on London's Hampstead Heath.

threw Richard II and put Henry IV, Duke of Lancaster, on the throne. It was during his reign that the first English heretic was burned at the stake. He was William Sawtrey, Rector of Lynn, in Dorset, and his heresy was preaching the Lollard Doctrines. Lollards were the followers of John Wycliffe, who rejected the Pope's authority and had the Bible translated into English so that any literate person could understand it. The persecution of the Lollards continued into the next reign when the movement, not organised enough to

lords and masters nervous and landlords became more wary about enforcing villeinage. Gradually the feudal system withered until it died.

The "Yeomen of Old England" who feature in some patriotic songs also emerged as a result of the 14th-century plagues. Landlords found it more profitable to rent out much of their land rather than pay labourers to tend it and in so doing they created a whole new class of yeomen farmers. The name originally meant simply "young men", presumably those with the energy to scratch a living from the often poor pieces of land and convert them, as they gradually did, into valuable smallholdings.

In 1399 the Lancastrian Revolution over-

withstand the pressure, went underground. The demands for change and reform in the Church would resurface successfully 100 years later, when they suited the purposes of the king.

The Wars of the Roses

Times were rarely peaceful during these centuries. Foreign wars were fought to gain or retain land and glory, while at home periodic attacks on the throne by rival contenders were equally bloody. Henry IV had to contend with the Rebellions of the Percys, a powerful Northumberland family, and the guerrilla warfare conducted by Owain Glyndwr (Owen Glendower, 1354–1416), a self-declared prince who was pressing hard for independence for Wales.

Henry IV's son, Henry V (1413–22), faced a conspiracy led by the Earl of Mortimer and, in 1455, after Henry VI had gone insane and government put into the hands of a Protector, rivalries between the powerful Dukes of York and Somerset led to the Wars of the Roses. This name was, in fact, coined by the 19th-century novelist Sir Walter Scott, but it is a convenient shorthand for these battles between the great House of York, symbolised by the white rose, and that of Lancaster, symbolised by the red.

Edward IV (1461–83) reigned for most of the duration of these wars. He has been called "a

of the young princes, Edward and Richard, said to have been smothered while imprisoned in the Tower of London in 1483. The guilt of their uncle, Shakespeare's hunchbacked Richard III, has never been proven and there is today a society dedicated to proving his innocence. Certainly, he's unlikely to have been as black as he was painted by Shakespeare – who, after all, was writing a melodrama calculated both to entertain and to conform diplomatically to the prejudices of his own time.

The circumstances of Richard's own death are also well known. He was killed during the Battle of Bosworth, in Leicestershire, where Shake-

man of gentle nature and cheerful aspect", although he did not extend his gentleness towards his brother, the Duke of Clarence, who incurred the king's displeasure, was found guilty of treason in 1478 and drowned in a butt of Malmsey wine.

One of the nastiest things about these wars was the number of people who were executed, with or without a trial, off the field of battle. Perhaps the best known of these murders was that

LEFT: Wat Tyler was beheaded by the Lord Mayor of London after the Peasants' Revolt, watched by King Richard (also seen on the right inspecting his troops). **ABOVE:** medieval jousting.

speare had him offering his kingdom for a horse, while his crown came to rest ignominiously in a nearby hawthorn bush.

The wars ended with the marriage of Henry VII (1485–1509), part-Welsh grandson of Owen Tudor and descendant of John of Gaunt, Duke of Lancaster, to Elizabeth of York. This united the opposing factions and put the country under the rule of the Tudors. Henry was something of a financial wizard and, determined to enrich a throne impoverished by years of war, proceeded to extort money wherever possible.

Through loans, subsidies, property levies and fines he refilled the royal coffers but, regrettably, most of the money was squandered by his son, Henry VIII on a series of French wars. These renewed hostilities gave the Scots an opportunity to ally themselves with the French and invade England. But they were terribly defeated at the Battle of Flodden Field, where James IV and 10,000 of his men were slaughtered.

The break from Rome

Henry VIII is the most famous of British kings. He was the hugely fat, gluttonous and licentious ruler who married six times, divorced twice and beheaded two of his wives. He is also famous as the man who brought about the Reformation, which made England a Protestant rather than a

Catholic country, because the Pope refused to annul his marriage to Catherine of Aragon, who could not oblige him by producing a male heir.

There are other well-known characters in this drama: one is Thomas Wolsey, Archbishop and Lord Chancellor, who had Hampton Court Palace built as an exhibition of his wealth and who was later charged with high treason for not giving sufficient support to his King. Another is Sir Thomas More, beheaded for refusing to recognise Henry as Supreme Head of the Church of England; and a third is Thomas Cromwell who, between 1536 and 1539, carried out the King's drastic wish to destroy the country's monasteries. But he made the mistake of

taking Protestantism too far for Henry's liking and was rewarded with decapitation on Tower Hill, while all the monastery lands and riches went to his ungrateful monarch.

The causes of the English Reformation were not, of course, quite so simple. Papal dispensation for the divorce was only withheld because Pope Clement VII was living in fear of Charles of Spain, the Holy Roman Emperor and Europe's most powerful monarch, who happened to be Catherine's nephew. A desire for Church reform had been growing for many years and now, encouraged by the success of Martin Luther (1483–1546), the great German reformer, many believed its time had come. The privilege and wealth of the clergy were also resented, even by those who had no doctrinal quarrels with the Church. And, of course, Henry needed the money to be made from the vast amounts of seized monastic lands and property.

"Bloody Mary"

Under Henry, Wales was joined with England in the 1536 Act of Union, which gave it representation in parliament. When he died in 1547, Henry was succeeded by his only male heir, Edward, a sickly 10-year-old who died six years later. His half-sister Mary then came to the throne and won herself the nickname "Bloody Mary", proving that a woman could be just as ruthless as a man when the occasion demanded. A devout Catholic, she restored the Old Religion and raised fears that her marriage to Philip II of Spain would lead to undue Spanish interference and the introduction of the dreaded Inquisition. During her rule the Marian Persecution, as it was called, saw at least 300 Protestants burned as heretics, including Archbishop Cranmer, who died at Oxford after first thrusting into the flames "the unworthy hand" which had earlier signed a recantation.

Mary is also remembered as the monarch who lost the French port of Calais, the "brightest jewel in the English crown" and the last British possession on the Continent, during a renewed war with France. More remorseful about the loss of land than the loss of so many lives, she declared that when she died the word "Calais" would be found engraved on her heart. ❑

LEFT: Cardinal Wolsey, Archbishop and Chancellor to Henry VIII (**RIGHT**). Wolsey was one of those beheaded by the much-married king.

THE GOLDEN AGE

Under Elizabeth 1, Britain ruled the waves and produced great literature.
But then power began to shift from the monarch to the politicians

The Elizabethan Age has a swashbuckling ring to it: the Virgin Queen and her dashing courtiers, the defeat of the Spanish Armada, and the exploits of the "sea dogs", Frobisher and Hawkins. Sir Walter Raleigh brought tobacco back from Virginia; Sir Francis Drake circumnavigated the world.

In this age of the renaissance man, even the great poets Sir Philip Sidney and John Donne spent time before the mast – although William Shakespeare, born six years after Elizabeth had been crowned queen, stayed at home, entertaining the crowds at the Globe Theatre in London's Southwark. Poetry, plays and pageants were the thing, and they accompanied the Queen on her tours of the country.

Conspiracies against the Queen

Elizabeth I, Henry VIII's daughter by Anne Boleyn whom he beheaded, may have had an interesting life at court but in fact she spent nearly 20 years of her long reign (1558–1603) resisting Catholic attempts to either dethrone or assassinate her. She had re-established Protestantism but was constantly challenged by those who wished to put Mary Stuart, Queen of Scots, on the throne and return to the Old Religion.

Mary had a colourful background. Sent to France as a child, she returned a young widow and in 1565 married her cousin, Lord Darnley. But she became far too friendly with her secretary, Rizzio, who was stabbed to death by her jealous husband at the Palace of Holyroodhouse in Edinburgh (tour guides point out the exact spot where it happened – some can even discern traces of faded bloodstains). Shortly afterwards Darnley himself was killed and, as Mary rather too swiftly married Lord Bothwell, suspicions were aroused, a rebellion mounted and Mary had to abdicate in favour of her son, James.

On fleeing to England, however, she was promptly incarcerated by Elizabeth and languished in prison while plots were fomented,

LEFT: the defeat of the Spanish Armada in 1588.
RIGHT: Elizabeth I, the "Virgin Queen".

mostly involving the assistance of Spain. The trial and execution of Mary in 1587 removed the conspirators' focal point and the defeat of the Spanish Armada the following year put an end to Catholic conspiracies against Elizabeth. It also gave England naval supremacy, which laid the foundations for a forceful future of flour-

ishing trade, expansionism and colonisation.

When Elizabeth died without an heir she was succeeded by Mary's son, James. He was James VI of Scotland, but James I in England, where he was the first of the Stuarts to take the throne. His succession brought a temporary union of the two countries but his reign, too, was bedevilled by religious controversy. The Puritans became prominent, believing that the Reformation had not gone far enough and calling for a purer form of worship. And the Catholics engineered a number of plots, one of which resulted in Sir Walter Raleigh's 13-year imprisonment in the Tower of London (his well-appointed rooms can be visited). Ironically, Raleigh was released by

James who was short of money and sent in search of gold in Guiana. The expedition failed and Raleigh, accused of treason, was executed.

The Gunpowder Plot

The most famous of the Catholic conspiracies was the Gunpowder Plot of 1605, when Guy Fawkes attempted to blow up the Houses of Parliament. The immediate result was the execution of Fawkes and his fellow-conspirators and the imposition of severe anti-Catholic laws. The long-term result has been an annual celebration on 5 November, when Fawkes is burned in effigy throughout the land and thousands of

seized in Elizabeth's reign after a series of rebellions had been brutally suppressed. Now they were redistributed among English and Scottish settlers. The county of Derry was divided up among 12 London merchant guilds and re-named Londonderry. Ulster became England's first important colony.

The Stuart period was one of conflict between Crown and Parliament. James I, a staunch believer in the Divine Right of Kings, a belief held by most European rulers of the time, would have preferred no Parliament at all and actually did without one for seven years. But, once recalled in 1621, the House of Commons re-

pounds-worth of fireworks go up in smoke.

The Puritan protests were more peaceful, but James had little sympathy with their demands. A new translation of the Bible into English (the "Authorised" or "King James" Version) was a rare concession. James said he would "make them conform or harry them from the land". Some left voluntarily. Going first to Holland, a small group who became known as the Pilgrim Fathers set sail in the *Mayflower* in 1620 and founded New Plymouth in North America, Britain's first toe-hold in the New World.

Meanwhile, in Ireland, events were taking place which would leave a long and bloody legacy. The lands of northern Irish lords had been

newed its insistence on political power in return for the taxes it was constantly asked to raise.

The Civil War

Under Charles I, relations with Parliament went from bad to dreadful. In 1628 he reluctantly accepted the Petition of Right, one of the most important documents in British history, which forbade arbitrary arrest and imprisonment and deemed that taxes should be raised only by an act of Parliament. But a year later he dissolved Parliament and initiated 11 years of absolute rule. Surprisingly, he managed very well and might have continued indefinitely had it not been for the over-zealous attempts of William

Laud, the anti-Puritan Archbishop of Canterbury, to impose the English Book of Common Prayer on the Scottish Church, or Kirk.

Influenced by the great French theologian, John Calvin (1509–64), the Scottish Church had become strictly Puritan, and was called Presbyterian because its elders were Presbyters, not Bishops. Laud's intransigence provoked a massive popular rebellion. The Covenanters, so-called because they had signed a National Covenant "to resist Popery", formed an army and invaded England.

THE WAR GOES ON

The Civil War has become romanticised, and a society flourishes today which re-enacts the principal battles.

Charles gained the support of the north and west of the country and Wales. Oliver Cromwell, member of Parliament for Cambridge and a stout defender of the Puritan cause, became leader of the Ironsides, backed by London and the southern counties and later joined by Scottish troops. Enormous damage was done to castles, churches and fortified houses during the war and when it was over many were "slighted" – either destroyed completely or made indefensible. Today the King and his Cavaliers are shown more sym-

LEFT: the execution of Mary, Queen of Scots in 1587.
ABOVE: Charles I also comes under the axe, in 1649.

Short of money and trained men, Charles was unable to cope. He had to summon a Parliament, but King and Commons were constantly at each other's throats and in 1641 discontented Irish Catholics took advantage of their disarray to attack the settlers who had taken their land. Thousands were massacred and the outcry in England was heightened by a belief that Charles had backed the Irish Catholic side. This belief, together with Charles's attempt to arrest the five members of Parliament most openly opposed to him, precipitated the Civil War.

pathy than Cromwell and his Roundheads – so called because of their short haircuts.

Cromwell's republic

King Charles's execution in 1649, on a scaffold erected outside Inigo Jones's new Banqueting House in Whitehall, has also become the stuff of which legends are made. He reputedly wore two shirts, so that he would not shiver in the January cold and cause people to think he was afraid. The poet Andrew Marvell, deeply moved by the event, wrote: "He nothing common did or mean/Upon that memorable scene."

As so often in politics, making a martyr of the enemy proved a big mistake. There was public outrage at home, while in Scotland Charles's son and namesake was crowned king. Young Charles, however, was not happy with the Presbyterian religion he was pledged to uphold. He marched into England where he was defeated at Worcester, was pursued south and, after many adventures, finally escaped to France.

Meanwhile, Cromwell and "the Rump" – the Parliamentary members who had voted for Charles's execution – declared England a Commonwealth. One of Cromwell's first acts was to exact reprisals for the massacres in Ireland by killing all the inhabitants of the towns of Drogheda and Wexford. Another was the sup-

pression of the Levellers, a group within his own army who did not believe that his democratisation had gone far enough. In 1653 Cromwell dissolved Parliament, formed a Protectorate with himself as Lord Protector and ruled alone until his death in 1658. Without him republicanism faltered and, in 1660, Charles II was declared king.

Britain prospered under Charles (1660–85), of whom it was said that he "never said a foolish thing nor ever did a wise one". True or not, one unwise thing Parliament was afraid he would do was become a Catholic. They therefore passed the Test Act, which excluded all Catholics from

PERSECUTION OF THE PURITANS

Puritans, who were known in the late 17th century as Nonconformists, aroused almost as much paranoia as Catholics and were subjected to a series of laws called the Clarendon Code after their instigator Edward Hyde, 1st Earl of Clarendon. These laws severely limited their participation in public affairs.

Two of the most famous literary works of the time were written by Puritans: John Bunyan's *Pilgrim's Progress*, which he wrote while in prison for "unlicensed preaching", and the blind poet John Milton's *Paradise Lost*, which was a thinly veiled lament for the Puritan cause.

public office of any kind. In 1678 Titus Oates (whose house can still be seen in the narrow high street in Hastings in Sussex) disclosed a bogus "Popish Plot" to assassinate the king. In the resultant hysteria, thousands of Catholics were imprisoned and no Catholic was allowed to sit in the House of Commons – a law that was not repealed for nearly 300 years.

Whigs and Tories

Fear of the monarchy ever again becoming too powerful led to the emergence of the first political parties. Both were known by nicknames: Whigs was a derogatory name for cattle drivers, Tories an Irish word meaning thugs. Loosely speaking, the Whigs opposed absolute monarchy and supported the right to religious freedom for Nonconformists, while Tories were the upholders of Church and Crown, the natural successors of Charles I's Royalists. The Whigs were to form a coalition with dissident Tories in the mid-19th century and become the Liberal Party. The Tories were the forerunners of the Conservative Party, which retains the nickname.

In 1685 Charles was succeeded by his brother. James II (1685–89) was not a success. Within a year he had imposed illegal taxation and tried to bring back absolute monarchy and the Catholic religion. Rebellions were savagely

put down, with hundreds being hanged and many more sold into slavery to the West Indies.

In desperation, Whigs and Tories swallowed their differences and in 1688 offered the crown to James's daughter, Mary, and her husband, the Dutch prince William of Orange. This became known as the Glorious Revolution and, although bloodless, a revolution it certainly was. By choosing the new monarch, Parliament proved itself more powerful than the Crown. This power was spelled out in a Bill of Rights,

LEFT: William of Orange defeats James II in Ireland at the Battle of the Boyne in 1690.
ABOVE: John Churchill, Duke of Marlborough.

which limited the monarch's freedom of action and ushered in a new era in which Divine Right and Absolute Monarchy had no place.

But James II had not yet given up hope. Backed by the French, he landed in Ireland in 1689, believing that the disaffected Irish Catholics would support him. This they did, but with disastrous results for both sides. At Londonderry 30,000 pro-William Protestants survived a siege lasting 15 weeks, but were finally defeated. Their Loyalist descendants still call themselves "Orangemen", and "No Surrender" is the Protestant rallying cry heard in Ulster's streets today. The next year, William's troops defeated James at the Battle of the Boyne. James fled to France, the south of Ireland was subdued and Protestant victory complete.

War with France dragged on, to be transformed in Queen Anne's reign into the War of the Spanish Succession, its aim being to put Charles, Archduke of Austria, on the Spanish throne. John Churchill, Duke of Marlborough, won a famous victory at Blenheim in 1704, for which he was rewarded with Blenheim Palace in Oxfordshire. In the same year Gibraltar was taken. Still in British hands, this remains a source of dispute with Spain today. The Treaty of Utrecht ended the war in 1713 and the Queen died without an heir the next year.

The birth of Great Britain

It was during Anne's reign that the name Great Britain came into being when, in 1707, the Act of Union united England and Scotland. The motives for this union were largely economic: the Darien Scheme, which was to have facilitated Scottish trade with the Indies, had failed, largely through opposition from the immensely powerful English-owned East India Company, and the duties on goods traded between Scotland and England had become exorbitant.

Under the Act the two countries were to share the same monarch and parliament while trade and customs laws were to be standardised, though Scotland was to retain its own Church and legislature. The Act did not, however, bring about instant friendliness and accord between the two nations, and it was largely the cause of the Jacobite Rebellions a few years later.

On Anne's death, a reliable Protestant monarch was needed in a hurry and George of Hanover, great-grandson of James I on his mother's side, but a Hanoverian through his father's line and German in language, upbringing and outlook, was invited to Britain. Throughout his 13-year reign he never learned to speak English fluently, nor did he have any great liking for his subjects.

Hanoverian Britain

The Hanoverian dynasty, under the four Georges, spanned a period of nearly 115 years. It was a time of wars with France and Spain, of expanding empire, industrialisation and growing demands for political reform. It also saw the last violent attempts to overthrow a British monarch, in the shape of the two Jacobite

Rebellions in support of the "Pretenders", descendants of James II.

The first rebellion, in 1715, in support of James, the "Old Pretender", was defeated near Stirling and its leaders fled to France. Thirty years later English war with France encouraged the Jacobites to try again. Charles, the "Young Pretender", popularly known as Bonnie Prince Charlie, raised a huge army and marched into England. Finding little support from English Jacobites, he returned north of the border where his Highland troops were savagely defeated in battle at Culloden by the Duke of Cumberland, nicknamed "the Butcher".

HANDEL COMES TO BRITAIN

The composer George Frederic Handel (1685–1719), who had been court conductor and composer in Hanover, Germany, came to London to try his luck. This annoyed his employer – an unfortunate enemy since that same employer followed him to London in 1714 when invited to become George I of England. After the coronation, Handel tried to placate him by playing the F major suite of his *Water Music* during a royal river procession in 1715.

Handel, whose *Messiah* remains a choral favourite, became a quintessentially English composer and is buried in Westminster Abbey.

Laws were subsequently imposed which removed the jurisdiction of the clan chiefs, forbade the wearing of national dress and ended the traditional Highland way of life forever. Charles roamed the highlands for several months as a fugitive before escaping to France.

No more "Pretenders" arose. From then on power struggles would be political ones, for it was with politicians and Parliament that real power lay. Monarchs were gradually becoming titular figures. Historians may talk about the reign of George III, but it was the policies of William Pitt or Lord Liverpool which mattered. Similarly, the Victorian Age was really the age of Peel and Palmerston, Gladstone and Disraeli.

The growth of London

What was London like when George and his queen, Sophia, arrived from Hanover in 1714? Despite the ravages of the Great Plague of 1665 which killed 100,000 Londoners, and a high infant mortality rate, the population had more than doubled since 1600 and stood at 550,000. This was largely due to migrants from poor rural areas who came in search of work as new farming machinery made them redundant.

The city had been partially rebuilt after the Great Fire of 1666, which started in a baker's shop in Pudding Lane and destroyed two-thirds of the cramped, timber-built city. But the sub-

in colonial trade which stimulated banking, insurance and share dealing. Quickly made fortunes could also be lost, as happened when the South Sea Bubble burst in 1720. In return for exclusive trading rights in the area, the South Sea Company had agreed to pay off part of the vast National Debt. But the shares crashed spectacularly and the City's first financial scandal left thousands ruined. Whig politician Robert Walpole (1676–1745), who helped restore public confidence, later became Chancellor of the Exchequer and Britain's first Prime Minister.

A flourishing trade and financial sector also created work for craftsmen and artisans, to fur-

sequent elegant buildings of Sir Christopher Wren (1632–1723), such as St Paul's Cathedral, were a far cry from the overcrowded and insanitary slums in which most people lived. In the more affluent areas, some streets were widened to allow carriages to pass and rudimentary street lighting was introduced in the mid-18th century. Westminster Bridge was illuminated by gaslight for the first time in 1813. But slums expanded, promoting squalor and degradation

London was then, as now, the country's leading commercial centre and fortunes were made

nish homes, build carriages and make clothes. At the same time it brought in service industries to cater for the *habitués* of the theatres, concert halls and newly fashionable coffee houses.

London was also the centre of court life and the seat of political power. The royal families spent their time at Buckingham House, Kensington Palace and at Hampton Court. George III was the first monarch to live in Buckingham House and George IV had it redesigned by John Nash into a Palace. A system of patronage flourished around Parliament, which met at Westminster, although not in the present building, which was built after a serious fire destroyed its predecessor in 1834. ❑

LEFT: the Jacobites face defeat at the Battle of Culloden.
ABOVE: slums depicted by William Hogarth in *Gin Lane*.

BRITANNIA RULES THE WAVES

Trade boomed, cities burgeoned, railways spread, the Empire swelled.

It was a great time to be British – unless you were poor

The treaty signed at the end of the Seven Years' War with France in 1763 allowed Britain to keep all its overseas colonies, making it the leading world power. The empire had been growing since 1607 when Virginia, the first British colony in America, had been established. In 1620 English Puritans had settled in Massachusetts and other settlements were made later in the century. By 1700 most were governed by a Crown official and incorporated into Britain's Atlantic Empire.

Throughout the 17th century the demand for goods – furs, rice, silk, tobacco, sugar – led to a series of wars with the Dutch and the French from which Britain emerged in control of much of West Africa, Newfoundland and Nova Scotia and some of the Caribbean islands. French and English battled for supremacy in Canada and India during the 18th century. By 1760 England had proved the clear winner: General James Wolfe's capture of Quebec ended French power in Canada and Robert Clive had beaten both Indians and French for control of the Indian subcontinent, a victory which made the East India Company a private colonial power.

Convicts and slaves

Britain's loss of its American colonies in 1783 was eased by the opening up of the Pacific. Captain Cook reached Tahiti in 1768 and then went on to New Zealand and Australia, where he landed at Botany Bay. When American Independence deprived Britain of a place to send its convicts, the harsh, undeveloped lands of Australia were the obvious alternative.

Colonial trade, unfortunately, went hand in hand with slavery. European traders bought slaves in West Africa, shipped them to the Americas under appalling conditions and sold them to plantation owners, often in exchange for produce which they took back home. The raw materials would then be converted into fin-

LEFT: the Battle of Trafalgar, as painted by Turner.
RIGHT: bustling trade with the New World from the quays of the Port of Bristol.

ished products and exported to other parts of the Empire. It was a neat trade triangle which meant high profits for some, misery and degradation for others. It was not until 1807 that the tireless efforts of William Wilberforce made the trade illegal and another 27 years before slavery itself was finally abolished in all British colonies.

The agricultural revolution

Radical changes took place in the English countryside in the late 18th century. Since Saxon times, large areas of land had been cultivated in narrow strips by tenant farmers, and common land had been used for grazing. Little was known about crop rotation or fertilisation and land would be worked until it was exhausted.

During the late 18th and early 19th centuries this system ended when the Enclosure Acts empowered wealthier landowners to seize land to which tenants could prove no legal title and to divide it into enclosed fields. This explains the patchwork quality of much of Britain's countryside, and the paintings of Suffolk by

John Constable (1776–1837) show that in some parts of the country little has changed.

A system of crop rotation meant land could be exploited to the full while the cultivation of fodder crops enabled livestock to be kept through the winter months. Artificial fertilizer and new agricultural machinery, such as the seed drill invented by Jethro Tull, also made arable farming more efficient and more profitable. But for the tenants evicted from their lands by the enclosures and the labourers thrown out of work by mechanisation, it was a disaster. Riots erupted in many areas but they could not prevent the march of progress. Many

This surfeit of capital was one reason why Britain was the first country to industrialise, but it was also helped by relative political stability, the security which came from being an island, from natural resources and from good trade arrangements. These fortunate circumstances combined to produce a genuine revolution, so rapid and complete were the changes it made.

The Industrial Revolution

The first steam engine was devised at the end of the 17th century but it was only when the Scottish inventor James Watt (1736–1819) modified and improved the design in the 1770s that steam

dispossessed peasant farmers had to leave their homes and look for work in the towns, which became hopelessly overcrowded. In Ireland and the Scottish Highlands the agricultural revolution led to mass emigration, particularly to America, and to lasting resentment.

Those who had done well out of new farming methods began to look for ways to invest their capital. They soon joined flourishing city bankers and merchants who had been made prosperous by international trade, to finance what we now call the Industrial Revolution.

THE LUDDITES

Attempts to wreck the hated power looms were made by "Luddites", named after Ned Ludd of Leicestershire. But the rebels lost the fight.

became an efficient source of energy, which would power trains and ships as well as factory machinery and make many later developments possible. The new steam pumps, for example, allowed speculators to drain deep coal mines, which vastly increased coal production, an important factor when opencast and shallow mines were nearly exhausted.

Textiles had long been a vital part of Britain's economy and the invention of the Spinning Jenny and the power loom in the 1770s and 1780s opened the way to mass production. As in agriculture, mechanisation destroyed the livelihood of those who could not invest in it. Handloom weavers, many of them women and children, were obliged to leave their homes and work in these "dark satanic mills".

Perhaps the most important element in speeding industrialisation was the breakthrough made by Abraham Darby of Coalbrookdale, Shropshire, who succeeded in smelting iron with coke, instead of charcoal. This hugely increased the production of iron which was used for machinery, railways and shipping. Here, in 1776, the world's first cast-iron bridge was built and can still be seen. Cast steel was first pro-

into disuse when the new railways proved faster and more efficient, but today, cleared out and cleaned up, they provide thousands of miles of leisure boating. There are more miles of canal in Birmingham than there are in Venice.

New roads were built. A process involving crushed stones and a layer of tar was named after its inventor, the blind Scot John Macadam, and gave us the road surface called "tarmac". By the early 19th century, men such as Macadam and Thomas Telford, whose masterpiece is the magnificent Menai Strait Bridge in North Wales, had created a road network totalling some 125,000 miles (200,000 km).

duced in the mid-18th century but it was another 100 years before the Bessemer process made possible the cheap mass production of steel.

It was, of course, pointless to produce goods or materials unless they could reach a market, so improved transportation ran parallel with production. The 18th century saw massive outlay on canal building. By 1830 all the main industrial areas were linked by waterways and Scotland was sliced in two by the Caledonian Canal. Unfortunately, most of these would fall

---

LEFT: coal mine in the Midlands at the start of the Industrial Revolution.

ABOVE: Turner's *Rain, Steam and Speed*, painted in 1844.

The Railway Age

But above all this was the age of the railways, when iron and steam combined to change the face of the country, and were romanticised in such vivid paintings as *Rain, Steam and Speed* by J.M.W. Turner (1775–1851). Isambard Kingdom Brunel (1806–59), who also designed the elegant Clifton Suspension Bridge across the Avon Gorge, laid down the Great Western Railway. The Stockton and Darlington line, designed by George Stephenson, inventor of the Rocket, was the first steam line to open, in 1825, followed five years later by the first intercity line, from Liverpool to Manchester. This historic occasion was marred when William

Huskisson, the President of the Board of Trade, was accidentally killed while officiating at the opening.

In the 18th and 19th centuries a whole new class of industrialists and entrepreneurs made fortunes to rival those of the aristocracy, who in turn looked down on them as *nouveaux riches*, with no breeding. But what about the workers? The new factories and mines certainly provided employment, but working conditions were dreadful. Fatalities in the new deepcast mines were high and those who survived sudden death often had their lives shortened by pneumoconiosis. Children as young as four were

employed underground and women worked alongside the men. In factories, too, employees of all ages were treated abominably, working 15-hour days in poor light and deafening noise.

It was not until 1833 that the first Factory Act made it illegal to employ children under nine and for women and under-18s to work more than 12 hours a day. Sixty years were to pass before another act dealt with health and safety at work, and then in a very minor way. These early industrial reforms were the initiatives of enlightened, liberal-minded men, acting on behalf of the under-privileged, often arousing great opposition from members of their own class for their "interference". It would be some

time before working people would be able to achieve benefits on their own behalf.

The Combination Acts of 1824 allowed workers to "combine" together to improve wages, but nothing else. The case of the Tolpuddle Martyrs, six Dorset men sentenced to deportation for their attempts to organise a more comprehensive union, demonstrated the need for workers to protect themselves against exploitation, but it was not until 1868 that the first Trades Union Congress met. Unions then went from strength to strength, although for a long time they largely benefited the so-called "Triple Alliance" of miners, railwaymen and transport workers, and they did little for workers in other areas.

The fear of revolution

The two events which most alarmed the British ruling classes in the closing decades of the 18th century were the American War of Independence and the French Revolution. In the former, people proved themselves willing to fight and die for equality, national identity and political representation. In the latter, they were prepared to remove the heads of the aristocracy and anyone else who denied them liberty, equality and fraternity.

Radical thinkers such as Edmund Burke (1729–97) and Tom Paine (1737–1809) enthused over the American people's struggle and Paine also supported the ideals of the French Revolution, although he later became sickened by its excesses. *The Rights of Man*, which he published in 1792, defended the people's right to reform what was corrupt. It attracted a lot of like-minded followers and seriously worried the government. Freedom of the press was suppressed, many radical leaders imprisoned, and Paine escaped to France to avoid retribution.

The fear of revolution was exacerbated by wars with France and Spain and the dissatisfaction provoked by the heavy taxes and loss of trade they caused. Known as the Napoleonic Wars, these hostilities began with the threatened French invasion of Belgium and Holland in 1793 and rumbled on, with only three years' break, until 1815.

These were wars which gave Britain two of its greatest heroes, Admiral Lord Nelson (1758–1805) and the Duke of Wellington (1759–1852) and some of its most famous victories. There was the Battle of the Nile in 1798, when Nelson annihilated the French fleet; the Battle of Trafalgar, where he himself was killed after reminding his men that "England expects that every man will do his duty"; Sir John Moore's inspired strike at Corunna, and Wellington's victory at Waterloo, which ended Napoleon's career in 1815.

However, political change in England was to come not through revolution but gradual reform. Between 1832 and 1884 three Reform Bills were passed. The first abolished "rotten boroughs", places which returned

THE CHARTISTS

This group lobbied for a secret ballot and votes for workers, but they were seen as dangerous revolutionaries and their movement finally fell into disarray in 1848.

had it not been for the determined and sometimes violent efforts of the suffragettes, led by Emmeline Pankhurst, and the role women had played in the workforce during World War I.

The 1829 Emancipation Act, which allowed Catholics to sit in Parliament, was another measure which frightened many of the old school, who feared it might pave the way for Popish plots and undermine both Church and State. And the controversial Repeal of the Corn Laws – the heavy taxes on imported corn

members to Parliament but had few or no inhabitants, and redistributed parliamentary seats more fairly among the growing towns. It also gave the vote to many householders and tenants, which was based on the value of their property.

The later reform acts extended the franchise more widely, but it was still property-based. Only in 1918 was universal suffrage granted and, even then, it was not quite universal: women under 30 were excluded and had to wait another 10 years. It is unlikely that women would have been enfranchised until much later

LEFT: naval hero Admiral Lord Nelson.
ABOVE: industry produced a new urban working class.

which were crippling trade and starving the poor – split the ruling Conservative Party. The "Peelite" faction, followers of the pro-repeal Prime Minister Sir Robert Peel, joined with Whigs to form the embryonic Liberal Party. This new grouping was committed to free trade, religious tolerance and a growing conviction that Ireland should be granted Home Rule.

The trouble with Ireland

The "Irish Question" was one to which no satisfactory answer could be found. The resentment of centuries bubbled to the surface after the potato famine of 1848, when about 20 percent of Ireland's population died of hunger and more than a million people emigrated to escape a similar fate. Hostility to Britain and all things British manifested itself in sporadic outbreaks of violence over the next decades. In 1885, after the extension of the franchise, 86 members of the Irish Party were elected to Parliament.

Under the leadership of Charles Parnell, the "Uncrowned King of Ireland", and with the backing of Prime Minister Gladstone and many of his Liberal Party, it seemed that their demands for Home Rule would be met. But Gladstone's bills were defeated and Parnell brought down by a personal scandal. It was not until 1914 that Britain agreed to establish an

ion status, not full independence, and obliged to accept the loss of six counties in the north which remained under British rule as Northern Ireland. Partition led to civil war in Ireland. In 1932, a new party, Fianna Fail, won the election and five years later the Prime Minister, Eamon de Valera, declared southern Ireland a Republic.

The age of Dickens

In 1848, as famine raged in Ireland, revolution broke out all over Europe. In Britain, once fear of the Chartists was quashed, the country entered a period of self-confidence and relative domestic harmony, despite the polarisation of

Irish parliament. But World War I intervened, delaying action, and Irish nationalists, tired of waiting, decided to fight.

At Easter 1916 a group of nationalists staged a rebellion. It was savagely repressed and the ringleaders executed. The severity of the reprisals swung Irish public opinion firmly behind the rebels, who established their own parliament, the Dail, and fought a guerrilla campaign against the British. This prompted a compromise: in 1921 Ireland was partitioned. The Irish Free State in the south was given Domin-

THE CRYSTAL PALACE

This showcase, conceived by Queen Victoria's beloved consort, Prince Albert, was built to house the 1851 Great Exhibition, highlighting Britain's industrial strengths. It was a roaring success.

rich and poor which Benjamin Disraeli, a later Conservative prime minister, called "the two nations" in his mid-century novel, *Sybil*. Poverty was nowhere more evident than in London, for many of whose citizens the squalor and crime which Charles Dickens (1812–70) portrayed so evocatively in his novels – which were first written for serialisation in popular newspapers – were all too real.

Fortunately, Dickens was not the only one who saw a need for improvement. Change, although slow, was on the way. The idea that public health was a public responsibility was gradually taking hold. After a cholera epidemic in 1832 claimed thousands of lives, health officials were appointed and measures taken to provide drainage and clean water.

The police force which Sir Robert Peel had established in 1829, and which took the nickname "bobbies" from him, was helping combat crime in London and other large towns. At the same time, Peel had abolished the death penalty for many petty crimes, such as pocket-picking, influenced perhaps by the ideas of Jeremy Bentham, the utilitarian thinker who believed there should be a balance between reward and pun-

founded by John Wesley (1703–91), who established the first Methodist chapel in Bristol, had become the religion of the working class. It is often said that the British Labour Party owes more to Methodism than to Marxism.

The working class

It is certainly true that working-class people, on the whole, were not attracted by revolutionary struggle and preferred to pursue their aims through trade union organisation and representation in Parliament. The first working-class member of Parliament in 1892 was John Keir Hardie, the Scottish miners' leader, and 14 years

ishment. Bentham founded University College, London and his corpse, fully clothed, still sits in a glass case in the entrance hall.

A newly created class of clerks, trades-people and artisans were adopting the values of thrift, sobriety and self-improvement which Samuel Smiles exhorted in his famous work, *Self-Help*. The Co-Operative Movement, which began in 1844 in Rochdale, Lancashire, was run on self-help lines, providing cheap goods and sharing profits with its members. Methodism,

later the British Labour Party won its first parliamentary seats. Although Karl Marx (1818–83) lived and worked in London for much of his life – his tomb can be seen in London's Highgate Cemetery – his ideas were known and shared only by a relatively small group of middle-class intellectuals.

Also largely ignored by the working man for whom he hoped to speak was John Ruskin (1819–1900), one of the founders of the Pre-Raphaelite Brotherhood of painters and writers which flourished in the late 19th century. William Morris, who devoted himself to the revival of medieval arts and crafts, shared Ruskin's anger at the social deprivation caused

LEFT: an election meeting in Blackburn, in the new industrialised Midlands. **ABOVE:** print by William Morris, who revived the taste for medieval arts and crafts.

by capitalism. Examples of his decoration and furnishings can be seen at Kelmscott Place, near Oxford, which was for a time the centre of the Brotherhood's activities. Fellow Pre-Raphaelites were Edward Burne-Jones, John Millais and Dante Gabriel Rossetti, artists who were perhaps less concerned with the social ills of the 19th century but equally convinced of the need to return to pre-Renaissance art forms. They eventually became establishment figures and their work is spread through galleries in London, Birmingham, Manchester and Liverpool.

Ruskin and Morris were among a growing number of those who believed that the lot of

working people would only be improved through education. Despite fears in some quarters that education for the masses was a dangerous thing, two Education Acts were passed towards the end of the century which made schooling free and compulsory up to the age of 13. The educational provision may have been rudimentary, but at least it was there – which put England on a more equal footing with Scotland, which had had state education since 1696.

Working-class life improved considerably during the last quarter of the 19th century. Many homes had gas lighting and streets were cleaned by the new municipal councils. The music hall provided inexpensive entertainment in towns.

Bicycles became a common method of transport and day trips by train to seaside resorts were the highlight of summer, even if most could not afford the bathing machines which allowed more affluent visitors to get into the water without any great loss of modesty.

Middle-class comforts

Middle-class life was comfortable and pleasant. Improved transport – including the world's first underground railway, opened in London in 1863 – enabled people to work in towns but live in leafy suburbs. Most of their new homes had bathrooms and the majority employed a maid.

Art and drama flourished. Aubrey Beardsley's fluid, sensual drawings were creating a stir. The Art Nouveau movement had reached Britain and influenced the work of Charles Rennie Mackintosh (1868–1928), who founded the Glasgow School at the end of the century, where he created his own strikingly simple style. At the theatre, audiences were being entertained by the plays of two Anglo-Irish writers: George Bernard Shaw believed in combining education with entertainment and introduced some of his radical politics into his work; Oscar Wilde, who would soon end his glittering career in a prison cell on charges of homosexuality, poked sophisticated fun at London's high society.

A complacent empire

All in all, Britain was feeling quite pleased with itself by the time of Queen Victoria's Diamond Jubilee in 1897, and continued to do so for another decade or so.

The Jubilee celebrated 60 years on the throne for the woman who had spent much of her reign as a black-clad widow and who had given her name to the age. She ruled over the biggest empire in the world. Atlases of the time showed vast areas coloured red, signifying that they were British colonies. The Punjab and much of Southern Africa had been added to earlier possessions. Egypt and the Sudan had become colonies – in practice if not in name – after Britain invaded in 1882 to protect its shipping routes to India through the newly built Suez Canal. Britannia did indeed rule the waves.

Then came the 20th century… ❏

LEFT: four generations of royalty: Victoria with future monarchs George V, Edward VII and Edward VIII.
RIGHT: the Crystal Palace, built for the Great Exhibition.

THE 20TH CENTURY

The British won their wars but lost their empire and then faced the big question:
did they really and truly want to join a United States of Europe?

All good things must come to an end. The Boer War of 1899–1902 ended in victory for Britain in South Africa but damaged its international reputation. France, Germany and America were competing for world markets. The newly united German state was the biggest threat, its education system putting it far ahead of Britain in scientific and technological developments. It had good reserves of coal and iron and was becoming the world's biggest producer of steel, which it was using to build battleships to rival those of the British navy.

Fear of Germany's growing strength forced Britain and France into an alliance. This, together with an earlier treaty which promised to guarantee Belgium's neutrality, plus the fear that Germany would overrun Europe and gain control of parts of the Empire, brought Britain into World War I in 1914. The Edwardian era, sandwiched between the turn of the century and the outbreak of war, is remembered as the zenith of prosperous stability, but its foundations had been shifting for some time.

The Roaring Twenties

World War I claimed over a million British casualties, most of them under the age of 25. The scale of the carnage shocked even such patriots as the writer Rudyard Kipling (1865–1936) who had been firmly committed to the aims of the war. But there were other effects, too. Men who had fought in France and been promised a "land fit for heroes" were disillusioned when they found unemployment and poor housing awaited them at the war's end. Women who had worked in factories while the men were away were not prepared to give up any of their independence.

There were strikes on the railways and in the mines and political unrest led to four general elections in just over five years, including one which brought the Labour Party to power for the first time. In 1926 a general strike paralysed the country but the unions' demands were not met and the men returned to work, much disgruntled and worse off than before.

There was another side to life, of course. For some, unaffected by gloomy financial reality,

these were the Roaring Twenties. Women with cropped hair and short dresses drank cocktails and danced to the new music, jazz, which had crossed the ocean from America. Silent films, another US import, were the wonder of the age. Writers such as Virginia Woolf and D.H. Lawrence were opening new horizons for the curious and daring – although it would be another 30 years before Lawrence's *Lady Chatterley's Lover* could be published in Britain.

The New York Stock Market crash of 1929 looked as if it would bring the party to an end. The effects soon spread throughout Europe and by 1931 Britain was entering the Great Depression. It ruined a few fortunes, but the principal

PRECEDING PAGES: Sir Winston Churchill, Britain's World War II leader. **LEFT:** bathing belles. **RIGHT:** Suffragette leader Emmeline Pankhurst arrested outside Buckingham Palace for campaigning for votes for women.

victims of the recession were in the industrial areas of northern England, south Wales, and Clydeside in Scotland. Three million people lost their jobs and suffered real misery with only the "dole", a limited state benefit, to keep them from starvation and homelessness.

In the south of England and the Midlands, the depression hit less hard and recovery was faster, mainly due to the rapid growth of the motor, electrical and light engineering industries. The bold, geometric designs of Art Deco, which began in Paris in 1925, could soon be seen adorning the spanking new factories which lined the main roads, roads which were starting

Mother, showed to their subjects during the Blitz, as the German bombing raids were called.

World War II

With memories of the "war to end all wars" still fresh in people's minds, there was great reluctance to enter another conflict. But by 1939 the policy of appeasement of German aggression was no longer tenable. Although Britain's island status saved it from invasion, the war involved civilians in an unprecedented way. German bombing raids tore the heart out of many cities. Coventry was particularly badly hit; its present cathedral, with its renowned John Piper win-

to fill with small, family cars.

In 1936, following the death of George V, the country was rocked by an unprecedented crisis. Edward VIII succeeded his father but was obliged to abdicate when family, Church and Government united in their refusal to let him marry a twice-divorced American, Mrs Wallis Simpson. The couple married in France and remained in permanent exile as the Duke and Duchess of Windsor. Edward's brother came to the throne and, as George VI, became a popular monarch, not least for the solidarity which he and his Queen, Elizabeth, later the Queen

LONDON'S BURNING

The Blitz by the Luftwaffe radically changed the face of London for the first time since the Great Fire of 1666.

dows, was built to replace the one that was lost. Ports and shipyards around the country were battered by repeated raids. Much of the modern building in British towns, not always blending too harmoniously, has been erected on former bomb sites.

Many London families spent their nights in the underground stations, the safest places during an attack, and a lot of people from cities and industrial areas were evacuated to the countryside during the worst of the Blitz. For children, sent to live with strangers while their parents remained behind, it was both a time of great loneliness and the first glimpse many of them had ever had of green fields and woodlands. For some of the country families on whom they were billeted, it may have been their first glimpse of the effects of urban deprivation.

Sir Winston Churchill had received massive popular support as a war leader, and he is still regarded by many people as Britain's greatest prime minister. But when hostilities ended in 1945 the electorate returned a Labour government, hoping that it would be able to sort out the problems of the war-torn country. The basis of the welfare state was laid, providing free medical care for everyone and financial help for the

autonomy during the next two decades, although many remained in the Commonwealth, with the Queen as their titular head. Jamaica and Trinidad did not gain independence until 1962, but they were two islands whose people were among the first black immigrants to Britain in the early 1950s, when work was plentiful and immigrants were welcomed to fill the labour gap. Newcomers from the Caribbean settled mainly in London at first, while later immigrants from the Indian sub-continent made their homes in the Midlands, where textiles and the motor industry offered employment.

The post-war years were ones of uneasy

old, the sick and the unemployed. The Bank of England, coal mines, railways and steelworks were nationalised. But these were hard years and wartime rationing of food, clothing and fuel continued into the early 1950s.

The end of empire
One of the most far-reaching consequences of the war was that it hastened the end of Britain's empire. Starting with India's independence in 1947, the colonies one after another achieved

LEFT: Underground stations were used as makeshift bomb shelters during London's Blitz, through which St Paul's Cathedral (**ABOVE**) miraculously survived.

peace. Britain joined the war against North Korea in 1950 and its troops, still a conscripted army, fought there for four years. In 1956, following Egyptian nationalisation of the Suez Canal, British and French forces conspired to attack Egypt, pleading bogus provocation. The imperialist action was widely condemned both at home and particularly in the United States.

These were also the years of the Cold War between the Soviet Union and the West, which prompted Britain to become a nuclear power. The first British hydrogen bomb was tested in 1957, two years after the world's first nuclear power station had opened in Cumberland (now Cumbria). The Campaign for Nuclear Disarmament was born in response and organised impressive protest marches.

But all was not gloom and doom. In 1947 Edinburgh had a highly successful festival of music and drama, which has gone from strength to strength. At the same time the first annual International Music Eisteddfod was held in Llangollen in Wales. Four years later the Festival of Britain was held in the newly built Royal Festival Hall on London's South Bank – the National Theatre was added to the concrete complex in 1964.

MOTORWAYS ARRIVE

As car ownership rose, the country got its first motorway, the M1 from London to Birmingham. The first stretch opened in 1959.

devices. New universities were built, with the aim of making higher education a possibility for more than just the privileged elite. Most people had two weeks' paid holiday a year and, alongside the traditional seaside resorts, holiday camps blossomed, offering cheap family holidays with basic accommodation, swimming pools, sports facilities and dance halls under one brightly-coloured roof.

Social attitudes were changing too, reflected in the rise of a group of writers known as "angry young men", including

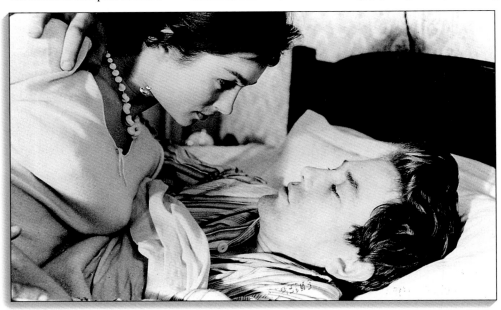

The Festival was designed to commemorate the Great Exhibition 100 years earlier and strongly signalled the beginning of the end of postwar austerity. In 1953, a new Elizabethan Age began as Elizabeth II was crowned in Westminster Abbey. Britain's Television Age began in earnest that day, too, as millions watched the coronation live on tiny flickering screens.

By the latter half of the decade things were definitely looking up. Harold Macmillan, the Conservative prime minister, declared in a famous speech that people had "never had it so good": unemployment was low, average living standards were rising. Increasing numbers of people owned TV sets and labour-saving

John Osborne and Arnold Wesker, whose plays challenged conventional attitudes and values. The popularity of these writers also marked the beginning of a move away from the dominance of the middle class in literature and of America in popular culture.

The Swinging '60s

The 1960s saw an explosion of new talent, much of it from the north of England. Alan Sillitoe and Stan Barstow wrote about working-class life in a way no one had done before. Northern actors, such as Albert Finney, achieved huge success and, in the cinema, directors Lindsay Anderson and Karel Reisz (best known for *If* and *Saturday Night and Sunday Morning*) made British films big box-office attractions. Pop music, as it was now called, underwent a revolution when the Beatles became world celebrities and turned their home town of Liverpool into a place of pilgrimage.

A relaxation of attitudes and the introduction of the contraceptive pill prompted a revolution in sexual attitudes. As poet Philip Larkin put it:

> *Sexual intercourse began*
> *In nineteen sixty-three*
> *(Which was rather late for me)*
> *Between the end of the Chatterley ban*
> *And the Beatles' first LP.*

member of the Common Market (now the European Union). Economic worries dominated as rising oil prices pushed up the cost of living, high inflation took its toll, and unemployment soared. An IRA bombing campaign brought home the seriousness of the situation in Northern Ireland, whose parliament was dissolved in 1972 as mounting violence forced the British government to impose direct rule from London.

Oil was discovered in the North Sea. But, although building oil rigs provided jobs, the oil revenues were largely soaked up in payments to the jobless. There was no economic miracle.

The 1970s also saw nationalism flourish in

It was a decade of optimism and national self-confidence was infectious: in 1966 England's footballers even won the World Cup.

The subdued '70s

It was during the winter of 1973, when an oil embargo and a miners' strike provoked a State of Emergency and brought down Edward Heath's Conservative Government, that the self-confidence collapsed. In the same year, with mixed feelings, Britain finally became a full

LEFT: Shirley Ann Field and Albert Finney in one of Britain's realistic 1960s films, *Saturday Night and Sunday Morning*. **ABOVE:** an oil rig in the North Sea.

Wales and Scotland. Plaid Cymru (pronounced *Plyed Cumree*) became a political force. Wales was given TV and radio channels in Welsh and the language was reintroduced into schools.

In Scotland, support grew for the Scottish Nationalist Party (SNP). In national elections it overtook the Conservatives and began to threaten the Labour Party, which had always done rather better north of the Border.

The Thatcher years

By 1979, unemployment had reached 3½ million and a wave of strikes plunged the country into what was called "the winter of discontent" – the media has a tendency to quote Shakespeare in times of crisis. The country lost confidence in its Labour government and an election returned the Conservatives to office under their new leader, Margaret Thatcher.

The impact of the West's first woman prime minister was enormous, but her personal popularity soon began to fade. It was dramatically revived in 1982 by the Falklands War when an invading Argentinian force was beaten off these South Atlantic islands, remnants of the empire.

The 1980s became known as the Thatcher decade. For many it was a decade of increased prosperity and bright new shopping centres sprouted up all over the country. Most ambitious

of all was the development of London's derelict docklands area into a new industrial site, with its own small airport and light railway system and prestige housing for young urban professionals carved out of former tea warehouses.

The nervous '90s

As the 1990s began, the City was no longer riding so high. Recession returned and many newly constructed luxury apartments remained empty. For others, particularly in the north, where steelworks, shipyards and mines had closed and much of the industrial infrastructure had collapsed, the 1980s had been a grim decade, and Disraeli's description of Britain as "two nations" was recalled. A long and acrimonious miners' strike in 1984 had weakened the unions, and coal mines, including most of those in South Wales, were subsequently closed. Most of Britain's nationalised industries were privatised, a move which a former Conservative prime minister, Harold Macmillan, likened to "selling the family silver".

After 11 years of Thatcherite rule, people began to tire of the Iron Lady's uncompromising style and she was finally voted out in November 1990 – not by the electorate, but by her own party. The Conservatives believed she had lost touch with the country, particularly over its role within the European Union, and that they might therefore lose the next election. She was replaced by a less combative leader, John Major.

Britain's technical status as an island was removed in 1994 when the first fare-paying passengers travelled by rail to Paris and Brussels through the long-awaited Channel Tunnel. But the big question remained: did Britain really feel European enough to be part of a full monetary union – perhaps even, one day, a political union?

That *fin de siècle* feeling

Two events in 1997 shook the nation out of its wary complacency. In a general election the Conservative Party was swept from power after 17 years as the Labour Party roared in with an unassailable overall majority of 179 seats in the House of Commons. The Conservatives were left without a single seat in either Scotland or Wales, both of which voted in subsequent referenda for a greater degree of self-rule. But Tony Blair's new government soon disappointed many by promoting unexpectedly conservative economic policies with evangelical fervour.

The second defining event was the death in a car crash in Paris of Diana, Princess of Wales. The wave of grief that swept the country took everyone by surprise, both the grievers who mourned all night outside Kensington Palace in London and the cynics who found echoes of *Evita* in the insistent public anguish.

Initially, the tragedy seemed to strengthen the monarchy as the Queen, like her subjects, began seriously to contemplate the changes that the 21st century might have in store. ❏

LEFT: Margaret Thatcher, who dominated a decade.
RIGHT: construction of the Channel Tunnel, linking Britain directly with Continental Europe.

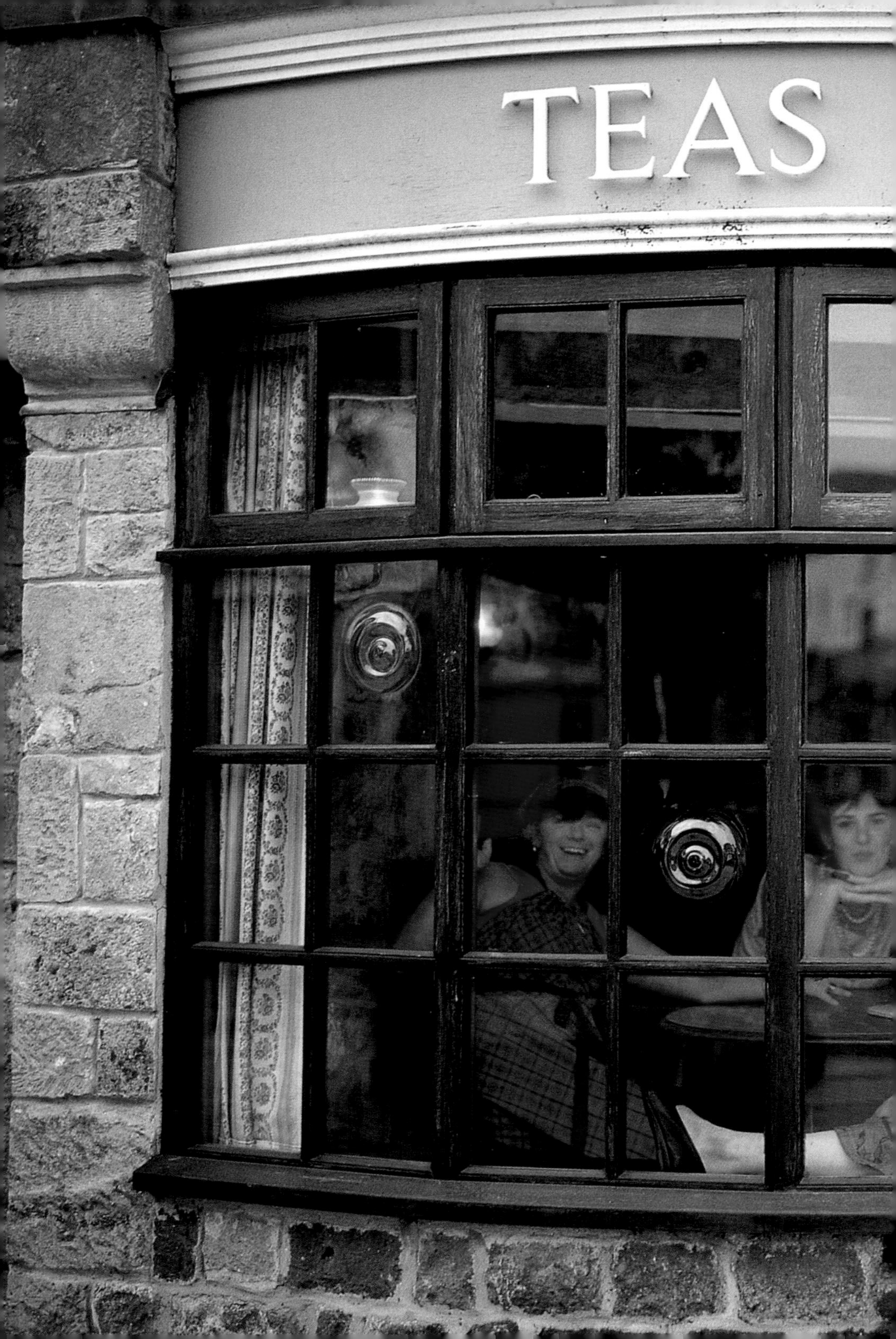
TEAS

CULTURE FROM A TO Z

The British psyche, like an iceberg, is mostly hidden from view. Here, in 26 essays, we reveal it in its totality

The British take a masochistic delight in hearing how bleak their outlook is. As Sir Winston Churchill put it, they "are the only people who like to be told how bad things are – they like to be told the worst." And it's certainly a conspicuous characteristic. Noel Coward lampooned it in the song "There are bad times just around the corner" – which, of course, became immensely popular.

Visitors find it hard to sympathise this self-deprecation, suspecting that it is really a cloak for rampant arrogance and realising that few countries are as rewarding to dip into. Take a pin and put it down on a map of Britain and you will find a different experience each time: different people, different houses, different scenery, different accents, different values, different views. Together they make up an astonishing island race, in whom the culture and customs are inextricably mixed; a character that is the sum of so many parts.

The A to Z of the nation and its foibles on the following pages can also be dipped into. These 26 short essays look at the ruling establishment of government, knights, lords and monarchy, and the role of the BBC. They examine the country's preoccupations with vicars, the weather and official secrets. They look at its hang-ups about accents, class and sex. They extol its games, its theatre and its pubs. They explain the particular peculiarities of tea-drinking and forming queues. The nation's notorious xenophobia is confronted head on. And the section finishes by trying to analyse the peculiar zeitgeist that has gripped post-imperial Britain – this "soggy little island huffing and puffing to keep up with Western Europe", as the American novelist John Updike once characterised it.

This alphabetical analysis does not explain everything that goes on either in public or behind closed doors between John O'Groats and Land's End. But it may shed light on some of the shadier areas of a society renowned for curious customs, mild eccentricities and an erstwhile ambition to rule half the world.

PRECEDING PAGES: tea-shop photo-call; Victorian elegance at a Welsh fair.
LEFT: modern choir girl.

Accents

When, in *Pygmalion* (later to be reborn as *My Fair Lady*), George Bernard Shaw set Professor Henry Higgins the task of passing off Eliza Doolittle, a common Cockney flower-seller, as a duchess at an ambassador's dinner party, there was no question about Higgins's first priority: he had to change her accent. Then, as now, a person's origins, class as well as locality, could be identified by the way he or she speaks and, as Shaw wisely observed, "it is impossible for an Englishman to open his mouth without mak-

ing another Englishman despise or hate him."

Although such snobbery is most associated with the English, the Welsh and Scots are not immune. The linguistically alert can detect a range of class differences between the North Welsh and the South Welsh, for instance, and the ambassador would much prefer a dinner party guest who greeted him in the soft-spoken tones of middle-class Edinburgh than in the rough vernacular of working-class Glasgow.

It is remarkable – given these social pressures, the small size of Britain and the smoothing influence of television – that a vast variety of regional accents continue to flourish. Yet they do: two Britons, one with a strong West Country accent and the other from Newcastle upon Tyne, would scarcely understand each other.

With Asian and West Indian immigrants having added to the variety of speech patterns in Britain, consensus about what constitutes "proper English speech" remains as elusive as ever. Pity the manufacturers of digitised voice generators: who in Glasgow wants their cooker to inform them in a Surrey accent that their roast is ready, or what Oxfordshire driver wants his car to tell him in a Norfolk accent to fasten his seat-belt? The same unsatisfactory solution again presents itself and machines, like BBC announcers, embrace Received Pronunciation.

BBC

The voice of Britain is often thought to be the voice of the BBC. Its tone is exemplified in its ponderous, impeccably pronounced radio World Service which broadcasts in 45 languages from Bush House in London's Aldwych. Its cultural aspirations are conveyed in the costume-drama exports of classic television sagas.

The British Broadcasting Corporation, set up in 1927, does not have a monopoly of the air waves, but it does have a good slice. It has five national radio channels plus a countrywide network of local radio stations, and two of the five terrestrial TV channels.

As an advertisement-free public service organisation, its powers and obligations are vested in the Board of Governors appointed by the government. These are exercised through a permanent staff headed by the Director General and the Board of Management. It must be impartial and free from political interference.

THE QUEEN'S ENGLISH

Although there is no "national" accent, many Britons are hostile to regional accents which differ from their own. Only 3 percent of the population uses the generally accepted "Received Pronunciation" associated with BBC announcers, yet the BBC is inundated with complaints when it employs on its national news bulletins an announcer with a noticeable regional accent. The royal family has an accent all of its own. A variant on the aristocrat's accent, it turns "stone" into "stain" and finds Prince Charles "abite the hice" when most people are "about the house". It's a gift to impersonators.

That is the theory. In practice, interested parties tot up the number of minutes' reporting of each side of an issue, looking for bias. The Left calls the BBC elitist and Conservative. The Right refers to the Bolshevik Broadcasting Corporation. But, having packed the Board of Governors with like-minded souls, the government of the day usually has less cause for complaint.

The Home Secretary has the power to intervene directly in broadcasting, as he did with the banning of interviews with members of terrorist organisations (aimed primarily at the IRA and its political wing, Sinn Fein). But government control is usually restricted to a quick chat, a

tap-dancing duo, the Lai Founs Chinese jugglers, and Miss Lutie and her pantomime horse. No wonder the "Aunty" image stuck.

There have been eccentricities, too – evidence that the Corporation is merely the nation talking to itself. One of television's early stars was Joseph Cooper and his silent piano; a long-running hit was a radio ventriloquist and his dummy, Archie Andrews.

But the BBC began to shrug off its Aunty image under Sir Hugh Greene, the director general during the 1960s, when satire bit deeply in *That Was the Week That Was*, hosted by David Frost and featuring such new young talents as

nod and a wink, which can leave the BBC looking ridiculous.

Unconcerned with pleasing advertisers, the BBC can give its audience what it should have rather than what it necessarily wants. Certainly that was the aim of John Reith, the BBC's first director-general, who shared the pioneering producers' passion to educate. A concession to audience taste was made in 1936 in one of the first variety programmes. It included a Chilean

John Cleese. Since then, funny BBC programmes have won large audiences, but they have, in the main, been undemanding. The most biting show of recent years, *Spitting Image*, was transmitted by a commercial channel.

Audience ratings still matter to the BBC, which is called to account when justifying the viewer's annual licence fee. Satellite television has begun to threaten audience figures. Still resolutely refusing to take advertising, the Corporation is constantly looking at ways of funding its output, from index-linked licences to pay-as-you-view TV. Always reliant on government for its funding, it must tread carefully; its future is never certain.

LEFT: boating and beer – two pleasures that accompany an Oxford education.
ABOVE: the traditional image of the British Broadcasting Corporation, guardian of "proper" English.

Class

A newspaper cartoon cunningly caught the British confusion over its social attitudes. "I don't believe in class differences," its well-heeled gentleman was explaining, "but luckily my butler disagrees with me."

The implication is that the lower classes, far from being revolutionaries, are as keen as anyone to maintain the status quo, and that they still embody the attitude to the upper classes parodied more than a century ago by W .S. Gilbert in the comic opera *Iolanthe*:

Bow, bow, ye lower middle classes!
Bow, bow, ye tradesmen, bow, ye masses!

From time to time, the class rigidities seem set to crumble, but the promise is never quite fulfilled, mainly because the British have a genius for absorbing dissenters into "the system" as surely as a spider lures a fly into a web. The Swinging Sixties promoted a new egalitarianism; but 30 years later such former threats to civilised society as Mick Jagger consort with the royal family. In the 1980s, the consensus among classes seemed again to be threatened, this time by Thatcherism, whose economic policies created stark inequalities between the

THE VALUE OF MONEY

Strangely enough, Britain's aristocracy is not especially ancient; it is said that only two non-royal families (the Ardens and the Berkeleys) can trace back their ancestry with certainty to before the Norman Conquest of 1066. Many later knights, barons, earls, dukes, marquises and viscounts bought their honours from kings or governments.

Within the aristocracy, intellectual ability is not highly valued – actors and sporting celebrities are much more likely to receive knighthoods and other honours than intellectuals are. And what lesser mortals would consider bad behaviour is common: upper-class parties display a fondness for noisy,

drunken and disorderly parties. As the essayist Hilaire Belloc put it:

Like many of the upper class
He liked the sound of broken glass.

Snobbery, "the pox Britannica", values attitude and position in society over money and the ability to make it. "Old" money, handed down over generations, is deemed superior to "new" money acquired through vulgar commerce. Thus a poor duke ranks higher in the social pecking order than a successful businessman. Within the middle classes, rank is assigned partly by a person's ability to act and speak like an aristocrat.

regions and swelled the ranks of the disgruntled unemployed; but, before any permanent damage could be done, the Conservative Party replaced Mrs Thatcher in mid-term with the more emollient John Major.

Mr Major's humble origins suggested that any working-class boy who applied himself diligently could become prime minister – surely a threat to the power of the upper classes? In reality, however, the true aristocrat is unperturbed by such irrelevancies, regarding a prime minister as the nation's equivalent to his butler.

The monarchy cements the social hierarchy; fringe aristocrats define their social standing in relation to their closeness to royalty, and the elaborate system of honours – from peerages and knighthoods to Companionships of the British Empire – transform achievement into much sought-after feudal rank because the titles (even though generally decided by the politicians of the day) are bestowed in person by the monarch.

The ruling class is a pragmatic coalition of middle and upper-class members. Generally, "they" (the people who seem to make all the decisions) remain strangely amorphous; common speech refers constantly to the fact that "they" have built an inadequate new motorway or that "they" have allowed some hideous glass skyscraper to be placed next to a Gothic cathedral – a peculiar dissociation from power in an avowedly democratic society. But "they" have certain characteristics in common: they tend to have been educated at any one of a dozen public schools and then to have progressed to either Oxford or Cambridge universities. From then on, the network is firmly in place and, with the help of dinner parties, country-house weekends and college reunions, the bush telegraph of power keeps lines of communications open. The "old school tie" has a durable knot.

Drama

In spite of its reputation, the West End of London is not always the place to find the country's dramatic cultural pearls. Here the tradition is as much of the theatre as of performances. This is

LEFT: classic image of the "two nations", as working-class boys watch Eton public school pupils wait for their chauffeurs at the start of their vacation.
RIGHT: William Shakespeare, still pulling the crowds.

where velvet and gilt Victorian playhouses were designed so that most of the audiences would peer down over the cast, where "the gods" (the seats high at the back) bring on vertigo and a concern that, had the buildings been conceived today, fire regulations would have ensured they never left the architects' drawing boards.

Nevertheless, the West End is still the place where companies aspire to put on their productions, because that is where the money is. Catering for audiences by the coachload, impresarios look to musical spectacles, revivals, and to plays that will please the widest range of tastes. As a result, such middle-of-the-road creative persons

as composer Andrew Lloyd Webber (Lord Lloyd-Webber) and the playwright Alan Ayckbourn have become both famous and very rich.

In general, the 1990s are showing no signs of danger. Peter Hall, the genius who, in his youth, brought Beckett's *Waiting for Godot* to the stage and who had an inspired reign at the National Theatre in London's South Bank, now directs more cautiously, though his organisational energy enabled him to set up a starry new repertory company in 1997 under his own name.

The new caution is in part due to the limited government subsidy, but it has more to do with trends. Funding, an annual complaint, need not affect quality and there is undoubtedly a continuing tradition of high-quality, committed drama throughout the country.

Shakespeare is certainly alive and well. The Royal Shakespeare Company, based in Stratford-upon-Avon and in the Barbican in the City of London, is basking beneath bright new directors such as Deborah Warner and Katie Mitchell and, as always, there is another wave of talented actors coming through. The theatre's continuing strength is highlighted as the curtain rises on a third generation of the great acting families, the Cusacks, Redgraves and Richardsons, while the tradition of acting companies which manage and direct themselves, as they did in

Shakespeare's day, has been reintroduced by Ian McKellen and Kenneth Branagh.

The National Theatre in London can still offer surprises, and should continue to do so under Trevor Nunn's direction. Notable productions can regularly be found at the Young Vic, the Gate, the Almeida and the Royal Court, home of *Look Back in Anger* and nurturer of radical writers such as David Hare and Caryl Churchill.

The backbone of British theatre lies beyond London, in the repertory companies of the provinces. The Manchester Exchange, Leicester Phoenix, Glasgow Citizens' and Edinburgh Traverse all have good reputations and in Liverpool a hive of talent has included the play-

wright Willy Russell and the actress Julie Walters. And the Fringe Festival in Edinburgh every August is where myriad actors and comedians clamour to show their earliest promise.

In the early 1990s, there were dire predictions that the British film industry was on the verge of collapse. But it has sprung back, thanks to successes like *Four Weddings and a Funeral* and *The Full Monty*, and to the injection of some of the profits of the national lottery.

Increasingly, television has not only bridged the gap between the film and theatre, but has also pushed drama into more exciting areas. Both the innovative Channel 4 and the BBC have commissioned films which would otherwise never have been made. Sometimes they are shown both on television and on the circuit, such as Peter Greenaway's *The Draughtsman's Contract*. Others are only shown on television after they have been distributed in the normal way, such as Granada Television's *My Left Foot*, which brought its star, Daniel Day-Lewis, international acclaim.

At the end of the day, theatre remains the great pull, and however far actors, directors and writers drift from it and feed the other media, there always seems to be a desire to return. Why, even old Joan Collins, famous beyond the dreams of avarice, has gone back to Britain's boards to find real success.

Elections

There are two main parliamentary political parties in Britain, Labour and Conservative, with the Liberal Democrats, Plaid Cymru (Welsh nationalists), the Scottish Nationalists and Ulster Unionists trailing a long way behind. The House of Commons, parliament's Lower House, is furnished with green seats, which distinguishes it from the red seats of the Lords in the Upper House. It can just about hold all 650 MPs, though the amount of committee work means there are often no more than a handful of members in the chamber at any one time. Like most British institutions, parliament is a male-dominated preserve with the air of a public school. Raucous behaviour is encouraged, although the Speaker, with her weary cries of "Order! Order!", endeavours to stamp out the worst excesses.

Unpardonable sins include accusing fellow

THE LUNATIC FRINGE

Anyone in Britain can form a political party. All that is required is a name for the party and a person to second the registration – and a £500 deposit, which is forfeited if the party receives less than 5 percent of the constituency vote. This stipulation is intended to deter frivolous candidates – but it doesn't. There are numerous hopeful parties, including the Greens, The Monster Raving Loony Party, the Natural Law Party (which runs on a platform of peace through meditation) and Sausages Against HP Sauce. On election night, candidates of all these parties appear briefly on television as the results are announced. It all adds to the gaiety of life and preserves the country's reputation as a safe haven for eccentricity.

MPs of lying (though they can be mendacious or "economical with the truth"). As recompense, they are free to libel members of the public without fear of prosecution – so long as they don't repeat the libel outside the House, in which case the courts are liable to take them for every penny they have. The ministers are answerable to the House, and the prime minister answers questions on Wednesdays. The business of actually getting a question asked is lengthy and an MP may spend years without once speaking.

Parliament has no written constitution. It relies on statutes and acts which have been passed over the centuries. The monarch has a right of veto but, wisely, none has used it since the 18th century. The Queen is not allowed to set foot in the chamber unless she is invited – which she is at the start of each session at the beginning of November, when she reads a speech prepared by ministers and civil servants outlining her government's plans for the nation's future.

A government may be in office for five years and the prime minister can call an election at any time within that period, giving six weeks' notice of the date. A prime minster who hangs on until the last possible moment – as John Major did in 1997 – has probably got good reason to feel insecure.

LEFT: Laurence Olivier in the title role of Henry V, the 1944 film that boosted morale in wartime Britain.
RIGHT: a striking tea-room sign in the New Forest.

Food

Few people contemplating a first visit to Britain would cite the cuisine as a major attraction. They may have heard disconcerting reports of soggy vegetables, tinned sauces and artificially flavoured puddings, and will certainly be aware of beef contaminated by "mad cow disease". But Britain has a sophisticated culinary tradition going back to the days of the grand Victorian country houses, and even earlier. In the Brighton Pavilion, visitors today can not only see the enormous kitchen and its

elaborate implements and fine copper serving dishes, but can read the menu for a banquet given in in 1817. More than 100 dishes feature, from delicate soups (a choice of four) to every kind of meat or game, including quail and wood pigeon. Puddings included miniature soufflés – chocolate, apple or apricot.

Victorian culinary knowledge was codified by a Mrs Beeton, who published her renowned *Book of Household Management* in 1861. She provided expert advice on everything from how to dry herbs to judging the age of a partridge, and her book, having been updated many times over the years, is still in print.

How, then, did the country acquire its reputation as a culinary wasteland? Britain's indigenous foodstuffs – lamb, potatoes, apples and pears, herbs, fish, eggs and cheeses – can be of very high quality, but they must be very fresh or stored under controlled conditions, and must be skilfully prepared. In Victorian times, most middle-class families employed servants, including a cook. But in the years leading up to World War II, changing social conditions led most people to give up their servants. Then came the wartime rationing of meat, eggs and butter. By the time these basic items were available once again, many traditional ways of cooking had been forgotten or,

without servants, were no longer practical.

In their place came an emphasis on convenience, with time-saving appliances and the modern supermarket with its rows of tinned and frozen foods. The neighbourhood grocer, butcher and fishmonger began to disappear – and with them, the attention to freshness and understanding of ingredients which had been taken for granted.

But the supermarkets had their advantages. Thanks to modern modes of transport, they could bring produce from sunnier parts of the world to the British masses, and at a reasonable price. Oranges, avocados and olive oil were once luxury items, and could now be

afforded by all. Very gradually, British chefs – and humble dinner party hosts – have learned how to incorporate the full flavours of the Mediterranean into the wholesome staples of the British diet. An army of foodies has goaded the supermarkets into providing fresh herbs year round, bread baked on the premises, and organic produce and meats.

Today one does not have to look very far to find examples of this "Modern British" cuisine. From Cornwall to Caithness you will see upmarket restaurant menus with dishes like roast cod with basil mash, roast rack of lamb with Provençal herbs, and raspberry profiteroles. The interest in cookery programmes on TV is so entrenched that there are now televised cook-offs and even game shows.

If, however, you don't fancy a seared tuna steak drizzed with a sun-dried tomato coulis, you can still find the fish-and-chip shops and kebab stalls which have made British food known the world over.

Games

G could also stand for Good Losers because the British, although they invented or developed a remarkable number of the world's most popular sports, pride themselves on the good grace with which they routinely accept defeat at the hands of former colonial subjects or various other over-zealous foreigners. It's playing the game that counts, as the old saying (or excuse) goes, not the winning.

That's certainly true of cricket, which has been described as "a game which the British, not being a spiritual people, had to invent in order to have some concept of eternity." The main purpose is simple: a bowler hurls a leather-covered ball at three wooden stumps in order to dislodge two strips of wood (bails) resting on top of them, and the batsman tries to deflect the ball with a paddle-shaped piece of willow. But the byzantine rules, first laid down by London's Marylebone Cricket Club in 1788, are best captured by a satirical definition: "You have two sides, one out in the field and one in. Each man that's in the side that's in, goes out and when he's out he comes in and the next man goes in until he's out. When they're all out, the side that's out comes in and the side that's been in goes out and tries to get those coming in out.

Sometimes you get men still in and not out. When both sides have been in and out, including the not-outs, that's the end of the game." Not surprisingly, an international match can take from three to five days to complete.

But cricket isn't really Britain's national game; it's England's. The Welsh much prefer rugby and the Scots soccer. Rugby, it has been said, is a thug's game played by gentlemen, while soccer is a gentleman's game played by thugs. Rugby Union (largely an amateur sport) and Rugby League (the professional variant) are both played with an oval ball and supposedly originated in England's Rugby School in 1823

Assoc. gave birth to the term "soccer".) In recent years, Britain has been in the vanguard of developing international soccer hooliganism.

The Scots, while football-mad, can lay claim to inventing the more placid game of golf in the 14th or 15th century, and the Royal and Ancient Golf Club of St Andrew's remains one of the golf world's governing bodies. Golf was also seen as a threat to archery, and the Scottish Parliament banned it in 1457. Mary, Queen of Scots took the game to France, where her attendants were known as cadets, hence "caddies".

So what happened to all the archers? They headed for the nearest pub and invented darts.

when a pupil playing football picked up the ball and ran with it. Rugby's rules are relatively simple, but it involves a lot of body contact.

Football, first played in England in the 12th century, puts the emphasis on kicking the ball rather than other players. So popular did it rapidly become that several English monarchs tried to ban it because it was diverting their subjects from the more military sport of archery. Its rules were finally codified in 1863 by the London Football Association (the abbreviation

LEFT: Terence Conran, the founder of Habitat who became one of London's high-profile restaurateurs.
ABOVE: cricket, the game that united the British Empire.

Heritage Industry

One reason why the British appear to live so much in the past is that they've got so much of it. Yet not until the 1980s, when corporatism and Margaret Thatcher took Great Britain Ltd by the throat, did anyone realise that The Past needed to be ruthlessly revalued on the national balance sheet. What's more, it needed a bright new image. So it changed its name. It became Heritage.

The tourist map of Britain took on a new aspect. Instead of the familiar counties and areas, there appeared Robin Hood Country, James Herriott Country, Rob Roy Country, Jane

Austen Country… Soon any area without such slick identification sought it. The depressed northeast, for instance, baptised itself Catherine Cookson Country – much to the confusion of tourists who turned up in South Tyneside in search of the mean streets that Ms Cookson had captured so well in her novels, only to find that they had long since been bulldozed.

Almost every week, somewhere in this economically declining country, a new museum opens. No aspect of life can escape being removed, rearranged, sanitised and preserved for profit. As the iron and steel industries wither away, the Ironbridge Gorge Museum flourishes. As coal mines close throughout Wales, the Big Pit mining museum at Blaenavon kits out tourists in hard hats and miners' lamps.

Critics complain that recreated "heritage" is often bogus history. Many new-wave industrial entertainments, said a former director of the Ironbridge Gorge Museum, tend to create a "curious, nostalgic, rose-coloured picture of a sort of Pickwickian industrial past which bears no relation to reality, but which we like to imagine. A lot of what is presented isn't based on scholarship at all but on attitude and emotion."

In the end, there are distinctions to be drawn. "Places like Jorvik in York, Beamish industrial museum in Durham and Ironbridge in Shropshire offer you 'real' artefacts as well as reconstructions," says Gordon Marsden, editor of *History Today* magazine. "But a themed museum like, say, the Oxford Story in Oxford is more like an Easter egg – hollow inside. You get a quick whisk through the past but then come out with nothing real to relate to."

It's all becoming rather Orwellian, people sometimes say. But even George Orwell might be taken aback to find that the subject of his 1930s study of recession in *The Road to Wigan Pier* has now become –what else? – the £3.5 million Wigan Heritage Centre.

Islands

Great Britain is the largest of the British Isles, an archipelago made up of around 2,000 islands. It is distinguished from the United Kingdom (of Great Britain and Northern Ireland) by the specific exclusion of any part of Ireland, and from the British Isles by the exclusion of the self-governing Isle of Man and Channel Islands.

The Isle of Man, in the Irish Sea midway between England and Ireland and 16 miles (25 km) from the Scottish coast, has a population of some 50,000. Its parliament, the House of Keys, is said to be the world's oldest. The Manx language, from the same root as Gaelic, was spoken by half the inhabitants at the end of the 19th century, but it has now died out. The island is famous for the tail-less Manx cat, and for the use of the birch, an instrument of corporal punishment employed by the courts.

The idea of being a king of an island is clearly attractive and whole islands do occasionally come up for sale. The reclusive Barclay broth-

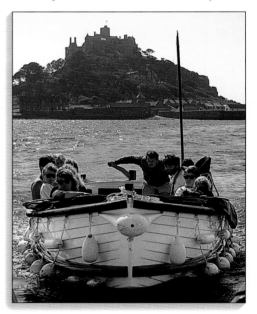

THE CHANNEL ISLANDS

Victor Hugo called the Channel Islands "pieces of France which fell into the sea and were gathered up by England." Best known as tax havens, the two main bank-laden islands are Jersey (45 sq. miles/117 sq. km) and Guernsey (24 sq. miles/62 sq. miles). The 2 sq.-mile (5 sq.-km) island of Sark is a feudal remnant, ruled over by an hereditary seigneur. The islands lie in the Gulf of St Malo just off the French coast and constitutionally are not part of the United Kingdom, yet their ambience is resolutely British. English holidaymakers like the slightly French ambience combined with the familiar English language.

ers, owners of *The Scotsman* and *The European* newspapers, bought Brecqhou, one of the Channel Islands, and fortified it to keep their castle-like mansion private. But most marketable islands are on the western side of Britain, from the Isles of Scilly off Land's End in Cornwall, past Anglesea in Wales to the more prolific Western Isles of Scotland. In the far northwest are the Hebrides; flying off the northeast are Orkney and the Shetland islands, where Britain's most northerly inhabited island, Muckle Flugga, is manned by brave lighthouse keepers.

Inter-island transport in these remote places is sometimes difficult and often exhilarating.

speculators and tycoons. Owning an island still has a poetic appeal, no matter what the cost. Accordingly, prices have spiralled. The islanders have grown nervous; when an island is sold, the futures of its residents hang in the balance. (In 1997, the islanders of Eigg breathed a sigh of relief when they finally managed, with the help of a benefactor, to pool together enough money to buy the island for themselves.)

When a new owner has taken possession of an island, he is only the lord of all he can see when the tide is high. When the tide is low, he is surrounded by the Crown, because the monarch owns the foreshore.

With Caledonian MacBrayne, the Scottish ferry company, it is possible to island-hop through 22 of the Western Isles. Loganair has the shortest scheduled flight in the world – a two-minute flight between two Orkney islands – and uses fields and even beaches as landing strips.

Some of the Scottish islands are getting their own private airstrips for the use of new owners. From having been traditionally the property of the landed aristocracy, many are now being bought by film stars, rock musicians, property

LEFT: St Michael's Mount, off the coast of Cornwall.
ABOVE: Benny Hill, whose smutty but inoffensive humour went down surprisingly well in America.

Jokes

For a slightly objective view of something so intensely subjective as humour, one could do worse than seek the opinion of George Mikes, a Hungarian who moved to England where he became a humorous writer. "Britain is the only country in the world which is inordinately proud of its sense of humour," he said. "In other countries, if they find you inadequate or they hate you, they will call you stupid, ill-mannered, a horse-thief or hyena. In England, they will say that you have no sense of humour. That is the final condemnation, the total dismissal."

Yet no monolithic British sense of humour exists. There are many varieties, of which five are most common:

Irony. To justify their view of themselves as good losers, to whom playing the game is more important than winning it – fortunately, given their usual performance – the British have developed a sophisticated self-mockery. It is a virtue to be able to laugh at oneself.

Satire. The satirist, who laughs at others, is nourished by the prevalence of hypocrisy in national life. Also, given the rigidity and conservatism of most national habits and institutions, it's easier to joke about them than to

change them. Political pamphleteering nourished that habit, which continued in such TV programmes as *Yes, Prime Minister*. The great visual tradition of vicious caricature, which reached its peak in the 18th and 19th centuries with James Gillray, George Cruikshank and William Hogarth, was continued in the TV puppet show *Spitting Image*.

Smut. Farces in which hilarity often relies on males losing their trousers remain popular theatre. Because the British are repressed about sex, dirty jokes abound and comedians such as the late Benny Hill built careers on a limited range of innuendo. "Mark my words," warned playwright Alan Bennett, "when a society has

to resort to the lavatory for its humour, the writing is on the wall."

Absurdity. Perhaps as a palliative against the national failings of formality and pomposity, surreal humour is highly developed. Lewis Carroll is the greatest literary exemplar, and there is a long tradition of nonsense verse. Modern examples are the radio *Goon Shows* of the 1950s (in which Peter Sellers made his name) and the *Monty Python's Flying Circus* TV comedies of the 1970s. Cruelty and sadism figure heavily in this form of humour, allowing people to channel nastiness and frustration into a socially acceptable outlet, smiling politely.

Wit. Shakespeare is full of it and Dr Johnson is still endlessly quoted ("A second marriage is the triumph of hope over experience"). The richness of the English language, with its wealth of homonyms and synonyms, encouraged verbal acrobats such as Oscar Wilde ("He hasn't a single redeeming vice.") and George Bernard Shaw ("An Englishman thinks he is moral when he is only uncomfortable."). But there's also ready wit to be found in most areas of national life, even in Parliament. In one famous exchange, Lady Astor spat at Sir Winston Churchill: "If the Rt. Hon. Gentleman were my husband, I'd put poison in his tea." To which Churchill replied: "If the Hon. Lady were my wife, I would drink it."

Knights

Twice a year, at New Year and on the Queen's official birthday in June, British newspapers carry two pages of tiny type – the Honours List of medals given out to the good, the worthy, the dedicated, the long-serving. Most simply receive medals (Order of the British Empire or Commander of the British Empire), a few are made lords, others will be made knights, to be called, for ever after, Sir or Dame.

This is what is left of the system of patronage and chivalry upon which wars were fought, taxes levied and monarchs, however mad or bad, could guarantee a faithful following. In the Middle Ages there were two kinds of knight: religious and secular. Religious orders, such as the Knights Templar, took monastic vows and devoted themselves to crusades against the infidel, while the secular knights enrolled in the services of noblemen. By the 14th century, however, knights had become merely wealthy landowners and anyone holding property worth more than £20 a year could buy a title.

There is no evidence of titles being bought in modern times, but a certain amount of sucking up to the political parties, including generous donations to party funds, is common. The Honours List is compiled by the civil service for the government of the day, although the public can also nominate worthy recipients in their communities. The Queen turns the winners into knights by dubbing them on each shoulder with a cermonial sword in the time-honoured way.

The recipients are something rather pre-

ours List, as she had done so little to support gays. But few minded Elton John becoming Sir Elton after he sang "Candle in the Wind" at the Princess of Wales's funeral service.

There are 10 different orders of knighthood. There is a better chance of becoming a lowly Knight Batchelor than joining one of the more obscure orders, such as The Most Eminent Order of the Indian Empire, a title not conferred on anyone since 1947. Most would be content with a less chivalrous Baronetage or Knightage with a title of Sir and, for Sir's wife, Lady, and the knowledge that they have joined an exclusive club of around 4,500. Membership is for

dictable, for the most part unknown beavers, busybodies and bureaucrats. Headlines focus on the sprinkling of knighthoods for people in the arts and sport, since the public might at least have heard of them. There is often a frisson of controversy. When the Beatles were given their Orders of the British Empire (knighthoods not included), disgusted colonels sent their medals back to the Queen. The actor and gay activist Ian McKellen was rebuked for accepting a knighthood in Margaret Thatcher's final Hon-

life unless, as in the case of the odd financier and businessman, they are jailed ("detained at Her Majesty's pleasure" is the euphemism), in which case Her Majesty can show her displeasure by demanding the title back.

Lords

Some Britons are born lords, some achieve their lordships, and some have lordships thrust upon them, but no longer is the monarch predisposed to carve up parcels of the kingdom for some lordly pals, for the kingdom has long since been accounted for.

LEFT: John Cleese, star of *Monty Python's Flying Circus* and *Fawlty Towers*, in the guise of a British bobby.
ABOVE: Roxburgh, a Scottish lord at home.

All Britain's aristocrats are lords, but not all lords are aristocracy. The pecking order of the nation's nobility, at last count, goes like this: royal dukes 5 (Edinburgh, Cornwall, York, Gloucester, Kent), ordinary dukes 24, marquesses 35, earls 204, viscounts 127 and barons 500. Kindly address a duke as "Your Grace" and a marquess as "Most Honourable". For the rest, "Right Honourable Lord" will do. What separates a duke from a baron is one yard of velvet and 3 inches of ermine trim, the difference between the length of train on the ceremonial robe each is entitled to wear.

In general, English lords take precedence over Scottish lords, of whom there are a disproportionate number; they include the Duke of Atholl, the only man in the realm allowed to keep a standing army, which he does in his 100-strong Atholl Highlanders.

The stately homes of many lords can now be visited. The burden of death duties, and of maintaining these crumbling piles, turned some of them into theme parks from the 1960s onwards. Otherwise, floating the odd Old Master or piece of furniture on to the art markets keeps them going for a year or two.

There are some 800 peers of the realm in all. With few exceptions their titles pass through the male side of the family. The heirs to a large chunk of Britain will undoubtedly attend a top public school, but not go to university, preferring instead officer training at the Royal Military Academy, Sandhurst, after which they would hope to be commissioned into one of the army's prestigious Guards regiments.

At the age of 21, they can take their places in Parliament's Upper House, the House of Lords. There they make speeches and pass or amend legislation sent for approval by the House of Commons. Theoretically they may speak their minds, but some conformity is expected. When John, Viscount Amberley, Lord Russell, spoke in the House in 1978 demanding the abolition of prisons, free goods in shops, free houses for girls aged 12 and the abolition of marriage, he was not allowed even to finish his speech.

In order to try to get some sense out of this place, and to try to bolster party support, Life Peers are created in the annual Honours List (*see Knights*). These peerages are often handed out to former politicians from the House of Commons who have been "kicked upstairs" for reasons either of age or of political expediency.

More properly called Life Barons, this is a junior award, made only for the holder's own lifetime and no title is passed on to the children.

There are around 400 Life Peers, added to which are the Archbishops of Canterbury and York plus 24 bishops, making up the Lords Spiritual, and 19 Law Lords, judges who are Lords of Appeal. That makes a total of more than 1,200 entitled to sit in the House of Lords, though at its most crowded (such as the day when the television cameras were first switched on) there will be barely 300 there. The various lords own so much of the country they can't be expected to run the damn thing, too.

ARE ALL LORDS LOADED?

Lords are not all rich and powerful. Every now and again a newspaper discovers one living in a bedsit or working as a railway porter. But death duties and other taxes apart, they don't have too much to complain about. One of Britain's wealthiest men is the Duke of Westminster who inherited his many millions-worth of Westminster and Belgravia property before he was 30, making him an exceptionally eligible bachelor.

Many lords still live in their stately homes, and among them are sumptuous museums of art and architecture, harbouring collections that would put many a big-city art gallery to shame.

Monarchy

"Her majesty's speech delivered upon the reassembling of parliament was, as usual, insipid and uninstructive. Its preferred topic was her majesty's approaching marriage, a matter of little importance or interest to the country, except as it may thereby be burdened with additional and unnecessary expense." That curt dismissal of Queen Victoria was written by a correspondent of *The Times* a century and a half ago. Since then the tribes of Britain have become noticeably more democratic, more plu-

richest woman and is the custodian of the world's largest private collection of art. Conscious of certain criticism, she recently began to pay tax and many "lesser" royals were removed from the Civil List, which provides public money towards their expenses.

Sometimes there is an outcry if lesser royals are seen to be living off the fat without putting in time on what can be an arduous stream of official engagements. But the British still regard the monarchy as a useful and desirable institution. By its very age it is a potent symbol of national identity; by being above party politics and not subject to election, it provides the State

ralistic, more educated, more informed and far more reverential to the family whom they continue to crown with the world's most valuable single piece of jewellery.

Her Majesty Queen Elizabeth II, descendent of both Kings Egbert of Wessex (AD 827–39) and McAlpine of Scotland (1057–93), and relative of the half-dozen remaining monarchs of Europe, earns around £1.8 million a day. It takes only the briefest whistle-stop tour of Britain's major palaces to realise that she is the world's

with a sense of last-bastion hope against the incompetence of often uninspiring politicians; and not least it is a darned good show.

Unlike Queen Victoria, who tried to interfere with her democratically elected prime ministers and became so disenchanted with the whole business of politics that she seriously considered packing her bags and ruling the Empire from Australia, her descendents who have reigned this century as the House of Windsor have been adept at keeping clear of the political arena. Never mind that, as builders, art patrons or setters of style, they have often seemed uninspired dullards.

The Queen passed retiring age in 1986 and

LEFT: Lord Denning, one of Britain's most distinguished law lords.
ABOVE: the Queen and Prince Philip.

she has made it known that, should the public want it, she would go. But opinion polls show that she retains broad support. The same cannot be said of her son and heir, Charles III (as he would be), who often seems ill-at-ease in public. Much mud was flung during the break-up of his marriage to Diana, Princess of Wales, and her tragic death in 1997 led to more calls that Charles should stand aside from the succession in favour of his eldest son, Prince William.

The ideal "image" of the royals in the 1990s is still a matter of debate. Nobody wants them to return to being the remote figureheads they were until the 1960s; Diana's overwhelming

made the TV show seem almost restrained. So will the royals survive into the 21st century? Will Charles ever make it to the throne? Stay tuned for tomorrow's exciting episode…

Newspapers

After listening to a journalist passionately defending the importance of a politically free and unfettered press in a modern democracy such as Britain, a character in Tom Stoppard's play *Night and Day* replies: "I'm with you on the free press. It's the newspapers I can't stand."

popularity certainly stemmed from her rejection of formal protocol and willingness to express her emotions as well as from her glamour.

But many people also question whether the insistence of Britain's tabloid press in treating the family as the cast of an action-packed soap opera, reporting sexual indiscretions in a way undreamt of a decade ago, has destroyed the mystique a hereditary monarchy needs to prosper in a democratic age. A savage TV puppet show, *Spitting Image*, lampooned them mercilessly, depicting Princess Margaret as a gin swiller and Prince Charles as an ecology freak. But the scandals surrounding the separations of Andrew and Fergie and Charles and Diana

THE SCANDAL SHEETS

The Sun, which unashamedly panders to Britain's lowest common denominator, remains the best-selling daily, with a circulation of nearly 4 million. The popularity of the tabloids makes them hard to ignore, but, even so, governments (whether Conservative or Labour) periodically threaten legal curbs when they feel the press is against them. The circumstances of the death of Diana, Princess of Wales in 1997 led to a sober re-assessment of journalistic values, particularly regarding the use of paparazzi photographs; all tabloid editors pledged not to use unauthorized pictures of Diana's sons.

Many share that ambivalence, and opinion polls show that journalists are rated in public esteem somewhere below tax inspectors and secondhand car salesmen. The old Humbert Wolfe rhyme is often quoted:

You cannot hope to bribe or twist,
thank God, the British journalist.
But, seeing what the man will do
unbribed, there's no occasion to.

One reason for such cynicism is that, while Britain has some of the best newspapers in the world (*The Times, The Guardian, The Independent,* the *Financial Times*), it also has some of the worst (*The Sun, The Star*).

By "worst", one means that objective news is consistently subordinated to highly imaginative stories about the sex lives of TV personalities, pop stars, footballers and the royal family, and that the few columns of genuine news are grotesquely sensationalised. Rupert Murdoch is generally credited with having started the downward slide with *The Sun*, best known for its photographs of topless models and its robust patriotism (its page-one headline after the sinking of the *Belgrano* during the Falklands War, with the drowning of many Argentine sailors, read simply "Gotcha!").

The saving grace is the diversity of Britain's papers. Ten national dailies (total daily sale: 14 million) and nine Sundays (total sale: 15 million) are distributed nationwide, augmented by a host of regional dailies and local weeklies.

One worry is concentration of ownership: Rupert Murdoch alone owns four national bestsellers – the top daily tabloid (*The Sun*), the second-ranking quality daily (*The Times*), the top Sunday scandal-sheet (*News of the World*, circulation: 4.5 million) and the top Sunday quality (the *Sunday Times*, 1.3 million). Within two years in the mid-1990s, Murdoch doubled the circulation of the *Times* by ruthless price-cutting; on some days it sold for 10p.

In Mrs Thatcher's time, most national newspapers were politically right of centre, but as Labour began to look electable, even Rupert Murdoch discovered a soft spot for Tony Blair, and the hitherto rabidly right-wing *Sun* backed Labour in the 1997 general election.

LEFT: avid readers of the world's best and the world's worst newspapers.
RIGHT: gardening is the nation's favourite hobby, and topiary is one of its more esoteric facets.

Outdoor Activities

Despite living on an island notorious for inhospitable weather, the British seem to enjoy spending a great deal of time out of doors – in their gardens or, increasingly, following more energetic outdoor pursuits. Exactly why they should prefer golf to basketball, and mountaineering to gymnastics, even after successive cold, damp sporting holidays, is a mystery.

Apart from gardening, the nation's most popular leisure activity is walking – or rambling, as it is often known. During the Industrial Revo-

lution, workers in the polluted northern mill towns fought for the right to roam the countryside on their days off. Rights of way from time immemorial were legally enshrined as public footpaths – which is just as well, as even in 1908 a member of the Commons and Footpaths Preservation Society complained in *The Times* that the motor car had made walking on narrow country roads too dangerous to contemplate.

Today, the Ramblers Association and affiliated groups have nearly 200,000 members and wage recurring battles against landowners who erect barbed-wire fences, plough up footpaths, or apply to abolish historic rights of way. Every local tourist authority can supply information on attractive walks in its vicinity, which generally pass conveniently close to a good pub.

Cyclists, too, are increasingly well catered for. Britain chose to celebrate the Millennium by criss-crossing itself with cycle routes from Elgin to Eastbourne and from Fishguard to Felixstowe. The routes are a combination of traffic-free paths and quiet roads, and are sometimes established on disused railway lines, now paved over.

For those of hardier disposition, there is also skiing in Scotland's Cairngorms, surfing and scuba-diving in the West Country, hang-gliding in any coastal or hilly area, and horse riding

everywhere. Many Britons find that the best way to meet nature on its own terms is simply by heading towards the nearest body of water and sinking a rod – if you are so tempted, do remember to buy a fishing licence.

Pubs

The best pub in England is called The Moon Under Water, and it hides down an unprepossessing side street in an old northern industrial town not far from Manchester. It has that indefinable richness of atmosphere that comes in part from its customers, who are mostly reg-

ulars and who attend not only for the beer but equally for the conversation, and in part from its uncompromisingly Victorian architecture and fittings, its dark-grained mahogany, ornamental mirrors and sparkling etched glass, its cast-iron fireplaces and ceiling stained yellow-brown by decades of nicotine, all combining to create the solid comfortable ugliness that often characterised the 19th century.

It has games, particularly darts, in its public bar, and good solid plain food at prices that would bankrupt a restaurant. It has barmaids who know everyone by name, and a delightful garden where, in summer, the customers drink under the shade of plane trees, while their children play at a decent distance on thoughtfully provided swings and slides.

The Moon Under Water is entirely free from modern miseries: from piped music, from plastic panels masquerading as oak, from the flashing lights of video games. It is always quiet enough to talk, if only to praise the excellence of the fine traditional English ale.

The Moon Under Water does not exist, and never did (although there is now a modern chain of pubs by that name). It was a figment of the imagination of George Orwell, the author of *Nineteen Eighty-Four*, who 50 years ago played a round of that perennially popular English game – dreaming of the perfect pub. There are 70,000 pubs in England and Wales and several thousand more in Scotland. Some are a great deal closer to perfection than others.

There are certain well-defined ground rules for what makes a *good* pub. In the English beer-drinker's Bible, the annual *Good Beer Guide,* author Michael Jackson wrote: "In a good pub, the greatest attention is given to the drink, and in particular to the beer. Sociability, on both sides of the bar, comes a close second. A good pub encourages social intercourse, and is not dominated by cliques. A good pub has a caring, responsive landlord, not an uninterested time-server or an arrogant buffoon. In a good pub, whatever further services are offered, there is always one bar (and preferably two) to accommodate those people who simply want to drink and chat without the distraction or inhibition induced by overbearing decor, noisy entertainment, or intrusive dining."

Most pubs have at least two bars: the "public bar" which is the basic drinking shop; and the "lounge bar". There may be a difference of a few pence in the drink prices; all pubs are required by law to put their price lists prominently on display.

Some would say that the public bar is for serious, usually male, drinkers, or for workers in dirty overalls. It will probably have a bare floor and a dartboard, or a pool table. Conventionally, the lounge bar is for sitting down, for entertaining women, for an evening out. It may have a piano or piped music.

The word "pub" is merely a shortened form of "public house", an indication that the earliest ale houses were simply private homes where the occupant brewed beer and sold it at the front

so much else in British life, the pub reached its zenith in Victorian times and the country is still immensely rich in opulent pub interiors from that period, despite all the efforts of philistine brewery corporations to rip them out in the name of "modernisation".

Pubs have been changing over the past few decades. More and more of them sell good, inexpensive food and are competing strongly with restaurants. Tea and coffee are often on offer and children are being made more welcome. The law says that no one under 14 may enter a pub, and between 14 and 18 they must be accompanied by an adult and may not buy or

door or across a table in the living room. To indicate that the house sold ale, the owner would hang out a sign, not saying "Ale", as the average Saxon peasant never graduated to literacy, but a pole topped with a bough of evergreen.

There is no shortage of claimants to be the Oldest Pub in Britain, but one with a stronger case than most is the Trip to Jerusalem, hacked into the rock beneath the walls of Nottingham Castle, and certainly in business at the time of the 13th-century Crusades, hence its name. Like

LEFT: enough open spaces remain to attract hikers – this one's in Ullswater in the Lake District.
ABOVE: the perfect pub also has the perfect barmaid.

WHAT MAKES A GOOD PUB

Every country has its drinking shop, but none has an institution quite like the British pub. The essence of a good pub (which modern buildings hardly ever achieve) is a feeling of intimacy. It must have nooks and crannies where conversations and assignations can take place without the world listening in. The beer must be pumped into the glass. Still alive and fermenting, it is drunk at the temperature of the cool dark cellar without refrigeration. It has no gas added to make it fizz, and it is brewed only from barley, hops and pure clear water. It should be golden or straw-coloured, and crystal-clear.

consume liquor. In reality some pubs, especially in country districts, welcome whole families. Some set aside special rooms for children, and where there are gardens they are almost always welcome. It is, in the end, up to the absolute discretion of the landlord, and how strictly the local police chief applies the law. In bigger cities, certain pubs have a predominantly gay clientele.

The most radical change, however, came about in the 1988 licensing laws which allowed pubs in England and Wales to open not just at lunch time and in the evening, but all day, from 11am to 11pm. (Scottish laws already permitted all-day opening.) About a third of the pubs take advantage of this. Twenty minutes' "drinking up" time is officially allowed after the closing time.

But drink-drive laws, health concerns and the rise of home entertainment have all hit the pub trade. Many small country pubs have closed, and the brewers have turned to every more bizarre "theme pubs" to woo younger drinkers.

Queues

"A man in a queue is as much the image of a true Briton as a man in a bull-ring is the image of a Spaniard or a man with a two-foot cigar of an American," wrote humorist George Mikes. "An Englishman, even if he is alone, forms an orderly queue of one."

Queue-jumping incurs severe social disapproval, though this takes no more serious form than tut-tutting and loud remarks such as: "I say, don't they know there's a queue?" The easiest response is to pretend one is a foreigner; the affronted queuers will then sigh, knowing that you know no better, poor soul, having been deprived of their cultural conditioning.

Some think that the orderly behaviour of most crowds is the only rational behaviour when one lives in a small, overpopulated island. Others see such conspicuous respect for order as the Germanic traits never far below the surface in the British character.

Ralf Dahrendorf, a German who became head of the London School of Economics, may have got to the heart of the matter when he said: "I have a feeling that this island is uninhabitable, and therefore people have tried to make it habitable by being reasonable with one another." Don't all rush to agree – there's a queue!

Race

Britons have the blood of many people coursing through their veins. Even before history was written, tribes were coming in from Iberia, central Europe and the Indian subcontinent. Romans were followed by waves of Jutes, Angles, Saxons, Scandinavians and Normans (originally Scandinavian Norsemen). What Prince Llewellyn was fighting for in Wales was not the original Celtic heritage, but the last bastion of a tribe driven up from Iberia and finally stopped by the Irish Sea. Robert the Bruce,

champion of the Scots, was descended from Robert de Bruis, a French Norman knight who arrived with William the Conqueror.

Trade, persecution and war brought Flemish weavers, French Huguenots, Chinese sailors, White Russians, patriotic Poles and German Jews. Hunger brought, among others, the Irish. In the 1950s Commonwealth citizens were enticed to Britain with job offers, but when they arrived, mostly from the West Indies, they found a welcome not quite as warm as they had been led to expect. There are around half a million West Indians now; many have become assimilated into British culture, although some of the latest generation have begun to reassert their

Afro-Caribbean heritage. Five black politicians made it to parliament in the 1997 election.

Asians came, too, from Africa and the Indian subcontinent, heading for the manufacturing cities of Birmingham, Bradford and Leicester. In 1972 Asians thrown out of Uganda were reluctantly allowed into Britain: increasingly, Her Majesty's Principal Secretary of State for Foreign and Commonwealth Affairs did not want to allow its Commonwealth citizens the right of abode – as many Hong Kong Chinese discovered when the colony reverted to China in 1997 – and the word "immigrant" became a euphemism for coloureds or blacks.

chip shops run as Chinese takeaways. There are around 868,000 Indians in Britain, 554,000 Pakistanis, 184,000 from Bangladesh and 123,000 Chinese. Other ethnic minorities include 484,000 Afro-Caribbeans and 73,000 Arabs.

Coloured ethnic groups make up just over 3 percent of Britain's 57 million population. Racial intolerance is not endemic but some nasty incidents are reported. Sometimes poor black communities are provoked; sometimes they erupt. In surveys over the years, race has been seen as a diminishing social problem, but the country still has a long way to go before it feels comfortable as a multi-racial society.

Many Ugandan Asians were professional businessmen and, though they had to start their lives again with nothing, some were able to build up highly successful companies which their sons are now inheriting. On a smaller scale, newsagents and local grocers' shops with long opening hours are often Asian-run; in towns and villages everywhere there are Indian restaurants, usually owned or managed by people from Pakistan or Bangladesh.

Also noticeable are the traditional fish-and-

LEFT: about 3 percent of Britain's population is coloured. ABOVE: sometimes the fickle weather does permit an outdoor *amour* in the park.

Sex

Time to consult George Mikes again. "Continental people," he said, "have a sex life; the English have hot-water bottles." The description is probably just as true of the Scots and Welsh, though of course there are exceptions, and the nation did have a brief affair with sex in the Swinging Sixties. But in the Aids era, the pendulum has swung back: *No Sex, Please, We're British* enjoyed an exceptionally long run in the West End.

Britons prefer their sex to be safe, a bit of a naughty joke rather than a dangerous affair.

There is a parallel with traditional British eating habits: performed when needs dictate, with minimum flair.

Just as Continental caterers have found scant competition in setting up the smaller, best-run restaurants and cafés, so generations of Continental men, faced with the British female on holiday, must wonder when their luck is going to run out. Why should the most insincere, banal compliment, even when garnished with a foreign accent, produce such instant success year after year? It must be because, whatever other qualities it may possess, British sexuality is sorely lacking in flattery and flirtation. More

DISCREET CHARMS

The British do not like overt sex displays. Not for them the garish shop windows of Dutch and German red-light districts. Every taste is catered for, particularly in the capital, but it is all reasonably discreet. No longer do street-walkers of both sexes ply their trade around Piccadilly Circus. The women left that scene decades ago and the boys' meat-rack was swept away by big police clean-ups more recently. But no telephone kiosk in town is without its "calling cards" tucked into every crevice, advertising a Roman-orgy range of vices for those who care to call.

often an initial encounter will involve insulting banter. Two young men, for instance, may approach two young women in the following manner. One youth will target the woman of his choice and give his companion a grotesque nudge. "Here!" he will shout merrily. "Don't think much of your one!" From this exchange, the young lady in question will understand that her swain fancies her very much indeed.

Traditionally, the attitude of the British to sex is prudish and repressive. They are supposed to be secretly addicted to spanking and other forms of corporal punishment for which public school has instilled a taste. They send each other childish postcards showing, perhaps, a puny, hen-pecked husband, his fat and unattractive wife and a beautiful big-busted bikini-clad passer-by. The printed jest is double entendre of the "Ooh, what a lovely pear" variety.

This is by no means old-fashioned humour, as any click of the radio or television switch will reveal. There is no better crash course of British sexuality than the *Carry On* films (28 in all, full of cosy sexual stereotypes, from tarty, pneumatic blondes to outrageously effeminate homosexuals) or a *Benny Hill Show*. Our Benny played the archetypal innocent abroad, leering hopelessly at lovely women. The "laddish" humour of the 1990s was louder and more aggressive but no more sexually mature.

Sex has never been a legitimate excuse for a crime of passion in Britain, but it haunts politicians. In 1963 the Profumo Scandal hastened the end of Harold Macmillan's Conservative government. The country was enthralled by the saga ("War Minister shares delights of call girl with Soviet naval attaché") and it still excited enough interest to be a successful film, *Scandal*, a quarter of a century later.

Tea

On average, Britons drink five cups of tea a day, consuming about one third of the total tea export market every year. The "real" cup of tea is, however, not always easy to find. Places to go looking are posh hotels that cater for the better-off tourist, low-budget cafés of the fish-and-chip variety that thrive in seaside towns, and native British homes that have not gone over to teabags.

The finest tea is made from the bud and first

two leaves of the tea bush. They should be steeped in boiled water for between three and five minutes. Traditionally, very strong Indian tea, rigid with tannin and probably jaw-clenchingly sweet, is favoured by burly men who work with their hands, while women, children and effete males like their cuppa watery-weak and China. But an occasional macho workman called out to fix something in a British home has reportedly voiced approval of delicately scented, pale Earl Grey.

WHAT HIGH TEA MEANS

High Tea is a full meal – an early supper which may contain ham and eggs, bread-and-butter with a variety of spreads and a good helping of cakes.

Notoriously cold British bedrooms inspired the Teasmade, a weird, rather outdated contraption – part alarm-clock, part Thermos, part eyesore – that promised a pre-programmed steaming cup of tea upon wakening. The taste does not live up to its technology, alas, but the idea of a solitary or marital cup taken in bed suits the national isolationism – in contrast, for example, with the early morning Italian espresso downed sociably, standing elbow to elbow with strangers.

Dipping a biscuit, cake or

There are as many ways of making a cup of tea properly as there are British residents and all methods involve mysterious and magical warmings and stirrings of the pot, exact timings and individual blends. Up North, they tend to put the tea in first, then add milk; down South they do the reverse and both halves of the country swear blind that theirs is the only way to make tea. Anyone with Far or Near East connections may well add a sneaky pinch of cardamom.

LEFT: Christine Keeler rocked the government in 1963 when her liaison with the War Minister coincided with a liaison with the Soviet naval attaché.
ABOVE: drinking tea involves a degree of etiquette.

burger in your teacup (dunking), or drinking from the saucer and blowing on your tea to cool it are socially out of order. It is also bad form to borrow someone else's spoon. Locals may call tea "tiffin", "char", "Rosie" (tea rhymes with Rosie Lee) or a "cuppa". They make it as a form of displacement activity, rather as a confused cat resorts to an unnecessary wash, at moments of high and emotional drama in their lives. Births and deaths require several gallons.

Diarist Samuel Pepys found his first cup of China tea such a novelty in 1660 that he gave it a special entry. In its early days, it was so expensive that it was locked away in metal caddies to stop the servants helping themselves. Adding to the price was the cost of transportation from the Far East on such speedy clippers as the *Cutty Sark*, now in dry dock at Greenwich, in London.

A cup of tea, without sugar or milk, contains only about four calories. Its stimulating effect is due to caffeine (weight for weight, tea leaves contain more than twice the caffeine of coffee beans). Its astringency and colour come from the tannin content, its flavour from volatile oils.

The habit of afternoon tea with cakes was started around 1840 by the Duchess of Bedford. The West Country's rich cream teas, with scones, jam, clotted cream and cakes to accompany the pot of tea, is inexpensive, delicious in a sickly way and packed with cholesterol. For a traditional afternoon tea, try a big hotel like the London Ritz, though you have to book. To work one off, find a Tea Dance where you can do the foxtrot to such nostalgic inter-war orchestral numbers as *Blue Moon* and *Smoke Gets In Your Eyes*. Such dances were once highly fashionable and are still popular with older people, the occasional member of parliament and anyone else with a little free time in the afternoon.

Union Jack

The flag of Great Britain is the same as the flag of the United Kingdom, which includes Northern Ireland. Most Britons do not know its proper name and they call it the Union Jack. The better informed call it the Union Flag, though a further name for it is the Great Union (not to be confused with the Grand Union, a pleasant north London canal).

The Union Flag was designed after the union

between England and Scotland in 1606, combining the red cross of St George (heraldically speaking, cross gules in a field argent) with Scotland's cross of St Andrew, a white diagonal cross on a blue background (saltire argent in a field azure). In 1801 the red diagonal cross (saltire gules in a field argent) of Ireland's St Patrick was added. No room is left for Wales's St Dewi, or David, whose emblem is a dove.

The constituent parts of the kingdom also have animals and plants for their own flags and heraldic devices: lions for both England and Scotland and a dragon for Wales; a rose for England, a thistle for Scotland and a leek for Wales.

HOW TO FLY THE FLAG

The Union Flag is a bit lopsided and may only be flown one way up. If hoisted incorrectly, particularly at sea, where mariners are well informed in these matters, it may be taken for a distress signal. The flag of any country hoisted on the jackstaff of a ship's bows is called the Jack. When the Union Flag is hoisted on a jackstaff it can be called the Union Jack. Tearing up or burning the Union Flag is impolite, but not an offence. During the funeral of Diana, Princess of Wales, the Union Jack was flown from Buckingham Palace at half mast – contrary to protocol, but in response to public demand.

Vicars

"What a pity it is that we have no amusements but vice and religion," said Sydney Smith. As a journalist as well as a clergyman, Smith, who was born in Essex in 1771, knew both the failings and the predelictions of the British. And, nearly two centuries after his death, the vicar is still portrayed as an object of affectionate ridicule. He is the stuff that farces are made of: a blathering, upper-class nincompoop who regularly looses his trousers or is otherwise compromised through misunderstandings. Or he is the sorry figure the tabloid press triumphantly unveils from time to time, accused of committing sins of the flesh.

In reality, the vicar who pops in for afternoon tea and lives in a large grace-and-favour vicarage is a disappearing breed. Although a slight upturn was detected in congregations in the early 1990s, they have dwindled, and Britain is no longer a nation of churchgoers. The Church is, however, a microcosm of society. Mosques, synagogues and temples co-exist beside cathedrals, churches and chapels. But it is the Church of England, with the Queen as its head, that is the backbone of Britain's moral society. The sovereign's role, established by Henry VIII,

women was one important issue on which some establishment figures could not yield – but instead of digging in their heels when women donned dog collars, they walked out and became Roman Catholic. The question of gay clergy has provoked a similar exodus but on a much smaller scale.

The church's Welsh and Scots counterparts are less flexible. The Scots Presbyterian Church is a stern church, Calvinist in its beliefs. Worshippers in the remoter parts of the country still regard cooking, washing up or reading a newspaper on Sundays as a cardinal sin. Scots Catholics, too, are far stricter than English ones.

gives her power to appoint (these days to approve) the two archbishops, of Canterbury and York, who are in turn responsible for their bishoprics and for the church's ruling body, the General Synod, which regulates church matters subject to parliament and royal assent.

On the whole, the Church of England, though rather stuck with a typically British misogynous establishment, is pretty easy-going. It has a liberal, ecumenical approach and prefers compassion to fire and brimstone. The ordination of

Nor is there such a liberal tradition among the ministry of Wales, where the utilitarian "chapel" is well attended. The chapels are Methodist, a movement founded by the 18th-century evangelist John Wesley, which urged thrift and hard work and appealed to the working class. It took hold in the working populations of northeast England, parts of Cornwall and, particularly, Wales where, linked with the Welsh language, Calvinistic Methodism evolved.

Unlike their English counterparts, none of these serious-minded clerics who watch from the side chapels of the realm are liable to be caught with their trousers down. If they were, it would be no laughing matter.

LEFT: patriotism shows its youthful face.
ABOVE: the Scots Presbyterian minister, who preaches a more robust Christianity than the Church of England.

Weather

"When two Englishmen meet, their first talk is of the weather," wrote Dr Samuel Johnson. Two centuries later, this relatively harmless national obsession is still going strong and no weather-related phrase is considered too banal or boring to merit use as a conversational opening gambit between strangers. Try "Hot/cold enough for you, then, is it?" "Looks like rain", "All right if you're a duck" and "Don't suppose this will hold much longer." All of these are useful, widely used phrases.

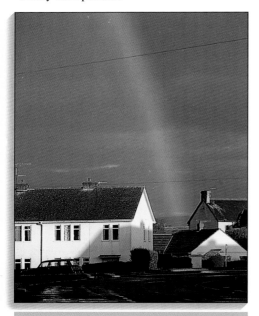

PEA SOUPERS

One famous British weather feature is, happily, gone: the noxious, sulphuric fog (from burning coal for heat) that used to blanket cities in chest-clogging yellow fumes and cause hundreds of deaths each year. It got everywhere, including the Royal Opera House where it was once so bad the audience could not see the stage. It became a stock favourite in films, wafting across lamplit, cobbled streets to denote 19th-century London. A sinister, cloaked stranger would collide with a policeman: "Terrible night, Guv, a real pea-souper"; another horrible murder was only moments away. In real life, the 1956 Clean Air Act put an end to these killer smogs.

Why should the British be so interested in the vagaries of their climate? The key lies in its unpredictability. Its swings of mood don't bear out its dull reputation at all. Far from always having the drizzly, mediocre summers and mild, wet winters of popular misconception, British weather can switch rapidly from drought to flood, damp cold to oppressive heat. Each dramatic change catches Britons on the hop.

The summer of 1976 contained the longest spell of continuous heat (followed by 1826 and 1995). In August 1990 temperatures reached the highest ever recorded: 98.8°F (37.1°C). Hurricanes in 1987 and 1990 caused several deaths and uprooted thousands of trees, Western film-style dust "devils" have blown through the lanes of Surrey, and waves higher than a double-decker bus submerged a seaside town in Wales.

Such violent extremes are made all the harder to bear because national habits, buildings and clothing are simply not designed to cope with them. Few homes or offices have fans or air conditioning to alleviate the summer's heat. In winter, heating and insulation systems work at half-cock, while road and rail networks inevitably come to a standstill in anything more than an inch of snow (one railway company, brought to a halt by one light snowfall, asserted – to general hilarity – it was the "wrong kind" of snow). Unwary motorists, villagers and livestock disappear under mounds of drifting snow in a manner that puzzles Continentals used to handling such seasonal hazards.

Older Britons take a strange pride in describing their childhood bedrooms in winter. These were often of such incredible coldness that parental false teeth and pet goldfish supposedly froze solid in their water overnight. Britons like to pretend to ignore the weather. They would prefer to pit themselves against the worst the elements can throw at them, rather than make themselves comfortable, which would be wimpish.

So, in summer's oven heat, they do not hide in tree-shaded piazzas or close their shutters to keep the tiled floor cool. Their cities are designed to ensure that streets become sweltering canyons, while overfurnished homes become more stuffy. Men sweat in summer traffic jams in heavyweight synthetic suits, tie only slightly loosened. In winter, people frequently dress inadequately, as if out of bravado. Well, you just can't trust those know-all weather forecasters, can you?

Hats (other than those expensive designer creations shown off at Ascot) are generally not taken seriously. Anyone spotted wearing something large and shady to fend off sunstroke or stop precious body heat seeping away is probably foreign.

Global warming may change British weather forever, creating very hot, long, dry summers. The writer Virginia Woolf thought that such weather might turn us all into outgoing Mediterraneans. But relentless, reliable sunshine is far more likely to provoke deep Scandinavian gloom, making us all sadder than SAD – Seasonal Affective Disorder, a condition diagnosed

waxed their coats, ugly folding plastic macs used to make rainswept holidaymakers look like film-wrapped, self-basting chickens. The small plastic rainhat, furled down to the size of a condom and secreted in the handbag, is still favoured today by older ladies with tightly permed, snowy hair.

Britons today keep a keen weather eye on their climate by frequently tuning in to radio and television forecasts. Traditionally, TV weathermen and women have been civil servants from the Meteorological Office in Bracknell, Berkshire, and some have compensated for their lack of media background by cultivating eccentric-

by doctors and normally produced by too little, rather than too much light.

For although the British have always dreamed of an empire upon which the sun never sets, dependable good weather spoils their "just-in-case" philosophy. Umbrellas, extra woollens and fold-up plastic raincoats are much-loved accessories. British women might have been considered as chic as Parisiennes were it not for their just-in-case cardigans flung inelegantly over summer dresses. In the days before golfing umbrellas were big and country people

LEFT and **ABOVE:** the weather, which constantly changes, is a constant topic of conversation.

ity. One cut-price cable channel carried the whole business to its absurd extreme by appointing a blonde with compelling physical attributes to read the weather in Norwegian.

Xenophobia

Like many island peoples, the British – and especially the working classes – have a profound distrust of outsiders, perhaps equating them unconsciously with invaders. It is not by chance that it took them so long to agree, reluctantly, to help finance a tunnel beneath the English Channel. The writer Nancy Mitford expressed an extreme version of this narrow-mindedness: "Abroad is unutterably boring and foreigners are fiends." The actor Robert Morley was more circumspect: "The British tourist is always happy abroad so long as the natives are waiters."

Even when dealing with their fellow Europeans, the British fall back on stereotypes. David Frost and Anthony Jay, in their book *To England With Love*, definitively summed up hell for the British as "a place where the Germans are the police, the Swedish are the comedians, the Italians are the defence force, Frenchmen dig the roads, the Belgians are the pop singers, the Spanish run the railways, the Turks cook the food, the Irish are the waiters, the Greeks run the government, and the common language is Dutch." Any odds on a federal Europe?

Youth

The teenager was invented in 1945 as a category of market research by 19-year-old Eugene Gilbert. Gilbert set up his copywriting company while still a student and made a fortune in America out of strategic use of phrases such as "dig this", "far out" and "groovy daddyo" to an impressed advertising industry. But when his London office opened and closed in the same year, his explanation was that "teenagers in Britain haven't found enough freedom or money to be commercially interesting."

The postwar world economy was built around the United States – the symbol of the future. Britain's wannabe rock-and-rollers even sounded as if they came from half-way across the Atlantic. But the authorities didn't make it easy for them to practise their accents: they banned Marlon Brando's 1954 film *The Wild One* for 13 years, and felt their caution justified when cinema riots greeted Bill Haley's *Rock Around the Clock*.

Thanks to full employment, British teenagers began to be more commercially interesting as the 1950s melted into the 1960s. They surprised their elders and betters by not only dancing to Tutti Frutti but by being able to spell it, too. They were better built, fed, clothed, housed and educated than ever before. Between 1938 and 1956 the number of children in secondary and higher education had doubled. With education came a conscience, a rejection of materialism,

nuclear arms and parental values. In life as well as literature, the anti-hero was "in".

Fighting was left to two gangs, the Mods and the Rockers, usually at seaside resorts on Bank Holiday weekends. Mods had short hair, wore suits and rode Italian motorscooters; the Rockers were oily bikers on Harley-Davidsons or British machines. Their encounters were seen as two mutually exclusive visions of the future: Europe's and America's.

The Merseybeat, the Beatles and their looka-likes from Liverpool, pulled the spotlight away from the capital for a while. But Mary Quant's fashions and the Rolling Stones soon had Lon-

don swinging again. Hippies and glam rockers in platform boots and glittery jackets came and went in the 1970s.

Then, just as things were beginning to look boring, in the long, hot summer of 1976 punk arrived. The music was loud and live and, like the clothes, designed to shock. Serious rebels adorned their bodies with safety pins and tattoos and dressed themselves in rubber, leather or bondage. Swastikas, swearing and spitting were the order of the day and everyone spoke with a fake working-class accent.

By the early 1980s punk had become a spiky-haircut postcard image to sell the tourists. Thatcher's children were growing up to become the Me generation of 18-year-old merchant bankers and stockbrokers who drove Porsches and lived in developments that rose from London's filled-in docks. These teenagers led the revolution of new money which supposedly would sweep the class system away.

But by the end of Thatcher's 1980s, the cycle of unemployment and inflation ushered in a more caring Britain. A new kind of music, which surfaced in Liverpool and Manchester, began to talk once more about global love and to exhort each other to "dig this, man". Teenagers, fuelled by the drug Ecstasy, packed into disused warehouses or farm buildings for

Zeitgeist

Taking a nation's spiritual temperature is as precise an art as palmistry, but a clue to Britain's confusing symptoms since World War II was provided by Dean Acheson, a US Secretary of State, who declared: "Great Britain has lost an Empire and has not yet found a role." Instead, it has embraced a wide repertoire of roles: in the 1950s, that of a respectable, middle-class spinster, strapped for cash but determined to maintain her dignity; in the 1960s, that of a buoyantly optimistic, fashion-conscious good-time girl; in

all-night dance raves. The Beatles were re-launched. Youth had turned another circle.

Today teenagers have freedom. They can join the army and get married at 16, the age of consent; at 18 they can vote and get drunk. They are commercially interesting to car manufacturers, record companies and food chains. Even parents listen to what they say. But Britain's politicians will never take the young 'uns seriously – not until they get a job, a vote and a mortgage.

***

LEFT: in the late 1950s and early '60s Mods fought with big-bike Rockers at seaside resorts on public holidays.
ABOVE: raves, such as this one in a London club, featured prominently in youth culture in the 1990s.

the 1970s, that of a lonely woman beset by financial worries, spurned by America and regarded by Europe as dowdy and old-fashioned; in the 1980s, a career woman, inspired by Margaret Thatcher to embrace a red-blooded success ethic; and in the 1990s there was a high-profile supporting role in America's all-action blockbuster *War in the Gulf*.

But where will the good roles be in the 21st century for an ageing player on the world stage? Her future is most likely to lie in European co-productions, sharing the smaller-print billing with her Continental counterparts. It hasn't the glamour of Hollywood, but times change – and well, a girl's got to eat. ❑

THE STATELY HOMES OF ENGLAND

Stately homes reflect more than privileged lives. They also illustrate centuries of social history, and of supreme artistic and architectural achievement

Britain's stately homes have a fascination that attracts visitors in their millions every year. Many have embraced the tourist theme enthusiastically, with such added incentives as safari parks, transport museums, historical re-enactments and adventure playgrounds, but at the heart of them all lies a house with a story. It may tell of great achievement in a palatial mansion crammed with priceless works of art;it may reflect centuries at the heart of a close-knit country community in the form of a rambling old manor house, crammed with centuries of acquisitions; it may even show how the servants and estate workers would go about their daily duties.

CHANGING TIMES

A house that may appear to be pure 18th-century neo-classical may well be hiding a medieval core and perhaps a Tudor fireplace where Elizabeth I once warmed her toes. Victorian high-flyers tended to confuse the issue by building convincingly fanciful medieval-style castles, complete with every convenience that the technology of the Industrial Revolution had made available to them.

The short Edwardian era saw both the carefree hey-day of the country house party and the onset of World War I, which marked the demise of the stately home in its traditional role. The revenue from opening to the public saved many splendid buildings and their contents from extinction and offers us the opportunity to explore a different way of life.

▷ LONGLEAT
The home of the Marquess of Bath, Longleat is the epitome of a Tudor English mansion. Set in vast parkland, it has also constructed a huge entertainment complex including a safari park with lions and gorillas.

△ PALATIAL SPLENDOUR
Castle Howard in Yorkshire is one of the most magnificent stately homes in Britain. It has been the home of the Howard family since it was built in the 18th century. The Great Hall rises 70 ft (21 metres) to an imposing domed ceiling.

◁ BLACK AND WHITE

Little Moreton Hall, near Congleton in Cheshire, is one of the finest timber-framed moated manor houses in the country. Begun in the middle of the 15th century, it still contains some of its original furniture. It has a knot garden.

▽ MANOR INTO PALACE

Knole, sitting in a deer park at Sevenoaks in Kent, is England's largest house. It was developed from a simple manor in the 15th century, courtesy of such owners as Elizabeth I. It has portraits by Reynolds and Gainsborough.

THE NATIONAL TRUST

It sounds like another stuffy government institution, but in fact the National Trust, founded in 1895, is a registered charity and receives no state grant. It was set up to acquire and preserve places of historic interest or natural beauty for the permanent enjoyment of the visiting public.

It now cares for 1,000 ancient monuments, over 200 historic houses, plus gardens, industrial sites, 550 miles (885 km) of coastline and 590,000 acres (240,000 hectares) of countryside.

Funded entirely by donations, legacies, admission charges and membership subscriptions, the Trust still runs at a loss, despite the willing efforts of its army of volunteers.

△ CORNISH MANSION

Lanhydrock House, near Bodmin in Cornwall, offers a complete picture of country house life in the 17th century, with kitchens, dairy, bakehouse and servants quarters also on show. It has formal and shrub gardens.

◁ ENGLISH VERSAILLES

The home of the Churchills, Blenheim Palace in Oxfordshire is a treasurehouse of works of art set in superb gardens and has a UNESCO World Heritage listing.

▷ THE SOLDIER DUKE

John Churchill was ennobled and well rewarded for his victory at the Battle of Blenheim.

PLACES

*A detailed guide to the entire country, with principal sites
cross-referenced by number to the maps*

In the early 1960s, before jogging and trainers were invented, Dr Barbara Moore began a brief craze of walking the length of the country, 874 miles (1,408 km) from John O'Groats in the northeast of Scotland to Land's End in Cornwall. (Even in this land of eccentrics she was thought rather crazy.) Though it took several weeks, it made the island seem small. Today a motorist could make the trip in not much more than a day, and it seems to have shrunk still further. But within that short distance there is an extraordinary variety of landscape, of peoples and places to see.

Apart from winter in the blizzard-blown Highlands of Scotland, getting around the country is very easy, particularly by car, and minor roads have always been good. Britain is, however, a crowded island: traffic can be bumper to bumper on motorways, especially such arteries as the M1, M4 and M6 and on London's orbital M25, while in the capital itself the average speed of traffic is the same as it was in the days of horse-drawn carriages.

Britain has its own favourite holiday haunts: the Lake District in the northwest, the Peak District in the Midlands, Devon and the Cornish Riviera in the West Country and the Pembroke Coast in South Wales. The Scots tend to head for the West Coast which is big enough to diffuse most crowds, while Blackpool, Britain's favourite seaside resort, creaks a bit under its 6 million annual visitors.

The tourist, rightfully, wants to see the classic sites, to visit the historic buildings, the university towns, to go on literary and artistic pilgrimages, to enjoy the splendour of castles, gardens and country houses. There is, however, pressure on these places and there is a continuing debate about limiting numbers. (Oxford, for instance, the third most visited city in Britain after London and Edinburgh, is concerned at the effect of around 3½ million visitors a year; it may follow the example of a Cambridge college which is is trying to reduce the numbers by charging an entrance fee.)

While this guide gives all the necessary information about these important and popular historic centres, it also suggests a host of other places to visit, places that are often missed but which give just as much insight into the life and culture of Britain. The chapters have been divided geographically in a way that makes each area easy to explore, and the Travel Tips section at the back of the book contains further recommendations that will help you gain an insight into Britain both on and off the beaten track.

PRECEDING PAGES: early winter in the north of England; Cornish fishing village; balloons over Leeds Castle, Kent. **LEFT:** a town crier in Norwich.

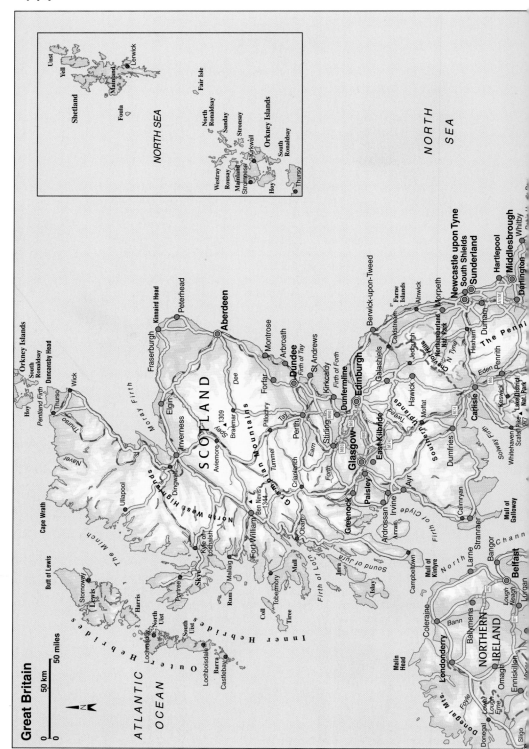

Great Britain

0 ___ 50 km
0 ___ 50 miles

ATLANTIC OCEAN

NORTH SEA

Shetland

Unst
Yell
Mainland
Lerwick
Foula

Fair Isle

North Ronaldsay
Sanday
Stronsay
Westray
Rousay
Mainland
Stromness
Kirkwall
Orkney Islands
Hoy
South Ronaldsay
Thurso

NORTH SEA

Orkney Islands
South Ronaldsay
Duncansby Head
Pentland Firth
Thurso
Wick
Hoy
Naver

Cape Wrath
Butt of Lewis
Stornoway
Lewis
Harris
North Uist
Lochmaddy
South Uist
Lochboisdale
Barra
Castlebay
Outer Hebrides
The Minch

Ullapool
Dingwall
Inverness
Elgin
Kinnaird Head
Fraserburgh
Peterhead
Aberdeen

Moray Firth
Spey
Dee
SCOTLAND
Grampian Mountains
Braemar
Aviemore
1309
North West Highlands
Kyle of Lochalsh
Skye
Portree
Mallaig
Rum
Tobermory
Mull
Coll
Tiree
Inner Hebrides
Jura
Islay
Campbeltown
Mull of Kintyre

Fort William
Ben Nevis 1344
Oban
Crianlarich
Tummel
Tay
Pitlochry
Perth
Forfar
Montrose
Arbroath
Dundee
Firth of Tay
St Andrews
Kirkcaldy
Firth of Forth
Dunfermline
Edinburgh
Stirling
Firth of Forth
Earn
Forth
Glasgow
East Kilbride
Paisley
Greenock
Firth of Lorn
Sound of Jura
Ardrossan
Irvine
Arran
Ayr
Firth of Clyde

Berwick-upon-Tweed
Coldstream
Galashiels
Tweed
Hawick
Jedburgh
Moffat
Southern Uplands
Dumfries
Cairnryan
Stranraer
Mull of Galloway
Solway Firth

NORTH SEA

Farne Islands
Alnwick
Morpeth
Newcastle upon Tyne
South Shields
Sunderland
Hartlepool
Middlesbrough
Darlington
Whitby
Northumberland Nat. Park
N Tyne
Hexham
Durham
Cheviot Hills
Penrith
Keswick
Carlisle
Eden
The Pennines
Lake District Nat. Park
Whitehaven
Scafell Pike 977

NORTH IRELAND
Londonderry
Malin Head
Coleraine
Ballymena
Bann
Omagh
Enniskillen
Lough Erne
Lough Neagh
Belfast
Bangor
Larne
North Channel
Donegal Mts.
Foyle
Lower Lough Erne
Donegal
Sligo

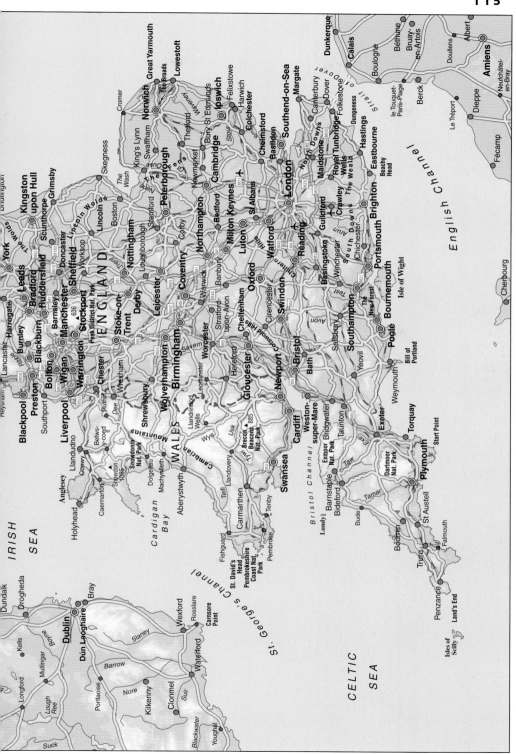

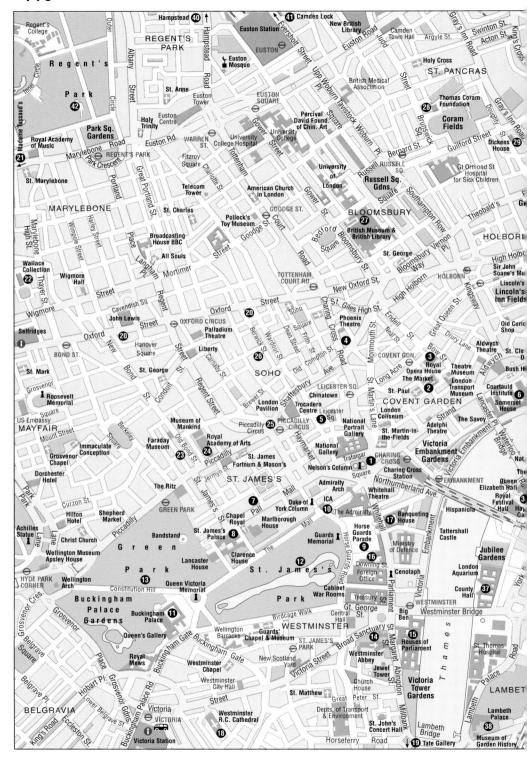

Regent's College

Hampstead 40

Camden Lock 41
New British Library
Euston Station
Camden Town Hall
Argyle St.
Acton St.
Swinton St.
King's Cross
Gray's Inn Road

REGENT'S PARK

Albany Street

Outer Circle

Hampstead Road

EUSTON

Euston Mosque

Upp. Woburn Pl.
Upp. Tavistock Pl.
Woburn Pl.
Judd St.
Euston Road

Holy Cross

ST. PANCRAS

British Medical Association

Thomas Coram Foundation 28

R e g e n t ' s

St. Anne

Euston Tower

EUSTON SQUARE

Gower St.
Gordon St.
University St.

Percival David Found. of Chin. Art

Tavistock Square

Bernard St.

Brunswick Sq.

Coram Fields

P a r k

Inner Circle

Holy Trinity

Euston Centre

University College Hospital

University College

Gt Ormond St Hospital for Sick Children

Gt Ormond St.

Guilford Street

Dickens House 29

Madame Tussaud's

42

Royal Academy of Music

Marylebone Road

Euston Rd.

WARREN ST.

University of London

RUSSELL SQ.

Russell Square

Southampton Row

Doughty St.

21

St. Marylebone

Park Crescent

Park Square Gardens

REGENT'S PARK

Great Portland St.

Portland Place

Tottenham Court Road

Russell Sq. Gdns.

Bloomsbury

St. George

Bloomsbury Way

Vernon Pl.

Theobald's

HOLBORN

MARYLEBONE

St. Charles

Telecom Tower

American Church in London

Gower St.

BLOOMSBURY

British Museum & British Library 27

Bloomsbury Row

High Holborn

Marylebone High St.

Wimpole Street

Harley Street

Place

St. Charles

Fitzroy Square

Charlotte St.

GOODGE ST.

Bedford Square

Bloomsbury St.

High Holborn

HOLBORN

Sir John Soane's Mu

Lincoln's Inn Fields

Wallace Collection 22

Thayer St.

Wigmore Hall

Broadcasting House BBC

All Souls

Langham Pl.

Mortimer Street

Pollock's Toy Museum

Goodge St.

New Oxford St.

St. Giles High St.

Kingsway

Great Queen St.

Lincoln's Inn Fields

Old Curio Shop

St. Cle
D

Bush H

Wigmore Street

Cavendish Sq.

John Lewis

Oxford Street

Soho Square

Phoenix Theatre

Endell St.

Neal's St.

Drury Lane

Aldwych Theatre

Selfridges

OXFORD CIRCUS

20

Palladium Theatre

Wardour St.

Dean St.

Frith St.

Charing Cross Road

4

Bow St.

Theatre Museum

Courtauld Institute 6

BOND ST.

New Bond St.

Hanover Square

Liberty

Carnaby St.

Berwick St.

SOHO

Old Compton St.

COVENT GDN.

Long Acre

Royal Opera House The Market

3

London Transport Museum

COVENT GARDEN

Somerset House

St. Mark

Grosvenor

20

26

Shaftesbury Ave.

Brewer St.

London Pavilion

Chinatown

Leicester Sq.

St. Paul

2

St. Martin's Lane

London Coliseum

The Savoy

Strand

MAYFAIR

Roosevelt Memorial

St. George St.

Conduit St.

Regent Street

Piccadilly Circus

25

PICCADILLY CIRCUS

Trocadero Centre

5

LEICESTER SQ.

Leicester Square

National Portrait Gallery

St. Martin-in-the-Fields

Adelphi Theatre

The Savoy

US Embassy

Museum of Mankind

Royal Academy of Arts

Haymarket

National Gallery

Victoria Embankment Gardens

Queen Elizabeth Hall

Royal Festival Hall

Hay

Immaculate Conception

Faraday Museum 23

Old Bond St.

24

Piccadilly

St. James Fortnum & Mason's

Nelson's Column

Trafalgar Square

CHARING CROSS

Charing Cross Station

Nat

Grosvenor Chapel

Mount Street

Berkeley St.

Jermyn St.

ST. JAMES'S

Admiralty Arch

Northumberland Ave.

EMBANKMENT

The

Dorchester Hotel

The Ritz

St. James's St.

7

Pall Mall

Duke of York Column

ICA

10

Whitehall Theatre

Banqueting House 17

Hispaniola

Hilton Hotel

Shepherd Market

Chapel Royal

Marlborough House

Horse Guards Parade

The Admiralty

Tattershall Castle

Park Lane

Achilles Statue

Christ Church

Wellington Museum Apsley House

GREEN PARK

St. James's Palace

8

Clarence House

The Mall

Guards Memorial

9

Ministry of Defence

Whitehall

Downing St. Foreign Office

16

Jubilee Gardens

London Aquarium

County Hall

37

HYDE PARK CORNER

Wellington Arch

Constitution Hill

G r e e n

P a r k

Lancaster House

Queen Victoria Memorial

St. James's Park

Horse Guards Road

Cabinet War Rooms

Treasury

Cenotaph

WESTMINSTER

Parliament St.

Big Ben

Westminster Bridge

Thames

Buckingham Palace Gardens

13

Buckingham Palace

11

Queen's Gallery

Wellington Barracks

Birdcage Walk

Guards' Chapel & Museum

Central Hall

WESTMINSTER

Gt. George St.

12

15

Houses of Parliament

St. Thomas's Hospital

BELGRAVIA

Royal Mews

Buckingham Gate

Westminster Chapel

New Scotland Yard

ST. JAMES'S PARK

Victoria Street

Westminster Abbey

Broad Sanctuary

14

Jewel Tower

Victoria Tower Gardens

LAMBETH

Grosvenor Gardens

Hobart Pl.

VICTORIA

Westminster City Hall

Church House

St. Margaret St.

Abingdon St.

Lambeth Palace

Belgrave Pl.

Eccleston St.

Buckingham Palace Rd.

18

Westminster R.C. Cathedral

St. Matthew

Great Peter St.

St. John's Concert Hall

Lambeth Bridge

Museum of Garden History

38

King's Road

Victoria Station

Depts. of Transport & Environment

Millbank

Horseferry Road

19

Tate Gallery

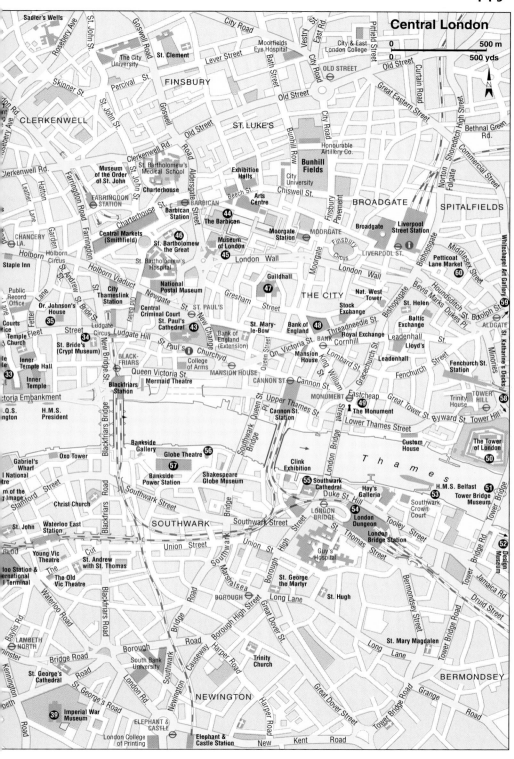

CENTRAL LONDON

London has enchanted visitors and residents for at least five centuries. There are few cities that offer such a variety of sights and sounds, few places that present a mood to suit just about any whim

Map, pages 118/9

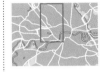

N o one has captured in words the excitement of London as well as Samuel Johnson, the doctor who had a literary cure for just about everything: "When a man is tired of London he is tired of life, for there is in London all that life can afford." Today, 200 years later, Johnson's words still ring true. There are few cities that offer such a variety of sights and sounds, few places that present a mood to suit just about any whim. London is there for the taking, so take and enjoy.

The pigeon-filled precinct called **Trafalgar Square** ❶ is a good starting point. Sitting at the core of London as one of the most impressive public squares in the world, it was laid out in the 1830s and '40s by Sir Charles Barry and dedicated to the memory of Admiral Lord Nelson and his decisive victory over Napoleon's fleet off Cape Trafalgar in 1805. The square is a paragon of the Classical style, enclosed by graceful white façades and dominated by the 162-ft (50-metre) **Nelson's Column** and four bronze lions. This is the strategic heart of London. The financial wizards of the City of London work to the east; the main shopping centres are to the west; the entertainment empire of the West End lies directly to the north; and the government palaces of Whitehall and Westminster stretch to the south along the River Thames.

PRECEDING PAGES: Big Ben and Houses of Parliament. **LEFT:** fountains in Trafalgar Square. **BELOW:** Piccadilly Circus.

Trafalgar Square is a transportation hub, traversed by a dozen bus lines and five different tube lines. The square is also the scene of London's annual New Year's Eve bash (not recommended for those who dislike crowds) and it has been the site of political demonstrations for more than 100 years. And in case there's trouble, the smallest police station in England sits in a lamp post at the southeast corner, with a direct telephone link to police headquarters at New Scotland Yard.

The French Crown Jewels are said to lie beneath Trafalgar Square: Madame du Barry, the mistress of Louis XV, brought them to London in 1793 and, the story goes, buried the stones in the grounds of the old Royal Mews, later demolished to make way for Trafalgar Square. Madame du Barry returned to France and lost her head upon the guillotine – but she never disclosed the whereabouts of the missing jewels.

Running along the north flank of Trafalgar Square is the **National Gallery** (open daily; Wed till 8pm; closed Sun am; free). Founded in 1824, the gallery has since grown into one of the most outstanding and comprehensive collections in the world, with a list of masters ranging from Leonardo and Rembrandt to El Greco and Van Gogh. In 1991 the "Sainsbury Wing", designed by Robert Venturi, was opened to house the rich Renaissance collection.

Around the corner, established in 1856, is the superb **National Portrait Gallery** (open daily; Wed till 8pm;

closed Sun am; free). Presenting an illustrated British history, it now contains the faces of more than 9,000 famous Britons, and it often stages photographic exhibitions.

To the right of the National Gallery is **St Martin-in-the-Fields** church, the oldest surviving structure on Trafalgar Square, built along simple but elegant lines by James Gibbs in 1722–6. The church became well-known during World War II when its crypt was a refuge from the Blitz. St Martin's is still the parish church for Buckingham Palace, with royal boxes at the east end.

St Martin-in-the-Fields might remind Americans of a New England country church – its distinctive style was copied widely in the 13 colonies before their independence.

BELOW: busker in Covent Garden.

Serendipitous Covent Garden

Northeast of Trafalgar Square begins the maze of narrow streets and tiny alleys called **Covent Garden**. There has been some type of market on this spot for more than 300 years, but the name actually derives from the convent garden that occupied the area until Henry VIII's Dissolution. At the centre of Covent Garden lies a cobblestone piazza and superb steel-and-glass market pavilions ❷ constructed in the 1830s to house flower, fruit and vegetable stalls. The market was moved to new quarters south of the river at Nine Elms in 1974, and in the early 1980s Covent Garden was refurbished into an area of restaurants, shops and cafés. It's now a showplace for buskers, or street entertainers, and a summer mecca both for office workers at lunchtime and for tourists. Covent Garden is also popular for afternoon shopping, especially cobblestoned **Neal Street** with a collection of speciality shops.

Candle-lit concerts are held in the last two weeks of July each year to celebrate the first Punch and Judy show, staged here in 1662. There is an antiques market on Mondays, and the popular Jubilee Market on weekends offers a colourful hotchpotch of arts and crafts, food stalls and puppet shows. But the action really heats up at night. Those with a taste for English tradition might imbibe at the many ancient pubs in the area such as the **Lamb and Flag** (on Rose Street, off Floral Street), a 17th-century pub once frequented by prizefighters and known as the "Bucket of Blood".

Covent Garden, backdrop for *My Fair Lady*, is synonymous with British theatre. Some of the names associated with its past are Sarah Bernhardt, Charlie Chaplin, Richard Sheridan and George Bernard Shaw. The **Theatre Royal** was established on Drury Lane in 1663 and is still a showcase for musicals. Nearby stands the majestic **Royal Opera House** ❸, home of both the Royal Opera and Ballet Companies, which began extensive refurbishment in 1997. On the other side of the piazza, actors are memorialized in St Paul's Church, which was designed by Inigo Jones in 1631.

Bibliophiles usually make haste for **Charing Cross Road** ❹, which marks the western boundary of Covent Garden district with a solid wall of bookshops. They range from **Foyle's** (the largest bookstore in London) to such specialist enclaves as **A. Zwemmer** (graphic design and photography). The secondhand bookshops have a great atmosphere.

For a change of scene, take a stroll through the **Photographer's Gallery** in Great Newport Street where there are changing exhibitions of video and photographs (open Mon–Sat from 11am; free). The gallery doubles as a café, so it's also a good place to quench a thirst or rest tired feet.

Charing Cross Road is on the east side of **Leicester Square ❺**. This is the domain of tourists, pigeons and buskers, a gaudy place filled with flashing neon and throbbing music that's home to another form of London entertainment – the cinema. More than a dozen movie houses are scattered around its leafy confines, and there's a statue of London-born Charlie Chaplin as The Little Tramp, and a Shakespeare fountain in its centre. It's traffic free except when stars' limousines arrive for premieres.

To the south of Covent Garden lies the Strand. Here, by Waterloo Bridge, is **Somerset House ❻**, built in 1770–1835. It now houses the superb Courtauld Institute collection of Impressionist paintings with works by Van Gogh, Gauguin and Cézanne (open daily; closed Sun till 2pm).

High-class club land

A much different atmosphere is found in **Pall Mall ❼**, on the west side of Trafalgar Square, a sedate and elegant avenue that runs through the heart of the St James's district. This is London's "Club Land" – the exclusive gathering place of English gentlemen behind the closed doors of the Athenaeum, White's, the Carlton and a dozen other private enclaves. The street takes its name from *paille maille*, a French lawn game imported to England in the 17th century and played by Charles I on a long green which once occupied this site.

Wedged between the wood-panelled halls of Pall Mall and the leafy landscape of Green Park are a number of stately homes. The most impressive of these, built by Henry VIII in the 1530s, is **St James's Palace ❽**. This was an official

Map, pages 118/9

In town let me live then, in town let me die, For in truth I can't relish the country, not I. If one must have a villa in summer to swell, Oh give me the sweet shady side of Pall Mall.
—CHARLES MORRIS, 1840

BELOW LEFT: waiting for Covent Garden's street show to start.
BELOW: Leicester Square.

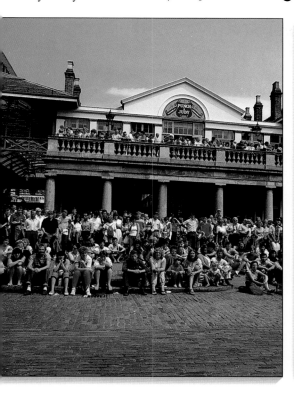

Most of London's ceremonial sites are located within easy walking distance of each other.

BELOW: Royal Horse Guard in Whitehall.
BELOW RIGHT: St James's Palace.

royal residence up until the 19th century. St James's is now occupied by Prince Charles and royal servants, although foreign ambassadors are still appointed to the Court of St James's. A cluster of royal mansions here includes **Marlborough House**, and the royal residences of **Clarence House** and **Lancaster House** where Chopin once played a royal command performance for Queen Victoria.

The Mall is London's impressive ceremonial way, a broad tree-lined avenue that runs from Buckingham Palace to the Admiralty Arch. The spectacular Trooping the Colour takes place on the Mall each June, as Queen Elizabeth rides sedately down the avenue in a horse-drawn carriage with an escort of Household Cavalry as part of a 200-year-old ceremony to mark the official birthday of the monarch. The legions mass on **Horse Guards Parade ❾**, a huge open space behind Whitehall, where the various royal units troop their regimental flags to the tune of marching music and thundering drums. The Household Cavalry can also be seen at 11.30am daily (alternative days in winter), as they ride down the Mall on their way to and from the changing of the guard at Buckingham Palace. They also mount a guard outside the old palace entrance on Whitehall.

Overlooking the Mall is the **Institute of Contemporary Arts ❿**, the cutting edge of modern painting, sculpture and the performing arts, housed in the Georgian-style Nash House (open daily, noon–7.30pm, Fri till 9pm).

Londoners have a love-hate relationship with **Buckingham Palace ⓫** (open Aug–Sept: daily, till 4.15pm; tickets at Green Park tube from 9am). To some, the Queen's home is one of the ugliest buildings in the capital, but it's also held in esteem as the symbol of Britain's royalty. The palace arose within a mulberry grove in the early 18th century as a mansion for the powerful Duke of Buckingham. It was purchased in 1762 by George III (who preferred to live in St

James's Palace) for £28,000. However, it wasn't grand enough for George IV (the Prince Regent), and soon after the building came under his control in 1820 he commissioned his favourite architect, John Nash, to rebuild it on a more magnificent scale. The improvements led to considerable controversy: Parliament authorised an expenditure that "might not be less than £200,000"; the work actually ended up costing more than £700,000. Despite all the alterations the palace wasn't occupied until Victoria became queen in 1837 and made it the official royal residence in London. In recent years the palace has opened to the public in August and September, and is well worth a visit.

Map, pages 118/9

Visitors gather in front of Buckingham Palace for the Changing of the Guard (normally 11.30am daily; alternate days in winter) and perhaps to snatch a glimpse of the Queen, who is in residence when the flag is flying. The more dedicated may decide to buy a ticket (from Green Park tube) to see the State rooms. Otherwise, only two sections of the palace are open to the public: the **Royal Mews** (stables), and the **Queen's Gallery** (open daily till 5pm). The gallery displays a rotating sample of paintings from the fabulous Royal Collection, which includes masterpieces by Vermeer, Leonardo and Titian.

The pelicans in St James's Park are fed at 3pm each day.

Bounding Buckingham Palace on the north and east are two of London's renowned green spaces – the arboreal tracts of St James's Park and Green Park. **St James's** ⑫ in particular has lush vegetation and a tranquil lake. Indeed, the park provides haven for a multitude of water birds, office workers and civil servants. The wooden footbridge across the lake gives a superb view of Buckingham Palace. **Green Park** ⑬ is a wild and rugged contrast. There are no tidy flower beds or ornate fountains – just rolling expanses of grass and woods where Charles II used to take his daily constitutional.

BELOW: Buckingham Palace ceremonial.

Westminster's grandeur

A short walk from the southeast corner of St James's Park is **Westminster**, the seat of English government for nearly 1,000 years. Westminster is also a holy place – the burial ground of English monarchs, the site of one of the greatest monasteries of the Middle Ages and the location of the most inspiring Gothic architecture in London. The area was a marshy wasteland inhabited by lepers until the 11th-century reign of Edward the Confessor, who took a distinct liking to Westminster and built both a great church and a palace upon the reclaimed land. **Westminster Abbey** ⓯ was consecrated on 28 December 1065; Edward died nine days later and was buried before the high altar. In December 1066, the ill-fated Harold (soon to lose his throne to William the Conqueror) was crowned as the new king during a special ceremony in the Abbey. This set yet another precedent, for since that day, all but two English monarchs have been crowned in the church.

Little remains of Edward's Saxon abbey; it was completely rebuilt under the Normans and then redesigned in flamboyant French-Gothic style 200 years later. The abbey's top treasures are the **Royal Chapels** (open Mon–Sat). The **Henry VII Chapel** is a 16th-century masterpiece of fan-vaulted ceilings in pure white stone, decked out in the colourful medieval banners of the Knights Grand Cross of the Order of the Bath. Behind lies the Royal Air Force Chapel, with a stained-glass window containing the badges of every squadron which fought in the 1940 Battle of Britain. **Poets' Corner** contains the graves of Chaucer, Tennyson and Dryden, plus monuments to Shakespeare, Milton, Keats, Wilde and many others. The abbey also houses the **English Coronation Chair**, built in 1300 for Edward I and still used for the installation of new monarchs.

ABOVE: typical fan vaulting in Westminster Abbey's Henry VII Chapel
BELOW: Westminster Abbey.

On the river side of Westminster Abbey rise the **Houses of Parliament** ⓰, an intrepid Gothic structure designed in the 1830s by Charles Barry and August Pugin to replace the old Westminster Palace built by Edward the Confessor. The building is one of the triumphs of Victorian England: 940 ft (280 metres) long with 2 miles (3 km) of passages and more than 1,000 rooms. At the south end is **Victoria Tower**, from which a Union flag flies whenever Parliament is in session, while on the north flank rises the majestic Clock Tower, commonly known as **Big Ben** after the massive bell, cast in 1858, that strikes the hours.

Within Parliament convene the two governing bodies of Great Britain, the House of Commons and the House of Lords, which moved into the old Palace of Westminster after Henry VIII vacated the premises in the 16th century. The Commons, comprised of the elected representatives of various political parties, is the scene of both lively debate and loutish heckling as MPs (Members of Parliament) wage verbal battle across their wood-panelled hall. You can watch from the safety of the **Visitors' Gallery** – and wonder, like so many others, how the British government ever gets anything accomplished (when Parliament is in session, queue at St Stephen's entrance from 5pm Mon, Tues & Thur (9.30am Wed, Fri); or request an entrance permit from your MP; free; tel: 0171-219 3000).

The lavish State Opening of Parliament takes place in the House of Lords each autumn, as the monarch reads a proclamation from a golden throne at the head of the room. The Lord Chancellor sits upon the Woolsack, a symbol of the importance of wool to the English economy during medieval times. One of the few relics of the old Westminster Palace to withstand a fire that all but destroyed the building in 1834 is **Westminster Hall**, a 240-ft (72-metre) long room built in 1099 with a sturdy hammer-beam roof of ancient oak. The hall has witnessed some of the most dramatic

Map, pages 118/9

Each of Big Ben's clockfaces is 23 ft (8 metres) in diameter.

BELOW: the 1,000-room Houses of Parliament.

moments in English history – from the tragic trial of Sir Thomas More in 1535 to the investiture of Oliver Cromwell as Lord Protector in 1653.

An exhibition about parliament in history is on show at the **Jewel Tower** (open daily; winter: till 4pm), a moated keep beside Westminster Abbey that held the king's jewels, clothing and furs until the reign of Henry VIII.

Whitehall is the broad and busy avenue that runs north from the Houses of Parliament to Trafalgar Square. Once the fulcrum of British colonial power, it is still home to the Foreign and Commonwealth Offices, the Treasury, Admiralty and Ministry of Defence – and the Prime Minister's 17th-century residence at **No. 10 Downing Street** ⓰ – but in fact much of the government has moved elsewhere to more modern and spacious locations.

In the Banqueting House, visitors push around little carts with mirrors on the top – to help them observe the Rubens on the ceiling.

For a startling contrast to the drab architecture of modern government take a detour into the **Banqueting House** ⓱, just beyond on the right, a brilliant relic of the old Whitehall Palace and a masterpiece of the English baroque (open Mon–Sat). Inigo Jones built the hall in 1622 at the request of James I. A decade later Peter Paul Rubens added the lovely allegorical ceiling.

Surprising modernity

BELOW: Whitehall from Trafalgar Square. **BELOW RIGHT:** the Prime Minister's residence in Downing Street.

Victoria Street shoots southwest from Parliament Square as an unexpected corridor of steel and glass skyscrapers in the heart of neo-Gothic London. Almost hidden between the corporate headquarters and banking houses is the terracotta bulk of **Westminster Cathedral** ⓲, England's premier Roman Catholic church. It arose in the 1890s in a bizarre Italo-Byzantine style, with a lavish interior of multi-coloured marble and an exterior in alternating red and white bricks. Climb the **Campanile Tower** for a superb view of Westminster and Belgravia.

Millbank follows the gentle curve of the Thames to the south of Parliament Square, first passing the sylvan **Victoria Tower Gardens** (home of Rodin's *The Burghers of Calais*) before sweeping round to the grand neoclassical mansion which is the **Tate Gallery** ⑲ (open daily; free). Take your pick from Picasso to Pollock or Matisse to Munch in this superb repository of 20th-century painting and sculpture. But don't forget, the Tate is also the nation's showcase for 19th-century British art with a host of old masters, including Constable, Hogarth and Reynolds. However, the highlight is the Clore Gallery, designed by James Stirling to house the extensive Turner collection.

Shopping and star-gazing

Just three stops on the tube from Pimlico station takes you to Oxford Circus. London's busiest shopping street is **Oxford Street** ⑳, which marks the boundary between **Marylebone** and the exclusive district of **Mayfair**. The **Marylebone** (pronounced *marly-bun*) district sprawls along the southern edge of Regent's Park, and was infamous in the 18th century for its taverns, boxing matches and cockfights. Now it is a staid neighbourhood of doctors, dentists and accountants.

You can't miss the long queues outside the **London Planetarium** and the adjacent **Madame Tussaud's Wax Museum** ㉑ on Marylebone Road (both open daily; combined tickets available). The waxworks were founded in 1802 by Marie Tussaud, a tiny woman who learned her craft in post-Revolution Paris – making wax effigies of the heads of guillotine victims. Today's effigies, which vary from the breathtakingly lifelike to the barely recognisable, cover celebrities from pop stars and sports heroes to popes. The appeal is that you can get really close to many of them – and there's no risk of being snubbed by a star.

Map, pages 118/9

TIPS

● In 2000 the Tate's modern collection will move to a new site at Bankside (see p. 145).

● Get to Madame Tussaud's first thing in the morning or buy a ticket in advance – the queues are the worst in London.

BELOW LEFT: Westminster Cathedral.
BELOW: the Beatles, Madame Tussaud's.

Shoppers' Paradise

One of the proud boasts by which Harrods made its name was that it could provide customers with anything they wanted. The pet department would not flinch at a request for a pair of hippopotami; the jewellery department would be sympathetic towards a sudden craving for Fabergé eggs.

Of course, most desires can still be satisfied in this world-weary city, but there are also many items waiting to give shoppers a surprise. Oxford Street is a good starting point. Between the Virgin Megastore in Tottenham Court Road (the hi-fi hub) and Marks & Spencer's premier branch near Marble Arch (the upmarket end of Oxford Street), every British chain store gets a look-in, led by the stalwart Selfridges and John Lewis. Little enclaves lead off it, such as St Christopher's Place, which beckons to a cluster of chic boutiques.

At Oxford Circus, Regent Street curves down to Piccadilly and here the old-style labels still dominate: Liberty's (the building

alone is worth a visit), Dickens and Jones, the glass and china shops of Waterford, Wedgwood and Villeroy & Bosch, and Garrard's, the royal jewellers. English clothes are sold at Jaeger, Austin Reed and Aquascutum. And all children love Hamley's, one of the world's largest toy stores.

South of Oxford Street and west of Regent Street is Mayfair and the aristocrats of the retail trade. Aspreys, Tiffany and Cartier sparkle, and Valentino, Chanel and Lagerfeld tease out the latest fashion styles, which should also be checked in South Molton Street. More than 400 antique and fine art galleries flourish in this area, including the auction houses of Sotheby's and Phillips, and the galleries of Cork Street which sell genuine paintings from Picasso on down.

Slip between the glittering parade of little shops in Burlington Arcade to Piccadilly and St James's, a traditional male preserve of bespoke tailors and shirt-makers. Women, though, are definitely allowed into Fortnum and Mason's to buy exotic groceries and partake of afternoon tea.

Piccadilly leads west to Knightsbridge and Harrods, where again the food halls are well worth a perusal. From Knightsbridge, the Fulham Road begins with a Golden Mile around the Conran Shop in the Art Nouveau Michelin building. Sloane Street, home to designers from Joseph to Yamamoto, runs from Harvey Nichols to Sloane Square and King's Road, still trendy after all these years.

Meanwhile, the centre of London can still offer good bets. Young designers such as Christopher New, John Richmond and Boyd & Storey have rediscovered Soho. Paul Smith and Nicole Farhi are worth searching out in Covent Garden.

Charing Cross Road, Cecil Court and Museum Street are the places to buy old and new books and prints: Foyle's is an astonishing maze of a bookshop. For antiques, the major weekly events are the Friday early-morning market at Bermondsey, and at Portobello Road on Friday and Saturday mornings.

On Sundays, hordes of people descend on the market stalls of Camden. The streets of Greenwich fill up, too, around four street markets, while Brick Lane and Petticoat Lane in the East End are famous for clothes and bargains of dubious origin. ❑

LEFT: tailored to perfection.

Hereford House in nearby Manchester Square contains the superb **Wallace Collection** , a treasure chest of 17th and 18th-century art and ornaments, among which there is Sèvres porcelain, Limoges enamels and antique French furniture. On the walls hang works by Titian, Rubens and Holbein (open daily; Sun: 2–5pm (11am–5pm in summer); free).

Voluptuous **Mayfair** is the hub of English wealth, the home of oil barons and property giants, of landed aristocrats and self-made nabobs. Its narrow streets are abuzz by day with the flow of cash, but at night the district slides into an eerie quiet as the financial wizards and fashion models retreat into their terracotta towers. By the mid-18th century, the powerful Grosvenor family had purchased the land and developed Mayfair into an elegant Georgian housing estate. This enticed the wealthy of dreary inner London to move out and settle in one of the city's first suburbs.

Today, Mayfair is known for its stylish shops and lavish auction houses. The names roll off the tongue as a testament to affluence: Cartier, Rolls-Royce, Floris, Gieves & Hawkes, Yardley and Smythson's. **Bond Street** ❷❸ is the kind of place where you can buy something for that person who already has everything. For a quiet walk, try one of Mayfair's elegant Victorian arcades, the tiny covered streets lined with a startling array of unique and interesting shops. The **Royal Opera Arcade** is the oldest, but the **Piccadilly**, **Prince's** and **Royal Arcades** are just as elegant. **Burlington Arcade** with its uniformed doormen is the most famous, only a few doors up from the **Royal Academy of Arts** ❷❹ (open daily). The Academy has changing exhibitions of major artists and its Summer Exhibition of amateur and professional artists (*see page 152*) provides light entertainment and perhaps the chance to pick up a bargain.

Map, pages 118/9

Mayfair was once farmland outside London. The name derives from the medieval May Fair, which took place each spring. For two weeks, the otherwise tranquil pastures sprang to life with fire eaters and eel divers, sausage tables and hasty-pudding stands.

BELOW LEFT: Sotheby's auction house. **BELOW:** Oxford Street.

A Night on the Town

Up West is where Londoners go for a night on the town. The West End is a mythical place, consisting of Shaftesbury Avenue shows, Covent Garden chatter, Leicester Square picture palaces and Trafalgar Square strolls. Many people find enough entertainment just by strolling around.

There are plenty of pubs and wine bars where Londoners meet their friends and decide what the evening has in store, sometimes by consulting the *Evening Standard* or the weekly listings magazine, *Time Out*. In summer people go for a drink on boats moored on the Embankment, or walk over Hungerford Bridge to the South Bank complex to watch jugglers and other street theatre – and perhaps even to go to the real theatre.

There is serious eating to be done Up West. At the top end is Albert Roux's Le Gavroche in Upper Brook Street which shines with Michelin stars, while Nico Ladenis's Chez

Nico on Park Lane is hard on its heels. Less exalted places can be found all around Soho; every ethnic cuisine is catered for, and there is an exciting Chinatown around Gerrard Street with dozens of authentic restaurants, predominantly Cantonese. People queue for hamburgers at Piccadilly's Hard Rock Café and Planet Hollywood near Leicester Square.

The music clubs in the West End have long been popular. The Astoria on Charing Cross Road is the place for the latest bands, while the 100 Club in Oxford Street majors in jazz. Ronnie Scott's at 47 Frith Street is London's most famous jazz venue.

Tickets to the most popular plays and musicals are usually hard to get, but with so many shows on offer there is always plenty of choice, even on the day. In Leicester Square, a booth opens at noon to sell half-price tickets for some of the evening's performances.

Leicester Square is also the capital's cinema centre, with several enormous cinemas. The Comedy Store, the city's main alternative cabaret venue, is also situated in Leicester Square. More risqué is Madame Jojo's in Soho, a remnant of the area's steamier days.

The club scene is thriving, but dress up rather than down as codes can be strict. Many clubs have "one nighters" featuring a particular style of music. To see who is going to be in tomorrow's gossip columns, head for Stringfellows in Upper St Martin's Lane. Leicester Square's Empire is one of the largest discos in Europe, or try the nearby Hippodrome with its amazing lightshow.

London's most exclusive night club is Annabel's, where the rich and the royal hang out. The WAG Club on Wardour Street is for heavy-duty dance music and the biggest gay club is Heaven in Villiers Street, but there are interesting night spots away from the centre: The Fridge in Brixton, south of the Thames, and Subterrania in Ladbroke Grove in west London.

Britain's licensing laws, which force pubs to shut at 11pm, and the departure of the last Underground train an hour or so later, mean the West End begins to feel dispiritingly empty by midnight and only those who know the scene can keep the party going till dawn. After spilling out of a club in the wee hours, they head for Bar Italia in Frith Street for the best cappuccino in town.

LEFT: the bright lights of Soho. ❑

Mayfair antiques and art are world-famous. **Christie's** in King Street auctions more than 150,000 objects a year, including furniture, armour, jewels and paintings, while **Sotheby's** in New Bond Street has been the scene of some of the most important deals in art history.

John Nash's curving **Regent Street** divides Mayfair from **Soho** as effectively as if there were an ocean between the two. Soho, long known for its low-life bars and sex clubs, has recently returned to being a neighbourhood of cosmopolitan foodshops and restaurants, with a population of East European émigrés, French, Italian and Greek restaurateurs and a thriving Chinese community. The sleazy side of Soho has all but gone. Raymond's well-established Revue Bar has terribly tasteful strip shows and a few hole-in-the-wall dens offer "live" entertainment.

Piccadilly Circus ㉕ is the spiritual heart of Soho, once a roundabout and now a frenzied junction which is forever crowded with black cabs, red buses and awe-struck tourists. The bronze statue of Eros stands atop a fountain on the south side of the mêlée, but is outshone by a neon curtain blasting advertising slogans to the masses. Nearby in Coventry Street is the **Trocadero** entertainment centre, whose attractions include **Segaworld**, the biggest hi-tech indoor entertainment theme park in the world, and **Madame Tussaud's Rock Circus**, a loud multi-sensory rock attraction.

In the heart of Soho is **Berwick Street** ㉖, the site of one of the best fruit and vegetable markets in London, excellent for both quality and price. Karl Marx used to live around the corner on **Dean Street** in the building now inhabited by an Italian restaurant, Quo Vadis. John Baird succeeded in transmitting the first pictures via wireless from a workshop in nearby **Frith Street** in 1926. His was a new-fangled invention that would soon be known as television.

Map, pages 118/9

Soho's multi-ethnic mix reflects the area's origins as a home to refugees – originally French Protestants who fled here in 1685.

ABOVE: wax rockers.
BELOW: meeting up at Piccadilly Circus.

The above marble from the Parthenon is one of millions of artefacts in the British Museum. The basis of the collection was laid by a physician, Sir Hans Soane (1660–1753).

BELOW: the British Museum.

Brainy Bloomsbury

For yet another drastic change in mood, hop on the tube at Piccadilly Circus and ride four stops to Russell Square. This will deposit you in **Bloomsbury**, the intellectual and scholastic heart of the city.

Bloomsbury is dominated by the **British Museum** ❷, one of the largest and best in the world (open daily; Sun from 2.30pm; free). The museum is both a priceless art collection and a monument to human civilisation, encompassing antiquities from almost every period and every part of the world – Egyptian, Assyrian, Greek, Roman, Indian, Chinese, Islamic and Anglo-Saxon. Among its multiple treasures are the Rosetta Stone from Egypt (the key that unlocked the secrets of hieroglyphic script), the great 7th-century Anglo-Saxon Sutton Hoo treasures, the Nimrud friezes from Mesopotamia and the Elgin Marbles, the remarkable figures that once graced the Parthenon in Athens. Don't expect to see everything in one day; it's impossible. But do expect to visit the museum every time you return to London.

The **British Library** was established within the same 19th-century building. However, the entire library of more than 9 million books – including a Gutenberg Bible, the Magna Carta and original texts by Shakespeare, Dickens and Leonardo da Vinci – has now been moved to a controversial £500 million edifice near King's Cross Station. The Reading Room (once the workshop of Karl Marx), redesigned for the millennium, will become an education and information centre.

The **Thomas Coram Foundation** ❷ at No. 40 Brunswick Square, is home of the Founding Hospital Art Treasures and the works of Hogarth, Gainsborough and Kneller (open Mon & Fri: 1.30–4.30pm only). Bloomsbury was the address of such intellectual figures as John Maynard Keynes (1883–1946) and

Virginia Woolf (1882–1941). But of all the writers and thinkers who have lived here one stands head and shoulders above the others: Charles Dickens. He lived with his family at **No. 48 Doughty Street** ❷ for almost two years (1837–39), during which time he wrote parts of *Oliver Twist*, *Nicholas Nickleby* and *Pickwick Papers*. The house is a small museum filled with portraits, letters, furniture and other personal effects of Victorian England's most famous novelist (open Mon–Sat).

East of Bloomsbury Square is the hardworking district of **Holborn** (pronounced *ho-bun*), which centres on the busy street and tube station of the same name. A pair of silver griffins on either side of Holborn High Street marks the official boundary of the City of London. Nearby is **Staple Inn** ❸, a timber-framed Elizabethan structure (the only one left in London) that once served as a hostel for wool merchants.

Legal London

Lying between Holborn and the Thames are the prestigious **Inns of Court** – the confluence of London's legal world since the Middle Ages. There were originally 12 inns, founded in the 14th century for the lodging and education of lawyers on "neutral" ground between the merchants of the City and the monarchs of Westminster. But today only four remain. Dr Johnson called the inns "the noblest nurseries of humanity and liberty in the Kingdom". Even today, no one can enter the legal profession in London without acceptance into one of the inns – a practice known as "passing the bar". **Gray's Inn** ❸ has a garden designed by Francis Bacon in 1606, a haven of plane trees and smooth lawns that provides a tranquil lunchtime retreat away from the hustle of the City. **Lincoln's Inn** ❸, north of

Map, pages 118/9

ABOVE: elegant Bloomsbury.
BELOW LEFT: the Royal Courts of Justice in the Strand.
BELOW RIGHT: barristers outside the Law Courts.

Fleet Street, has a medieval hall and a 17th-century chapel by Inigo Jones. The leafy expanse called **Lincoln's Inn Fields**, once a notorious venue for duels and executions, is now restricted to picnics and summer sunbathing. On the north side of the fields at No. 13 is the **Sir John Soane Museum**, an outlandish mansion which is a sort of British Museum in miniature, housing Soane's remarkable collection of antiquities, paintings and architectural designs (open Tue–Sat; free). Nowhere else in London can you see such an odd assortment of artifacts under one roof. The **Old Curiosity Shop** – made famous by Charles Dickens – sits on Portsmouth Street near the southwest corner of the fields.

The most fascinating of the inns is the twin complex of the **Inner** and **Middle Temples ㉝**. The name derives from the Knights Templar, a medieval religious fraternity that occupied this site until the early 14th century. The temple has changed little: it is still a precinct of vaulted chambers, hammerbeam roofs and lush wood panelling. In the 16th-century Middle Temple Hall, Shakespeare's own company once performed *Twelfth Night* for the Elizabethan court.

The 12th-century **Temple Church** is one of only four "round churches" left in England. The lawyers and judges who now inhabit the Temple may seem as anachronistic as the buildings, for they can still be seen rushing about clad in white wigs, flowing black robes and highwing collars.

Fleet Street takes its name from the Fleet River, which once flowed from Hampstead River into the Thames. Until the 1980s, the street was the centre of the national newspaper industry. Then computerised typesetting arrived, the power of the old print unions was broken, and the papers built new printing works in Docklands and moved their editorial offices to cheaper locations. Not a single national newspaper remains in Fleet Street. **St Bride's ㉞** is the official

The unique three-tiered steeple of St Bride's was used by a local baker as the model for his wedding cakes – a design now copied all around the world.

BELOW: a pub on the tourist trail. **BELOW RIGHT:** Sir John Soane Museum.

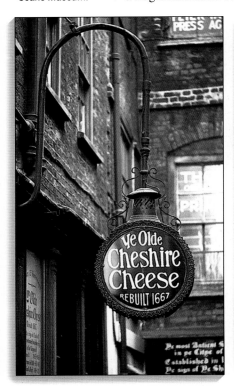

parish church of the British press, an impressive 17th-century church built by Christopher Wren.

Dr Johnson compiled his famous *Dictionary* and the *Complete Works of Shakespeare* in the attic of a house at **No. 17 Gough Square ⑤**, just north of Fleet Street (open Mon–Sat from 11am), where he lived from 1748 to 1759. Between bouts with pen and ink, Dr Johnson did his drinking nearby at **Ye Olde Cheshire Cheese**, a charming pub that still stands in Wine Office Court.

South Bank

Londoners look at the **South Bank Complex ⑥** (across Waterloo Bridge from Somerset House) in two ways: as the greatest fine arts forum in Europe, or as an uninspired mass of concrete that should be put out of its misery. The truth lies somewhere in between. The **Royal Festival Hall** plays host to the London Symphony and Philharmonic Orchestras, a spacious arena that is famed for its acoustics and visibility. Next door are the **Queen Elizabeth Hall** and the **Purcell Room**, used for a variety of events, from chamber music to poetry readings.

The **National Film Theatre** sits in the shadow of Waterloo Bridge, presenting an ever-changing bill of vintage and foreign-language films as well as the London Film Festival each November. Nearby is the highly imaginative **Museum of the Moving Image** (open daily), which covers television as well as cinema; here, children can have a go at flying over London like Superman.

The huge **National Theatre** is known for the high quality of its drama productions and its enthusiasm for new playwrights. The **Hayward Gallery**, with changing exhibitions of contemporary art, rounds off the South Bank show (open daily; Tue, Wed till 8pm).

Map, pages 118/9

"When a man is tired of London, he is tired of life," said Dr Johnson, "for there is in London all that life can afford."

BELOW: the Royal Festival Hall.

Close by, in the majestic **County Hall ㉗**, built in 1909–33 and seat of the Greater London Council until it was abolished in 1986, is the new **London Aquarium**, whose 41 exhibits range from sharks to stingray (open daily).

Upriver from the South Bank Complex, beyond Westminster Bridge, is **Lambeth Palace ㉘** which has been the London residence of the Archbishop of Canterbury for nearly 800 years.

Another great landmark south of the river is the **Imperial War Museum ㉙**, situated in Lambeth within the remains of the "Bedlam", the old Bethlehem Hospital for lunatics (open daily). The museum, completely redesigned in 1989, houses weapons, vehicles, paintings, uniforms, decorations and scale models, and you don't have to be a warmonger to find it fascinating.

Village Hampstead and Regent's Park

Adjacent to Hampstead Heath is Highgate Cemetery. Among the luminaries laid to rest here are George Eliot, Michael Faraday, Christina Rossetti and Karl Marx.

BELOW: Hampstead Heath. **RIGHT**, a popular local pub.

To visit one of London's loveliest and most historic "villages", head north on the Northern Line from Waterloo Station. For more than 300 years **Hampstead ㊵** has attracted men of arts and letters. John Keats' house is open to the public (Keats Grove; open daily; closed 1–2pm; free), as is the house where Sigmund Freud spent his last year (Freud Museum, 20 Maresfield Gardens; open Wed–Sun). Today, Hampstead is populated by a mixed bag of music, stage and cinema stars who maintain the district's trendy and transient flavour. Despite the steady encroachment of suburbia, Hampstead retains a certain village atmosphere, aided no doubt by the proximity of 790-acre (310-hectare) **Hampstead Heath**. For the visitor, Hampstead is best viewed on foot, window shopping along the **High Street**, or exploring the elegant Georgian and Regency mansions along **Church Row**, **Flask Walk**, **Downshire Hill** and **Holly Hill**.

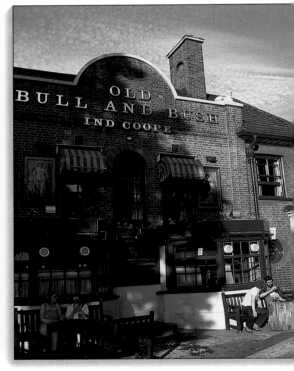

An 18th-century decree forbade building on the Heath, thus preserving a rambling tract of dark woods and lush meadows. The 18th-century **Kenwood House** is the only large structure on the Heath. It now houses the Iveagh Bequest, a rich collection of English and Dutch paintings that includes works by Rembrandt, Reynolds and Vermeer (open daily (Oct–Mar: till 4pm); free).

Haverstock Hill runs from Hampstead into **Camden Town**, a journey which takes you from the literary past into the rag-tag present. Camden became famous in the 1960s as a gathering place for hippies, street artists and various vagrants, who set up small shops and stalls around **Camden Lock** ⍟. The market is now one of the most popular London weekend attractions. Browse through the antiques, crafts, old clothes and military surplus goods, and listen to the talented buskers who gather in the cobblestone courtyard beside the Lock.

Just west of Camden Town is **Regent's Park** ⍟, a massive green space with a long and chequered history. Henry VIII established a royal hunting ground here on land seized from the Abbess of Barking. Later, in the early 19th century, the park became part of the Prince Regent's (later George IV) great scheme for a huge processional thoroughfare and palace complex to stretch from Pall Mall to Primrose Hill. The Prince commissioned John Nash to design and develop the scheme, but the dream got only as far as the famed Regency terraces on the southern fringe of the park, which represent Nash at his best.

London Zoo was founded in Regent's Park in 1826 by Sir Stamford Raffles, who also founded Singapore. Tommy, the first chimp, arrived at the gates in a stagecoach, while the first giraffes were unloaded at London Docks and carried through the City, startling pedestrians. Among the zoo's features today are the aviary designed by Lord Snowdon and the 1930s penguin pool (open daily). ❏

Map, pages 118/9

Regent's Canal runs for 8½ miles (14 km) from Paddington in west London to Limehouse in Docklands. The whole length can be walked.

BELOW: London's parks are often far from crowded.

LONDON: THE CITY AND SOUTHWARK

The City is the oldest part of London, a trading post the Romans called Londinium. Rebuilt since the devastation of World War II, today it is Europe's financial powerhouse

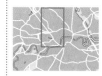

Map, page 118/9

Fleet Street sweeps from London's theatreland into Ludgate Hill and the **City of London,** that history-packed square mile that sits atop the remains of both Roman and medieval towns. The City has long been the domain of merchants and craftsmen, a powerful coalition of men who helped force democracy upon the English monarchy and then built a mercantile empire on which the sun never set. Despite the encroachment of modern office blocks and computers, the City retains something of its medieval ways: the square mile is still governed separately from the rest of London, by the ancient City Corporation and its Court of Common Council – relics of the medieval trade and craft guilds.

Wren's masterpiece

Sitting at the top of Ludgate Hill is **St Paul's Cathedral** ⑬, dominating the skyline of the City like no other structure, the massive dome punching upward through the forest of highrises that has come to surround it since World War II. After the Norman St Paul's was destroyed in the Great Fire of 1666, Charles II asked Christopher Wren to design a new cathedral to befit the status of London. Wren's first plan was rejected as too radical, but he then responded with a brilliant blend of Italian baroque and classical influences – a huge cruciform building whose stone cupola takes it to a height of 365 ft (111 metres). Only St Peter's in Rome has a bigger dome.

St Paul's arose in 1675–1710 as the first cathedral built and dedicated to the Protestant faith, and was the crowning achievement of Wren's career. It played host to Queen Victoria's Diamond Jubilee ceremonies in 1897; Winston Churchill's funeral in 1965; and the wedding of Prince Charles and Lady Diana Spencer in 1981. The cathedral miraculously survived the Blitz, though the neighbourhood around it was destroyed by German bombs and missiles. St Paul's is also a notable burial place; among those entombed within are Wellington, Nelson, Reynolds, Turner and Wren himself. The cathedral's interior displays the work of the finest artists and craftsmen of the late 17th century: iron grillework of Tijou, wooden choir stalls by Grinling Gibbons, and the murals inside the dome by Sir James Thornhill. Around the inside of the dome stretches the **Whispering Gallery**, so called because you can easily comprehend the voices of anyone standing on the opposite side of the void. A winding stairway leads to the outside of the dome, where there is a panoramic view of London.

Sprawling north from St Paul's is the futuristic **Barbican** development ⑭, a startling contrast to the maze of twisting streets and ancient buildings that surround

LEFT: St Paul's still dominates the City's skyline. **BELOW:** the Lord Mayor in his coach.

CITY OF LONDON

BELOW: the Bank of England.

the cathedral. This urban renewal project arose from the rubble of an old neighbourhood that had been destroyed in the Blitz. One of the Barbican's many showcases is the **Museum of London** , a superb collection devoted to the history of the city from prehistoric to modern times (open Tues–Sun; closed Sun am; entrance fee, free after 4.30pm). There are models of old buildings, reconstructed shop fronts, audio-visual shows, a reference library, antique vehicles and a number of historic artifacts such as the Lord Mayor's State Coach. The Barbican Arts Centre is also the London base of both the Royal Shakespeare Company and the London Symphony Orchestra.

Nearby is **St Bartholomew-the-Great** ⑥, a Norman church which has also served as a stable, factory, wine cellar, coal store, and even as Benjamin Franklin's London printworks during its 1,000-year history.

In the shadows of the Barbican's skyscrapers is the **Guildhall** ⑦, one of the few buildings to survive the Great Fire and now the home of the government of the City. Largely restored, this ornate Gothic structure was built in 1411 with funds donated by various livery companies, the medieval trade and craft guilds that held sway over the City. Within the Guildhall is the famous **Great Hall**, decorated with the colourful banners of the 12 livery companies and the shields of all 92 guilds (open May–Sept: daily; Oct–Apr: closed Sun; free).

Britain's financial heartland

A short walk east along Gresham Street brings you to the **Bank of England** ⑧, a building of powerful classical design. The Bank still prints and mints all British money, administers to the national debt and protects the country's gold reserves. Nearby stands the old London **Stock Exchange**, founded in 1773 but now housed in a skyscraper at the junction of Threadneedle and Old Broad Street. The trading floor is no longer used – shares are now traded electronically – but there's an exhibition on the history of stocks and securities.

Directly opposite the Bank are the **Royal Exchange** (obviously modelled on the Parthenon) and **Mansion House**, the official residence of the Lord Mayor since the 1750s. Many of the City's treasures are housed within this Palladian-style palace, which is generally closed to the public: the 15th-century Mayoral Chain of Office; the 18th-century Great Mace; and an extensive collection of Corporation plates, tapestries and crystal.

King William Street leads south from the bustling Bank intersection to London Bridge and the Thames. Just before you reach the river, a huge fluted column peers over the helter-skelter of rooftops: the 202-ft (60-metre) **Monument** ⑨ – Wren's memorial to the Great Fire of 1666. Climb to the summit for a superb panorama of central London (open daily; Sat, Sun from 2pm; winter: Mon–Sat till 3.40pm; entrance fee).

The torturous tower

Lower Thames Street traces the medieval banks of the river past the old Billingsgate Fish Market and the elegant Custom House. A squat stone building commands this southeast corner of the City, a pensive medieval fortress known as the **Tower of London** ⑩ (open daily; entrance fee). The Tower has served, over the centuries,

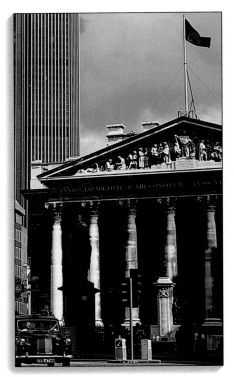

as fortress, palace, prison and museum, as well as arsenal, archive, menagerie and treasure chest. It's the most alluring of London's many monuments, attracting millions of tourists a year; so expect queues.

William the Conqueror built the inner keep (the **White Tower**) as both a military stronghold and a means of impressing his new subjects in England. Constructed between 1078 and 1098, it was the largest building in Britain and soon symbolised royal domination. It remained a royal residence until the 16th century, when the court moved to more comfortable quarters in Westminster.

The Tower then became the storehouse for the Crown Jewels and the most infamous prison and execution ground in London. After 1747 the Tower became the Royal Mint, Archive and Menagerie – until the elephants, lions and bears were moved to the new Regent's Park Zoo a century later. German spies were executed here in both world wars.

The White Tower houses the diminutive **St John's Chapel**, built in 1080 and now the oldest church in London. Beneath Waterloo Barracks is a vault containing the **Crown Jewels**, including the Imperial State Crown which sparkles with 3,000 stones and the **Royal Sceptre**, which centres around a 530-carat diamond called the Star of Africa. Also worth seeing are the **Crowns and Diamonds** exhibition in the Martin Tower, the **Regimental Museum's** permanent display of weapons from the mid-17th to mid-19th centuries, and the **New Armouries**, which is given over to temporary exhibitions.

Beefeaters

The Tower is protected by the Yeomen Wardens or Beefeaters, so-called not because of their carnivorous habits, but because they were founded in the 16th century as the

Map, page 118/9

ABOVE: one of the Beefeaters who guards the Tower of London (**BELOW**).

boufitiers or guardians of the king's buffet. An authentic chopping block sits upon Tower Green – yes, you may place your head on it for photographs.

The most spectacular of London's many spans is **Tower Bridge** , a striking Gothic profile opened in 1894. Perhaps its most infamous moment came in 1954 when the warning lights failed and a double decker bus became wedged between the open spans. The inside of Tower Bridge is open to the public (open daily; entrance fee); it contains a museum of London bridges and superb views.

Southern ways

On the south side of Tower Bridge is the restaurant-lined **Butler's Wharf** and the Conran Foundation **Design Museum ❷**, whose changing exhibitions are aimed at provoking visitors into an appreciation of good, commercial design (open daily from 11.30am; closed Sat, Sun am; entrance fee). Heading upstream again, the riverside walk between Tower Bridge and London Bridge passes by **HMS *Belfast* ❸**. Commissioned in 1939 as the largest cruiser in the British Navy, it is now a maritime museum (open daily; entrance fee).

Continuing past more renovated warehouses towards London Bridge, the **London Dungeon ❹** provides a gruesome account of life in medieval London – children love it (open daily; Oct–Mar: till 4.30pm; entrance fee).

Beyond London Bridge rises the majestic **Southwark Cathedral ❺**. Augustinian canons erected the original church in the 13th century, but the cathedral has been much altered since then. Adjacent, in the St Mary Overie Dock, is a replica of Sir Francis Drake's galleon, the *Golden Hinde*. Close to Southwark Bridge is a replica of the 1599 **Shakespeare's Globe ❻**, a theatre-in-the-round which stages the Bard's plays on the site where they were first performed (guided

ABOVE: Southwark Cathedral. **BELOW:** Tower Bridge.

Map, page 118/9

tours; daily from 9.15am; Tue–Sat: till 12.45pm; Sun till 2.45pm; Mon till 3.45pm; entrance fee). Starting in 2000, the Tate will display its modern art in the converted **Bankside Power Station** ➄.

Back on the north bank of the river, downstream from Tower Bridge, lie **St Katharine's Docks** ➄. Built in 1828 as a shipment point for wool and wine, the docks were renovated in the early 1980s and have become a posh residential and commercial district. The complex contains a shopping arcade, a yacht harbour, pub, hotel and several old warehouses (such as the Ivory House) now converted as modern offices and flats. It is the most successful of the docklands developments which extend east from here to the Isle of Dogs where the Canary Wharf tower (Britain's tallest office block) marks their modern ambitions.

Mansell Street leads north from the Tower into the warren of narrow streets that marks the start of London's **East End**, traditionally the City's working-class district. **Whitechapel** and **Spitalfields** – both at the north end of Mansell Street – are where 19th and early 20th-century European immigrants settled, though the Jewish population has long dispersed.

The **Whitechapel Art Gallery** ➄ in Whitechapel High Street (by Aldgate East tube) is a beautiful piece of *fin-de-siècle* architecture, and is one of London's most exciting galleries, hosting regular exhibitions by living artists (open Tues–Sun from 11am; Wed till 8pm; free).

Petticoat Lane ➅, once the domain of old clothes dealers, is the most famous East End market. Today, the traders – a mixed bag of Cockneys, West Indians and Asians – prove every Sunday morning that racial harmony is indeed possible. The stalls along Middlesex Street are a chromatic jumble of clothes, antiques, food and just about everything else you can think of. ❏

Shakespeare's Globe is an octagonal construction. It has a thatched roof and an open centre, where the standing audience can participate much as they did in Shakespeare's day. There is also seating capacity for 1,500 on wooden benches; cushions can be hired.

BELOW:
Shakespeare's re-created Globe.

LONDON: CHELSEA AND KENSINGTON

Home to some of Britain's best and brightest – and wealthiest – Chelsea and Kensington offer the visitor fine museums, lovely streets to stroll along, and superlative shopping.

Map, page 148

In the 19th century Chelsea was an avant garde "village" just outside the sprawl of central London. Among its more famous residents were Oscar Wilde, John Singer Sargent, Thomas Carlyle, Mark Twain and T.S. Eliot. Cheyne Walk, a row of elegant Georgian terraced houses just off the river, has long been Chelsea's most popular residential street. George Eliot, Turner and Carlyle lived there in the 19th century; J. Paul Getty and Mick Jagger in the 20th. Chelsea is where England swung in the 1960s, with boutiques such as Mary Quant's Bazaar, and where punk began in the 1970s with Vivienne Westwood and Malcolm McClaren's boutique, called 'Sex'.

The **King's Road ❶** is Chelsea's famous thoroughfare and one of London's most curious. It started life as a tranquil country lane but was later widened into a private carriage road from St James's Palace to Hampton Court on the order of King Charles II. Down on the riverfront is **Chelsea Royal Hospital ❷**, Sir Christopher Wren's masterpiece of the English baroque style, opened as a home for invalid and veteran soldiers in 1682 to match his hospital for sailors at Greenwich. A few hundred army pensioners still reside there, and parade in their famous scarlet frockcoats on Oak Apple Day (29 May). Nearby, tracing the history of the British military from the 15th century, is the **National Army Museum** (open daily; closed bank hols; free). **Ranelagh Gardens** stands adjacent to the Royal Hospital, the site of the Chelsea Flower Show held each spring.

On Royal Hospital Road is the strange little **Chelsea Physic Garden**, a botanical laboratory from which cotton seeds were taken to the American South in 1732 (open Apr–Oct: Wed, Sun pm only). Walk across either Albert or Chelsea Bridges and enjoy the lush expanse of **Battersea Park ❸** on the south bank, with gardens designed as part of the Festival of Britain in 1951 and the Buddhist Peace Pagoda, commemorating the 1985 Year of Peace.

Belgravia: where the really rich live

Having crossed the Thames again and returned to King's Road, leave Chelsea by proceeding east, crossing Sloane Square and entering the elegant district of **Belgravia**. The area was used for grazing until Thomas Cubitt developed it as a town estate for aristocrats in the early 19th century. The district retains this exclusive quality as the home of diplomats, senior civil servants, celebrities and the occasional duke or baron. Belgravia is littered with grand Regency terraces and squares, bound by cream-coloured mansions and carefully tended gardens. Behind these grand façades lie the

LEFT: Georgian town house, Chelsea.
BELOW: a Chelsea pensioner.

diminutive mews, tiny cobblestoned alleys that once served as stables. This is London's most expensive residential district.

North of Belgravia via Sloane Street is the bustling neighbourhood of luxury shops and first-class hotels at **Knightsbridge**. This is the home of **Harrods ❹**, London's most famous department store. At night, its light-spangled façade resembles an enormous Victorian birthday cake. As in the British Museum, you could spend days wandering the aisles of Harrods and still not see everything. But be sure to visit the food halls, which display more than 500 varieties of cheese, 140 different breads and 160 brands of whisky. The Victorian tiles underfoot are under a preservation order, which means they cannot be removed or altered without government permission.

Museums and more museums

South Kensington tube station (one stop after Knightsbridge) is the jumping-off point for Exhibition Road's cluster of fine museums. The **Victoria & Albert ❺** is the most famous of these, housing a marvellous collection of millions of

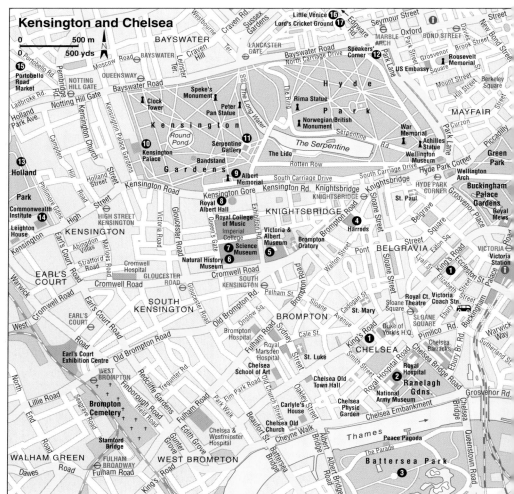

see map opposite

items dedicated to the fine and applied arts of all nations, eras and styles. It has been called a vast box of delights and indeed there must be something for everyone within its brick walls. The maze-like interior includes 7 miles (11 km) of galleries, with exhibits that range from furniture and paintings to textiles and armour (open daily; closed Mon am). Highlights include the Raphael "Cartoons", the Great Bed of Ware from 1590 and the TT Tsui Gallery of Chinese Art.

For pterodactyls, try the **Natural History Museum** ❻ in Cromwell Road (open daily; Sun from 11am). It has one of the best dinosaur and prehistoric lizard collections anywhere. The Life Galleries section of the museum also has fascinating exhibits on early man, Darwin's theory of evolution, human biology, birth and whales (including a life-size model of a blue whale). In the Earth Galleries (geology section) you can experience a simulated earthquake, or examine a piece of the moon. The Discovery Centre is popular among children, as is the adjacent **Science Museum** ❼, which has items ranging from Puffing Billy (one of the oldest surviving locomotives) to spacecraft and satellites (open daily).

One of Victorian England's greatest monuments also lies within South Kensington. Queen Victoria laid the foundation stone for the **Royal Albert Hall** ❽ in 1867 in memory of her late husband, Prince Albert who was responsible for many of the South Kensington institutions. The circular 7,000-seat auditorium is still one of the largest theatres in London, and stages a varied programme from pop concerts to brass band competitions. However, the Albert Hall is most famous for the BBC-sponsored summer Promenade Concerts – the Proms – a marvellous showcase of both classical and more modern music. The final concert is traditionally a playful combination of serious music-making and boisterous audience participation. This "Last Night of the Proms" is broadcast live on BBC television, and millions across the nation tune in for their annual dose of flag-waving, fancy dress and old-fashioned sing along.

ABOVE: the Royal Albert Hall. **BELOW:** Harrods.

Across Kensington Gore, and undergoing restoration until 1999, sits the **Albert Memorial** ❾, a flamboyant Gothic monument that rises suddenly from the plane trees of Kensington Gardens and Hyde Park. When visible, Prince Albert sits under a lavish canopy, forever reading the catalogue from the 1851 Great Exhibition, which he engineered on the site.

Palaces and gardens

A short walk away through the prolific and tranquil gardens is **Kensington Palace** ❿ (open May–Oct: daily; guided tours only). Christopher Wren refurbished the mansion for William and Mary in the late 17th century, and for nearly 100 years it served as the principal private royal residence in London. Queen Victoria was born within its brick walls in 1819. Today it is the London residence of several members of the royal family, including Princess Margaret, and was, until her death, the home of Diana, Princess of Wales. Another popular spot in the park is the **Serpentine Gallery** ⓫ (open daily during exhibitions; free), a tiny art museum beside the bird-filled lake of the same name. In the northeast corner of Hyde Park is **Speakers' Corner** ⓬, where, particularly on Sundays, you will find orators passionately defending all manner of causes and beliefs.

TIP

The Notting Hill Carnival takes place on the August Bank Holiday weekend. The children's costume parade is on Sunday, and the adults' on Monday. The crowds can be tightly packed and the music deafening. Beware of pickpockets as well.

Holland Park House 𝟙𝟛, just west of Kensington Palace via Kensington High Street, gives its name to leafy Holland Park, one of the least known but more interesting green spaces in London. Sir Walter Cope, James I's Chancellor of the Exchequer, built the lavish Jacobean manor upon the site in 1606; through his daughter's marriage, it became the property of the Earls of Holland, who surrounded the house with 55 acres (22 hectares) of exotic gardens. Only the east wing of the house survived the bombing of World War II.

By the park in Kensington High Street, the **Commonwealth Institute 𝟙𝟜** marks a complete contrast in style and mood, for this futuristic building is dedicated to the resources, culture and economies of former British Empire outposts. The Institute includes a reference library, cinema and several exhibition galleries such as the Commonwealth Experience with a "Heliride" over Malaysia (open daily; closed Sun am).

Notting Hill's Street Carnival

North of Holland Park is **Notting Hill**, one of London's most highly sought-after residential districts with handsome white stucco Victorian terraces and villas. However, the relative calm which prevails throughout the year is shattered every August Bank Holiday when the streets explode with music and colour as the city's huge West Indian population stages the largest street carnival in Europe. The atmosphere is electric as thousands flock to see the wild and exciting costumes of the procession which moves to the rhythmic beat of steel bands and reggae music. The district's other famous attraction is the **Portobello Road Market 𝟙𝟝**. On Saturdays the whole street becomes jammed: at the top end with tourists in search of antique treasures, whilst, at the far end, those with an eye for

BELOW: Portobello Road Market.

a bargain rummage through the second-hand clothes and bric-a-brac stalls. Fine objets d'art can be found, but at a price. In the middle of it all locals battle to buy their fruit and vegetables.

East of Notting Hill and on the north side of Hyde Park is **Bayswater**, a district that is both trendy and posh, a transport hub and a shopping mall. Bayswater stretches up to **Paddington Station**, the mainline station for trains to the west of England and soon to have a direct rail link with Heathrow Airport. To the north of Paddington begins a network of man-made waterways that once linked north London with Oxford and the Midlands. The posh residential district of **Little Venice** ⑯ lies at the junction of the Grand Union, Regent's and Paddington Canals and residential moorings for barges here are much sought after.

Refurbished canal barges operated by the **London Waterbus Company** (Apr–Oct: daily; Nov–Mar: Sat & Sun; tel: 0171-482 2660) run east from Little Venice to Regent's Park through another exclusive neighbourhood, **St John's Wood**. The Rolling Stones sang about it; the Beatles crossed Abbey Road in the middle of it. Now St John's Wood is populated by an offbeat collection of diplomats, record company executives, pop stars, and Porsche-driving businessmen.

Lord's Cricket Ground ⑰ is tucked away in the heart of the Wood. Lord's is the grand shrine of cricket *(see page 82)*, the best-known ground in the world and the home of the famous Marylebone Cricket Club (MCC), the governing body of the sport for more than a century. The **Cricket Museum** is filled with sporting memorabilia, stretching back to the time of Thomas Lord, the grounds-man who founded the club in 1787 and moved the field here in 1816 (two-hour guided tour daily: noon and 2pm, also 10am on major match days; tel: 0171-289 1611). ❑

London's double-decker buses are traditionally red, but nowadays you may see buses in other colours as well.

BELOW: Lord's cricket ground, St John's Wood.

THE ENGLISH SEASON

The Season is when high society is on display.
The events are mostly sporting, but a sense of style
is far more important than a sense of fair play

The English Season was an invention of upper-crust Londoners as a series of mid-summer amusements. This was the time when young girls "came out" at society balls, at which eligible young men would be waiting to make a suitable match. Mission accomplished, the families would repair to their country homes. The presence of royalty is an important ingredient, and the royal family has long taken a keen interest in the sports highlighted by the Season.

The events are completely insignificant compared to their importance as social gatherings. People who care nothing for rowing attend Henley Regatta in the first week of July; philistine amateurs flock to the Royal Academy's Summer Exhibition; the musically challenged die for a ticket to Glyndebourne's opera season on the south coast; and ill-informed people queueing for tickets to Wimbledon often seem to think it's the only tennis tournament in the world.

Eliza Dolittle, played by Audrey Hepburn in *My Fair Lady* (right), summed it up when, beautifully dressed by Cecil Beaton for the Royal Enclosure at Ascot, she forgot she was supposed to be a lady and urged a horse to "move yer bloomin' arse!". Such working-class passion is not welcome at an event where decorum, good breeding and a fancy hat take precedence over anything as vulgar as sporting enthusiasms.

▷ **HENLEY REGATTA**
Striped blazers and boaters are *de rigueur* at this Edwardian, public-school outing among the beer and Pimm's tents on the banks of the Thames in Oxfordshire.

▽ **ROYAL ASCOT**
Hats are the main talking point of Royal Ascot in June, and the Royal Enclosure is the only place to be on this fine flat race course near Windsor.

△ **POLO IN THE PARK**
International Polo Day at the Guards Polo Club, Windsor Great Park, is the height of this sport of kings (Prince Charles is a keen player) and rich South Americans. The pitch here – and the one in Richmond Park – is usally lined by Range Rovers and Rolls-Royces.

THE ALTERNATIVE SEASON

△ GLYNDEBOURNE

Charmingly set on the South Downs near Brighton, this summer opera location is renowned as much for its lavish picnic hampers as it is for its star performances, which are now staged in a new, enlarged building.

▽ CROQUET

The Hurlingham Club, by the river in Fulham, is host to the national championships of England's eccentric and surprisingly vicious game of croquet, otherwise played on country-house lawns.

Muddy fields and dripping camp sites don't dampen the spirits of those attending the "alternative" season – the annual round of music festivals. The larger ones attract the best bands from around the world and you don't have to be a hippy, crustie or a member of a youth tribe to attend. Many people take a tent to the large weekend events, some come only for one day.

The largest rock event, the Glastonbury Festival in Somerset, takes place at the end of June. More than 1,000 performances are given on 17 stages by more than 500 bands. It's fast becoming *the* place to be seen, and therefore tickets sell out quickly.

If you can't get to Glastonbury, try the four-day Phoenix festival which takes place in mid-July at Stratford-upon-Avon. This is a family-oriented event, with a crèche and seven music stages vying with comedy, circus and funfairs.

The best world music festival is Womad, held in Reading in mid-July. There are workshops and arts and crafts, with good facilities for families. The Reading Festival in late August attracts some of the best US rock groups. Smaller events are the July Cambridge Folk Festival and the Irish Fleadh, in Finsbury Park, north London, in June.

▽ CHELSEA FLOWERS

The Chelsea Flower Show in the grounds of the Royal Hospital Chelsea in May is an early taste of the Season. It can be a terrible crush but thousands find it rewarding.

△ WIMBLEDON FORTNIGHT

The stream of people pouring out of Southfields tube station every July contains a large number of young girls, who act like pop fans, coming to root for their favourite player.

Thames Water
Thames Conservancy Division

When the Lock-keeper is off duty

THE LOCK MAY BE HAND OPERATED AS
FOLLOWS

(1) Ensure that both pairs of gates are properly closed.

(2) Fill the lock as necessary by lowering the selector
lever (on the left of the operating pedestal) to
'SLUICE' position and rotating handwheel (clockwise)
to open or (anti-clockwise) close the sluices.

(3) When water levels are correct raise the selector
lever to 'GATE' position and rotate the handwheel
(clockwise) to open or (anti-clockwise) close the
gates.

**PLEASE LEAVE THE LOCK EMPTY
WITH THE GATES CLOSED.**

DAY TRIPS ALONG THE RIVER

*The Thames has played a central role in London's history, and you
can travel along it by boat to a variety of fascinating places,
including Greenwich, Kew Gardens and Hampton Court*

Map,
page
158/9

The capital spreads out from the centre seemingly for ever, as more than seven million people find space to live over 610 sq. miles (1,570 sq. km). Liberally sprinkled among this human mass are many parks, palaces and museums which offer rest and respite from the hustle and bustle of the big city. The River Thames is its biggest breathing space. From Greenwich to Richmond, every suburb along the river has its own personality, and each can be reached by local London transport, as well as by riverboats. Eastwards, London's Docklands have been greatly renovated, but beyond a few remaining local pubs, it will be a long time before they find any real character. To the west, however, the river is a focus of pleasure: in summer, oarsmen and yachtsmen pit their wits against its tides, people stroll along its towpaths and the pubs are wet with warm beer and enlivened by warm company.

PRECEDING PAGES:
Windsor Castle.
LEFT: Mill End Lock
on the Thames.
BELOW: all the
swans belong to the
monarch or to City
of London guilds.

Royal Greenwich

Greenwich ❶ can best be reached by train from Cannon Street or London Bridge train stations. Alternatively, a boat service runs downriver from Westminster (tel: 0171-930 4097) and Charing Cross Piers (0171-987 1185), leaving every 30 minutes in peak season and taking about an hour. Or take the Docklands Light Railway from Tower Bridge or Bank tube stations to Island Gardens, and walk through the pedestrian tunnel beneath the river. A good time to visit Greenwich is on Sunday, when there is a crafts market.

There have long been settlements here. In the 11th century Vikings pulled their longboats ashore here, slew Archbishop St Alfege, and ravaged London. In 1427 Bella Court Palace was built on the riverside and it became a royal retreat. Henry VI made it his favourite residence and subsequent Tudor monarchs – Henry VIII, Elizabeth I and Mary – were all born at Greenwich, and it was here that Sir Walter Raleigh is supposed to have laid his cloak over a pool of mud so that Queen Elizabeth would not get her feet wet.

James I had the old palace demolished and commissioned Inigo Jones to build a new private residence for Queen Anne. The result was the **Queen's House**, completed in 1637, a masterpiece of the Palladian style and perhaps the finest piece of Stuart architecture in England. Next door is the **National Maritime Museum**, an excellent seafaring collection, swelled with Millennium funds. Here the 1805 Battle of Trafalgar is re-lived and the glory of the nation's maritime tradition unfolds, with boats, paintings, and memorabilia from heroic voyages. A short distance up the hill (by foot or shuttle bus) is the **Old Royal Observatory**, constructed at Greenwich by Charles II in 1675 in order to perfect the arts of navigation and astronomy. Since that time, the globe's longi-

The real character of old docklands London can be found in its pubs: the Trafalgar Tavern at Greenwich, the Angel at Bermondsey, the Mayflower at Rotherhithe, the Grapes at Limehouse and The Prospect of Whitby at Wapping Wall, said to be London's oldest pub, dating from 1520.

tude and time zones have been measured from the Greenwich Meridian, which cuts right through the middle of Flamsteed House, now a museum of astronomical instruments and timepieces. (The Royal Observatory, Maritime Museum and Queen's House are open daily, last entrance 4.30pm; combination entrance tickets available.)

Greenwich has been associated with British sea power for the past 500 years. Just downstream is the **Royal Navy Dockyard** at Chatham (*see page 217*), which flourished under Henry VIII and Elizabeth. In the late 17th century, Sir Christopher Wren built the **Royal Hospital for Seamen** at Greenwich, an elegant complex in the baroque style that became the **Royal Naval College.** Its highly-decorated chapel and Painted Hall, decorated in the early 18th century by Sir James Thornhill, are open to the public (open 2.30–4.45pm daily; free).

On the waterfront are anchored two of England's most famous ships. The *Cutty Sark*, built in 1869, was the last of the great China clippers, a speedy square-rigger that once ran tea from the Orient to Europe. It has been superbly preserved and now contains a small museum and a collection of ship figureheads. Its own figurehead is of the hag who pursued Tam O'Shanter in the Robert Burns poem, getting so close she pulled off his horse's tale: she is wearing a "cutty sark" – a cut-down shift. Nearby sits the tiny *Gipsy Moth IV*, the yacht in which Sir Francis Chichester sailed solo round the world in 1966.

Take the river boat further downstream, past the site of the Millennium celebrations ❷ and catch a glimpse of the **Thames Barrier** ❸. This great shining steel wall, which stretches 1,700 ft (520 metres) across the width of the River Thames, protects London from the danger of flooding. (Open daily, entrance fee, nearest train station is Charlton, 20 mins walk.)

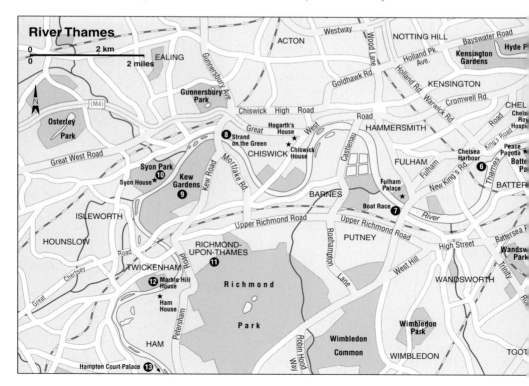

see map below

Upstream: gardens and grand houses

River boats go upriver from Charing Cross, too, past Westminster and Lambeth to Battersea and Chelsea, followed, on the north bank, by the District tube line, and on the south bank by the overground train line from Waterloo. Opposite the Peace Pagoda in **Battersea Park ❹**, erected for the 1985 Year of Peace by Japanese Buddhists, is Sir Christopher Wren's **Chelsea Hospital ❺** and beyond, the upmarket development at **Chelsea Harbour ❻**. But the leafy riverbank does not really begin until **Putney ❼**, where the University Boat Race between Oxford and Cambridge University begins each March. Putney can be reached by river boat, or by taking the District Line to Putney Bridge.

Beyond is Hammersmith Bridge. The Piccadilly and District tube lines go to Hammersmith, the starting point of a riverside walk that leads to Chiswick and has a number of popular riverside pubs, such as the Dove on Upper Mall. This historic 18th-century tavern is where *Rule, Britannia* is supposed to have been written by Thomas Arne. **Strand on the Green ❽**, just beyond, has lively Georgian houses and charming fishermen's cottages. After your walk, try one of the good riverside pubs, including the Bull's Head and City Barge, both nearly 400 years old.

A further diversion at Chiswick is **Hogarth's House** (open Tues–Sun pm only; tel: 0181-994 6757), a 17th-century mansion now filled with engravings and personal relics of one of England's most famous artists. **Chiswick House**, an early 18th-century Palladian villa designed by the third Earl of Burlington, is even more delightful. (Train from Waterloo to Chiswick, or District or Piccadilly tube lines to Turnham Green; open Apr–Sept: daily (Sun from 2pm); Oct–Mar: open Wed–Sun; tel: 0181-995 0508).

ABOVE: The Peace Pagoda in Battersea Park, erected by Japanese Buddhists.

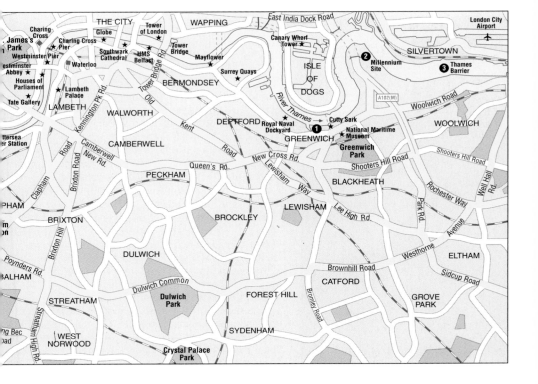

Tropical house in Kew

Kew, a quiet suburb upstream and across the Thames from Chiswick, plays host to the Royal Botanic Gardens, often called simply **Kew Gardens** , 300 acres (120 hectares) of exotic plants from around the world (open daily). The gardens were first planted in 1759 under the direction of Princess Augusta, who was then living on the site. In 1772, George III put Kew in the hands of botanist Sir Joseph Banks, who had just returned from a round-the-world expedition to collect plant specimens with Captain Cook, and the collection grew and grew. Today there are special areas given over to redwoods, orchids, roses, rhododendrons, alpine and desert plants. But the most famous of Kew's nurseries is the **Palm House**, a vast Victorian pavilion of steel and glass that contains hundreds of tropical plants. Sadly, the Palm House had to be restored following damage sustained in the storms of 1987 when many of Kew's old and rare species of trees were damaged or lost, but it is once again open to the public. The latest addition to the greenhouses is the ecologically correct and energy-saving **Princess of Wales Conservatory**, opened in the same year.

Across the Thames from Kew is another famous botanical centre – **Syon Park**. The Dukes of Northumberland built a great mansion on the site in the 16th century while the lush gardens were added later by the great English landscape gardener, "Capability" Brown. Syon now offers a number of interesting attractions: the **National Gardening Centre**, the **Living Butterfly Museum** (open daily; entrance fee), and **Syon House** itself, which has a lavish baroque interior and vivid conservatory (house open Apr–Sept: Wed–Sun and public hols; tel: 0181- 560 0881; entrance fee). To reach Syon Park from central London, take the District Line to Gunnersbury, then the 237 or 267 bus to Brent Lea Gate. From Kew, cross Kew Bridge and take the bus.

Richmond (reachable by train from Waterloo or via the District tube line, or on foot along the towpath from Kew) retains its village atmosphere with its cluster of book and antique shops, tea salons and charming riverside pubs. The Three Pigeons and the White Cross are two of the most popular. The Victorian-style **Richmond Theatre** sits on the edge of the green and is an important showcase for big-name productions on their way to the West End. **Richmond Park** was enclosed by Charles I as a royal hunting estate and is now the only royal park that keeps a large stock of deer. On the way to the park, a walk up Richmond Hill from the centre of town leads to a magnificent view west over the Thames.

Bus 65 or 371 from Richmond will take you to the flamboyant 17th-century **Ham House**, an annex of the Victoria and Albert Museum (open Easter–Oct: from 1pm Sat–Wed; tel: 0181-940 1950; entrance fee). Ham House contains a rich collection of period paintings (including Reynolds and Van Dyck), tapestries, furniture, carpets and clothing. Cavaliers and Roundheads do fierce battle each spring on the Ham House grounds as part of a three-week Richmond Festival.

Richmond Bridge leads across to **Twickenham**, known for its many mansions. It is also the home of English rugby (international games are staged in winter at the huge Twickenham Rugby Football Ground). The 18th-century **Marble Hill House** on Richmond Road is a

The Royal Botanic Gardens played a key role in the introduction of plant species to Britain's colonies: breadfruit to the West Indies, quinine to India and rubber trees to Malaysia.

BELOW:
Kew Gardens.

Palladian-style dwelling that has long provided a retreat for the secret affairs of the Crown. Both George II and George IV kept their mistresses in this mansion. Today the house contains a fine picture gallery and a lovely garden, the scene of outdoor Shakespeare productions and concerts during the summer months (open daily; Oct–Apr: till 4pm). Riverside Twickenham offers a number of worthy pubs including the White Swan, the Eel Pie and the Barmy Arms.

An exemplary Tudor palace

Above Twickenham is Teddington, the first lock which marks the end of the tidal Thames, and then **Hampton Court Palace 13**. Its two distinctive architectural styles make it both the paragon of the Tudor style and the self-proclaimed English version of Versailles (open daily; mid Oct–mid Mar till 4pm; tel: 0181-781 9500; entrance fee). In the early 16th century, Hampton Court was built by Cardinal Wolsey as the finest and most flamboyant residence in the realm. When Wolsey fell from grace, he gave the palace to Henry VIII in a futile attempt to regain favour. The king instantly fell in love with it and moved there with Anne Boleyn. He ordered the construction of the Great Hall, the Clock Court and the Library, and enlarged the gardens. It is said that Elizabeth I used Hampton Court as an illicit love nest away from the prying eyes of Westminster. She also planted the gardens with exotic trees and flowers brought to England from the New World by Sir Francis Drake and Sir Walter Raleigh.

In the 1690s, the sumptuous **State Apartments** were designed by Wren for William and Mary, who also commissioned the famous Maze and the Tijou grillework atop the entrance gates. Today the 1,000 rooms are filled with paintings, tapestries and furnishings from the past 450 years. ❑

Map, page 158/9

TIP

The quickest way to reach Hampton Court is by train from Waterloo (30 minutes). If you have 3–4 hours to spare, though, the boat journey from Westminster Pier is pleasant (tel: 0171-930 4721).

BELOW: Hampton Court Palace.

Map, page 165

THE THAMES VALLEY

Winding its way across the western Home Counties of Bucking-hamshire, Berkshire and Oxfordshire, the Thames crosses some of the gentlest and most quintessentially English of landscapes

The banks of this historic waterway have seen civilisations come and go. On the twin hills of Sinodun, south of Dorchester-on-Thames, the early Britons built a major camp as early as 1500 BC. (*Dun* means fort in Celtic.) After the arrival of Caesar, the Romans did the same, and the remains of both settlements can be seen today. The Thames is a river of plenty and has made its valley a fertile farmland. In the Middle Ages the river was so thick with salmon even the poor ate it as a staple. Great abbeys and monasteries flourished here, and kings and queens have made it their home.

To fly-fishermen, the Thames Valley begins at Bell Weir Lock just a mile north of **Staines**, south of the M4 beside the orbital M25. From Bell Weir north to the river's source (a muddy patch in a field near Coates in Gloucestershire), the river is bordered almost continuously by hills. On the west side of the motorway is Egham and the riverside meadow at **Runnymede ❶** where, on 15 June 1215, King John signed the Magna Carta. Tradition maintains that the barons encamped on one side of the Thames while the king's forces occupied the other. Magna Carta Island, the larger of the two river islands, was the neutral ground on which they met. Above is **Cooper's Hill**, which affords a panoramic view of Windsor Castle to the north. Of this hill Alexander Pope wrote:

On Cooper's Hill eternal wreaths shall grow,
While lasts the mountains or while Thames shall flow.

At the bottom of the hill lies the Magna Carta Memorial, an uninspiring structure presented by the American Bar Association. Nearby is the John F. Kennedy Memorial – three plush acres that the Queen gave to the United States in 1965 in perpetuity.

A pleasant diversion from Runnymede follows the riverside road from Staines to **Datchet ❷**. This was once the Datchet Lane mentioned in *The Merry Wives of Windsor* – the road that Falstaff was carried along in a dirty linen basket to be ducked in the Thames.

Windsor's royal castle

From Datchet across the river is England's most famous castle, **Windsor ❸** (50 mins by train from London's Waterloo (direct) or Paddington (change at Slough); open daily till 4pm; Nov–Feb: till 3pm; tel: 01753-831 118). Since the reign of Henry I in the 12th century, Windsor has been the chief residence of English and British sovereigns. William the Conqueror founded the original structure, a wooden building that consisted most likely of a motte and two large baileys enclosed by palisades. The stone fortifications were built in the 12th and 13th centuries. Rising dramatically on a chalk cliff above the Thames, the castle you see today incorporates additions by nearly every sovereign since. In the 19th century, George IV and Queen Victoria spent

LEFT: Eton oarsman.
BELOW: the Thames at Cliveden.

In the choir of St George's Chapel are the tombs of Henry VIII, Jane Seymour and Charles I. The Albert Memorial Chapel, built by Henry VIII as his own mausoleum but later converted by Victoria as a monument to her husband, Prince Albert, houses more tombs of royalty.

almost £1 million on additions. This century has seen great restorations of the interior, in particular of **St George's Chapel** (closed Sun), the worst casualty of a disastrous fire in 1992.

Part of the Lower Ward, St George's Chapel is one of the finest examples of Perpendicular architecture in England (rivalled only by King's College Chapel at Cambridge and the Henry VII Chapel at Westminster). Dedicated to the patron saint of the Order of the Garter, the chapel displays in the choir stalls the swords, helmets, mantles and banners of the respective knights.

In the Upper Ward are the **State Apartments**. These serve as accommodation for visiting foreign sovereigns and are occasionally closed to the public. Lavishly furnished, they include many important paintings from the royal collection, including works by Rubens, Van Dyck, Canaletto and Reynolds. There are also drawings by Holbein, Michelangelo, Leonardo and Raphael.

The Round Tower is what everyone thinks of as Windsor Castle. Climb the 220 steps for the wide valley view, but don't try to see the east side of the Upper Ward which houses the Queen's private apartments. Instead, venture outside and south of the castle to the **Great Park**, more than 2,000 acres (800 hectares) of lush greenery. The **Savill and Valley Gardens** have the world's biggest collection of rhododendrons.

As a complete contrast, **Lego Land Windsor**, 2 miles (3 km) from the town centre on the B3022 Bracknell/Ascot road, is a theme park based around the children's building blocks – in this case, millions of them. Its 150 acres (60 hectares) of wooded landscape include rides, shows and workshops. Lego is a contraction of two Danish words, *Leg Godt*, meaning "Play well" and the park puts a worthy emphasis on learning. (Shuttle buses run from Windsor; Greenline

BELOW:
Windsor Castle.

buses run from London Victoria; open Apr–Sept: daily; mid Jul–Aug till 8pm; Oct: open certain days only; tel: 0990-04 04 04).

see map below

Eton across the river

Across the river from Windsor is **Eton College**, that most famous of English public schools, founded in 1440 by 18-year-old Henry VI. The original set of buildings included a collegiate church, an attached grammar school and an almshouse. It was Henry's intention that the church and school become a place of pilgrimage and devotion to the Virgin. The Wars of the Roses cut him short. Henry was murdered in the Tower of London and every year on the anniversary of his death an Etonian lays a wreath of lilies in the cell in which he died.

To the visitor, Eton is a cluster of red-brick Tudor buildings with little towers and hulking chimneys. The **School Yard** (the outer quadrangle), the **Long Chamber** and the **Lower School** all date from the 15th century. The chapel, in Perpendicular style, has 15th-century wall paintings depicting the miracles and legends of the Virgin. Most of the windows were damaged in World War II, but some of the modern installations are interesting. The cloisters dating from the 1440s are stunning; beyond them stretch the fields of which the Duke of Wellington is said to have made his famous remark that Waterloo was won on the playing fields of Eton.

Stoke Poges ❹, north of Eton and on the far side of **Slough** (a town to avoid) was the inspiration for Thomas Gray's most famous poem, *Elegy in a Country Churchyard*. The statue erected in 1799 commemorates him with a maudlin inscription, though the sheer beauty of the churchyard – its old lychgates, its rose bushes and its garden of remembrance – are what brings visitors.

TIP

Windsor Castle's Changing of the Guard at 10.30am has more pizzazz than the one at Buckingham Palace.

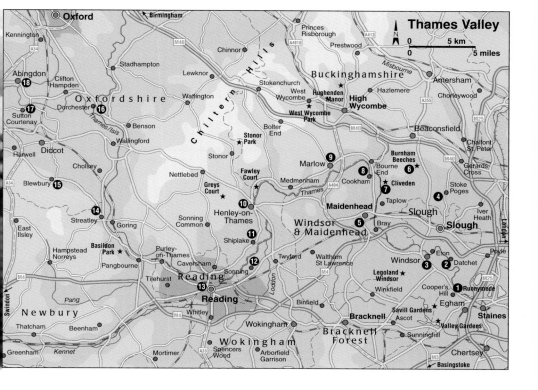

The shell fountain at Cliveden. A scandal erupted in the early 1960s when defence minister John Profumo slept with a girl he met there, Christine Keeler, who was also bedding a Russian diplomat.

BELOW:
Cliveden House.

Half a dozen miles (10 km) upriver from Eton lies **Maidenhead ❺**, the starting point of some of the most beautiful countryside in the valley. Known in medieval times as "Maydenhythe", meaning maidens' landing place, its bridges are its most interesting feature: the 128-ft (38-metre) arches of Brunel's railway bridge are the largest brick spans ever constructed.

From Maidenhead the A423 goes 8 miles (13 km) direct to Henley, but there are several picturesque villages and towns clustered on either side of the river nearby. **Bray**, nestled in a bend in the Thames just south of Maidenhead, has a lovely church that dates from 1293. The **Jesus Hospital**, founded in 1627, is also interesting, and still cares for 26 older citizens from a trust set up by its originator.

Taplow is another pretty village on the north side of the Thames opposite Maidenhead. From Taplow a road leads through Burnham to **Burnham Beeches ❻**, a pastoral stretch of 375 wooded acres (150 hectares).

Upstream from Maidenhead is **Cliveden Reach**, another wooded tract, this one owned by the National Trust. The house called **Cliveden ❼**, once the home of a Prince of Wales, several dukes and the Astor family, is poised dramatically above cliffs. Before World War II Nancy Astor turned it into a meeting place for politicians and celebrities. Today, Cliveden is run as a luxury hotel. The main rooms are viewable part of the year (Mar–Oct: Thur, Sun; 3–6pm). The gardens are open to the public and are decorated with Roman fountains, temples and topiary (open daily, Easter–Dec from 11am; Dec till 4pm: tel: 01628-605 069). Maps, available at the entrance, show suggested walks through the woodland with spectacular views of the Thames.

Cookham ❽ is yet another picturesque riverside village, though it's perhaps better known as the home of the artist Stanley Spencer (1891–1959). Spencer's

**Map,
page 165**

portrait of Cookham Bridge hangs in London's Tate Gallery. Cookham has a gallery dedicated to his work, housed in the King's Hall on Cookham High Street where he attended Sunday School (open Easter–Oct: daily; Nov–Easter: Sat, Sun). A copy of his painting of the *Last Supper* hangs in the church, parts of which date from the 12th century though it is mentioned in the Domesday Book, a survey compiled in 1086. The 15th-century tower is unusual; it is one of the few church towers with both a clock and a sun dial.

Six miles (9 km) upriver is **Marlow ❾**, the town in which Mary Wollstonecraft wrote *Frankenstein*. In 1817 she lived in West Street ("Poets' Row") with her husband, the poet Shelley, while he wrote the poem *The Revolt of Islam*. Marlow goes back to Saxon times, when it was known under the name of "Merelaw" but what you see today is comparatively new, like the suspension bridge and **All Saints Church**, which both date from the 1830s. The rustic walks along the river below Marlow Lock are refreshing, as is **Quarry Wood**, 25,000 acres (10,000 hectares) of beechwoods on the Berkshire bank.

Crew capital of the world

Henley-on-Thames ❿ has been known for its races since 1839, when it was host to the world's first river regatta. The four-day Henley Regatta, usually held in the first week of July (*see page 152*), attracts oarsmen and women from all over the globe. Just as interesting as the crews are the spectators, an audience of near-Edwardian elegance – white linen dresses, straw hats and bottles of bubbly. Less celebrated regattas are held on weekends throughout the summer.

There are several stately homes around Henley, but the most exquisite is **Greys Court**. West of Henley on the road to Peppard, this well-preserved Tudor house

In the Middle Ages, all swans on the Thames belonged to the Crown. Two London guilds, the Worshipful Company of Vintners and the Dyers, were later allowed to own swans as well. Each July, in the ceremony of "swan upping", the beaks of non-royal cygnets are marked to show ownership.

BELOW:
Henley-on-Thames.

OXFORD TO STRATFORD

Maps, pp 174, 179 & 188

The triangle of Britain between Oxford, Warwick and the River Severn contains a history, culture and architectural style which seem to grow out of the ground. At its heart are the Cotswolds

The Cotswolds are part of a range of limestone hills which stretch from the Dorset coast northeast to Lincolnshire. What distinguishes them here is oolite. Oolite, called egg-stone because it looks like the roe of a fish, is the fine-grained freestone that has given a special character to the houses, barns, churches and pigsties from the hills' edge above Chipping Camden to the southern full stop at Bath. More than in any other region of Britain, the buildings here are organic, shaped by local hands.

The stone takes on colours from gold to blue-grey, and responds with different hues to changing weather conditions in a quite remarkable way. In Oxford these stones glisten wet after a noontime shower, and none of their warmth has left those that were used to build the rose-covered cottages of Stratford-upon-Avon, or the castle and the timbered Tudor houses beneath the castle at Warwick.

As if to reinforce the idea of a natural triangle, this area of the west Midlands is now enclosed by motorways on its three sides: the M4 from London to Bristol at its base; the M40 from London to Birmingham via Oxford and Warwick on the eastern side; the M5 from Birmingham to Bristol on the west. A good hopping-off point to the region is Oxford, which is about one hour's drive (60 miles/95 km) from both London and Birmingham. London's Paddington station serves the region.

PRECEDING PAGES: Castle Combe in the Cotswolds. **LEFT:** Oxford High Street. **BELOW:** the Radcliffe Camera.

City of dreaming spires

When Britain's noblest river passes through **Oxford ❶**, it cannot be called the Thames as it is everywhere else. Instead it is called the Isis. Another river flows into it, the Cherwell (pronounced *Charwell*), and rising from the confluence of these muddy banks are the spires of that most mythologised of cities.

However you arrive, you will see them: the spire of Christ Church Cathedral, Tom Tower and Magdalen Tower. This is Oxford, the city that has given its name to many things from marmalade to movements, where undergraduates, cycling around corners, trail their gowns in the wind. But Oxford is also the site of the first Morris Motors works and since World War II it has been an industrial city as much as an academic one. Yet the twain rarely meet and, despite the arrival of a McDonald's in Cornmarket Street, Oxford has weathered the late 20th century amazingly unscathed.

A tour of Oxford is essentially a tour of the colleges, and a good starting point is **Carfax Ⓐ**. (The name derives from the French, *Quatre Voies*, "four ways".) This is the old centre of the city, around the pedestrianised area, where the four main streets meet: Cornmarket, High Street, Queen Street and St Aldate's. The tower at the northwest corner, all that remains of St Martin's Church, dates from the 14th century, and from

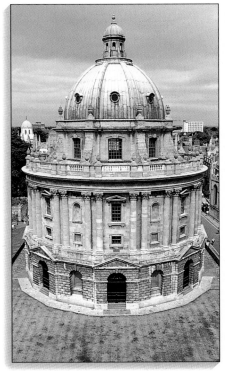

The seven-ton bell hanging in Tom Tower, Great Tom, sounds 101 strokes at 9.05pm for the original 101 college members. And the time? Oxford is 1° 15' west of Greenwich, so that when London's clocks show 9.05 it is deemed to be 9pm in Oxford.

the top of it you take in a good view of the city (open Easter–Oct: daily; Sun from 2pm; Nov–Dec: till 4pm.) From Carfax, walk south along St Aldate's (passing the impressive, neo-Jacobite Town Hall on the left) to **Christ Church** **B**, the grandest of the colleges (open Mon–Sat; Winter: till 4pm; closed noon–2pm.)

Known simply as "The House", Christ Church was founded in 1525 by Cardinal Wolsey (his pointed hat is the House's insignia), on the site of an old priory said to have been established by the Saxon princess, St Frideside. **Tom Tower** was built by Sir Christopher Wren in 1681. **Tom Quad**, the largest quadrangle in Oxford, has splendid grace and magnitude, and it was in the pool here, which is known as Mercury, that Anthony Blanche was dunked in Evelyn Waugh's 1945 novel *Brideshead Revisited*.

Christ Church chapel is also the **Cathedral** of Oxford. The 144-ft (43-metre) spire is one of the earliest in England, dating from the 13th century. As well as the reconstructed tomb of St Frideswide, the cathedral also contains some exquisite stained glass, including works by the Pre-Raphaelite artist, Edward Burne-Jones. Lining the south side of the Tom Quad is the enormous **Hall** of Christ Church, with its magnificent hammerbeam ceiling, while away to the north is the neoclassical Peckwater Quad and the smaller Canterbury Quad, where the **Picture Gallery** has a fine collection of Renaissance paintings and drawings (open daily; closed 1–2pm and Sun am; Oct–Easter: open till 4.30pm). South of the college, extending down to the confluence of the Thames and Cherwell, is the glorious **Meadow** where cows graze. Along the Thames are the University and college boathouses. It's here, at the end of May in Eights Week, that the summer college races take place.

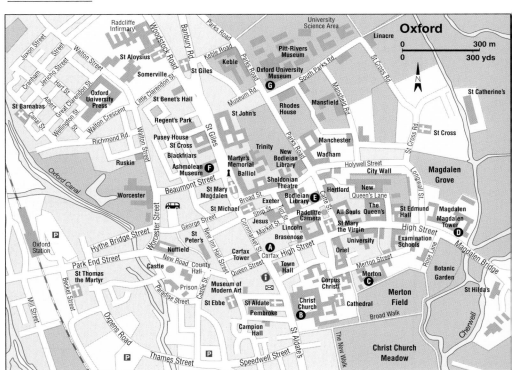

College tour

From the Broadwalk, the wide path running east-west across the Meadow, there's a path cutting north to **Merton College**  (open daily till 4pm; Mon–Fri: from 2pm). Founded in 1264, Merton has some of the oldest buildings in Oxford. Its library in Mob Quad (the oldest complete quadrangle in Oxford) was built in the 1370s (open Mon–Fri, 2–4pm). The library's 16th-century bookshelves make it the first Renaissance Library in England, one where the books were set upright instead of being kept in presses. One of Merton's illustrious graduates was the writer and caricaturist Max Beerbohm (1872–1956), and in Mob Quad is a set of rooms decorated with his memorabilia.

see map opposite

Opposite Merton are **Corpus Christi** (open 1.30–4.30pm except when conferences are held) and **Oriel** (open 2–5pm during term), smaller colleges both, though no less picturesque. The chapel at Corpus has an altarpiece ascribed to Rubens. Merton Street turns left at the top and takes you into the **High Street** where **Magdalen Tower**  (pronounced *maudlin*) rises to the right.

Magdalen was founded in 1458 by William of Waynflete. The chapel is a fine example of Perpendicular architecture and the cloisters are stunning. Behind them is the **Grove**, Magdalen's deer park, and the lovely **Water Walks**, a maze of garden and stream-side paths. On the opposite side of High Street is the **Botanic Garden**, which has an endless variety of roses (open daily; winter to 4.30pm).

Walking west along High Street you pass on the left the **Examination Schools**, built in 1882 in the style of a Jacobean country house with classical and Gothic elements, and on the right **St Edmund Hall** (entrance in Queen's Lane; open daily till dusk). This was incorporated as a college in 1957. Before that, it remained the sole survivor of the once numerous residential halls of the

University dignitaries emerge from the Encaenia, the honorary degree ceremony held at the Sheldonian Theatre each June.

BELOW: Magdalen College.

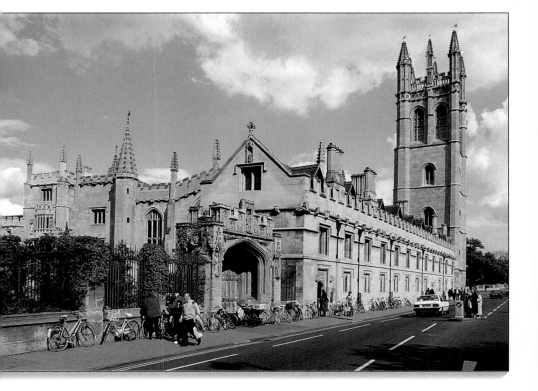

Busts such as the Emperors' Heads (or Bearded Ones) put up in 1669 outside the Sheldonian Theatre were often used in antiquity to create boundaries.

BELOW: the Venetian Bridge of Sighs in Queen's Lane.

medieval university. St Edmund Hall came into existence in the mid-13th century, and its name honours Edmund of Abingdon, who died in 1240 and was the first Oxford graduate to become Archbishop of Canterbury and be canonised.

Further west along High Street are **University College** on the left (with a Shelley memorial) and **All Souls** on the right, the only college with no undergraduates (open Mon–Fri, 2.30–4.30pm; closed Aug). But a winding stroll along Queen's Lane will take you to the rear of **New College**. The chapel and cloisters of both are stunning, as is the garden with the remains of the medieval town wall. The lane curves and suddenly you stand beneath the Venetian bridge (built in 1903) that connects the new and old buildings of **Hertford College**.

A camera and millions of books

From here there is a lovely view of the round **Radcliffe Camera** (1749) on the left and Wren's **Sheldonian Theatre** (1669) straight ahead. Dominating the scene, however, with the magnificent **Old Schools Quadrangle** as its centrepiece, is the **Bodleian Library** . This is one of the world's largest libraries, founded in 1602 by Sir Thomas Bodley. Having agreed to receive a copy of every book registered with Stationers' Hall in 1610, the library now houses more than 6 million volumes, including 50,000 precious manuscripts. The Bodleian has never been a lending library; even Charles I was once refused the loan of a book. Beyond the main entrance of the library is the old **Divinity School**, with its fine vaulted ceiling. Although the library is not open to the public, tours can be booked at the Divinity School which include a brief look into the main hall.

The best known place to actually buy books in the city is **Blackwell's** in Broad Street. Nearby, Magnus Magnusson is the taped commentator for *The Oxford*

Story, an audio-visual show relating the history of the University. Opposite **Balliol College** (open daily during term) a cross in the road marks the point where the Protestant Martyrs, bishops Cranmer, Latimer and Ridley, were burnt at the stake in 1555 and 1556. Around the corner at the top end of St Giles, they are further commemorated by the **Martyrs' Memorial**, which was erected in 1841.

The neoclassical building opposite the Martyrs' Memorial, and the oldest public museum in Britain, is the **Ashmolean Museum** Ⓕ (open Tues–Sat: till 4pm; Sun: 2–4pm; closed Mon except bank hols; free). It houses a superb collection of Italian Renaissance, Dutch still-life and modern French painting. It also has an impressive collection of 16th and 17th-century tapestries, bronzes and silver; Greek, Roman and Egyptian sculpture; a Stradivarius, ceramics and jewellery.

North along St Giles is **St John's College**, founded in 1555. Its lovely gardens, landscaped by "Capability" Brown, rival those of Wadham and Trinity as the prettiest in Oxford (open 1–5pm daily). Behind St John's stretches Parks Road, with the **Oxford University Museum** Ⓖ built in 19th-century neo-Gothic to the taste of the art critic John Ruskin (1819–1900). The museum is a storehouse of zoological, entomological, mineralogical and geological odds and ends (open Mon–Sat, 12–5pm; free).

Around Oxford

There are several villages worth visiting nearby. **Iffley**, south of the city, has a well-preserved Norman church that dates from 1170 and stands gracefully and timelessly above the river. The thatched cottage is the old church school. Some 16 miles (25 km) further southwest is the market town of **Wantage** ❷, birthplace of King Alfred (AD 849–99), and 3 miles (5 km) further west is Uffington

**Maps,
pages
174 & 179**

TIP

Most of the colleges are open daily to visitors (usually in the afternoons). However, they tend to close at exam times, and some close at the end of term when conferences are held. Check noticeboards outside each college for opening times.

BELOW: Oxford University Museum.

where the 360-ft (110-metre) **White Horse** was carved in the Iron Age at the highest point in the Berkshire Downs.

Eynsham ❸, 8 miles (13 km) west of Oxford along the A40, is a picturesque village with the remains of a once famous abbey. Further northwest via Witney is **Minster Lovell ❹** which has a 15th-century cruciform church and the romantic moated ruins of Minster Lovell Hall. The remains of this 15th-century manor house stand above the Windrush with a gloomy beauty. Francis, the 9th Baron Lovell, went into hiding here and starved to death in 1487.

Eight miles (13 km) north of Oxford on the A34 is **Blenheim Palace ❺**, the destination not only of admirers of Sir Winston Churchill, but of those who like the natural-style gardens of Britain's best known landscape gardener, "Capability" Brown. An afternoon stroll at Blenheim, with tea afterwards in the handsome village of Woodstock, is a quintessentially English country excursion (open mid Mar–Oct: daily till 4.45pm; tel: 01993-811 091).

Britain's largest private house, covering 7 acres (2.8 hectares), including the courtyards, the Churchills' family home is the masterpiece of the playwright and architect John Vanbrugh (1664–1726). The exterior of the palace is an orgy of the baroque style, with both Doric and Corinthian columns. Inside is a maze of magnificent state apartments and, on the ground floor, the small bedroom where Winston Churchill was born in 1874. There's also an exhibition of Churchilliana, including manuscripts, paintings, books, photographs and letters. When the house is closed, there is still the 2,500-acre (1,000-hectare) park to enjoy. Originally designed in the ornate French style by Henry Wise, the landscaping was completely redone in 1764 by Brown, who constructed a dam across the River Glyme and created the majestic lake which can be seen today.

ABOVE: the church at Minster Lovell.
BELOW: Blenheim Palace, home of the Churchill family.

Cotswolds villages: caught in time

Shaking off the clay of Oxford's vale, the roads west climb gradually to the heights of the edge facing the Severn and the distant mountains of Wales. Here are the Cotswold hills, broken by steep wooded valleys and rushing streams, Coln and Churn, Windrush, Dikler, Leach and Evenlode. They thrust out like fingers and detach themselves in isolated humps. Height and defensibility made their tops the towns of prehistoric man. Their pastures and rivers provided subsistence in Roman times, and wealth for medieval peoples in the production of wool and cloth. Cirencester, 40 miles (65 km) west of Oxford, was second only to London in size in Roman Britain, and Burford, half way between the two, had its wool-merchants' guild before the Norman Conquest. Thus, the architecture of Cotswold villages was subsidised by the profits of the clothing industry. With its collapse, the Cotswolds went to sleep till pricked awake by the tourist.

The churchyard at **Burford** ❻ has tombs in the shape of wool bales. Wool merchants' houses of the 14th to 16th centuries can often be found hiding behind later fronts. Just south of Burford, at Filkins, is **Cotswold Woollen Weavers**, a fully working 18th-century woollen mill with a permanent exhibition of the industry (open daily; closed Sun till 2pm; free).

Just south of Filkins, **Lechlade** ❼, 22 miles (36 km) west of Oxford on the A420/A417, on the upper Thames, makes a good starting point for a circuitous tour. Below St John's Bridge cabin cruisers pass, and trout wait beside the 13th-century **Trout Inn**. No doubt William Morris, the utopian craftsman, dropped in here from his house just downstream at **Kelmscott Manor** (open Apr–Sept: Wed only, 11–1pm, 2–5pm; open 3rd Sat of month, 2–5pm; tel: 01367-252 486). A typical Cotswold stone-built house, the manor has a roof of split stones, of

see map below

ABOVE: the Trout Inn at Lechlade.

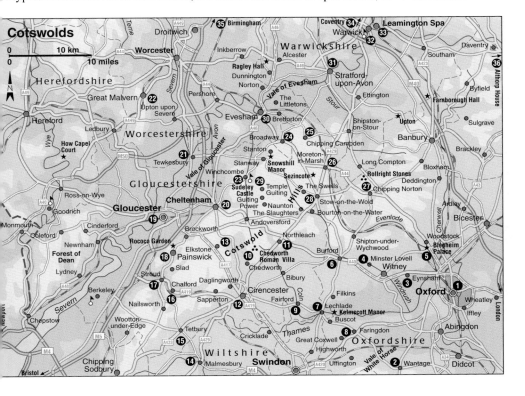

and the Romans "Corinium", though locals call it Ciren. Second only in size and importance to London under the Romans, its fortunes flourished under the wool merchants, and floundered during the 19th century. Today, the medieval character of this "capital of the Cotswolds" is remarkably preserved. One of the best examples of Perpendicular in the country, the porch of the church of St John Baptist (open daily), once doubled for the town hall. Of the 12 bells in the tower, the ninth is called the "Pancake Bell", because it is always rung on Shrove Tuesday. The story of Roman Cirencester is compellingly told at the **Corinium Museum** (open Apr–Oct: daily; Sun 2–5pm; Nov–Mar: closed Mon) and substantial remains of the town walls remain, along with a well-preserved amphitheatre.

Ermin Street is now the A417 leaving the town to the northwest, where two village churches are not to be missed. First is **Daglingworth**, 4 miles (6 km) away, with Saxon sculptures, including a crucifixion of compelling simplicity. Then, high up, 5 miles (8 km) further on, is **Elkstone's** church , with a view to its east window under low Norman arches like a limestone cave.

Malmesbury lies 12 miles (20 km) southwest of Cirencester on the A429. Two distressing things have happened here. A woman was once killed by a tiger, and the abbey became a factory. The woman was Hannah Twynnoy, who died in 1703. As her tombstone records: "For Tyger fierce took life away … And here she lies in bed of clay". The tiger was from a visiting menagerie. At the Dissolution a rich clothier bought the abbey in a package deal which allowed him to convert it into a weaving-shed, and the parishioners to use the nave for services. Enough remains, especially a richly decorated porch and inner door, to give a good idea of the abbey's former glory.

Cirencester Park, home of the Earl Bathurst, shows a green wall to the town – a horseshoe hedge of yew so high it must take a fire-man's ladder to reach for clipping.

BELOW LEFT: Cirencester. **BELOW RIGHT:** Tetbury.

Five miles northwest of Malmesbury, in **Tetbury ⑮**, a fine 17th-century market hall recalls the one-time bustle of trading in wool that was conducted in the pillared open space beneath it.

Map, page 179

Gorgeous valley

Returning north 10 miles (16 km) beyond Tetbury, the A46 arrives at Nailsworth and the start of the gorge-like valleys of Stroudwater, of wheels now still and looms long silent. There are still one or two cloth mills here, and cottages hug the terraces above the steep streets.

At **Chalford ⑯** the descent into the **Golden Valley** begins. Curiosities are both here and further east at **Sapperton.** One is a round house with conical roof and Gothic windows on the banks of the canal opened in 1789 to link the Thames with the Severn. At Sapperton the canal disappears into the hillside under a triumphal arch. From where the River Frome breaks through the western wall of the Cotswolds, **Stroud ⑰**, on its hill, looks across to the mountains of Wales. The country's cloth industry was concentrated here in the Stroudwater valley in the 16th century, and England's armies went to war in uniforms of scarlet and blue cloth from these mills.

Take to the heights to the east of the A46, and you are in a "Little Switzerland" of swift-flowing streams and wooded ravines. **Slad**, on the B4070, is the village on which the novel *Cider With Rosie* by Laurie Lee was based. His cottage and pub are still there, but the school has taught its last children.

On the A46, 3 miles (5 km) north of Stroud, is **Painswick ⑱**, whose traditions include weaving, tomb-carving and "clipping". The mills have closed and the masons have put down their tools, but the clipping (meaning "embracing")

ABOVE: statue in the Rococo Garden at Painswick. **BELOW:** bucolic scene at Selsey, near Stroud.

Originally signs were graphically designed because few people could read. This newer example is in Gloucester.

service is still held every September when children join hands to encircle the church. Just north of Painswick on the B4073 is the **Rococo Garden** (open Feb–mid-Dec: daily), restored to its former glory as depicted in a painting of 1748.

Kings, queens and tailors

The nearby county town of **Gloucester ⑲** is a cathedral city and inland port and has been a strategic centre guarding the route to Wales since Roman times. Alfred held a parliament here in AD 896, Canute signed a treaty and William the Conqueror ordered the Domesday survey from the Chapter House. Henry I died here of eating lampreys (a kind of eel), Henry III was crowned and crook-backed Richard III reputedly ordered the murder of his nephews. Charles II took out his spite on the city for opposing his father, by having its walls demolished. Queen Victoria stayed here in a pub. Of the Roman walls, vestiges remain; of the medieval town, very little. The Victorian warehouses in the old docks have been renovated and include an antiques centre with a street of period shops, the **National Waterways Museum** (open daily) and the **Museum of Advertising and Packaging** (open Mar–Sept: daily; Oct–Feb: closed Mon).

The cathedral remains the city's focal point. The nave is Norman, and the windows in the south transept are in earlier Perpendicular style. Fourteenth-century stained glass fills the largest east window in England and over the choir is a complicated cross-ribbed vault. Pilgrims once came to the richly ornamented tomb of Edward II, who was murdered at nearby Berkeley Castle. There is marvellous fan vaulting in the cloisters and even the Monks' Lavatory has its appeal. In the town there is a **Folk Museum** with a reconstructed Double Gloucester dairy (open Oct–June: Mon–Sat; July–Sept: daily). There are Turners and Gains-

BELOW: narrowboats at the National Waterways Museum.

boroughs in the **City Museum and Art Gallery** (open Oct–June: Mon–Sat; July–Sept: daily). The **Tailor of Gloucester Museum** recalls Beatrix Potter's famous story, which was based on real people and events (open Mon–Sat: free).

Just 8 miles (13 km) northeast is **Cheltenham ㉒**, a spa town which makes a good base for the Cotswolds. Lord Byron came here, as did George III. The discovery of the mineral spring in 1718 started it, but it was the visit of George III and his queen 70 years later that made the spa fashionable as a summer resort. Like Bath, it was fortunate in its architects, J.B. Papworth and J.B. Forbes, who chose Cotswold building stone or stucco, and in the lightness and gaiety of the Greek revival style. **Lansdowne Terrace, Place** and **Crescent** as well as **Suffolk Square** and the **Pittville Estate** are the staged backdrop to the individual performances of the **Rotunda** and the **Pittville Pump Room** where the waters can be tasted (open Wed–Mon till 4.30pm). For a frisson of the surreal, walk the street of statues, the caryatids of **Montpelier Walk**. The **Promenade** is a walk of a different kind, with lots of trees, shrubs, flowers and shops. Orchestras play, and so do fountains: there is a well established music festival in July.

Cotswold limits

The Cotswolds's western limit is 10 miles (16 km) north at **Tewkesbury ㉑** where the Avon joins the Severn. Here stone gives way to attractive timbered cottages, many of them serving as pubs, such as the 17th-century Bell Inn. In 1473 the Battle of Bloody Meadow, the last of the Wars of the Roses, was fought here, spilling over into the abbey itself. Even the monks took a hand. In that building there are many monuments, and from the square tower there are views over the river valleys to the Malvern Hills and the mountains of Wales.

Map, page 179

The composer Gustav Holst, best known for his Planets Suite, was born in Cheltenham and there's a museum to his memory at 4 Clarence Road (open Tues–Sat, 10am–4.20pm).

BELOW: the Pittville Pump Room at the spa town of Cheltenham.

Twelve miles (20 km) north of Tewkesbury is **Great Malvern** , from which there are magnificent views over 10 counties. This is another health resort and the hills are the source of bottled mineral water.

If ghosts walk at all, they must walk at **Sudeley Castle** at Winchcombe ㉓, 6 miles (10 km) northeast of Cheltenham on the A46 (open late Mar–Oct: daily from 11am; tel: 01242-604357). This great, castellated house, just south of Winchcombe, has been carefully restored, and displays a fascinating collection of royal relics and paintings.

Two villages further along this road to Broadway are **Stanway**, with scallop shells over the rather pretentious gateway to the manor, and **Stanton**. Nearly every cottage here is built in the best period of Cotswold architecture, from the mid-16th to the mid-17th century. **Snowshill Manor**, in a valley south of Broadway, belonged to Catherine Parr, last wife of Henry VIII. Tudor beneath the skin, it houses a magpie collection from musical instruments to toys (open late Mar–Oct: Wed–Mon 1–4.15pm; July, Aug: daily; tel: 01386-852410).

Broadway ㉔ is the Cotswolds' show village, and a broad street it is. Houses and cottages face one another across an expanse of green on the road from London to Worcester, all in the same style and mostly in the same honey-coloured stone. The **Abbot's Grange** dates from the 14th century and the **Lygon Arms** (one of the Cotswolds' best restaurants) from the 16th. Charles I and Cromwell stayed there, but of course not at the same time. **Broadway Tower** on the escarpment above is the second highest point in the Cotswolds (open Apr–Oct: daily).

Chipping Campden ㉕, 5 miles (8 km) northeast of Broadway, has a long main street lined with fine stone houses dating from before the 17th century, when this was one of the most prosperous wool towns. Especially interesting are the

almshouses and church, the town hall, and William Grevel's house. Grevel, a wool merchant, died in 1401, and his memorial brass in the church remembers him well.

Turning back eastwards towards Oxford on the A44, the circuitous route reaches **Moreton-in-Marsh** ㉖, which took to linen weaving when the woollen industry failed. A mile or two west is **Sezincote**, a house in the Indian style, which gave the Prince Regent his ideas for Brighton Pavilion (house open May–July, Sept: Thur, Fri; 2.30–5.30pm, no children; garden Thur, Fri all year).

"Chipping" means market and 8 miles (13 km) further on is **Chipping Norton** ㉗. Beside many 18th-century houses is **Bliss Tweed Mill**, looking like a country mansion with a factory chimney on top (now private luxury apartments). The town is handy for an excursion to the **Rollright Stones**. These are a big circle of 70 Bronze-Age standing stones on a hilltop, called the King's Men, a smaller group called the five Whispering Knights and a lone menhir called the King. Like Stonehenge, their origins are unknown. According to legend, the king and his knights were turned to stone by a local witch. The stones are on private land, but can be viewed from the roadside.

Secret valleys

The hill town of **Stow-on-the-Wold** ㉘, 4 miles (6 km) south of Moreton-in-Marsh, was once the scene of great sheep fairs. Daniel Defoe recorded as many as 20,000 sheep being sold on one occasion. Like sheep, 1,000 defeated Royalists were penned in the church after the last battle of the Civil War in 1646. To the west of the town are the Swells, **Upper Swell** and **Lower Swell**, villages on the River Dikler. They owe their odd name to "Our Lady's Well", but they are pure Cotswold. The Guitings, **Temple Guiting** ㉙ and **Guiting Power**, in thick woods on the Windrush a few miles further west, are a little too perfect. Between them, the **Cotswold Farm Park** offers a chance to see rare but local farm animals like Cotswold lions – sheep with fleeces like lions' manes – and pigs such as Tamworth Gingers (open Mar–Sept: daily).

Over the hill, just below the Swells, are **Upper Slaughter** and **Lower Slaughter**, with fords on the tiny Slaughterbrook, dovecots and mills. Nearby is **Bourton-on-the-Water**, one of the best of the Cotswold stone villages. Set on the river Windrush, it has all the ingredients of fairyland: miniature footbridges over streams and under willow trees, sweet smells in the perfumery, a motor museum in a barley mill, a model railway, and a model village. Also nearby, the **Birdland Park** covers 4 acres (1.5 hectares) of ponds, groves and aviaries; this setting is the home to hundreds of species of exotic birds (open daily; winter: till 4pm).

On their northern side, the Cotswolds merge into the **Vale of Evesham**, part of the Avon valley where the climate is ideal for growing fruit and vegetables which have given the town of **Evesham** ㉚ a prosperous air.

Above Evesham the A439 follows the Avon for 14 miles (22 km) to **Stratford-upon-Avon** ㉛. William Shakespeare was born here in Henley Street on 23 April 1564. He was christened in the local Holy Trinity Church and went to the local school; at 18 he married 16-year-old Anne Hathaway and they had three chil-

Map, pages 179 & 188

ABOVE: at Cotswold Farm Park. **BELOW:** Chipping Campden.

dren. In 1597, after his extraordinary career as a playwright in London, he bought New Place in Chapel Street where he lived for the last half dozen years of his life. He died on his 52nd birthday and is buried at Holy Trinity.

In spite of the numbers of tourists, the town, of half-timbered buildings beside the river, still manages to evoke the atmosphere of the times of its most famous son. His birthplace is the starting point for a tour of the town. The entrance is through the modern **Shakespeare Centre Ⓐ** on Henley Street, the headquarters of the Birthplace Trust (open daily; winter: till 4pm). Shakespeare's granddaughter married Thomas Nash and they lived in **Nash's House Ⓑ** on Chapel Street, which is now a museum of the town (open daily; winter till 4pm). Nash's House was next door to New Place, of which only the foundations remain, preserved in a garden. The living legacy of the playwright can be found at the **Royal Shakespeare Theatre Ⓒ** and the smaller **Swan Theatre**, where the Royal Shakespeare Company stages its often controversial performances. There is a collection of RSC theatre items, and backstage tours can be arranged.

Between Shakespeare's birthplace and Nash's House is **Harvard House Ⓓ** (open daily; winter till 4pm). Built in 1596, this was the home of Katherine Rogers whose son, John Harvard, founded the US university.

In **Shottery**, a mile or so to the west of the town, is **Anne Hathaway's Cottage Ⓔ** (open daily; winter: till 4pm). She lived in this thatched and much-restored cottage during the 16 years Shakespeare was in London. Their life together resumed when he returned to settle down in New Place.

Stratford fills up in summer, but there are other towns nearby which are well worth seeing. Eight miles (13 km) north of Stratford, just off the A46, is **Warwick ㉜**. Despite a serious fire in 1694, many buildings from the Tudor period

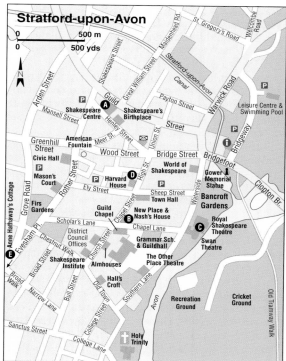

Stratford-upon-Avon

0 — 500 m
0 — 500 yds
N

remain standing. First fortified in 914 by Ethelfleda, the daughter of Alfred the Great, **Warwick Castle** has had a rich history (open daily; tel: 01926-495 421). Although only a mound of earth remains of the original Saxon structure, the 14th-century towers standing today are the proud features of England's finest medieval castle. For centuries England's most powerful families lived at Warwick. A collection of paintings, including portraits by Rubens, Van Dyck and Holbein, is complemented by sets of arms and armour. The graffiti in the dungeon and torture chamber is attributed to Royalist soldiers from the Civil War. Bordering the River Avon, the castle's 60-acre (25-hectare) gardens landscaped by "Capability" Brown are impeccably maintained.

Lord Leycester's Hospital by the West Gate was originally founded as a guildhall in 1383. In 1571, Robert Dudley, Earl of Leicester, had the buildings renovated as almshouses. Today the hospital is a museum and the home of ex-servicemen.

Adjacent to Warwick, **Leamington Spa** ㉝ is a spacious Regency and Victorian spa town that has prided itself on its amenities since spa developments began in the late 18th century. The A46 continues another 8 miles (13 km) to **Coventry** ㉞. This is a car manufacturing town that was terribly bombed during World War II, when all but the steeple of its cathedral was demolished. The **New Cathedral**, by Sir Basil Spence, was completed in 1962 and is highly imaginative with immense stained-glass windows and a richly coloured interior.

To the west of Coventry, **Birmingham** ㉟ had become an manufacturing centre long before the Industrial Revolution of the late 18th century. The canals and railways of that era confirmed its importance, while in more recent times it has become the focus of the national motorway network. A city founded on the metal and engineering trades, Birmingham is in the process of reinventing itself as a great centre for services, shopping and cultural activities, claiming for itself not merely a national, but also a European role as it looks to the future.

At the centre is **Victoria Square**, an enormous pedestrian esplanade dotted with contemporary sculptures and flanked by the classical **Town Hall** and the Renaissance-style **Council House** with its mosaic and pediment relief entitled *Britannia Rewarding the Manufacturers of Birmingham*. The nearby **Museum and Art Gallery** (open Mon–Sat, Sun pm) is famous above all for its matchless collection of Pre-Raphaelite paintings.

The restored canalside developments to the west of the centre include the National Indoor Arena and the **National Sea Life Centre** (open daily), while to the northwest, the fascinating Jewellery Quarter has a **Discovery Centre** (open Mon–Sat) which demonstrates the skills of the jewellers and their contribution to Birmingham's reputation as "workshop of the world".

To the east of the region now, where **Althorp Park** ㊱, off the A428 northwest of Northampton, is the family estate of the Earl of Spencer (who pronounces it *Althrup*), and the burial place of his sister, Diana, Princess of Wales. Althorp House, a 121-room mansion built in 1508, its gardens and a museum dedicated to Diana can be visited in July and August only. The small island on which Diana is buried can be viewed from the other side of the oval lake designed in the 1660s by André le Nôtre, the architect responsible for the gardens at the Palace of Versailles. ❑

**Maps,
pages
179 & 188**

The post-Diana Althorp Park was opened to the public in July and August 1998, with tickets costing £9.50 and sold in advance. Tel: 01604-592020. Website: www. althorp-house.co.uk

BELOW: Althorp House and the island on which Diana, Princess of Wales, is buried.

CAMBRIDGE AND EAST ANGLIA

Once cut off from the rest of England by forest and uncrossable marshland, the countryside and historic towns of East Anglia have managed to retain their other-worldliness

Maps, pages 194 &196

Edinburgh

London

E ast Anglia, the four counties of Norfolk, Suffolk, Cambridgeshire and Essex, bulging into the North Sea between the Thames estuary and the Wash, has the least annual rainfall in all of Britain. You would not know this, however, since it is also a region of fens and great rivers, of lakes, called meres or broads, and bird-filled coastal marshes. The beauty of East Anglia is not a typical one. Few places rise higher than 300 ft (90 metres) above sea level. Charles Dickens' young hero, David Copperfield, noticed this upon his first visit to Yarmouth: "It looked rather spongy and soppy… and I could not help wondering, if the world were really as round as my geography book said, how any of it could be so flat."

No one passes through East Anglia; nowhere lies on the other side. Road and rail connections with the rest of the country are poor. To East Anglians, emigration means moving 5 miles (8 km) down the road. To the south the A12 leads northeast from London to Colchester, famed for its oysters, and on to Ipswich before heading north to the seaside towns of Lowestoft and Great Yarmouth. From east London the M11 runs up to Cambridge 53 miles (85 km) directly north, from where the A11 goes northeast to Norwich and the A10 continues to King's Lynn and the fenlands around the Wash. The main rail routes run from London's Liverpool Street station.

In the 11th century, when the area was surveyed by the compilers of the Domesday Book, the four counties of East Anglia were some of the richest and most highly populated in the country. Today, with a population density less than half the national average, East Anglia resolutely refuses to follow the nation's trends.

Land of church builders

In the Middle Ages, a huge forest in the south (a fraction of which remains today as Epping Forest) and a strip of uncrossable marshlands in the north (the Fens) separated East Anglia from the rest of the country. The region became a sanctuary from the power struggles that wracked the rest of the emerging kingdom, and it was to East Anglia that many religious orders fled for peace. They left a legacy of churches, cathedrals and abbeys; in Norfolk alone there are 600 churches.

East Anglia was also a region of gentry, whose houses still mark the landscape much as the churches. **Audley End ❶** in the medieval town of Saffron Walden, 15 miles (24 km) south of Cambridge, was built for a Lord Treasurer and said by James I to be "too large for a king". As it stands today the house is large, but it is only a fraction of the original; much of it was demolished in

PRECEDING PAGES: Swan Hotel, Lavenham. **LEFT:** the Bridge of Sighs, Cambridge. **BELOW:** King's College, Cambridge.

ABOVE: Cambridge
traditions – pubs
and graduation.

1721. The interior decoration, by Robert Adam, and the immaculate gardens, landscaped by "Capability" Brown, are classics of English country design (open Apr–Sept: Wed–Sun am only; tel: 01799-522 399).

Despite the backwater quality about East Anglia, it is still a region of wealth. Farmers here drive luxury cars, and the modern gentry, casually dressed but rich nonetheless, host grouse shoots for their southern cousins who cannot spare the time to go to Scotland. University brainpower has been harnessed in the hi-tech industries of Cambridge's science parks. But what the visitor feels most in East Anglia is the sense of isolation. It has changed little since the 11th century.

Undisturbed by both the sooty touch of the Industrial Revolution and the bombs of World War II, many villages and towns remain unspoiled, apart from noise pollution around the airforce bases at Mildenhall and Lakenheath. The only element that destroys East Anglia is the sea, which is devouring the eastern shores. East Anglia harbours myriad landscapes that range from the flat wilds of north Norfolk to the rolling green tranquillity of south Suffolk, an inch of land for every mile of sky. Gainsborough and Constable both declared that the beauty of Suffolk landscape – its winding lanes, sloping fields and still waters – was what spurred them to paint.

University town

An Elizabethan historian once described the fen dwellers as "brutish, uncivilised and ignorant". Today's Oxford undergraduates invoke this claim when they scornfully refer to the university at **Cambridge** ❷ as the "Fenland Polytechnic", but some of the world's finest thinkers, artists and architects matured in this fenland town.

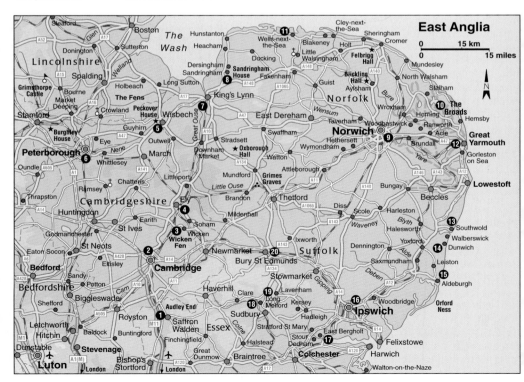

Cambridge, which takes its name from the River Cam, was founded in the 12th century by a settlement of Franciscans, Dominicans and Carmelites. In 1209, a handful of scholars hurriedly fled Oxford after a disagreement with the town authorities and settled in Cambridge. It was this – and the founding in 1281 of the first college, Peterhouse, by Hugh de Balsam, Bishop of Ely – that established the university.

Other colleges were soon founded under the patronage of local gentry and a succession of monarchs. In 1441 Henry VI founded **King's College A** central to the University on King's Parade. Five years later, **King's College Chapel** – considered the glory of Cambridge – began construction, which took nearly 70 years. Chapel services are open to visitors, and it is worth standing in the ancient pews alongside Rubens' *Adoration of the Magi*, listening to the voices of the superb choir float up along the curves of the magnificent fan-vaulting and gazing at the series of 25 16th-century stained-glass windows, which portray the story of the New Testament.

From the top of **Great St Mary's Church B** opposite King's Chapel visitors can see the whole of Cambridge, including the distant gaunt tower of the **University Library**. Like the Bodleian at Oxford, the University Library at Cambridge by law receives a copy of every book published in the United Kingdom. Opposite St Mary's is the dignified **Senate House** – the university parliament, built by James Gibbs between 1722 and 1730.

The beauty of Cambridge is its compactness; a few steps in any direction will take you past a piece of history, whether it be the Anglo-Saxon tower of the tiny church of St Benét's (eclipsed by the college buildings, but 250 years older) or the Cavendish Laboratory, the site of the first splitting of the atom.

Map, page 196

TIP

Visitors are generally free to walk through the college grounds. Colleges on King's Parade have a small entrance charge; others, on the town's outskirts, are free.

BELOW: Fountain in the Great Court at Trinity College.

The choristers of St John's, like those of King's, have achieved international renown through recitals, recordings and concert tours. Visitors can hear them sing at evensong, held in the chapel (above) during term time.

In the gardens of **Christ's College** ● a tree supposedly planted by the poet John Milton (1608–74) still stands. It was while at Christ's that Milton composed the *Hymn of Christ's Nativity* as a college exercise. The Great Court at **Trinity** is the largest university quadrangle in the world, but look closely at the figure of its founder, Henry VIII, above the gateway: instead of a sceptre he holds a chair leg. Trinity's library, seen from the riverfront, was built by Sir Christopher Wren. Further north is **St John's** ●, founded in 1511 by Lady Margaret Beaufort. Its three-storey gatehouse, decorated with carvings of heraldic beasts, is magnificent. Behind it, along the river, is the **Bridge of Sighs** (1831), modelled on its more famous namesake in Venice. Across Bridge Street from St John's is the **Holy Sepulchre Round Church** ●, one of only four round churches in England. This one was founded in 1130 by the Knights Templar and was connected with the Crusades. The shape is based on that of the Holy Sepulchre in Jerusalem.

Queens' College ●, hidden behind St Catharine's, has an unusual and seemingly rickety half-timbered President's Lodge. A little beyond the town centre along Trumpington Street stands **Peterhouse** ●, the oldest and most traditional of the colleges. Next door is the **Fitzwilliam Museum**, a spectacular collection including works by Turner, Titian and Rembrandt, and a fine selection of manuscripts, including William Blake's original poems (open Tues–Sat; Sun from 2.15pm; free). Beyond the Fitzwilliam the **Botanic Gardens** make a haven for tired tourists and students alike. In Castle Street is a delightful **Folk Museum** ● (Apr–Sept: open daily; Sun from 2pm; Oct–Mar: closed Mon), and around the corner, the **Kettle's Yard Art Gallery** (open Tues–Sun, pm only; free) has an eclectic collection of modern works.

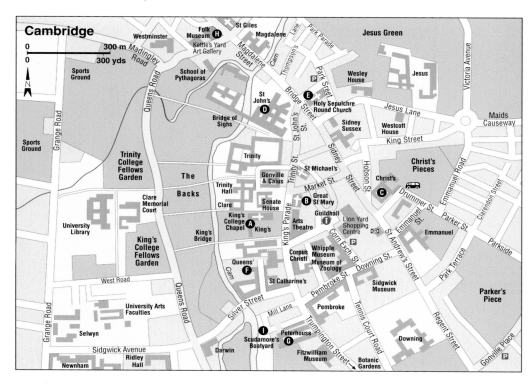

The best way to see many colleges is to hire a punt from **Scudamore's Boat-yard ❶** at the end of Mill Lane. Drift down the "Backs" (only undergraduates try to speed) from Charles Darwin's House to the Bridge of Sighs, gliding between the willows at the backs of the colleges.

The wetlands

Flat, spongy and soppy the Yarmouth area may have seemed to young Copper-field, but the **fenland** is flatter, spongier and soppier still. The village names – Landbeach, Waterbeach, Gedney Marsh and Dry Drayton – all tell the same story. Never marry a fenland woman, runs the saying, because on the wedding night you may discover she has webbed feet. For centuries no one tried to cross the marshes, let alone build on them, yet today the black fenland soil is some of the most productive land in the country.

The Romans were the first to try to drain the 2,000-sq.-mile (5,200-sq.-km) marsh that stretched from Cambridge to Lincoln, but success came only in the 16th century, when the Dutch engineer Vermuyden cut rivers through the marshes. Even he was not prepared for the dramatic land-shrinking that resulted. Today's fields are often 10 ft (3 metres) below the rivers that were cut to drain them. Only one fen remains undrained; at **Wicken Fen ❸** (signposted off the A10, 17 miles/27 km north of Cambridge) the windmill works to keep 600 acres (240 hectares) of marshland wet, preserved by the National Trust.

Where the A10 approaches **Ely ❹**, 16 miles (25 km) north of Cambridge, the everlastingly flat skyline is broken. **Ely Cathedral** (completed in 1351) domi-nates the fens from its perch on the top of what used to be called the Isle of Eels – after the staple diet of the villagers. The Isle, a knoll of dry land, was selected

Maps, pages 194 &196

ABOVE: the wetlands.
BELOW: the unique lantern in Ely Cathedral.

as a cathedral site by St Etheldreda in AD 673. Some 400 years later it made an ideal refuge for Hereward the Wake from the pursuit of William the Conqueror. Hereward seemed unreachable on Ely (then an island), but eventually the monks tired of the siege and showed the conqueror's men the secret pathway through the marshes, giving Hereward away.

The splendour of Ely Cathedral lies in its unusual situation and in its unique lantern. In the evening, the lantern – an octagon of wood and glass built high on the back of the nave in an extraordinary feat of engineering – reflects the rays of the dying sun. By night its glass gleams with the light within.

The A1101 on the left, 5 miles (8 km) north of Ely, crosses the unimaginatively named Hundred Foot Drain and passes between the rows of marching crops to **Wisbech ❺**, a market town that styles itself as the capital of the fens. The two imposing Georgian streets (Southbrink and Northbrink) illustrate the prosperity fen drainage brought, and Market Square is full of the produce it provided in abundance. In the eccentric **Fenland Museum** on Museum Square are pictures of Wisbech in its heyday and the complete furnishings of a Victorian post office (open Tues–Sat; winter: till 4pm; free). West of Wisbech on the A47, **Peterborough ❻** is worth a visit for its Norman cathedral, built in 1116–99.

While Wisbech has been preserved by a lack of economic development, **King's Lynn ❼**, 12 miles (20 km) northeast along the coast, has marched on. Much of the town has been rebuilt since the late 1950s. Many of the historic buildings worth seeing lie in the streets bordering the River Ouse with **King Street** marking the heart of the old town.

Eight miles (13 km) northeast of King's Lynn, **Sandringham House ❽** was embellished by a king and is still used as a royal country retreat. Edward VII,

ABOVE: Father Time at Sandringham House.
BELOW: the gardens at Sandringham.

when Prince of Wales, built Sandringham in 1861, but it is decorated in styles ranging from Jacobean to Regency. The house is closed when a member of the royal family is in residence, but the 7,000-acre (2,800-hectare) parklands are kept open (house/grounds open Mar–Sept: daily from 11am; closed: first week August; tel: (01553) 772 675).

Map, page 194

City of spires

A city that retains its sense of history alongside economic success is a rare place, yet **Norwich** , the county town of Norfolk, manages to do both. It has a church for every week of the year and a pub for every day, they say, and every vista of this surprisingly hilly town confirms it. Within the city walls 32 medieval churches still stand, though some now have secular purposes. **St James'** is a puppet theatre; the imaginative **Elizabethan Theatre** at the Maddermarket is a combination of chapel and warehouse; and **St Peter Hungate** at the top of Elm Hill is a museum of ecclesiastical treasures.

Besides the **Cathedral** and its fine **Cloisters**, the **Cathedral Houses** in the Close and **Pull's Ferry** (last used as a river-crossing in 1939) are worth seeing. With no source of fuel readily available to drive machines, Norwich, once the third richest town in England, was left behind by the Industrial Revolution. The city became self-sufficient and today continues to prosper, with a relatively low percentage of unemployment compared with other areas of the country. Retailing became the profession of the prosperous, and it was a succession of wealthy grocers who, century by century, added to **Strangers' Hall**. The result today is a charming museum (closed at present) with 23 rooms designed in a bewildering variety of styles. The earliest parts of the house date from 1320.

There are 119 Saxon flint round towers in Norfolk. The Normans, however, considered the local stone undramatic, so, to build Norwich Cathedral, they shipped white stone from Normandy across the Channel and up the River Wensum.

BELOW:
Norwich Cathedral.

CATHEDRALS OF EAST ANGLIA

Three enormous Norman cathedrals, all started around 1100, grace the region. Founded in 1081, Ely is best known for its massive, octagonal lantern, built by Alan de Walsingham to cover the crossing of the nave and transepts when the Norman tower fell down in 1322. But the whole interior, with its 250-ft (76-metre) long nave is magnificent, reflecting various architectural styles, from Norman, through the Early English, Decorated and Perpendicular Gothic styles to the early Renaissance.

Peterborough Cathedral was begun in 1118 and is in part a good example of the late Norman style, though it was added to in virtually every succeeding architectural period. The cathedral was severely damaged by Oliver Cromwell's troops in the 17th century. Visitors today, however, can still marvel at its painted wooden ceiling, which dates from 1220 though it has been repainted twice.

Norwich Cathedral was founded in 1096. The original wooden roof of the nave was replaced in the 15th and 16th centuries by stone vaulting and embellished by carved and painted bosses illustrating scenes from the Bible. Easier to view – and even more delightful – are the 400 vault bosses in the adjoining cloisters. Norwich's spire, at 315 ft (96 metres), is second only to that of Salisbury.

ing the summer, and it is also home to common and grey seals which bask on the sands at low tide. **Wells-next-the-Sea**  is a genuine working port, with coasters along the quay and fishing boats bringing in whelks, crabs and shrimps.

In the 1880s the Great Eastern Railway Company published *Holiday Haunts in East Anglia*. The new railway network opened up a dozen resorts on the sunny coastline. But today, with many routes no longer in service and with travel abroad easier than ever, few holidaymakers come to the East Anglian coast. Some of the smaller beachside resorts have been all but forgotten, thus preserving their Victorian atmosphere. Two such spots are **Sheringham** and **Cromer**, in north Norfolk, a coastline lashed by winter storms. In 1855–56 there were 500 wrecks off this shore. Even today almost every village has its own lifeboat. The one at Cromer is famous. Henry Blogg, a crew member for 53 years, helped save 873 lives. Meanwhile, at Sheringham, fishermen haul their boats up to the top of the cliff with tractors.

Midway around the coast, **Great Yarmouth**  has kept its popularity with the tourists. Once the scene of great activity with the arrival of herring, today it is a tacky place; the golden sands of the beach are hidden behind the spires of the helter-skelters and the walls of the roller-coaster.

So changed is Yarmouth that the 1969 film of *David Copperfield* had to be shot in the resort of **Southwold** , 20 miles (32 km) south. This town has a dignity and refinement that Yarmouth lacks. Its manicured appearance is due partly to a fire in 1659 which destroyed much of the fishing village and allowed careful planning in reconstruction. In the magnificent Perpendicular church, Southwold Jack, a figure in armour, rings in the services by striking a bell with his sword. Despite the dominance of tourism, Southwold has one of the few estuary ports

ABOVE: crabs, a local delicacy.
BELOW: bowling at Great Yarmouth.

still used by fishermen. It also has what must be the cheapest passenger ferry in the country which sails across to **Walberswick**, an attractive village frequented by painters. The ancient capital of **Dunwich** ⑭ at one time had eight churches; now the sea has swept the town away.

Artists' inspiration

Across the Blythe estuary from Walberswick to **Aldeburgh** ⑮ is a rewarding, though long, walk. Benjamin Britten (1913–76) made the fishing village his home and in 1948, together with the tenor Peter Pears, started the prestigious annual music festival that runs for two weeks every June. Since then, Aldeburgh has become fashionable indeed. The village was also the birthplace of George Crabbe (1754–1832), whose poetry inspired Britten.

Some 25 miles (40 km) southwest of Aldeburgh is the Suffolk county town of **Ipswich** ⑯, once described as a load of old bricks that fell off a lorry between Norwich and London. It has little to recommend it apart from an atmospheric Victorian dockland, complete with lightship and sailing barges, on the River Orwell. George Orwell, the author of *1984,* took his pen name from the Orwell, but the Stour, which meets the Orwell at its mouth around the North Sea passenger and cargo ports of **Harwich** and **Felixstowe**, is the more famous of the two rivers, thanks to the work of a much-loved British artist.

Constable country, as the Suffolk countryside alongside the Stour is called, is exactly that. John Constable (1776–1837) painted the river, the trees and the villages with a love that has made this landscape familiar even to those who have never been there. The artist was born in the grand village of **East Bergholt** ⑰ (just off the A12 between Ipswich and Colchester), where the bells of the

Map, page 194

The "house in the clouds" at Thorpness shows how to turn a water tank into an object of interest.

BELOW: the Old Moot Hall at Aldeburgh.

MARKET CROSS

church tower, never finished, are housed in a shed in the graveyard. His father was the mill owner at **Flatford**, just down the hill. The setting had great sentiment for Constable, and when he recreated it in the painting *The Hay Wain*, he postponed his marriage for a month simply to finish the work. The water mills of nearby **Stratford St Mary** were another favourite subject. In fact, all along the River Stour is Constable's element. He wrote: "The sound of water escaping from mill dams, willows, old rotten planks, slung posts and brickwork … these scenes made me a painter."

The village of **Dedham**, only a few miles up the banks of the Stour from Flatford and best approached that way, has changed little. The row of neoclassical houses that faces the church is pristine. And yet Dedham is not entirely unmodern; inside the timeless church one of the pews is decorated with medallions from the first moon landing.

ABOVE: teashop in Lavenham and,
BELOW, the village's Little Hall.

Woollen finery

Unspoilt as Dedham may seem, the villages inland are even more so. In **Kersey, Hadleigh** and **Lavenham**, many of the timbered houses that lean over the streets date from the early 16th century. This is wool country, and these villages were well known and wealthy for 700 years after the Norman Conquest (Kersey cloth is mentioned by Shakespeare). The rich mill owners lived in grand halls and worshipped in magnificent churches, all built with their profits.

Fine examples of both of these are at **Long Melford** ⑱ (north of Sudbury). The village's Tudor houses present a pleasing visage of turrets and moats; the two best examples are Melford Hall and Kentwell Hall. In the village of **Lavenham** ⑲ almost all the houses are at least 400 years old. The townspeople have

removed the telegraph poles and buried the wires underground to preserve the village's Tudor appearance.

Timber-framed houses give the villages their beauty, but flint and brick dominates at **Bury St Edmunds** ⑳, the cathedral city of the area, midway between Ipswich and Cambridge on the A14. But the city is no backwater, and the narrow streets around the **Buttermarket** are jammed with people, as is the **Nutshell** on The Traverse, said to be the smallest pub in England.

On Cornhill, the **Moyse's Hall Museum** built in the 12th century, is considered the oldest Norman house in East Anglia (open daily; Sun 2–5pm). It is also said to have been the house of a Jewish merchant, or even a synagogue, but with no evidence to support the claims. Inside are Bronze Age and Saxon artefacts found in the area, plus relics of the grisly Red Barn murder. At the centre of the town in Market Cross is a beautiful building by Robert Adam housing the **Bury St Edmunds Gallery** which stages temporary exhibitions (open Tues–Sat except during exhibit preparations).

The gem of Bury is the ancient **Abbey** and **Cathedral**. The beautiful grounds, laid out as formal gardens, are twice the size of the city centre, and the surrounding walls exclude the noise of the town. Below the Cathedral, built in the 12th century, lie the remains of the Abbey swathed in grass. Originally founded in the 7th century, it was an important place of pilgrimage after the body of Edmund, last king of the East Angles who was killed by the Danes, was placed there in about 900. In 1214 a group of barons swore before the altar to raise arms against King John if he refused to set his seal to the Magna Carta. He did, unwillingly, a year later, and today Bury still celebrates this – and Edmund's burial – in its motto: Shrine of a King, Cradle of the Law. ❑

Map, page 194

ABOVE: memorial window in Long Melford's Perpendicular Church.
BELOW: the abbey ruins at Bury St Edmunds.

THE SOUTHEAST

Kent and Sussex offer the hedonist a deckchair on a sunny beach, the delights of rolling countryside, the thrill of walking in high places, and the discovery of churches and rambling country houses

Map, page 210

The counties of **Kent** and **Sussex** in the southeast corner of England lie south of the Thames estuary, between London and the Channel. Any part of them can be seen on a day trip from the capital, particularly their historic centres such as Canterbury, Rye, Brighton and Chichester which are best explored on foot. From London's orbital M25 motorway the M23 leads south to Brighton, principal resort of Sussex, while the M2 and M20 head for the Channel ports of Folkestone and Dover in Kent. Victoria and Charing Cross stations provide the rail links.

The Kent coast is 21 miles (34 km) from France, and in 1875 the two countries were proved to be within swimming distance by Captain Matthew Webb (it took him 21 hours and 45 minutes). As the nearest point of the country to the Continent, this is the way invaders came: Romans, Angles, Saxons and Britain's last conquerors, the Normans, who scorched the date of 1066 into the history books with their triumph at the Battle of Hastings. Towers, castles and moated mansions were built to withstand later invasion attempts by France, Spain and, in the 20th century, Germany, while cathedrals rose at Chichester and Canterbury, the Church of England's spiritual home and the focus of centuries of pilgrims.

The counties have a common geology in which all the strata run east to west. Kent's North Downs mirror the Sussex South Downs and the filling in this cake is greensand, Weald clay and sandstone, repeated in reverse order. All contribute to a rich variety of landscape in a relatively small space. The chalky South Downs, with a walking trail along their summit, were hailed somewhat exaggeratedly by the eminent 18th-century naturalist Gilbert White as "a chain of majestic mountains". They reach the sea at the spectacular white cliffs at Beachy Head, near Eastbourne; the North Downs end at Dover.

In between the North and South Downs is the Weald, an excellent area for fruit growing, particularly apples, and grapes for white English wines (the chalk Downs are the same geological strata that runs through the Champagne region of France). Hops grown for beer were once picked by London's East Enders in a holiday mood but barely 50 hop farms remain.

PRECEDING PAGES: thatching is an intricate craft. **LEFT:** chalk cliffs at Beachy Head. **BELOW:** a thatcher at work in Sussex.

King Canute's shore

To the west lies the county town of **Chichester ❶** where the cathedral spire rises like a beckoning finger above this typical English rural town of notable Georgian houses. The **South Downs** provide a backdrop and the creeks and marshes of its harbour nearly lap its walls. The 227-ft (70-metre) 14th-century spire, the only one in the country visible from the sea, was rebuilt in 1861 after a storm had brought it down. Inside, the modern altar tapestry by John Piper (born 1903) is a

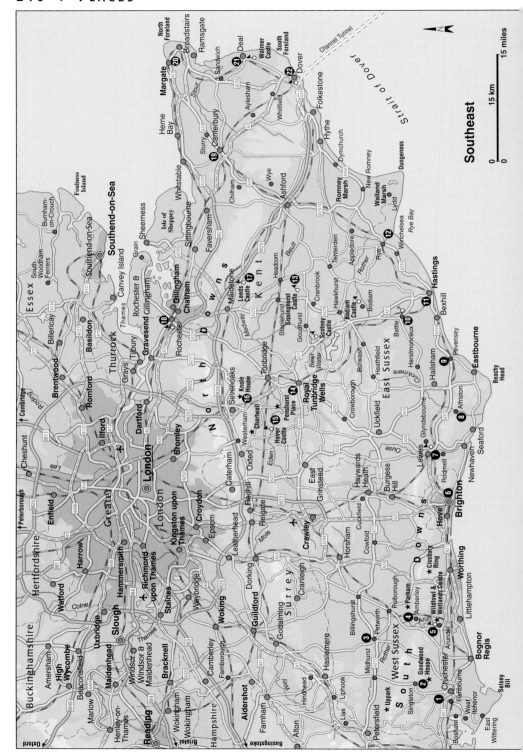

Southeast

dramatic surprise. Among many fine carvings and relief work the most remarkable is the 12th-century *Raising of Lazarus* which can be found in the south side of the choir.

The 15th-century **Market Cross** is one of the finest in the country. Good local pubs with accommodation include the 15th-century Dolphin and Anchor in West Street and The Ship in North Street. To the north of the town is the **Festival Theatre**, a theatre in the round, where Laurence Olivier was the first director.

Little of Chichester's Roman walls remain, but at **Fishbourne**, a mile to the west, Britain's largest Roman palace was uncovered in 1960. It is worth seeing for its well preserved mosaics as well as to appreciate its formidable scale and size (open daily; mid Dec–mid Feb: Sun only). The estuary it stood beside has receded and Chichester's harbour now has myriad muddy inlets (harbour tours from **West Itchenor**), the most attractive being at **Bosham**.

In the South Downs up behind Chichester is **Goodwood**, site of a racecourse and country house (for opening times, tel: 01243-774 107). At the summit is the hill fort of the Trundle, giving wonderful views before dropping down to **Singleton ❷** and the **Weald and Downland Museum** (open Mar–Oct: daily; Nov–Feb: Wed, Sat, Sun). For this ambitious open-air project, buildings from throughout the ages have been collected from the region.

Continuing north for 6 miles (9 km) the A286 arrives at the elderly market town of **Midhurst**, where a right turn on to the A272 leads another 6 miles to **Petworth ❸**. Here narrow streets are twisted and turned by the walls of the great 17th-century **Petworth House**, seat of the Percys, Earls of Northumberland (open Apr–Oct: Mon–Wed, Sat, Sun: 1–5.30pm; tel: 01798-342 207). It has a deer park landscaped by "Capability" Brown and an exceptional art collec-

see map opposite

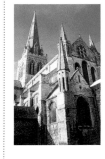

ABOVE: Chichester Cathedral. **BELOW:** Goodwood House.

Virginia Woolf has strong associations here. Her sister, Vanessa Bell, lived with Duncan Grant a few miles from Rodmell at Charleston, a mellow farmhouse they enhanced with murals and a

BELOW: Eastbourne.

to the river. At **Bull House**, Thomas Paine, author of *The Rights of Man*, lived from 1768 to 1774. In the same High Street, 10 men and women were burned at the stake during times of religious intolerance.

From Lewes the A27 to Eastbourne passes near **Glyndebourne**, the celebrated opera house, where it is fashionable to go during the summer season. The area on the opposite, southern side of the highway could be described as rural Bloomsbury. At **Rodmell** Leonard and Virginia Woolf lived in Monk's House from 1919 (open Apr–Oct, Wed & Sat, 2–5pm; tel: 01892-890 651).

From Berwick the River Cuckmere runs south to **Alfriston ❽**. Next to the church is the thatched Old Clergy House and in the village are former smuggling inns. Chalk cliffs, called "the Seven Sisters", lead to **Beachy Head**, at 530 ft (160 metres) the highest cliff on the coast, and the smart resort town of **Eastbourne**, with its pier, fortress and numerous other attractions including Devonshire Park, where the famous Lawn Tennis Championships are held just prior to Wimbledon each year.

William the Conqueror's country

In the levels to the east, **Pevensey ❾** has the most considerable Roman monument in Sussex, but the Roman fort was incomplete and could not withstand the landing in 1066 of William, Duke of Normandy, the last man successfully to invade Britain. The Norman Conqueror did not meet up with Harold of England until some 10 miles (16 km) inland; the spot where Harold fell, his eye pierced through by an arrow, was marked by William who built upon it the high altar of the abbey church at **Battle ❿** as a thanksgiving. An imposing 14th-century gatehouse leads to the grounds and ruins of the abbey.

The place where William prepared for battle is 6 miles (9 km) southeast of Battle. **Hastings'** ⓫ hilltop Norman castle, above a warren of caves where smugglers' adventures are re-enacted, is now a ruin, though a siege tent inside re-tells the battle story on which the town has thrived. On the Stade tall, weatherboarded sheds used by the fishermen for storing nets are architectural fantasies.

To the east is **Winchelsea**, which, like neighbouring **Rye** ⓬, has suffered from floods and the French and now lies high and dry. Edward III (1327–77) gave Rye its walls and gates. The **Landgate** and **Ypres Tower** survive, as well as much half-timbering. Today Rye is a pottery town and there is an active artists' colony whose work can be seen at the Stormont Studio in East Street (open Wed–Sat; free), and the Easton Rooms in the High Street (open daily; free).

From Rye the land lies flat across the great expanse of **Romney Marsh**, a strange, haunted area of a special breed of sheep, of water weeds and wading birds such as the Kentish plover.

Weavers and the Weald

But before continuing in this direction, a detour back up from Rye on the B2082 to the white weatherboard town of **Tenterden**, home of a small historic railway, leads towards the **High Weald**. The region to the west of here was made rich by Flemish weavers, notably around **Cranbrook**. Daniel Defoe wrote *Robinson Crusoe* here (1719).

Some 50 years later, during the Seven Years' War, 23-year-old Edward Gibbon, who wrote *The Decline and Fall of the Roman Empire*, was guarding French prisoners held in **Sissinghurst Castle** ⓭ (open Apr–mid Oct: Tues–Fri 1–6.30pm; Sat–Sun 10–5.30; tel: 01580-715 330), 2 miles (3 km) to the east.

Map, page 210

Oast houses are a typical feature of the Kent countryside. They were used as kilns for hops.

BELOW: a colourful corner in the old Channel port of Rye.

TIP

Many of England's finest vineyards can be found between Tenterden and Penshurst. Look out for signs offering winery and cellar tours, after which you can taste the wines.

The 16th-century manor house was in ruins when it was bought by Vita Sackville-West (1892–1962), poet, novelist and gardener extraordinary, and her politician husband Harold Nicolson in 1930. The beautiful gardens which they created are among the most visited in Britain, though belated revelations about Vita's love life no doubt have helped to bring the curious. The most famous part is the White Garden, with its stunning array of white foliage and blooms.

Eight miles (13 km) west is **Goudhurst**, peaceful enough now, but in 1747 the villagers locked themselves in the church while a gang of smugglers from nearby **Hawkhurst** fought the local militia in the churchyard. From this half-timbered town there are wonderful views south over hop and fruit country and nearby are several places worth visiting. **Bodiam Castle**, to the south beyond Hawkhurst, is a classic medieval fort set in a 3-acre moat (open mid Feb–Oct: daily; Nov–Dec: closed Mon; tel: 01580-830 436) while **Scotney Castle**, 5 miles (8 km) southwest, has been described as one of the loveliest surviving landscapes in the 18th-century pictorial tradition (open May–mid Sept: Wed–Fri: from 11am; Sat, Sun: from 2pm; gardens open Mar–Nov; tel: 01892-891 081).

Taking the waters in Tunbridge Wells

Half way down the A21 between London and Hastings lies **Royal Tunbridge Wells** , a place supposedly full of blimpish retired colonels who write letters to *The Daily Telegraph* and sign themselves "Disgusted".

Dudley, Lord North, a hypochondriac, brought fame and fortune to the town in 1606 when he discovered the health-giving properties of a spring on the common. Court and fashion followed, and the waters, rich in iron salts, were, and still are, taken at the Pantiles. This terraced walk, with shops behind a colonnade, is named after the original tiles laid in 1638, some of which are still there. Eight years earlier, Henrietta Maria, wife of Charles I, came here after the birth of Prince Charles; she was obliged to camp in a tent on the common.

BELOW: the Pantiles in Tunbridge Wells.

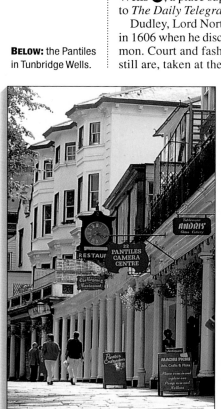

The former home of the novelist William Thackeray in London Road (known simply as Thackeray's House) is now a restaurant and wine bar with a good reputation. There are also a number of good second-hand bookshops in the old part of town. **Penshurst Place**, just to the northwest of the town, is one of Kent's finest mansions, dating from 1340 (open Apr–Sept daily from 11.30am; Oct–Mar: Sat, Sun only; tel: 0189- 870 307). Home of the Viscount de L'Isle, it was for two centuries the seat of the Sidney family, notably Sir Philip Sidney, the Elizabethan soldier and poet.

A few miles to the west lies **Hever Castle** ❺ (open Mar–Nov: from noon; Oct–Nov: till 4pm; tel: 01732-865 224). Henry VIII, who first met Anne Boleyn in this, her father's house, seized Hever after her execution and murdered her brother. William Waldorf Astor (1848–1919) applied his American millions to make massive and sympathetic improvements to the moated castle, 35-acre (15-hectare) lake and gardens where flower beds are laid out exactly as they were 400 years ago in Tudor times.

Some 10 miles (16 km) to the north on the B2026 is **Westerham**, a town that commemorates General James

Wolfe, who decisively drove the French from Canada when he stormed Quebec in 1759. South of the village is **Chartwell**, Winston Churchill's home from 1924 until his death in 1965. There is often quite a queue to see his home and studio where many of his paintings are on display (open end Apr–Oct: Wed–Sun: 11am– 4.30pm; tel: 01732-866 368).

Sevenoaks is the town 5 miles (8 km) to the east on the far side of the A21 and on its outskirts is **Knole** ⓰, one of the largest private houses in the country (open Apr–Oct: Wed–Sun (Thur from 2pm); tel: 01732-810 378). It was the Archbishop of Canterbury's residence until confiscated by Henry VIII, and Elizabeth I gave it to Thomas Sackville who greatly extended it. It has 365 rooms, 52 stairways and seven courtyards. There are exceptionally fine portraits of the Sackville family by Gainsborough and Van Dyck, as well as some rare furniture. In the 1,000-acre (400-hectare) deer park is a fascinating Gothic folly birdhouse.

Kent's pride and joy lies to the east, six miles (10 km) beyond the county town of **Maidstone**. **Leeds Castle** ⓱, the castle of the queens of medieval England, is a fairytale place built on islands in a lake. It has 500 acres (200 hectares) of parkland and is a popular day out (open daily; tel: 01622-765 400).

Maidstone lies on the River Medway which empties into the Thames estuary between **Rochester** ⓲ and **Chatham** 10 miles (16 km) to the north. Chatham grew around the Royal Navy dockyard established by Henry VIII. The dockyard, closed in the 1980s, is now a working museum with a naval theme. Charles Dickens lived at 11 Ordnance Terrace in Chatham as a boy, when his father worked for the navy. The writer is remembered at the **Charles Dickens Centre** (open daily) in Rochester, where you can see the Swiss chalet he used as a study. A Norman castle and keep stand above the river at Rochester (open daily).

Map, page 210

Loose, once a milling village, is now a pleasant suburb of Maidstone. Local women prefer the name to be pronounced as in "lose".

BELOW: the ballroom at Knole, one of Britain's largest private houses.

The cradle of English Christianity

Canterbury ⑲ is the cradle of English Christianity. The Conqueror's Castle, the cathedral and its Thomas à Becket Shrine were a magnet for pilgrims for centuries, and in St Margaret's Street the **Canterbury Tales** (open daily) promises a "medieval adventure" with the sights, sounds and even the smells of the journey made by five of Chaucer's characters.

Despite German aerial bomb attacks in 1942, much of the town's medieval character remains, and there are a number of good pubs in its narrow streets. The town's delights include the remains of the original Roman wall which once enclosed it. Also worth visiting are the excavated ruins of **St Augustine's Abbey** near the grounds of **St Augustine's College** where Anglican clergy are trained. Farther east along Longport is **St Martin's Church** which was used for Christian services even before the arrival of Augustine. In the 4th century this area was the selected by rich Romans for their villas, and remains can still be seen. The town's **Heritage Museum** is located in Stour Street (open Mon–Sat; June–Oct: also Sun from 1.30pm).

Further east lies **Margate** ⑳, which the railway opened up to East Enders as one of the capital's most popular seaside resorts. Bathing machines were invented here by a local Quaker and it still has a breezy holiday air. A couple of miles away is **North Foreland**, the tip of the duck's tail of Kent and Britain's most easterly spot. Immediately below is **Broadstairs**, a more up-market resort which has a sandy bay and landscaped cliffs, which Dickens described as being "left high and dry by the tide of years". When he knew it, the clifftop **Bleak House** was called Fort House. He spent his summer holidays there in the 1850s and 1860s (open mid Mar–Nov: daily; June–Aug: till 9pm).

BELOW: Canterbury Cathedral.

BECKET'S CATHEDRAL

Canterbury Cathedral is a hotchpotch of styles. The oldest part is the crypt, which dates from 1100, but there are traces of still earlier work. The first church on the site was established in AD 597 by St Augustine who had been sent by Pope Gregory the Great to convert the heathen English. In 1170, Archbishop Thomas à Becket, who had been quarrelling with King Henry II, was murdered in the cathedral by four of the king's knights. Becket was canonised in 1173, and after Henry II had performed public penance at his tomb in 1174, the cathedral became one of Christianity's most important shrines, attracting pilgrims from across Europe. In 1220, Becket's bones were transferred to a shrine in the Trinity chapel, the place of pilgrimage which Chaucer described in the prologue to the Canterbury Tales. In 1935, the shameful murder of Thomas à Becket was recounted in verse by T.S. Eliot.

The cathedral's glorious, soaring nave (the longest medieval nave in Europe) was rebuilt in 1400 and the main Bell Harry Tower was added a century later. The stunning stained glass rivals the best in France. But visitors will also want to see the crypt, particularly to admire the capitals of the columns, with their intricate foliated decoration and carvings of beasts.

Sandwich lies along the River Stour, 2 miles (3 km) from the sea. As long ago as the 9th century it was an important port, but by the 17th century the progressive silting up of the estuary left it high and dry, and it is now surrounded by a 500-acre (200-hectare) coastal bird sanctuary. In the 11th century, Sandwich became one of the original Cinque Ports, a string of safe harbours from here to Hastings which were specially fortified against invaders. **Walmer Castle** (open Easter–Oct: daily; Nov–Easter: Wed–Sun; closed Jan; tel: 01304-364 388) in **Deal ㉑** is still the official residence of the Lord Warden of the Cinque Ports. On the beach of this small resort Julius Caesar landed in 55 BC and on the shingle beach, from which there is good fishing, is a plaque commemorating the event. The latest attack on the town came not from the sea but from an IRA bomb smuggled into an army barracks in 1989.

Sandwich, Deal and **Dover ㉒** are now billed as "**White Cliffs Country**", and at Dover, Britain's busiest passenger port, the chalk massif of the South Downs dramatically drops into the sea. On these cliffs the Romans built a lighthouse, the Normans a **castle** (open daily), and from here Calais can be seen. The **White Cliffs Experience** (open daily) brings to life the story of Dover, from Roman times to the present day, with an especially vivid re-creation of the town during the dark days of World War II bombing raids.

But it is near the neighbouring Channel port of **Folkestone** that the Continent comes more sharply into view. Here, dried dogfish is called "Folkestone beef", and the town has a large market on Sundays. But it has become more famous for the nearby Channel Tunnel, which since 1994 has provided fast train and car shuttle services between England and France. It is a development which makes all the coast's castles, towers and parapets look even more ancient. ❑

Map, page 210

BELOW: the Isle of Thanet from Broadstairs.

HARDY COUNTRY

*Wessex, in central southern England, was immortalised by the
novelist Thomas Hardy. It is especially rich in history and
its ancient monuments include Stonehenge*

Map,
page
224/5

Edinburgh

London

No literary works bear the impress of place so strongly as the novels of Thomas Hardy (1840–1928) and no place has had its character and the character of its people revealed as Wessex has by Dorset's most famous son. Wessex is in fact an ancient kingdom, rather larger than the one in which the novelist's trail winds. This was the kingdom of the West Saxons, who had supremacy in England from AD 802 to 1013. It extended across the modern counties of Hampshire, Wiltshire, Dorset and Somerset and even for a short while included Devon and Cornwall which were conquered from the Welsh.

The M3 motorway southwest of London leads to the ancient capital of Winchester in little more than an hour, and beyond it the urban sprawl of Southampton, once a transatlantic liner port. Skirting it, the A31 continues through the New Forest to the smart seaside town of Bournemouth and then to Dorchester, centre of the Hardy tours. To the north, the A303 leaves the M3 at junction 8 and heads for Salisbury Plain and Devon. Trains to London arrive at Waterloo.

There is no hurry about Wessex. The pace of life here is dictated by the cattle on its farms and the slow cycle of its growing crops. Its economy is largely agricultural, and industry, where it does raise its head, is discreet. Wessex is for wandering. Roads are generally minor and invariably go the long way round. There are great houses such as Longleat and Stourhead, and plenty of ruins, among them Corfe Castle, about which the painter Paul Nash wrote: "No mood of nature or human intrusion can affect that terrific personality." Maiden Castle's vast earthwork is another such "personality".

Dorset provides most of the coastline. To be lulled, go to Lyme Regis or Weymouth; to be threatened, go to Chesil Beach or Portland; to be overawed, go to the cliffs of Lulworth and Purbeck. Wessex seaside, like the country that lies behind, puts on a great show.

England's second capital

Winchester ❶ was England's first capital, as well as capital of Wessex, until all decision-making was moved to London in the 17th century. William the Conqueror had to be crowned in both places, though whether he had tea at the Old Norman Palace Tea Rooms is not so certain. Beneath the medieval and modern city is a Roman town, and a Norman **cathedral** replaced the Saxon. Older than Canterbury and the longest in Europe, its Norman transepts and tower survive, but nave and choir were modernised by William of Wykeham in Perpendicular style towards the end of the 14th century. The organ's first notes were heard at the Crystal Palace in London's Hyde Park in 1851. The palace, cloisters, colleges and mill are all breathtaking. The

PRECEDING PAGES: Salisbury's spire and sunny meadows. **LEFT:** cottages in Milton Abbas. **BELOW:** Winchester Cathedral.

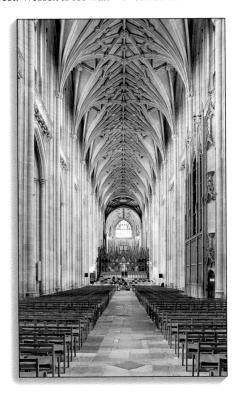

tant centre in Wessex and the burial place of two Saxon kings, it retains a medieval flavour. You almost expect old conflicts between townsfolk and monks to flare again or to come upon Sir Walter Raleigh and his wife in their seats in the abbey chapel. In the airy conservatories at **Compton House**, butterflies fly free in what, for want of a better word, is called a farm, and silkworms produce the thread for silk (open Easter–Sept: daily; tel: 01935-474 608).

At Yeovil **9**, 5 miles (8 km) west of Sherborne, you stray into Somerset for a visit to **Montacute**, an Elizabethan house begun by the lawyer who opened the prosecution at the trial of Guy Fawkes. In golden Ham Hill stone, the ornamental gazebos or lookouts at the corners of the forecourt are exquisite mansions in miniature with latticed windows (open end Mar–Oct: Wed–Mon from noon; tel: 0891-335 222).

In the church at **East Coker**, 3 miles (5 km) to the south, are the ashes of T.S. Eliot (1888–1965). The poet's ancestors emigrated from here to America. "In my beginning is my end," he wrote in the poem named after the village.

There is a warm briny wind at **Lyme Regis ⑩**, just east of the Devon border. This old fishing town was once as fashionable a resort as Bath, and it was popular 100 years before Bournemouth was even thought of. Regency bow windows and trellised verandas on Victorian villas line the **Parade** on the way to the tiny harbour and its curved protecting arm, the **Cobb**, where the Duke of Monmouth landed in 1685, aspiring to the crown. Its sea-lashed walls were a supporting role for Meryl Streep in the 1981 movie *The French Lieutenant's Woman*. "Granny's Teeth", its stone steps, are described by Jane Austen in *Persuasion*, and it was here that Louisa Musgrove tumbled. The story goes that when the poet Tennyson was shown the exact spot where the Duke landed, he

said: "Don't talk to me of Monmouth, show me the exact spot where Louisa Musgrove fell!"

Austen's house, **Bay Cottage** (now a café) is near the harbour end of the parade, and she wrote much of her book here. During a visit in 1804, she stayed at Pyne House at 10 Broad Street. Charles II's illegitimate son, Monmouth, stayed at the George, in the town, and his blue ensign flew in the market place.

The road that hugs the sea to the east has a precarious footing above the landslips, descending to Charmouth and Jane Austen's "happiest spot for watching the flow of the tide". Hereabouts the cliffs reveal the existence of earlier visitors, like the elephant and rhinoceros, not in zoos, but in fossils. Ichthyosaurus turned up here in 1811. **Bridport ⓫** ("Port Bredy" to Hardy) is 2 miles (3 km) from the sea, yet there is no denying its marine character. Rope and cordage, nets and tackle, this was the stuff of Bridport's prosperity.

West Bay is Bridport's improbable harbour. A narrow channel dug in the shingle bank and flanked by two high piers only feet apart offers a needle-threading operation for the small craft that lie uneasily in the little basin. In the old days coasters had to be hauled in with Bridport ropes. Visit on a Saturday and enjoy the outdoor market.

The shingle finger of Portland

The next town east, nearby **Burton Bradstock**, is warmly summed up in thatch and smoky stone, flowers everywhere and a stream that trickles to the sea below Burton Cliff. It turned the wheel of the flax mills until the last one closed in 1930.

The dreaded Chesil Bank begins here, curving away eastwards to where it becomes the slender link that makes the **Isle of Portland** only a courtesy title. It is

Map, page 224/5

ABOVE AND BELOW LEFT: hunting for fish. **BELOW RIGHT:** Punch and Judy puppet shows are still performed on some local beaches.

in fact, only a peninsula. The pebbles of the steeply shelving bank increase in size towards Portland, and at night, local fisherman docking at any point on the 16-mile (25-km) ridge can tell exactly where they are from the size of the pebbles. The bank has no mercy. To drive a boat in here spells almost certain disaster. **St Catherine's Chapel**, on a green hill above the bank at **Abbotsbury** ⓬, leads a double life. A place of prayer for 500 years, it is also maintained as a mark for seamen. On the land side it overlooks the most fascinating miscellany of monastic ruin, a swannery and sub-tropical gardens. The 15th-century abbey barn, bigger and more splendid than many a parish church, was built as a wheat store. Further along the same road, by the salt water of Fleet, is the swan sanctuary founded in the 14th century.

George III did **Weymouth** ⓭ a good turn when he went there in 1789 for his convalescence after a serious illness. The grateful citizens responded by erecting the highly coloured statue that ends the half-mile esplanade. The king bathed from his "machine" to the music of his own anthem. Fanny Burney records the occasion in the diary she kept while Second Mistress of the Robes to Queen Charlotte. George can be seen in chalk outline on a neighbouring hillside astride a horse. There is much of the character of the 18th-century watering place about Weymouth today. Stuccoed terraces still front the esplanade, the sands are golden and the sea is blue. There are museums of sea life, diving and shipwrecks. From Weymouth's jetty, ferries maintain a regular service to the Channel Isles.

Thomas Hardy's heartlands

To the south of Weymouth a narrow strip of land carries the road to the "island" of **Portland**. Thomas Hardy observed that the people who lived on what he

During the Civil War Abbotsbury's Benedictine abbey was used to store gunpowder, and the explosion which reduced most of its buildings to ruins provided the whole neighbourhood with material for new houses. The vicarage, farm and countless cottages in the village have the tell-tale white stones in their walls.

BELOW: St Catherine's Chapel.

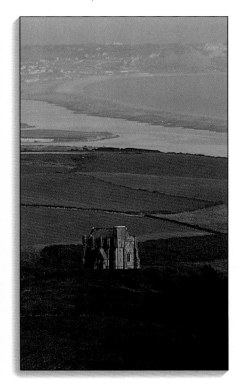

THE GENIUS OF THOMAS HARDY

Film makers today continue to be drawn to *Tess of the D'Urbervilles* and *Jude the Obscure*, finding that their strongly drawn characters and melodramatic situations translate very effectively to the screen. Yet when the novels first appeared, in the 1890s, reviewers condemned them for their pessimism and immorality. Certainly, they are much darker than Hardy's early novels such as *Under the Greenwood Tree* and *Far from the Madding Crowd*, published in the 1870s, although even these more pastoral stories convey a strong sense of the utter indifference of fate towards their protagonists – a defining characteristic of Hardy's writing.

Thomas Hardy (1840–1928) was born at Higher Bockhampton, near Dorchester, the son of a stonemason, and trained as an architect. All his major novels are set in Wessex and, despite their frequent bleakness of outlook, Hardy draws their rustic characters movingly and with evident affection. He is also an acute observer of the natural surroundings, about which he writes poetically.

It was to poetry that he turned in his later years, with collections such as *Wessex Poems* (1898) and *Satires of Circumstance* (1914). Like his novels, his poetry has grown in critical stature with the passing of time.

called "the Gibraltar of Wessex" had manners and customs of their own. The sheer structure of Portland makes it a place apart. Everything is stone: buildings, walls, quarries – heaps of it everywhere. This is the stuff of which most of London's best loved buildings are made: Portland Stone. The lighthouse on the island's south tip overlooks the broken water of the treacherous Portland Race.

The green of the high hills inland of Weymouth comes as a welcome relief. Dorchester, 8 miles (13 km) north, is best approached from the great hill of **Maiden Castle**, *Mai Dun* ("great hill" – probably the world's largest earthwork), just before the town on the left. Excavations have shown that the hill was occupied 4,000 years ago, and a clever maze conceals the hill fort's entrance.

Dorchester ⓮, Dorset's county town, is well aware of its past, and the pace of life here, beyond the fast motorways, is noticeably slower. Thomas Hardy, Judge Jeffries and the Tolpuddle Martyrs all try to catch the visitor's eye. Hardy's statue commands his "Casterbridge" from the top of the High Street. The judge of the 1685 Bloody Assize which dealt so harshly with the followers of Monmouth's rebellion invites visitors to drink tea where he lodged, and the men of Dorset, sentenced to transportation here in 1834 for asking for a wage increase, left a courtroom in the **Shire Hall** remarkably unchanged since (open Mon–Fri; closed noon–2pm). Hardy's is perhaps the most potent influence. He was apprenticed to an architect at 39 South Street, and after he left the practice in 1885, he used his knowledge to design his own house, **Maxgate**, on the Wareham Road, where he died in 1928 (open Easter–Sept: Mon, Wed, Sun, from 2pm only: entrance fee). There is a memorial collection devoted to Hardy in the **Dorset County Museum** on High West Street, a cast-iron building of 1880, delightfully decorated in bright primary colours. Stunning finds from Maiden Cas-

ABOVE: Hardy's statue in Dorchester. **BELOW:** his study in the town's museum.

Map, page 224/5

A geologist's paradise, the coast between Weymouth and Swanage is full of surprises – like the tiny circular bay between steep cliffs at Lulworth Cove, and the neighbouring Stair Hole, the oozing black layers of shale at Kimmeridge (long a source of oil) and the great cliff at Worbarrow.

tle are here, too (open Mon–Sat; July–Aug: daily). Thomas Hardy was actually born in the cottage his great-grandfather built at **Higher Bockhampton**, just north of Dorchester in 1840. *Far From the Madding Crowd* and *Under the Greenwood Tree* were written here (Hardy's Cottage open Easter–2 Nov: open Sun–Thur: 11am–dusk).

The village of **Milton Abbas** ⓯ off the A354, 12 miles (20 km) to the northeast, annoyed Viscount Milton. It interfered with the view from his rebuilt mansion, **Milton Abbey** (open during daylight hours), so in 1752 he moved the village as well, half a mile away, sticking to the rustic tradition of cob and thatch.

The 30-mile (48-km) coast from Weymouth east to Swanage, below Poole Harbour, is strictly for walking, army operations permitting, but approachable by car at **West Lulworth** ⓰, Kimmeridge and Worth Matravers.

Towards the east, the chalk hills around the **Isle of Purbeck** break at **Corfe Castle** ⓱ (open daily; Nov–Mar: 11–3.30pm), a too-picturesque ruin haunted by treachery, cruelty and murder. Here King Edward was murdered by his stepmother in AD 978, French prisoners were starved to death in the dungeons by King John, and the castle was traitorously handed over to the Roundheads in 1646 who pulled a large part of it down.

Swanage ⓲ ("Knollsea" to Thomas Hardy) "was a seaside village, lying snugly within two headlands as between a finger and a thumb". Look out for the stone globe, 10 ft (3 metres) in diameter, weighing 40 tons, and flanked by panels lettered with sobering information on the nature of the universe. **Old Swanage**, sitting on the hilltop, traps between its stone houses a millpond.

Around Poole Harbour's creeks, mud flats and islands is **Poole** ⓳ itself, most beautiful on the quay and overlooking ships and shipyards, yachts and

BELOW: the cliffs at Durdle Door near Lulworth.

chandler's stores. Curving steps meet under the portico of the **Custom House** with its coat of arms representing an authority the Dorset smuggler never acknowledged. The town is also famous for its pottery.

Beyond Poole are the hotels and elegant terraces of **Bournemouth** ⓴, the sedate resort built at the end of the 19th century. To the northwest lies **Wimborne Minster** ㉑, where the church has a fine 13th-century clock. It has no hands, but rather the planets revolve with winged angels in attendance. Just east of Bournemouth is **Christchurch** on the mouth of the Avon, which goes back more than 100 years. There is a turret at the **Priory** with a deliciously interlaced pattern of Norman arches that strongly recalls Pisa's leaning tower.

Hampshire haunts

Good rivers and harbours make this popular yachting country. **Lymington** ㉒ is the next safe port of call and on the River Beaulieu (pronounced *Bew-lee*) 6 miles (10 km) beyond, **Buckler's Hard** was famous for shipbuilding from the mid-18th century. Many of Nelson's warships took to the water here, launched between the two rows of shipwrights' cottages. At the end of the Napoleonic wars it all came to an abrupt end, but the **Maritime Museum** captures the flavour of the good old days (open daily; Easter–Sept: till 6pm; winter: till 4.30pm; tel: 01590-616 203). **Beaulieu**'s church is unique; the monks' dining room was transformed into a pulpit. Lord Montagu runs Britain's best-known **Motor Museum** at Palace House in Beaulieu (open daily; tel: 01590-612 345), and the local wine should be sampled.

To describe the wild, dense 100 sq. mile (260 sq. km) woodland of the **New Forest** ㉓, which lies behind this coast, as "new" would seem to support the tra-

Map, page 224/5

ABOVE: old Georgian architecture at Lymington. **BELOW:** Corfe Castle.

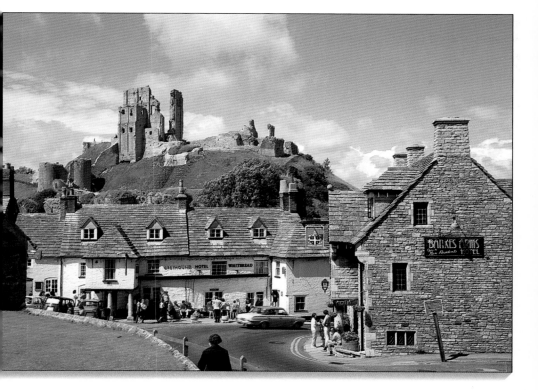

ditional belief that William the Conqueror had a hand in its creation. But this was always forest; William merely enforced measures to protect his deer. There is no evidence to suggest he destroyed villages and churches to achieve his objective, although there are few of either in the area. When driving through, remember that wild ponies have priority. Alice Lydell, Lewis Carroll's real Alice, is buried at **Lyndhurst**, the forest's capital, 8 miles (13 km) north of Lymington.

Miniature England on an Island

From Lymington a regular ferry crosses to the **Isle of Wight** ㉔ in 30 minutes (from 5.55am to 9.30pm daily). The 147 sq. mile (380 sq. km) island is shaped like a kite, with the capital, **Newport**, just about where you might attach a string. Close by is **Carisbrooke Castle**, built by Elizabeth I as a defence against the Spanish Armada and remembered chiefly as the prison of Charles I (open daily; winter: till 4pm; tel: 01983-522 107). He was taken back to trial and execution from here, having made the mistake of thinking he would get protection from the local governor. No such luck – the governor's father-in-law was one of Cromwell's close allies. Tragically, Charles's daughter, 15-year-old Princess Elizabeth, died here in captivity and is commemorated by a monument in Newport church. **Cowes**, at the mouth of the Medina River, lives once a year (every August) for Cowes Week – the yachtsman's Ascot.

ABOVE: Nelson's HMS *Victory*, Portsmouth.
BELOW: the Needles Lighthouse.
RIGHT: the River Fleet, Hampshire.

Osborne House is highest Victorian, Queen Victoria's favourite residence, and left very much as it was in her lifetime (open daily; Easter–Oct: till 4.30pm: winter: check times 01983-200 022). The chalk cliffs of the island shatter spectacularly in the Needles at the eastern end. Tucked behind them is **Alum Bay**, where sands come in all the colours of the rainbow, and are carried away in bottles as souvenirs. Tennyson took walks on the chalk downs above Freshwater, where he lived for 30 years, and declared the air "worth sixpence a pint". That was Champagne money. Keats took inspiration from the woods at **Shanklin**, and countless holidaymakers take to Sandown's pier. Pretty bays, thatched villages, roses and honeysuckle – England in miniature.

One way to return from Cowes is up the long arm of Southampton Water to **Southampton** ㉕. The armies that won the battles of Crécy and Agincourt embarked from here, the tiny *Mayflower* sailed for America, and many great ocean liners have followed since. The image was blemished by the bombing of World War II, but the city rose again, and there is vivid history all around in the surviving Norman walls, gates and houses.

Ferries also cross the Solent from the Isle of Wight to "Pompey", the important naval base of **Portsmouth** ㉖. This, too, was heavily bombed in the war, but the naval tradition could never be destroyed. The Royal Navy's museum is here, at the **Historic Dockyard** (open daily; winter: till 4.30pm; tel: 01705-727 652), but most visitors head for Admiral Lord Nelson's flagship *Victory*, on which he died at the Battle of Trafalgar in 1805, and the hulk of *Mary Rose*, Henry VIII's "favourite warship", dredged up in 1982 (open daily; entrance fee; tel: 01705-839 766). Charles Dickens was born here in Commercial Road in 1812, but of Thomas Hardy there is no longer any sign. ❑

THE ENGLISH GARDEN

*Britain's temperate climate encourages an amazing
diversity of gardens which blend the grand
and the homely in a cosmopolitan range of styles*

The formal gardens of great houses have both
followed fashion and set the style for the nation's
favourite hobby. In medieval times, fruit trees, roses
and herbs were grown in walled enclosures:
Elvaston Country Park in Derbyshire is a good
example. In the 16th century, aromatic plants were
incorporated in "knots" (carpet-like patterns).
Tudor Gardens (like those at Hatfield House in
Hertfordshire and Packwood House in Warwickshire were enclosed squares of flowers in geometric
patterns bordered by low hedges and gravel paths.

The Renaissance gardener also liked snipping
hedges into shapes: the most inventive examples are
at Hever Castle in Kent. A taste for small flower
beds persisted through the 17th and 18th centuries
when fountains and canals began to be introduced.

THE ART OF THE LANDSCAPE

In the 1740s a rich banker, Henry Hoare, inspired
by Continental art during his Grand Tour, employed
William Kent (1685–1748) to turn his gardens at
Stourhead in Wiltshire into a series of lakes dotted
with grottoes and buildings in the classical style.
This was the birth of the landscape garden, known
as *le jardin anglais*, that was an entirely English
invention. The style was a direct reaction to the
formal gardens made in France for Louis XIV at
Versailles. Nature instead of geometry was the
inspiration, and the idylls of landscape painters
became the idylls of gardeners too.

"Capability" Brown (*see panel, right*) rejected
formal plantings in favour of natural parkland and
restricted flowers to small kitchen gardens. But
Humphry Repton (1752–1815) reintroduced the
formal pleasure
garden. The
Victorians put the
emphasis on
plants and
Gertrude Jekyll
(1843–1932)
promoted the idea
of planting
cycles to ensure
that colour lasted
through the year.

△ **COTTAGE GARDENS**
Such gardens are the pride
and joy of thousands of
people all over Britain. They're
labour-intensive: perennials
need to be planned, borders
restocked, plants dead-
headed and weeds removed.
But it's a labour of love.

▷ **TRESCO ABBEY GARDENS**
Thanks to the influence of the
Gulf Stream, sub-tropical flora
can flourish at England's
south-western tip. These
gardens, on the Isles of Scilly,
were laid out on the site of a
Benedictine priory and contain
many rare plants.

◁ **GARDEN STATUES**
The classicists favoured
populating gardens with
assorted Greek goddesses
and coy nymphs, and the
trend gradually evolved
to include strikingly
modern sculpture. At a
more demotic level,
brightly painted
garden gnomes
have their
adherents.

THEY CHAMPIONED CHANGING STYLES

△ **HIDCOTE MANOR**
This 17th-century Cotswold house at Mickleton in Gloucestershire, has one of the most beautiful English gardens, mixing different types of plot within various species of hedges. Although covering 10 acres (4 hectares), it resembles a series of cottage gardens on a grand scale, conveying an impression of what Vita Sackville-West called "haphazard luxuriance".

Lancelot Brown (1715–83) was nicknamed "Capability Brown" when he rode from one aristocratic client to the next pointing out "capabilities to improvement". His forte was presenting gardens in the natural state, and his lasting influence lay in his talent for combining simple elements to create harmonious effects.

Brown liked to create elegant lakes for his parks, as at Blenheim Palace in Oxfordshire. He was also involved with the gardens at Stowe in Buckinghamshire, which the National Trust today describes as "Britain's largest work of art", and with the gardens at Kew, Britain's main botanical establishment, just outside London.

One of the 20th century's most influential gardeners was Vita Sackville-West (1892–1962), below, who developed her gardens at Sissinghurst Castle in Kent. She revived the 16th-century idea of dividing a garden into separate sections, combining a formal overall style with an informal choice of flowers.

◁ **STOURHEAD**
This Wiltshire garden, birthplace of England's landscape movement, is dotted with lakes and temples and has many rare trees and shrubs. The artful vistas were created in the 1740s, and their magnificence contrasts with the severe restraint of the Palladian house (1721–24).

△ **THE KNOT GARDEN**
This example at Henry VIII's Hampton Court Palace outside London showes the Tudor liking for knots – small beds of dwarf plants or sand and gravel laid out in patterns resembling embroidery. Topiary, statues and mazes provided a counterpoint to the mathematical order.

THE WEST COUNTRY

*Like their splendid landscape, the people of Cornwall, Devon
and Somerset are a blend of rugged power and muted tranquillity –
and this sets them apart from many other peoples of Britain*

Map,
page 240

Edinburgh

London

The mystique of the West Country transcends its reputation as Britain's most popular holiday region. Beneath the Bristol Channel and Wales and on the edge of the moderating Atlantic, the peninsula is made up of Somerset, Devon and Cornwall, rural counties tucked away with hidden fishing hamlets and Britain's warmest winter weather.

The West Country is also steeped in legend. This is the land of King Arthur, Camelot and the Holy Grail; the land of Jack the Giant Killer and the myth of an ancient Druid who gave weary travellers sips of water from a golden cup. History here takes on a romantic quality, with facts obscured by time and fictions embellished with tales of piracy, smuggling and shipwrecks.

West Country people have always considered themselves special, celebrating their Celtic origins and taking pride in their self-reliance. There's a certain island mentality here – in fact Cornwall itself is almost an island. The River Tamar flows along all but 5 miles (8 km) of the Devon border. Old traditions flourish, like the Helston Furry Dance in early May when people fill the town with flowers and dance in the streets.

Historically, the West Country has been cut off from the mainstream of British culture both by geography and choice. The peninsula was settled by hard-working Celts from Brittany who scraped a living off the essentials of the land. They dug tin and copper, grazed their sheep and cattle on windswept moors, and braved treacherous currents to take fish from the sea.

The tip of the peninsula, Land's End, is 290 miles (465 km) from London. The main artery into the region is the M5 which comes down from Birmingham, meeting the M4 from London at Bristol, and continuing down to Exeter. On a good day the 175-mile (282-km) drive from London to Somerset will take three hours. Tourist routes are well signposted and walkers can make the most of the 500-mile (800-km) coastal footpath which extends from Minehead in Somerset to Poole in Dorset. The region is served by train from Paddington station in London.

PRECEDING PAGES:
St Just, Cornwall.
LEFT: Port Isaac,
Cornwall. **BELOW:**
the Avon at Bristol.

Points of departure

A jumping-off point into the region could be the old Atlantic port of **Bristol ❶**, much of it now in the hands of the heritage industry. John Cabot set off for Newfoundland from here in 1497. Greatly rebuilt after World War II, the city manages to keep some interest around its port, such as the 17th-century **Llandoger Trow** pub in King Street which Robert Louis Stevenson supposedly used as a model for the inn favoured by Long John Silver in *Treasure Island*. Opposite is the Bristol Old Vic's **Theatre Royal** (1766), while the **Arnolfini Gallery** has also been making its name as an

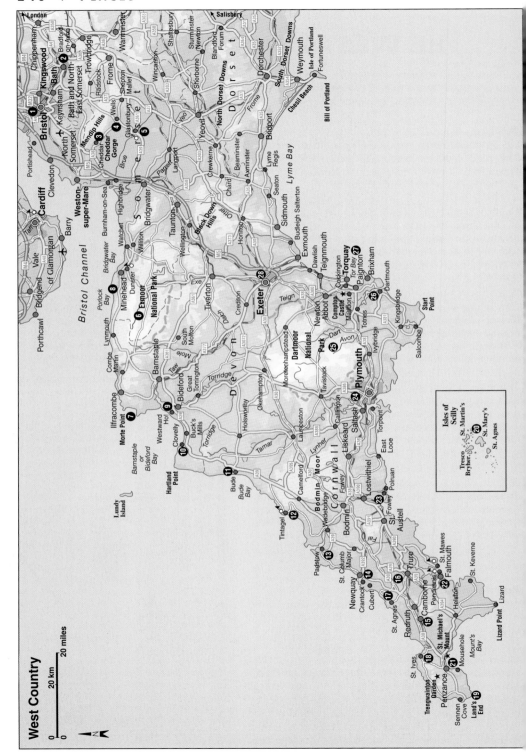

West Country

0 — 20 km
0 — 20 miles

arts venue in this lively university city. Britain's most famous engineer is celebrated here: Isambard Kingdom Brunel (1806–59) designed the world's first ocean-going propeller ship, **SS *Great Britain***, and she can be seen in her original dock. Brunel was also responsible for the superb **Clifton Suspension Bridge** which majestically spans the Avon gorge.

Map, page 240

Another jumping-off point for the West Country is 10 miles (16 km) southeast, at the more leisurely and salubrious **Bath ❷**, Britain's most celebrated spa town. It owes its good looks to Bath stone and the genius of two men, the elder and younger John Wood, who in the 18th century gave its streets, squares and crescents a harmony that recent development has done its best to disturb. The limestone they used is well suited to their neo-Grecian style.

Prince Bladud, father of King Lear, started it all back in the mists of time. The mud bath cured his pigs, and him, of scrofula. The Romans came, enjoyed the waters and went. King Offa founded the abbey some 200 years before King Edgar was crowned King of All England there in 973. But the baths were forgotten until the 18th century when the business of bathing became fashionable.

Bath's architectural heritage has been wonderfully preserved, and the Theatre Royal and International Music Festival in May ensure that the strong cultural tradition is maintained. Among the many things that must be seen, viewed preferably from the **Parade Gardens**, is Robert Adams's **Pulteney Bridge** which has houses on it like old London Bridge. John Wood junior designed the **Royal Crescent** from where the playwright Sheridan eloped with Elizabeth Linley.

ABOVE: Isambard Kingdom Brunel.
BELOW: the Great Bath by torchlight.

The Circus, at the town's centre, **Assembly Rooms** (open daily; free), **Queen Square** and **Cross Bath** must also be seen. But the steamy core of it all are the **Roman Baths** (open daily), at basement level to the modern city, and the adjoin-

ing **Pump Room** where the hot springs erupt and where the water, good for rheumatism, can be drunk.

Americans can feel at home at **Claverton Manor** (open Apr–July, Sept–Oct: Tues–Sun & public hols; Aug: daily; tel: 01225-460 503), high above the Avon valley, 4 miles (6 km) south of Bath. This houses the **American Museum**, whose period furnished rooms and displays of folk art offer an absorbing picture of American domestic life between the 17th and 19th centuries.

The Mendip Hills, just east of the coast and south of Bristol, mark an abrupt end to the flat, cultured landscape of the Avon Valley and the start of the wild expanses of the West Country. Across the crest of the hills runs the **West Mendip Way**, a popular hiking trail that twists from Wells, 20 miles (32 km) southwest of Bath, to the Bristol Channel and offers superb views of the countryside.

Much of the natural scenery here is simply breathtaking; **Cheddar Gorge ❸** 12 miles (20 km) northwest of Wells, is carved by a river that now runs underground. The sheer limestone cliffs, 450 ft (135 metres) above Cheddar village below, cut through the Mendips for more than a mile. In the village itself you can visit vast underground caverns (open daily).

On the Holy Grail trail

The pride and joy of **Wells ❹**, at the southern tip of the Mendip Hills, is the **Cathedral**, a massive Gothic shrine started in about 1185 and finished four centuries later. Unlike other English cathedrals, the two main towers were built outside the church proper, thus extending the western facade into a massive gallery for 400 individual statues. More than 25 percent of the sculpture has been destroyed (most by rampaging Puritans in the 17th century) but the remaining

South of Cheddar along the A371 is the Ebbor Gorge. Formed 270 million years ago, this is the most beautiful gorge of the Mendips, a lush mix of elms, oaks and ash trees, mosses, fungi and ferns. Caves here contain the remains of Stone Age pots, axes and reindeer.

BELOW: soaring above Bath's Royal Crescent. **BELOW RIGHT:** Gough's Cave, Cheddar.

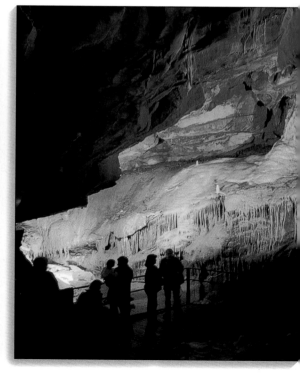

group is an array of bishops and kings, saints and prophets, angels and apostles. The interior is no less spectacular, especially the "hour-glass" arches at the junction of the nave and transept. These were constructed in the 14th century after the cathedral threatened to collapse under the weight of a new central tower.

Map,
page 240

Outside the cathedral, the **Vicar's Close** beckons to a row of 14th-century buildings (the only complete medieval street remaining in Britain). The exteriors have changed little from their original design. But the **Bishop's Palace** (open Easter–Oct: Tues–Fri, Sun & public hols; Aug: daily) south of the cathedral, is outstanding. One of the oldest inhabited houses in England, the Palace is home to the Bishop of Bath and Wells. The high wall surrounding it dates from the beginning of the 13th century. Swans glide across the broad moat and, since Victorian times, have been trained to ring a bell for their food. By the Cathedral Green the **Wells Museum** (open Easter–Sept: daily; Oct–Easter: Wed–Sun) houses plaster casts of the cathedral statues.

It's a pity that the abbey at **Glastonbury ❺**, 6 miles (10 km) southwest, has not been preserved in the same way, for it was once the richest and most beautiful in England. Little remains of the great complex – a few ruined pillars and walls. But these remain an impressive monument to the power of the Roman Catholic church in England before Henry VIII's dissolution of the monasteries.

Like much of West Country history, the origins of Glastonbury Abbey are shrouded in myth and legend. One story claims that St Patrick founded the original abbey and that St George killed the famous dragon nearby. The most popular legend says that Joseph of Arimathea, the man who gave his tomb to Christ, sailed from the Holy Land to Britain to convert the heathens in AD 60. Joseph was leaning on his staff on Wearyall Hill, when it magically rooted and flow-

ABOVE: the Cheddar Gorge experience.
BELOW LEFT: Wells Cathedral. **BELOW:** Glastonbury's abbey.

ered. To Joseph, this was an omen that he should settle and found the abbey. Joseph brought with him the chalice from the Last Supper, the Holy Grail. In the 6th century King Arthur came to Glastonbury in search of the Holy Grail, and tradition says Arthur and Guinevere were buried under the abbey floor.

A short walk to the steep, conical hill called **Glastonbury Tor**, which rises up from the flat Somerset plain, is worthwhile for the view from the top, surmounted by remains of the 15th-century St Michael's Church).

The boundary between Somerset and Devon falls within the confines of **Exmoor National Park** , 265 sq. mile (690 sq. km) filled with the sights and sounds of Richard Doddridge Blackmore's novel, *Lorna Doone*, the story of a 17th-century family of outlaws. The landscape of the park, dotted with pretty villages, transforms itself from windswept ridges covered with bracken and heather, to forested ravines carved out by white-water streams.

The undulating Somerset and Devon Coast Path, stretching more than 30 miles (48 km) along the shore, north of the A39, is the most fascinating of Exmoor's many hiking trails. Hugging tightly to cliffs and coves, it offers splendid views of the Bristol Channel and the far-off Atlantic.

Snatches of sandy beaches, like **Morte Pointe** ❼ northwest of **Barnstaple** (as the name implies, not for swimming) and **Porlock Bay** ❽, 6 miles (10 km) west of Minehead, are good for birdwatching. Just east of Minehead the village of **Dunster** is a pleasant stopping-place. Dunster has been a fortress site since Saxon times, but the present castle dates from the 13th century. Most of the original structure was destroyed after Charles I's execution in 1649. The graceful turrets and towers seen today are the work of Anthony Salvin, a 19th-century architect. The village itself is considered a perfect replica of feudal times, largely

Exmoor ponies, direct descendants of the prehistoric horse, are the most ubiquitous inhabitants of the moor, but there are also red deer, sheep and Devon Red cattle.

BELOW: Glastonbury Tor. **BELOW RIGHT:** Clovelly cobbles.

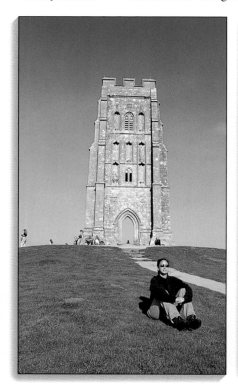

because one family, the Luttrells, owned it for 600 years until 1950. The parish church of warm pink sandstone is one of the West Country's finest.

Map, page 240

King Arthur's country

Where Devon turns to Cornwall, a chain of fishing villages and hidden beauties lie beside the A39 running down to Tintagel. **Westward Ho!** ❾, by Bideford, is a popular seaside resort named after the novel by Charles Kingsley (1819–75). It has 3 miles (5 km) of sandy beach. **Clovelly** ❿ is probably the most well known of these hamlets in Bideford Bay. Cars are banned from the village and donkeys carry visitors' luggage. The steep cobbled street descends 400 ft (120 metres) to the sea in a series of steps. A romantic 2-mile (3-km) walk west from the harbour leads to a magnificent range of cliffs. Nearby **Buck's Mills** is an unspoiled village of thatched cottages.

Farther south and into Cornwall, the rolling waves at **Bude** ⓫ have long attracted surfers. For those who prefer calmer swimming, **Summerleaze Beach** in the town is a good spot, a sheltered sandy expanse north of the River Neet.

The legend of King Arthur comes alive at **Tintagel** ⓬, a wild and romantic castle on the north Cornwall coast about 18 miles (29 km) south of Bude. Tradition claims that Arthur was born or washed ashore at Tintagel, where he built a sturdy castle for Guinevere and the Knights of the Round Table. In fact, all that remains at Tintagel are the ruins of a 6th-century Celtic monastery and a 12th-century bastion (open daily), most of it washed away by the sea. In the town itself, the old slate-built post office is interesting. This 14th-century manor house is now owned by the National Trust (open Apr–Oct).

Some 20 miles (32 km) south on the A39 and then west along the A389 is

King Arthur's presence is strong at Tintagel, though it isn't backed by archaeological evidence.

BELOW: Tintagel Point.

Cornwall offers some of the best surfing in Britain. It is at its exhilarating best at Fistral Bay, Newquay, and Porthmeor Beach, St Ives.

BELOW: Padstow.

Padstow , the only safe harbour in north Cornwall and an important port for more than 1,000 years. The town is named after St Petroc, a Celtic missionary who landed here in the 6th century as the first of numerous Irish and Welsh priests who came to convert the heathen Cornish. The Vikings sacked Padstow in AD 981, but it later grew into a fishing centre and mineral port. The primary industry these days is tourism, especially during the summer, when Padstow overflows with families and couples attracted by Cornwall's abundant sunshine.

Clustered around the harbour are the historic **Abbey House**, **St Petroc Church**, the **Harbour Master's Office** and **Raleigh Cottage**, where Sir Walter collected port dues as the Royal Warden of Cornwall. Every May Day the town fills up when a bizarre Hobby Horse festival creates a carnival atmosphere.

Continuing south along the coast, **Newquay** ⑭ is Cornwall's Malibu – the beach where Britain's surfers cruise the waves. Famous in the 18th and 19th centuries as a pilchard port, Newquay exported dried fish to Spain and Italy. Newquay also has Cornwall's only zoo, in **Trenance Park**.

Worthwhile excursions south of Newquay include the ancient Norman church at **Crantock**, a village once notorious for its involvement in contraband. Crantock Beach is lovely, too. Still further south is **Cubert**, which features a church tower shaped curiously like a bishop's mitre. The interior of the church preserves fine Norman and 14th-century carvings and a font.

The corridor between the neighbouring towns of Redruth and **Camborne** ⑮, 18 miles (29 km) southwest and inland, was the fulcrum of Cornish tin mining for more than 200 years. Little active mining remains, but you can get some idea of what tin meant to the region's economy by visiting the **Camborne Museum** (closed Thur & Sun) housed in the library. It also has exhibits relating to Richard

Trevithick, the "Father of the Locomotive", who manufactured the first high-pressure steam engine in 1797. Four years later he attached his engine to a four-wheeled carriage and drove 10 friends up Beacon Hill in Camborne; they were the first people ever transported by steam power.

Tin-smelting capital

Truro ⓰, 10 miles (16 km) east, is the cathedral city of Cornwall and the county's unofficial capital. In the 18th century it was both a centre for tin smelting and a society haunt that rivalled Bath. **Lenion Street**, laid out around 1795, features fine Georgian architecture and is complemented by **Walsingham Place**, an early 19th-century crescent off Victoria Place. One of Cornwall's oldest and most famous potteries, **Lakes**, still operates in Chapel Street, and is open to visitors. The neo-Gothic cathedral was begun in 1880.

Out to the coast again on the A390, St Agnes Beacon, outside the village of **St Agnes ⓱**, offers a view of 32 church towers and 23 miles (40 km) of coast from 628 ft (190 metres) above. Now owned by the National Trust, much of the surrounding area was once mining land. Today the old buildings and scars of industry give the area a melancholy beauty.

One of the last ports of call on this north coast is **St Ives ⓲**, a classic Cornish fishing village popular with artists since the end of the 19th century. Among them was the sculptor Barbara Hepworth who lived and worked here from 1949 until her death in 1975. Her home is now a museum. Locally inspired art has been further bolstered by the **Tate Gallery St Ives** (both museums open daily; Oct–Apr: closed Mon), an offshoot of the London gallery which opened in 1993 in a much acclaimed new building.

Map, page 240

Truro's cathedral, built by J.L. Pearson, is a particularly refined example of the late Victorian era's Gothic revival.

BELOW: St Agnes coastline.

Cornwall's other important minerals, china clay has become its primary economic product, supplying more than 80 percent of the world's raw material for porcelain. The harbour is dominated by the great bulk carriers and machinery that move clay out of the port. But Fowey is also a snug harbour for numerous pleasure craft and fishing boats. The ancient town centre remains intact (visit the 18th-century **Town Hall** and 14th-century **Toll Bar House**) and is still recognisably a Cornish "village". Take the ferry across the harbour to **Polruan**, a quaint and hilly little village.

Drake territory

Plymouth ㉔, on the Devon-Cornwall border, is a relic of the Age of Exploration, the city of Drake, Raleigh and the Pilgrim Fathers, a town where young Englishmen have long gone in search of seafaring adventure. But today's Plymouth is more than a history book, for it's still a thriving port, industrial centre, market town and cultural mecca, the largest city west of Bristol. Plymouth is at its best on Sunday morning, when the office workers still lie snug in their beds, the shops are closed and the streets are all but empty. Only then does the town recover its purely nautical self. Stand atop the green lump called the Hoe, 120 ft (37 metres) above the sea, and gaze into the wide Sound.

Francis Drake has long been Plymouth's favourite son. He sailed from the port in 1577 on his renowned global circumnavigation, and upon his return the citizens of Plymouth elected him as mayor.

The Pilgrims sailed from Plymouth's West Pier in 1620 aboard the fragile *Mayflower* to the New World. (They originally launched from Southampton, but bad weather damaged their ship and they called at Plymouth for repairs.)

When the Spanish Armada was sighted off Plymouth's coast in 1588, Francis Drake was playing bowls on the Hoe. Legend says that he insisted on finishing the game before doing battle, but in fact he had to wait for the outgoing tide.

BELOW:
Sir Francis Drake.

While at Plymouth, the Pilgrims took shelter in the wine cellars of the firm of James Hawker, which still carries on business today.

The Hoe still dominates Plymouth as it did in Drake's day. **Smeaton's Tower** is a red-and-white striped lighthouse that offers excellent views of the Sound. Nearby is the **Royal Citadel** (open May–Sept: daily), a fortress built in the 17th century by Charles II to stall any Republican comeback. Well landscaped into the front brow of the Hoe is the **Dome** (open daily), an innovative multi-media presentation of Plymouth's past and present. Down by the port is an Elizabethan quarter known as the **Barbican**, a mixture of cobblestoned streets, medieval houses and bustling piers. Many of Plymouth's historic voyages started out here and the 16th-century **Island House** is where the Pilgrims spent their last night in England. There's a fish market on the far quay, and plenty of shops, taverns and art studios to keep visitors occupied.

A walk in the wilderness

Directly inland from Plymouth is **Dartmoor National Park** ㉕, an expansive 365 sq. miles (915 sq. km) of forest and moorland that protects the largest of the West Country's wilderness areas. Beneath all that heather and bracken is a solid core of stone, one of five granite masses that form the geological heart of the West Country. There are hundreds of miles of public footpaths and hiking trails across the moor, walked by an estimated 8 million people each year. The visitors tend to overwhelm Dartmoor's indigenous population, the 30,000 people who live in and around the park. But the villagers still have grazing rights to the open grasslands on the moor, and they can also collect peat, stone and thatching straw for their homes. Dartmoor remains much as it has been for 1,000

Map,
page 240

The famous Dartmoor ponies are related to Stone Age horses which have lived on this land for millions of years. The Galloway and Highland cattle and black-faced sheep are later imports.

BELOW:
Dartmoor ponies.

years: a harsh landscape of open moors, rocky outcrops, wooded vales and muddy bogs broken only occasionally by a village or farm.

Dartmouth ㉖, directly east of Plymouth, is yet another of the West Country's famous ports. The town retains much of its seafaring heritage in the form of **Britannia Royal Naval College**, which has trained such officers as Prince Charles and the Duke of Edinburgh for the Royal Navy. (Even Chaucer's pilgrim Shipman was a Dartmouth man.) Dartmouth Harbour is lined with 16th-century merchant's houses and half-timbered taverns. **Pannier Market** still sells fresh fruit and vegetables on Friday mornings, but the rest of the week it becomes a cluster of art and craft stalls.

Just a stone's throw up the coast lies **Torbay** ㉗, a conurbation of Torquay, Paignton and Brixham which likes to bill itself as the English Riviera because of its mild climate, lengthy beaches and scattered palms. **Brixham** is the only one that maintains something of its fishing village ambience. The Dutch king William of Orange, son-in-law of James II, landed here in 1688 to begin the Glorious Revolution, which, with the support of parliament, bloodlessly unseated James from the throne and established the constitutional monarchy upon which British government is still based.

West of Torbay (and within walking distance) is **Cockington**, a pretty thatched-cottage village. Three miles (5 km) on is **Marldon**, with a lovely old church, and still one mile farther is **Compton Castle** (open Apr–Oct: Mon, Wed & Thur). This manor house, still the seat of the Gilbert family, was originally built in 1340. Sir Humphrey Gilbert (1539–83) was the founder of Newfoundland, the first British colony to be set up in North America, and the half-brother of Sir Walter Raleigh.

ABOVE: Exeter Cathedral. **BELOW:** changing huts at Torquay.
RIGHT: Mevagissey harbour.

Cathedral city

Exeter ㉘ is many things to many people: a lively university town, the cathedral city of Devon, and still the most important city in the West Country after Plymouth. The immense **cathedral** dominates the skyline and is the finest structure in all Devon, built from the 11th to 14th centuries in Norman Gothic style. The exterior displays a remarkable collection of stone statues, the largest surviving group of 14th-century sculpture in England. The lavish interior is dominated by a striking vaulted ceiling which is carved to resemble the radiating branches of a palm tree. Among the church's treasures are the 14th-century Bishop's Throne and the *Exeter Book of Old English Verse*, compiled between AD 950 and 1000.

Outside the cathedral, much of Exeter pales in comparison. But the **Maritime Museum** (open daily) comprises more than 100 historic vessels displayed in two warehouses and along both banks of the River Exe, ranging from Arabian dhows and Polynesian dugouts to Chinese sampans. A 17th-century building on the quay displays work by Devon's craftsmen, with regular demonstrations. Also interesting are the 11th to 16th-century rooms of **St Nicholas Priory** (open Easter–Oct: Mon–Sat pm), **Rougemont House** and the castle ruins. Exeter is a market town in properous dairy country, and is an ideal place to sample Devon's cream teas. ❑

Wales

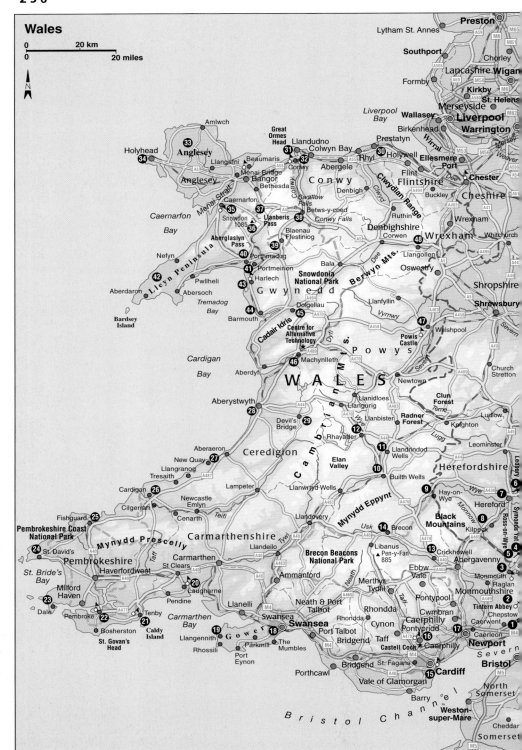

0   20 km
0   20 miles

N

Lytham St. Annes **Preston**
Southport   Chorley
Formby   **Lancashire Wigan**
Kirkby
St. Helens
Merseyside Wallasey **Liverpool**
Birkenhead **Warrington**
Liverpool Bay   Prestatyn
Holyhead Amlwch   Great   Llandudno   Rhyl **Holywell Ellesmere**
34 Ormes **31** Colwyn Bay   **30** **Port**
33 Anglesey Head Llandudno **32** Conwy Abergele **Flint** **Chester**
Langefni Beaumaris **C o n w y** Denbigh **Flintshire** Buckley **Cheshire**
Anglesey Menai Bridge   Swallow Betws-y-coed Ruthin **Wrexham** Whitchurch
Bangor   Falls   Conwy Falls **Denbighshire** **Wrexham**
Caernarfon Bethesda Caernarfon **37** **48**
Bay **35** Snowdon **38** Blaenau Corwen Llangollen *A495*
36 1085 Llanberis Ffestiniog Oswestry
Nefyn   Aberglaslyn Pass Pass **Shropshire**
42 **40** Porthmadog Bala *Berwyn Mts.*
Lleyn Peninsula Pwllheli **41** Portmeirion Llanfyllin **Shrewsbury**
Aberdaron Abersoch **43** Harlech **Snowdonia** *Vyrnwy*
Tremadog   **National Park** **47**
Bardsey *Bay*   **G w y n e d d** *A483* Welshpool
Island   **44** Dolgellau   **Powis**
Barmouth Centre for **Castle**
Cardigan Cadair Idris Alternative **P o w y s** Newtown Church
Bay Technology ★ Stretton
46 Machynlleth **Clun**
Aberdyfi   **W A L E S** **Forest** Ludlow
Aberystwyth Llanidloes *Teme*
28 Llangurig Knighton
Devil's **29** Llanbister **Radnor** Leominster
New Quay Bridge   **Forest**
27 Rhayader **11** Llandrindod **Herefordshire**
Aberaeron Elan **12** Wells
Llangranog **Ceredigion** Valley **10** **Hereford**
Tresaith   Builth Wells **9** Hay-on- **7**
Cardigan **26** Lampeter Llanwrtyd Wells Wye **6**
Cilgerran Newcastle **Black** **8**
Fishguard **25** Emlyn *Usk* **Mountains** Kilpeck **5**
Pembrokeshire Coast Cenarth Llandovery **14** Brecon **13** Crickhowell **4**
National Park *Teifi* Libanus Abergavenny **3**
24 St. David's **Mynydd Prescelly** Llandeilo **Brecon Beacons** Pen-y-Fan Monmouth **2**
St. Bride's Haverfordwest **Carmarthenshire** *Tywi* **National Park** 885 Ebbw **Monmouthshire**
Bay Milford St Clears Ammanford Merthyr Vale Raglan **Tintern Abbey**
23 Haven Carmarthen *Neath* Tydfil Pontypool Caerwent **1**
Dale Pembroke Laugharne **Neath & Port** Rhondda **Caerphilly** Cwmbran Caerleon
22 Pendine Llanelli **Talbot** *Cynon* Pontypridd **17** **Newport**
Bosherston **21** Tenby *Carmarthen* **M4** Swansea Port Talbot **Taff** Castell Coch **16** *Severn*
St. Govan's Caldy *Bay* **19 Gower** **18 Swansea** Bridgend Caerphilly **Bristol**
Head Island Llangennith Parkmill The Mumbles Bridgend St. Fagans **15 Cardiff**
Rhossili Port **Vale of Glamorgan** **North**
Eynon Porthcawl **Somerset**
Barry **Weston-**
B r i s t o l   C h a n n e l **super-Mare** Cheddar
Somerset

THE WYE VALLEY AND SOUTH WALES

This chapter begins by following the Wye Valley into Wales from Chepstow, then crosses to Cardiff and Swansea and continues up to the beautiful Pembroke Coast

Map, page 256

The principality of Wales, the mountainous land which points to the Irish Sea, is little more than 135 miles (216 km) long and at one part less than 35 miles (56 km) wide. The border runs from the mouth of the Dee in Liverpool Bay in the north to the mouth of the Wye on the Severn estuary in the south. It roughly follows the lines of the dyke built to contain the Celts by Offa, the powerful Anglo-Saxon king of Mercia from 757 to 796

This 168-mile (269-km) frontier earthwork provides walkers with an introduction to Wales (a good place to start is Knighton, at about the halfway mark). Some 300 years after Offa, the Normans drove the Welsh further into the hills, establishing the Marches and the powerful Marcher Lordships along the border.

Traditionally, Wales is a melodic land of green hills and welcoming valleys, of Welshcakes, crumbling castles, poets and song. It has sweeping sandy beaches and dramatic coves, sheep for shawls, lamb for the pot and ponies for trekking over hills. It is less populous than England, though its accessibility from southern, central and northern parts of the country make it a popular holiday haunt.

From London the M4, skirting Bristol, crosses the second Severn Bridge (opened in 1996) and plunges immediately into Wales, following the industrial south coast, past Newport, the capital at Cardiff, and Swansea towards the cliffs and beaches of Pembroke. Halfway up the M5 between Bristol and Birmingham, at junction 8, the M50 leads west towards the pretty town of Ross-on-Wye, where it meets the A40 from Gloucester, crosses the border at Monmouth and dives between the Black Mountains and Brecon Beacons before heading back down to the Pembroke coast. Mid Wales can be approached from here or from the M54 which leaves the M6 at junction 10A just north of Birmingham. The A5 takes the road on to Shrewsbury, crosses the border at Welshpool and makes its way down to Aberystwyth, the town of the University of Wales on Cardigan Bay.

PRECEDING PAGES: Porthmadog Railway Station. **BELOW:** Tintern Abbey, Britain's most complete ruined monastery.

The Wye Valley

Commanding the mouth of the Wye, where it empties into the River Severn near the suspension bridge, is **Chepstow ❶**. The castle's Norman keep, set on a high rock, stands out against the limestone cliffs. The old town wall, which in some places is 7 ft (2 metres) thick, was originally designed as an extension of the castle.

Wordsworth did not exaggerate when he wrote his eulogy of **Tintern Abbey ❷**, 6 miles (10 km) north of Chepstow on the A466. It is an extraordinarily lovely spot. Built by Cistercian monks in 1131, the abbey (open Mar–Oct daily) is the most handsome and most

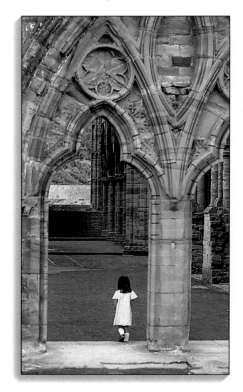

complete of Britain's ruined monasteries. Outside it is The Anchor Inn which was probably the abbey's watergate; an arch dating from the 13th century links it with the slipway.

Some 10 miles (16 km) further north on the A466 is **Monmouth** , a market town at the confluence of the Wye and Monnow rivers. At òne time a Roman settlement, it became home to Breton lords. Henry V, who spent several years of his reign putting down the Welsh revolt of Owain Glyndwr, was born here in 1387. The 11th-century castle has magnificent decorative ceilings. **Raglan Castle** (open daily) is 7 miles (11 km) southwest of Monmouth on the A40. During the Wars of the Roses it was a fortress and it later became the home of the Earls of Worcester. Now mostly a ruin, it retains an elegant hexagonal moated keep.

A few miles east of Monmouth is **Coleford** in the **Forest of Dean**. In the 17th-century Speech House, now a hotel, Verderers, keepers of the forest, conduct their business as they have always done. This former royal hunting ground (40 sq. miles/105 sq. km) is mostly of oak and beech and there are good views from the trails. A **Museum of Forest Life** (open Apr–Oct daily, Nov–Feb Sat & Sun) is sited on the forest's northeast side at **Camp Mill** near **Cinderford**, where there are echoes to the old coal and iron industry.

Just to the north is **Symonds Yat** , a dramatic outcrop 400 ft (122 metres) over a loop in the Wye valley. The river twists along to the east of the A40 for another 8 miles (13 km) to **Ross-on-Wye** , a town whose situation and quaintness ensures it is full of visitors in summer. It centres on an arcaded market hall.

Black-and-white, half-timbered Tudor buildings are a speciality of these Welsh border towns. Above Ross are **Ledbury** , which has a renowned herring-bone patterned Market House, and **Hereford** , 10 miles (16 km) distant.

TIP

Beneath Symonds Yat, the village of Symonds Yat East is a popular centre for outdoors enthusiasts. Canoes and kayaks can be hired for a day or part day for excursions up or down the River Wye.

BELOW: twin heroes in Monmouth: Henry V and early aero-engine maker Henry Rolls.

Hereford **cathedral** was founded by King Offa, and its greatest treasure is the *Mappa Mundi*, one of the first maps of the world, dating from around 1300. The city is also centre of a cider-making industry.

While in Hereford, it's well worth visiting **Kilpeck ❽**, 8 miles (13 km) south-west off the A465 Abergavenny road. It has the most wonderfully ornate Norman church in Britain, built around 1140. The River Wye heads west from Hereford, up towards the Cambrian mountains in the heart of Wales.

Just off the A438, 23 miles (38 km) west of Hereford, is **Hay-on-Wye ❾**. It was transformed into a "book town" in the 1970s when the eccentric Richard Booth, seeing shops and cinemas close as they lost business to bigger towns nearby, converted them into bookstores in a bid to focus tourism. A crafty publicist, he went on to declare Hay-on-Wye an independent country, with himself as monarch, but he hit financial difficulties and other booksellers moved in. Most of the town is in Wales. William de Braose, a Marcher Lord, built a castle here to replace the one burned down by King John. Owain Glyndwr destroyed it in the 15th century, though a gateway, the keep and part of the wall remain.

Beckoning hills

The next major town on the Wye is **Builth Wells ❿**, 20 miles (32 km) west. This is pony trekking, walking and fishing country. The Royal Welsh Show, the principal agricultural event, is held here in July. Seven miles (10 km) to the north is **Llandrindod Wells ⓫**, a spa town which in its Victorian heyday attracted some 80,000 visitors a year. Its wide streets have Georgian houses and a number of hotels. The land here is 1,000 ft (305 metres) above sea level.

To the west, near to the source of the Wye, lies the little tourist town of

Map, page 256

ABOVE: Richard Booth, the man who turned Hay-on-Wye into a book town, and, **BELOW**, part of his legacy.

John, Marquess of Bute, embodied Victorian confidence as mayor of Cariff in 1890. He was the driving force behind the building of the city's docks.

BELOW: Cardiff Castle, proud as a peacock.

the mountains that bear its name, is an old market town of narrow streets at the confluence of the Usk and the Honddu. Its cathedral has only been such since 1923, though a church of some kind has occupied the site since the 12th century. Much of the present building was restored in the 19th-century. The **Brecon Beacons National Park Information Centre** (tel: 01874-624437) in the town and the **Mountain Centre**, off the A470 at **Libanus** 4 miles (6 km) south of Brecon, provide information on climbing, pony trekking and reservoir sailing.

King coal

Between the mountains and the industrial south coast run the valleys whose names – Merthyr, Ebbw Vale, Rhondda, Neath – were once synonymous with mining, making **Cardiff ⓯** the world's greatest coal port. But by the beginning of the 1990s only a handful of deep mines remained. Cardiff is the capital of Wales, with a population of 280,000. **Cardiff Castle** (open daily) brings together all the strands of the city's history. The outer walls contain Roman stonework and the Norman keep, built by Robert Fitzhamon at the end of the 11th century, still stands tall. At the height of Cardiff's prosperity, between 1867 and 1872, the Marquis of Bute (responsible for building much of the docks) added to the castle, with a clock tower and many elaborate banqueting halls. The Marquis was also responsible for **Castell Coch** (Red Castle), a folly-cum-hunting lodge above the River Taff 5 miles (8 km) north of the city

The **National Museum of Wales** (open Tues–Sun) has much evidence of the principality's history and its **Art Gallery** has an Impressionist collection plus works from both English and Welsh painters. But for those who really want to know about Wales **St Fagan's Museum of Welsh Life** (open daily), 4 miles (6

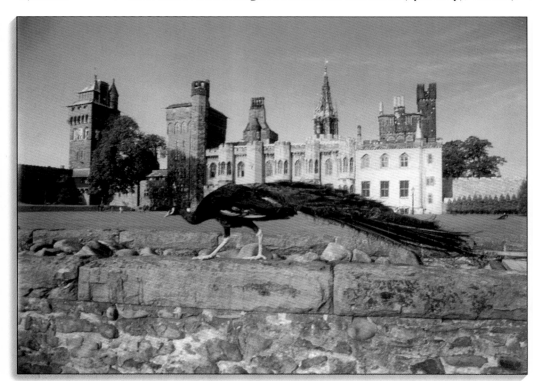

Map, page 256

km) west of the city, is a must. Set around the Tudor **St Fagan's Castle**, it has brought together buildings of interest from all over the country – cottages, a toll gate, chapel, cock pit – and there are demonstrations by rural craftspeople.

Europe's largest urban renewal scheme at **Cardiff Bay** is reuniting the city with its docks and coastline. Work is in progress to construct a barrage which will create a new basin in the dock area by raising the water level. The scheme can be explored in full at the futuristic **Cardiff Bay Visitor Centre** (open from 9.30 am or 10.30 am on weekends and public holidays).

The Bay already houses a Norwegian stave church, originally built to serve the religious needs of the world's sailors, and **Techniquest** (open Mon–Sat), Britain's largest hands-on science exhibition centre. It offers nearly 200 experiments, which enable you to make yourself appear to disappear, play a harp with no strings, design a tree, create flight and make a painting without paint. It also has a planetarium, science theatre, laboratory and library.

Following the demise of the Cardiff Opera House project, it is now proposed that the Bay should be the site for the Wales Millennium Arts and Entertainment Centre. The centre will contain a theatre for musicals, opera and dance, Waterfront Museum and 3-D Imax cinema.

Caerphilly 🔟, 5 miles (8 km) north of Cardiff, is where the famous white cheese comes from and it also has the remains of one of Britain's most extensive castles, covering 30 acres (12 hectares). To the east of Cardiff is the industrial town of **Newport** 🔟 on the mouth of the Usk where the exceptional tide led to the bridges being built high in the air. The main A48, more attractive than the M4, here follows the old Roman road towards Chepstow, arriving, after 10 miles (16 km) at the Roman walled town of Venta Silurum, near **Caerwent**. Some of its remains are among the important collection in the Newport **archaeology museum**, while just outside the town, up the Usk Valley at **Caerleon** is the remains of a fortress, Isca Silurum, and the most complete surviving Roman amphitheatre in Britain.

As a capital city, Cardiff is a youngster when compared with either London or Edinburgh. It was designated a capital only in the 1950s.

The Gower Peninsula

The second largest city in Wales is **Swansea** 🔟, 40 miles (64 km) west of Cardiff, on the mouth of the Tawe, which gives it its Welsh name, Abertawe. It has been scarred by World War II bombs and subsequent industrialisation, and Dylan Thomas (1914–53), Wales's most famous poet, called it "an ugly, lovely town... jerry villa'd and smug suburbaned by the site of a long and splendid curving shore". He was born here at 5 Cwmdonkin Drive, close to Uplands. The city's main attraction is its regular **market**, the largest in Wales, where such traditional local food as cockles and laverbread (a delicacy made with seaweed and eaten fried with bacon) can be bought.

On the southern edge of Swansea Bay is **The Mumbles** where there are good boating and water skiing facilities. The town claims to have inaugurated the world's first passenger-carrying railway when, in 1807, it ran a horse-drawn tramway into Swansea.

The Mumbles is the start of the **Gower peninsula**, a small finger of land 20 miles by 5 (32 by 8 km) which juts out into Carmarthen Bay. This area has some of

BELOW: fairground organ at St Fagan's Folk Museum.

*Dylan Thomas.
(1914–53) supported
his poetry with
journalism, radio
work and film making.
His drinking binges
were legendary, and
one preceded his
death in New York.*

BELOW: Mumbles
Head, start of the
Gower Peninsula.

Wales's best scenery and it contrasts starkly with industrial Swansea. There are good surfing beaches on its southern coast, much of which is given over to a nature reserve. Five miles (8 km) west of The Mumbles on the A4118 is **Parkmill** where sand dunes are reputed to have buried two churches and are threatening to do the same to the ruins of **Pennard Castle**. At the west end of the peninsula is the gracious 3-mile (5-km) sweep of **Rhosilli beach** and above it **Llangennith** ⑲ where traces of antiquity are sited on Atlantic-facing slopes. In the 6th century St Cenydd built a monastery here and Norman monks adopted it as their home 600 years later. **Llanmadoc Hill**, just north of Llangennith, is topped by a hill fort – the best viewpoint at this end of the peninsula.

On the mainland behind the peninsula, the River Tywi forces the road inland to **Carmarthen** and, 9 miles (15 km) beyond, skirts the River Taf on which **Laugharne** ⑳ lies. Anyone who has read or heard *Under Milk Wood*, his memorable play, may feel themselves to be in familiar territory, though Dylan Thomas, who lived here from 1949, probably based his play on New Quay on the Cardigan Bay coast. The young, drunken, bad-boy, poet-angel has left his mark on this cockle-fishing village. The boat-house on the "heron-priested shore" where he lived and worked is now a museum. His friend Richard Hughes (1900–76), the author of *A High Wind in Jamaica*, lived in the castle nearby.

The Pembroke Coast

Pembrokeshire, in the extreme southwest of Wales, has long been called "Little England beyond Wales" because of the numbers of English who have settled there. It is renowned for its rugged coastline. The **Pembrokeshire Coast National Park** stretches from Amroth in Carmarthen Bay around St David's

Head and up to Cardigan in Cardigan Bay, taking in 160 miles (260 km) of spectacular coastal scenery.

Tenby ㉑ is the first major resort on this coast. In Welsh the town is **Dinbychy-pysgod** ("Tenby, little fort of the fished") and it has retained its town walls and the remains of a castle. Its 15th-century prosperity shows in the **Tudor Merchant's Hall** (tel: 01834-842279). Boats leave here for **Caldy Island**, 2½ miles (4 km) offshore, where Cistercian monks produce scent from flowers.

The coast around **St Govan's Head**, 12 miles (20 km) west of Tenby, is a popular section of the park. Just inland is **Bosherston**, famous for its waterlily ponds and mere from which, some believe, came King Arthur's sword, Excalibur (Merlin, the Welsh wizard of Arthur's court, is said to have originally come from Carmarthen). **Pembroke** ㉒ is a few miles north at the head of an estuary in the large natural harbour of **Milford Haven**, a major oil terminal. There are many boating facilities in the area, particularly around **Dale** ㉓.

Pembroke is dominated by its inspiring castle (open daily), birthplace of the wise and thrifty Henry VII, England's first Tudor monarch. It has a fine circular stone keep, which was harder to undermine than the old square towers. Beneath the Great Hall is a cave, called The Wogan, leading to the harbour.

St David's and Fishguard

A toll bridge leads over Milford Haven, otherwise the road around the valley via the market town of **Haverfordwest** is circuitous. The coast west of here is drawn in to sandy **St Bride's Bay** with St Ann's Head and the bird sanctuary islands of Skomer and Skokholm in the south, and Ramsey Island and St David's Head, Wales's western extremity, in the north.

Map, page 256

TIP

The best way of seeing the coast is to follow the Pembrokeshire Coast Path. It provides dramatic views of the sea cliffs and endless opportunities for watching gannets, fulmars, puffins, cormorants and other wildlife which thrives in the region.

BELOW: Dylan Thomas's study in Laugharne.

ABOVE: High summer on Anglesey.

way of life and the small, lime-washed cottages with slurried roofs. A warning of the island's eccentricities comes just after crossing the Straits when the A5 passes the village of **Llanfairpwllgwyngyllgogerychwyrndrobwllllantysili- ogogogoch**; its name is an accurate description of the place: "St Mary's Church by the white aspens over the whirlpool and St Tysilio's Church by the red cave".

Beaumaris, with its fine moated castle and the nearby Penmon Priory, is towards the eastern end of the island, while **Caernarfon** ❸❺, the largest town in the area, is at the opposite end of the straits on the mainland. With its city walls and towers intact, Caernarfon is a fine resort, popular with yachtsmen. Its strategic position meant it was an important settlement long before the present castle was built. The Romans arrived in AD 78 and built a fortress, Segontium; some excavated remains can be seen. Begun in 1283, the **Castle** (open Mar–Oct daily) was the largest of Edward I's network of fortifications. The exterior walls and three towers remain intact and are hugely impressive, though most of the interior has been lawned. Queen's Tower houses the fascinating **Regimental Museum** of the Royal Welsh Fusiliers.

Mountain scenery

BELOW: Snowdon sunset at Capel Curig.

Immediately behind these coastal resorts is Eryri, the Place of Eagles. This is **Snowdonia**, Wales's most mountainous region. Fourteen summits are above 3,000 ft (1,000 metres) and **Snowdon** ❸❻ itself, some 12 miles (19 km) as the eagle flies east of Caernarfon, is the highest at 3,560 ft (1,085 metres). Sculpted by glacial activity, these mountains have been a playground for generations of climbers and walkers. Rolling green foothills rise into sheer crags, and stone sheepfolds cling impossibly to high slopes. Simply driving around Snowdonia

is an exhilarating experience. Roads such as the A4086 through the sheer-sided Llanberis Pass to the east of Caernarfon, the A5 through the stunning **Ogwen Valley** between Capel Curig and Bethesda, and the A498 south of Capel Curig via the **Pass of Aberglaslyn** to Porthmadog on the coast, offer breathtaking views of the mountain scenery, which is studded with brilliant lakes. A mile (1.6 km) north of the Pass of Aberglaslyn is **Beddgelert**, a tiny, compact village nestled in the middle of beautiful scenery. The name means "the grave of Gelert". According to legend, Gelert was a loyal dog mistakenly killed by Prince Llewellyn after it had rescued his son from a wolf.

Purists insist that, like the poet William Wordsworth, visitors should climb Snowdon in order to see the dawn. The easiest path to the summit starts on its northern side at **Llanberis** ❸ and is 3½ miles (5.5 km) long. But the most popular paths are the **Miners' Track** and the **Pig Track**, both of which start at the Pen-y-Pass car park at the top of the Llanberis Pass.

Betws-y-coed ❸, situated at the junction of the A5 and the A470 and at the meeting point of three valleys, Lledr, Llugwy and Conwy, is another popular centre for outdoor enthusiasts. In the Wybrnant valley 3½ miles (5 km) southwest, is a small cottage called **Ty Mawr Wybrnant** (open Mar–Sept Thur–Sun pm, Oct–Nov Thur, Fri, & Sun pm), the birthplace of Bishop William Morgan (1545–1604) who first translated the Bible into Welsh. The National Trust runs nature trails from here in summer. Two miles (3 km) west of Betws-y-coed on the A5 towards Capel Curig are the famous **Swallow Falls**.

Snowdonia is full of stupendous natural scenery, but man has also left his mark on the area. Slate quarrying was once the most important industry of northwest Wales, and the huge heaps of slate spoil which overshadow places like Llanberis and Bethesda, and, most famously, **Blaenau Ffestiniog** ❸ on the A470 to the east, are its enduring legacy. Though the mountainsides are scarred, they do become eerily beautiful when wetted by the rain which falls so plentifully here. The legacy of slate has also given rise to some of the region's best tourist attractions, including the **Welsh Slate Museum** at Llanberis (open daily), where the sight of workmen splitting and dressing slate is guaranteed to make any idle onlooker feel clumsy; and, in Blaenau Ffestiniog, the **Llechwedd Slate Caverns** (open daily), where visitors can take a tour on Britain's deepest underground railway.

From Blaenau Ffestiniog, slate was transported by rail to **Porthmadog** ❹. Porthmadog was the creation of William Maddocks (1773–1828), a local mill owner and parliamentarian. He constructed the mile-long embankment, called the Cob, across the river mouth which reclaimed 7,000 acres (2,800 hectares) and gave rise to the lovely town. In its industrial heyday, slate was shipped from the quaysides here to all over the world. The old **Ffestiniog Narrow Gauge Railway** (Mar–Oct, tel: 01766-512340) was rescued from oblivion in 1954 and is today a must for visitors. The 13½-mile (22-km) journey from Porthmadog to Blaenau Ffestiniog up the beautiful the Vale of Ffestiniog provides spectacular views of the mountains from the carriage windows.

The architect Sir Clough William Ellis had an even more vivid imagination than Maddocks when, in 1926,

Map, page 256

TIP

Less energetic visitors can get to the summit of Snowdon on the Snowdon Mountain Railway, a rack railway which starts in Llanberis.

BELOW: Ffestiniog Railway driver at Porthmadog.

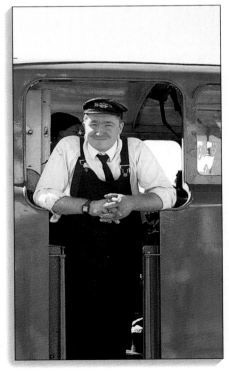

he decided to build an Italianate village beside Porthmadog in the Dwyryd estuary. This elaborate folly **Portmeirion** ❹ (open daily), incorporates a hotel and its surreal setting was used as the backdrop for Patrick McGoohan's influential TV series *The Prisoner*.

Wales is sometimes depicted as an old lady throwing a ball out to sea. Her head is Anglesey, her leg Pembroke and the **Lleyn Peninsula** ❹ is her arm (with Porthmadog in her armpit, so to speak). Caernarfon lies on her shoulder and from **Aberdaron**, at the tip of the peninsula, **Bardsley Island**, her ball, can be reached. In the 7th century monks came to settle on the island. It is said that 20,000 saints are buried here; certainly the island feels like a holy place.

Around the peninsula are tiny coastal harbours such as **Porth Dinllaen** and **Nefyn**. Travelling north of Nefyn on the B4417, the 1,850-ft (560-metre) mountain **Yr Eifl** appears large on the left. On its eastern peak is the site of **Tre'r Ceiri**, one of the oldest Iron-Age forts in Britain. Nearer to Porthmadog, the pleasant resort of **Criccieth** is dominated by its **castle** (open daily), which has been a ruin since it was besieged by Owain Glyndwr in the early 15th century.

Men of Harlech

At the other side of Tremadog Bay lies **Harlech** ❹, the perfect place from which to view the Lleyn Peninsula and Snowdonia in one breathtaking gaze. The castle (open Mar–Oct, daily), perched on a promontory looking out to sea, fell to Owain Glyndwr in 1404, though it was recaptured by the English within five years and went on to feature in the Wars of the Roses, when the siege (and subsequent surrender) by the Lancastrian garrison inspired the now famous marching song *Men of Harlech*.

Many millions of people know Portmeirion as the village where "No. 6" was kept in Patrick McGoohan's cult television series from the 1960s, "The Prisoner".

BELOW:
Harlech Castle.

CASTLES

There are two distinct kinds of castle in North Wales: "native" structures and those built by Edward I following his successful campaigns against the Welsh in the late 13th century. Those in the former category, such as Powis and Criccieth, were built by Llywellyn the Great (d.1240), who as Prince of Gwynedd devoted his life to securing the territorial integrity of Wales. His grandson, Llywellyn the Last, sought to establish his own authority as Prince of Wales, but his refusal to pay homage to Edward I resulted in the invasion that put an end to any hopes of independence.

The last of the Welsh castles to fall was Castell y Bere on the western flanks of Cadair Idris, in 1283. Long since abandoned to the elements, the ruins lack the grandeur of other castles in Wales, but remain today one of the most poignant reminders of Welsh resistance, made all the more so by the magnificent mountain scenery in which they lie.

Edward's own castles at Conwy, Beaumaris, Caernarfon and Harlech, supported by fortified town walls, are fine examples of medieval military architecture. Their theatrical siting to guard strategic points against Welsh resistance would have intimidated any enemy. Even so, all except Caernarfon were taken, if only briefly, by the Welsh rebel Owain Glyndwr's uprising at the start of the 15th century.

Eleven miles (18 km) south of Harlech is the holiday resort of **Barmouth ㊹**, attractively built up against towering cliffs and offering superb views of **Cadair Idris** at the other side of the estuary. From here the road turns inland up the Mawddach Valley to **Dolgellau ㊺**, an excellent base for exploring the Cadair Idris range. It's the epitome of a sturdy, close-knit Welsh community.

South of Dolgellau on the A487, 3 miles (5 km) north of Machynlleth, is the much-praised **Centre for Alternative Technology** (open daily), whose numerous outdoor displays highlight the advantages of an environmentally friendly approach to modern living. **Machynlleth ㊻** itself is a pleasant market town at the southern edge of the Snowdonia National Park. The principal attraction here, on Aberystwyth Road, is **Celtica** (open daily), an audio-visual exhibition which vividly brings to life the sights and sounds of Wales's Celtic past.

From Dolgellau, it's a 37-mile (60-km) drive east to **Welshpool ㊼**, county town of Powys. There are unexpected red-brick Georgian houses here, but there are also ancient, timbered, lopsided hotels and pubs. A mile southwest is **Powis Castle** (open Apr–Oct: Wed–Sun 12–4pm; also open bank hol. Mon, and Tues in June–Aug), built by Welsh princes around 1300. The terraced gardens, created between 1688 and 1722, are arguably the most dramatic in the country.

Thirty miles (48 km) to the north of Welshpool is **Llangollen ㊽**, home of the **International Musical Eisteddfod** and regarded as the centre of Welsh culture and music. Its two most famous residents were eccentric gossips, Lady Eleanor Butler and the Hon Sarah Ponsonby, the "Ladies of Llangollen", who from 1780 lived at **Plas Newydd** cottage (open Mar–Sept pm except Sat, Oct–Nov Fri & Sun pm) at the end of Castle Street and entertained anyone passing through what is now the A5 road to Dublin via the Holyhead ferry. ❑

Map, page 256

BELOW: Eisteddfod ceremonial.

Formed in Liverpool in 1960, the Beatles learned their trade through gruelling engagements at the city's Cavern Club and at venues in Hamburg. They shot to fame under the management of local record shop owner Brian Epstein, signing a recording contract and producing such records as She Loves You and Love Me Do.

BELOW: the Beatles remembered in Liverpool.

and '80s. But some rejuvenation has taken place, notably in the **Albert Dock**. The warehousing area has become a complex of small shops and museums, including the **Tate Gallery Liverpool** (open Tues–Sun) and **The Beatles Story**, an "experience" of the city's illustrious sons which is naturally open "eight days a week" and features the Yellow Submarine and a stroll down Penny Lane. The **Merseyside Maritime Museum** (open daily, also in Albert Dock) incorporates a Customs and Excise museum with contraband such as fake Rolex watches and lets you try your hand at being a customs officer.

The city's architecture is on a grand scale and includes the imposing 295-ft (90-metre) **Royal Liver Building** by the docks, and two new churches – the circular **Roman Catholic Cathedral**, designed by Sir Edwin Lutyens and Sir Frederick W. Gibberd, consecrated in 1967, and the **Anglican Cathedral**, Britain's largest, by Giles Gilbert Scott, completed in 1978. The **Liverpool Museum** and the **Walker Art Gallery** (both in William Brown Street, and open Mon–Sat, and Sun pm; free), are worth a visit.

There is also a good Pre-Raphaelite collection at the **Lady Lever Art Gallery** (Mon–Sat and Sun pm). This is an excuse to take the much sung-about ferry across the Mersey to the Wirrall peninsula which protrudes between this estuary and that of the Dee to the south. Alternatively, you can drive through the Mersey Tunnel to emerge on the Wirrall at Birkenhead. The gallery is nearby in **Port Sunlight**, a model workers' village founded by Lord Leverhulme (1851–1928) for his soap empire. From the Wirrall there are good views across the Dee estuary to the enticing hills of North Wales.

North of Liverpool are Lancashire's sandy resorts of **Southport**, **Lytham St Anne's** and **Blackpool** ❹, Britain's most popular seaside resort. Up to 6 million

FOUR LADS WHO SHOOK THE WORLD

Merseyside and Shropshire

people come here each year, their numbers swelled by trades union and political party conferences. The promenade, all 7 miles (11 km) of it, centred on a 518-ft (160-metre) Eiffel-style tower, is lit up in the autumn and these "illuminations" are an event in themselves.

In fact **Morecambe**, a resort in the bay of the same name to the north, claims to have started this idea as a way of extending its summer season. The beaches all down this coast are wide and long, and sand yachting is popular at the more up-market resort of Lytham St Anne's.

Border towns

South of Liverpool, at the head of the Wirrall peninsula and at the end of the 40-mile (64-km) M56 from Manchester, is **Chester ❺**, the most northerly and the most exciting of the timbered Tudor towns of the Welsh Marches, the hilly country bordering Wales. Its particular architectural character can be seen by walking down Eastgate, Watergate or Bridge Street with their **Rows**, double tiers of shops and covered walkways, one on top of the other. The oldest dates from 1486, and most of them were built in the following century.

In Roman times Chester was an important stronghold called Deva and part of an **amphitheatre** can be seen just outside the city walls by St John's Street. The **Grosvenor Museum** (Mon–Sat and Sun pm) records the Roman legacy with models of the fortress city. Under the Normans Chester was a near-independent state governed by a succession of earls. The tidal estuary of the Dee allowed the city to flourish as a port up until the 15th century when it began to silt up; after that, shipping was transferred to the large natural port of Liverpool.

The 2-mile (3-km) round trip of the **city walls** helps orientation. This is one of

Map, page 278

TIP

Be sure to try some Morecambe Bay shrimps, gathered in nets taken across the sandy beaches by horse and cart.

BELOW: Chester, a border town with a distinctive style.

the few British cities with its medieval walls still intact, those on the north and east sides following the original Roman plan. The **Cathedral**, off St Werburg Street, was a Benedictine Abbey until Henry VIII's Dissolution of the Monasteries. Unusually squat, it has a short nave and a massive south transept featuring a grand, Victorian stained-glass window. Two miles (4 km) north of the city is **Chester Zoo** (open daily), the largest outside London.

It is worth making a special expedition to **Little Moreton Hall ⑥** (late Mar–Oct: Wed–Sun pm, and public holiday Mon; Nov–Dec: Sat & Sun pm; tel: 01260-272 018), due east of Chester via the A54 and A34. The ornately decorated, half-timbered, moated manor house was built in 1450–1580.

Just a few miles further south lies **Stoke-on-Trent ⑦**, main town of The Potteries, the region that has supplied Britain with its finest china since the 17th century. Royal Doulton, Royal Grafton, Coalport, Minton, Spode … all the well-known porcelain and china factories are here and may be visited. A good starting point is the **Potteries Centre** by the station, where the products of two dozen local manufacturers are on display. At Barlaston, just off the A34 to the south of Stoke, is the Wedgewood Visitor Centre (open daily), with a museum, a shop and demonstrations by potters and decorators.

Engineers, scientists and poets

From Stoke, head south on the M6 and then west on the A518 to **Telford ⑧**, a new town named after the 18th-century engineer Thomas Telford. Begun only in the 1960s, the ambitious project takes in **Coalbrookdale**, where coke was first used to smelt iron, and **Ironbridge** on the River Severn, where the world's first iron bridge was built by Telford in 1773. The **Ironbridge Gorge Museum** (*see*

ABOVE:
Chester Town Hall.
BELOW: Shrewsbury
Cathedral.

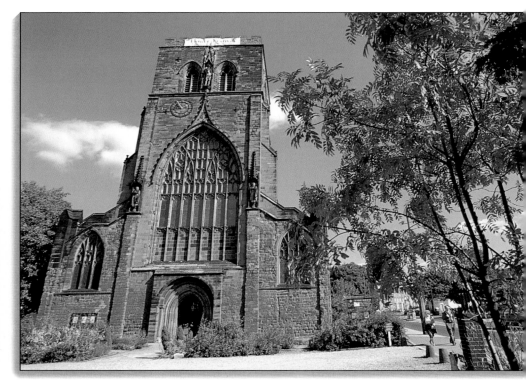

page 282), open all year, has Abraham Darby's original coke furnace from 1709, as well as warehouses and other industrial heritage.

Shrewsbury ❾, home of the scientist Charles Darwin (1809–82) and the World War I poet Wilfred Owen, is 12 miles (20 km) due west of Telford. The county town of Shropshire is beautifully situated on a meander in the River Severn, crossed by the English bridge and the Welsh bridge, it has houses dating back to the 15th century, plus fine parks and gardens. The pink sandstone **castle**, near the station, was converted into a house by Telford and now incorporates the **Shropshire Regimental Museum** (open Tues–Sat).

Shrewsbury is also the home of the poet A.E. Housman (1859–1936) who eulogised the dreamy slopes of this agricultural land in *A Shropshire Lad*. These lands of the Marcher lords, also captured vividly in the novels of Raymond Williams (1921–88), have been the scene of much bloodshed and have a flavour unlike anywhere else in Wales. It was in this area that the native culture mingled most thoroughly with that of the Roman and Norman invaders, giving rise to a fascinating Celtic and foreign mix. All down the border, the hills roll softly towards England and can be explored by paths, bridleways and woodland trails.

Perhaps the loveliest of these border towns is **Ludlow** ❿, where Housman's ashes lie. The centre of the town is remarkably consistent architecturally, with 13th-century taverns and Tudor market buildings. It was at **Ludlow castle**, the former seat of the presidents of the council of the Marches, that John Milton's masque *Comus* was first performed in 1634. Sixteen miles (25 km) west of Ludlow is **Knighton** ⓫, the centre for exploring Offa's Dyke. This 8th-century earthwork, built by the Saxon King Offa to protect England from Welsh marauders, now carries a long-distance footpath. ❏

Map, page 278

Above: shopfronts in Shrewsbury.
Below: Ludlow Castle.

THE IRONBRIDGE GORGE AND COALBROOKDALE

During the 18th century, the Ironbridge Gorge was the scene of some remarkable innovations which helped drive forward the Industrial Revolution

Situated on the River Severn in the heart of Shropshire, the Ironbridge Gorge is named after the world's first ever cast-iron bridge, constructed over the river in 1779. Before then, the whole area had been known as Coalbrookdale. Rich in natural resources and benefitting from river transport, this had been a centre of mining and ironworking since the time of Henry VIII. But by the end of the 17th century, the wood used to make the charcoal to fuel the simple bloomery furnaces was becoming scarce, and a cheap and plentiful alternative was needed.

ABRAHAM DARBY AND HIS LEGACY

The problem was solved by Abraham Darby, a Bristol brassmaker, who in 1709 used a Coalbrookdale furnace to pioneer the smelting of iron with coke made from local coal. This process allowed him to produce cheap but high-quality cast-iron pots on a large scale, and Coalbrookdale rapidly became the busiest industrial centre in the world.

Developments that continued under Darby's heirs included the production of cast-iron cylinders made for for steam engines (1722); the first iron railway wheels cast for use on a colliery line (1729); the first iron rails (1767); and of course the famous bridge. With the advent of canals, and later railways, iron making at Coalbrookdale was superseded by other industrial areas, but the Darby company remained. There were also other thriving industries in the gorge, including the Coalport china works and the tile works at Jackfield. Today, they are all part of the Ironbridge Gorge Museum.

△ **WONDER OF THE AGE**
Begun in 1779 by Abraham Darby III, the Iron Bridge was designed by Thomas Farnolls Pritchard, a Shrewsbury joiner turned architect. The giant ribs for the structure were cast in open sand and raised with the aid of scaffolding. Intriguingly, the joints in the ironwork are based on traditional carpentry methods, including dovetails, wedges, mortises and tenons.

◁ **BLISTS HILL FURNACES**
The Bedlam furnaces (right) were replaced in the mid-19▮ century by the furnaces at nearby Blists Hill. Already an▮ established mining centre in the area, Blists Hill was opened up to expansion at th▮ end of the 18th century by th▮ arrival of the Shropshire can▮ and the subsequent construction of William Reynold's ingenious Hay Inclined Plane, which linked the canal to the transport system of the River Severn.

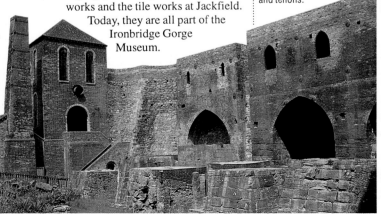

▽ BLAST FROM THE PAST

In early blast furnaces, air was supplied by water-driven bellows. The advent of the steam engine to drive enormous blowing cylinders (such as this one in the Blists Hill blast furnaces) meant that a furnace could be provided with more air and a greater output could be achieved.

◁ IRONBRIDGE TOWN

The completion of the Iron Bridge spawned the rapid development of the town on the north bank of the Severn. Schemes included the Tontine Hotel, built to cater for the numerous visitors from all over the world. Having been advertised in the 1870s as "The Brighton of the Midlands", in the 20th century Ironbridge became neglected, but almost every house has now been restored.

△ FINE CHINA

The Coalport China Museum occupies part of the old china works established by William Reynolds in 1793; for over a century it was one of the most successful works in the world.

◁ BEDLAM ON THE SEVERN

"Coalbrookdale by Night" by Philip de Loutherbourg (1801) symbolises the awesome qualities of the Industrial Revolution. It shows the Bedlam furnaces by the River Severn.

BLISTS HILL OPEN AIR MUSEUM

Together with the Iron Bridge itself and the excellent Iron Museum on the site of the Darbys' Coalbrookdale ironworks, the principal attraction of the Iron Bridge Gorge is the Blists Hill Open Air Museum. Until the 1860s, Blists Hill was a thriving industrial site, but then decline set in, and by 1960 it was completely abandoned.

Acquired by the Ironbridge Gorge Museum Trust, it was opened as an open air museum in 1973. The original furnaces, foundry and brick and tile works are part of this working museum, but around them a "Victorian Town" has been created.

Designed to show a variety of trades dating from the late 19th century, most of the buildings have been dismantled from elsewhere and rebuilt. Staffed by costumed demonstrators, they include a tinsmith, a cobbler, a printer, a leather workshop (pictured above), a carpenter, a decorative plasterer and a candlemaker.

Visitors can change money into pre-decimal currency at the Lloyds Bank and spend it at the local pub with its sawdusted floor, at the bakery with its fine pies and pasties, or even at the chemist's shop.

At the end of the site are the Squatters Cottages which show the effects of the Industrial Revolution on the lives of working people.

ABOVE: the Pavilion
Gardens, Buxton.
BELOW: family
outing in a Peak
District village.

Each Shrove Tuesday, Ashbourne hosts a no-holds-barred football match in which up to 300 players a side try to score goals by touching the walls of Sturston Mill and Clifton Mill, 3 miles (5 km) apart.

Ashbourne is also a convenient place to stay for families visiting **Alton Towers ❸**, a theme park with some notoriously hair-raising rides (open Mar–Nov: daily; tel: 01538-702 200).

From Ashbourne, take the A515 north into the Park, taking the left turn down the quiet lane that twists through **Dovedale**, a gentle limestone glen dubbed "little Switzerland". Sheep densely populate these dales and sheepdog trials are popular summer distractions. Black-and-white collie dogs, obeying a farmer's every whistle, round up the black-faced sheep, expertly guiding them into pens.

A few miles further along the A515 – or, for the adventurous, after a delightful mystery tour through unclassified country lanes – **Buxton ❹** is a resort whose thermal springs made it a kind of English Lourdes in medieval times. Today it markets the product of its nine springs by claiming that it doesn't have the disagreeable smell and taste of some spa waters. You can swim in an indoor spa-water pool at the **Pavilion Gardens**.

Between 1570 and 1583, Mary, Queen of Scots sought treatment in Buxton for her rheumatism, a complaint doubtless aggravated by her imprisonment in a succession of draughty establishments. The ravine of the **Wye** provides a beautiful limestone route for walkers, but the town itself never succeeded in outshining Bath, as the fifth Duke of Devonshire intended when, at the end of the 18th century, he planned and built his grand crescent.

Chapel-en-le-Frith ❺, on the A625, is a small market town. "Frith" means "forest," but little of that is left today. Nearby, north of the A625, is **Edale**, a

tidy village huddling at the foot of the peat-covered **Kinder Scout** peak, the challenging start of the Pennine Way.

Further along the A625, **Castleton** ❻ is a centre for subterranean exploration. Situated at the foot of **Winnats Pass**, **Speedwell Cavern** (all caverns open daily) is so high that rockets have gone up 450 ft (138 metres) without hitting the roof. The **Treak Cliff Cavern** has the most spectacular formations and is one of the few sources of the semi-precious Blue John stone. The blackened ceiling in the entrance to the **Peak Cavern** dates from the time when it was occupied by a community of rope-makers. High above the village, **Peveril Castle** (open daily) was the setting for Sir Walter Scott's *Peveril of the Peak*.

Hathersage ❼, on the same road, is the hillside village that inspired "Morton" in Charlotte Brontë's *Jane Eyre*. Little John, the outsized lieutenant of the outlaw Robin Hood, is a native and he is supposed to be buried in a 14-ft (5-metre) grave in the churchyard.

To the north of Hathersage is **Stanage Edge**, the longest of the Peak's gritstone edges and a playground for climbers and hang-gliders. A diversion south along the B6001 leads to **Eyam** (pronounced *Eem*), a pretty village remarkable for the action of its villagers in 1665. Finding that plague germs had arrived in a box of cloth sent from London to the local tailor, they completely sealed off the village to confine the disease; within a year, three-quarters of the 350 inhabitants were dead.

Palladian palace

Near Baslow, off the A619, is **Chatsworth House** ❽, "the Palace of the Peak", a vast Palladian mansion built between 1687 and 1707 and set in a spacious deer

see map opposite

The Treak Cliff Cavern is one of the few sources of the semi-precious Blue John stone, which is sold locally.

BELOW: in the gardens of Chatsworth.

ABOVE: Bakewell puddings.

Sheffield's fame as a blade-making town reaches back to Chaucer and the Canterbury Tales, *in which a miller carried a Sheffield knife in his stocking.*

park with gardens landscaped by "Capability" Brown (open mid Mar–Oct: daily; tel: 01246-58 22 04). It houses priceless collections of books and furniture, as well as fine paintings by Rembrandt and Reynolds. Chatsworth boosts business by staging an angling fair, a brass band festival, show-jumping and horse trials. Half-a-million people visit it every year; the current duchess calls it "a town".

Heading back south, the A6 trunk road passes through **Bakewell** ❾, a stone-built agricultural town with two medieval bridges over the Wye. Two miles (4 km) to the southeast, **Haddon Hall** (open Apr–Sept: daily; closed Sun July–Aug; tel: 01629-812 855) is one of Britain's best preserved and most atmospheric old houses, dating in parts from the 12th century. Nikolaus Pevsner, chronicler of architectural excellence, called it "a large, safe, grey, lovable house of knights and their ladies".

Cutlery and crockery

Yorkshire's largest city, **Sheffield** ❿, lies to the east of the Peak District. Sheffield prospered at the foot of the Pennines, using the cascading water to drive grindstones manufactured from their millstone grit. Efforts during the 20th century to tame the furnaces have worked: the depth of dust on one nearby golf course measures less than 1 percent of what it did 30 years ago, and it now claims to be the cleanest industrial city in the world. But there were also many factory closures during the 1970s and '80s: Sheffield steel may still be best but Korean cutlery costs less.

Today's shopping centre is emphatically modern, neat suburbs cling to steep gradients, and the **Crucible Theatre** has a national reputation. The **Sheffield City Museum** (open Wed–Sun; free) on Glossop Road has many of the most

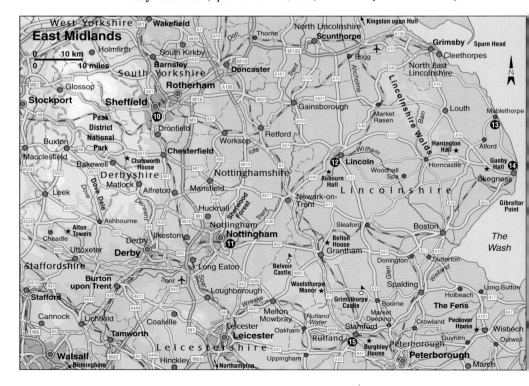

Map, pages 288 & 290

important archaeological finds in the Peak District as well as natural history exhibits, while the adjoining **Mappin Art Gallery** has a fine collection of the work of local artists. Out to the west on Abbeydale Road South is the **Abbey-dale Industrial Hamlet** (closed Mon except public holidays), a living museum of Sheffield's industrial past, where craftsmen regularly come to show their traditional skills. Silverware is on show in the appropriate setting of the 17th-century **Cutlers' Hall** opposite the **Cathedral**.

Derby and Nottingham to the southeast are also coal mining areas. **Nottingham** ⓫ is where D.H. Lawrence (1885–1930) grew up and where the sheriff used to be continually outwitted by the legendary outlaw Robin Hood. The sheriff's castle is no longer intact, but a statue of *Robin* is by the old walls and **The Tales of Robin Hood** (open daily) whisks you back to the middle ages to smell, see and browse through the outlaw's era.

East of Sheffield, Lincolnshire has several important sights worth seeking out. Around 125 miles (200 km) away on the A57, **Lincoln** ⓬ itself is a Roman city, with some well-preserved medieval buildings which attest to the wealth it derived from a flourishing wool trade with Europe. The Cathedral, in a mixture of Norman and Gothic styles, is one of Britain's best.

A similar distance again will take you to the North Sea coast, where there are a number of resort towns, including **Mablethorpe** ⓭ and **Skegness** ⓮.

If you are heading back down south, take the A1, A15 or A16 to **Stamford** ⓯, 47 miles (76 km) south of Lincoln. There you will find one of Britain's most spectacular Elizabethan stately homes, **Burghley House** (open Apr–Sept: daily; tel: 01780-52451), built in 1560–87 by William Cecil, first Lord Burghley. The lavishly painted ceilings make the house well worth a detour. ❑

ABOVE: Lincoln Cathedral. **BELOW:** the beach at bracing Skegness.

YORKSHIRE AND THE NORTHEAST

Map, pages 296 & 300

The lands of the northeast are wild, wide-open spaces, littered with evidence of a turbulent past, but they shelter some picture-book villages, bustling towns and the historic city of York

Long before Sunday-afternoon strollers trod Pennine millstone grit and mountain limestone, it was pounded by the feet of armies. The region's history is as turbulent as the sudden storms that rage on the high moors; no other part of the country has more fortifications.

In AD 122, the Roman emperor Hadrian built a fortified wall for 73 miles (117 km) across the country from sea to sea to keep back barbarian Scots. The Borders region, known as the "Debatable Lands" from the Middle Ages to Elizabethan times, was in a state of constant feuding. The Wars of the Roses (1455–85) saw the Houses of Lancaster (red rose) and York (white rose) locked in a struggle to win control of the throne. The Civil War in the 17th century divided local allegiances between king and parliament.

Other revolutions took place here, too. The seed of Christianity in Britain was planted in AD 634 on Lindisfarne, off the coast of Northumberland, and in Jarrow on Tyneside the Venerable Bede first wrote down the history of England.

At the southern extremity of the region, on the edge of the industrial north which spreads out from Greater Manchester, is Leeds, 190 miles (305 km) from London. York is 196 miles (315 km) from the capital and Newcastle is 275 miles (440 km) – just 46 miles (75 km) short of the Scottish border. The A1(M) goes all the way to Newcastle and then on up the coast to Edinburgh. A faster route north is on the M1 to Leeds. The A61 will then take you the scenic way to the A1. Fast trains run to Leeds, York and Newcastle from King's Cross station in London.

PRECEDING PAGES: dawn in the Aire Valley, Yorkshire. **LEFT:** Hadrian's Wall. **BELOW:** Bolton Abbey in the Dales.

Living traditions

Although most of the north's industries have been in upheaval, traditional life goes on. At Huddersfield, to the north of the Peak District and 15 miles (24 km) south of Leeds, the famous choral society has performed Handel's *Messiah* every year since 1836. In the ranks of the Black Dyke Mills Band, Britain's most celebrated brass band, are weavers, shotfirers and furnacemen.

Victorian thrift is alive and well in local towns, made manifest by the numerous building societies, which borrow money from small savers in order to lend to house buyers. Few of the societies build anything these days; many are shedding their mutual status and becoming public limited companies (plc). The largest, the Halifax, takes its name from the town 10 miles (16 km) northwest of Huddersfield. In 1997, the Halifax also became a plc.

Halifax ❶ earned its wealth from textiles. Today, one of its main attractions is the award-winning **Eureka**, Britain's first "hands-on" museum designed especially

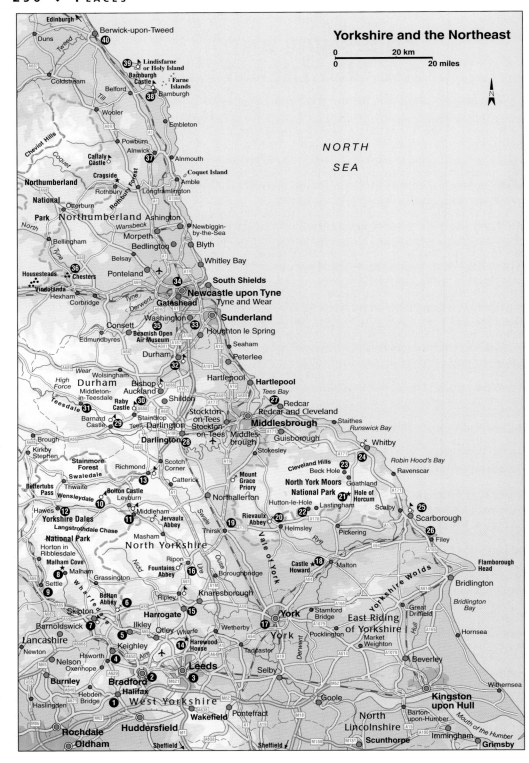

Yorkshire and the Northeast

NORTH

SEA

for children (open daily; tel: 01422-330 069). In nearby **Bradford ❷**, the 19th-century textile barons built solid dependability and vigour into every brick of the city's Italianate Town Hall and its Gothic Wool Exchange. One of the richest, Titus Salt, enshrined his ideals in a model village near the town, providing it with mill, hospital, school, library, church and almshouses, but religiously excluding pubs. He called it **Saltaire**. (These days, alcohol *is* on sale.) The village is worth a visit, especially as it now features a major collection of the work of contemporary artist David Hockney (who grew up locally) in the **1853 Gallery** (open daily; free) .

Northern attractions

Many recent immigrants have been attracted by the wool trade, which is still important. Asians make up 20 percent of Bradford's old city and the Muslim influence is strong. Bradford's tourism promoters, who call themselves "The Myth-breakers", have opened a **J.B. Priestley trail**, tracing the early life of the novelist and playwright who was born in the town in 1894 and immortalised it as "Bruddesford" in *The Good Companions*. Festivals feature the music of Frederick Delius (1862–1934), also a native. Another famous sons is the contemporary playwright Alan Bennett.

The **National Museum of Photography**, **Film and Television** (open Tues–Sun) has a screen five storeys high by 96 ft (30 metres) wide, as well as the Kodak Museum's collection of cameras and pictures. The mills have been eclipsed, but 50 mill shops strenuously promote their wares.

Leeds ❸, the town's larger next-door neighbour and Yorkshire's main city, has developed into a world centre for ready-made clothing. Its big tourist attrac-

see map opposite

Bradford-born J.B Priestley was noted for his varied output and shrewd characterisation – both in his books and in his plays

BELOW: a sheepdog and his master.

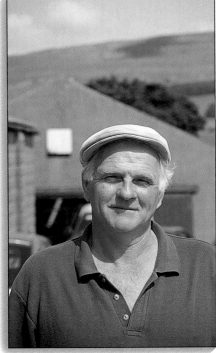

TIP

On the A65 between Ilkley and Leeds, you can dine at the world's biggest fish and chip shop, Harry Ramsden's 1. It has chandeliers, plush decor, parking for 400 cars, plus a coach park.

tion, at Clarence Dock, is the **Royal Armouries Museum** (open daily), displaying 3,000 years of arms, from musket balls and jousting equipment to an elephant's suit of armour and parts of Saddam Hussein's supergun. Built on the site of a derelict wharf by the River Aire, the museum is architecturally striking, both inside and out.

Presented with the matchless raw material of the Brontës, Yorkshire's tragic literary family, the engine of tourism has shifted into overdrive. The steep cobbled streets of **Haworth ④**, a hill village of grey stone houses 14 miles (22 km) west of Bradford on the B6144, are tramped by 700,000 visitors a year. A babble of nationalities queue to file through the **Parsonage**, now a museum, where Charlotte, Emily, Anne and Branwell grew up (open daily).

Haworth station is the headquarters of the **Keighley and Worth Valley Railway Preservation Society** (open July–Aug: daily; Sept–June: weekends and public holidays), which runs steam locomotives on a 5-mile (8-km) track between **Keighley** and **Oxenhope**.

A dozen miles north of Haworth, **Ilkley ⑤**, a Victorian inland spa for the prosperous burghers of Leeds and Bradford, has immortalised its rugged climate in the Yorkshire anthem *On Ilkla Moor baht 'at* which, translated, tells you that it is not prudent to venture forth on Ilkley Moor without a hat.

The undespoiled Dales

To the north of Ilkley lies the expanse of the **Yorkshire Dales**, characterised by their dry-stone walls, bustling market towns, lonely farmhouses and cathedral-like caverns. The motorist can do worse than abandon a fixed itinerary and explore at will. The easiest excursion from Ilkley takes you into surrounding

BELOW: the stationmaster at Haworth.

BRONTË COUNTRY

Not all the relics on display at the Parsonage in Haworth may really have been owned by the Brontës: visitors gazing at a boot jump to the conclusion that the author of *Jane Eyre* must have had exceptionally small feet. But the tiny manuscripts are a poignant reminder of the secrecy with which the three sisters surrounded their work.

In the town, the church where the Brontës' father was parson scarcely exists; it was rebuilt by his successor in 1879. All the Brontës except Anne, who was buried in Scarborough, lie in the family vault near to where the Brontë pew stood in the old church. Still very visible is the congestion of old tombstones in the burial ground, recalling mid-19th-century conditions here, when average life expectancy was 28 and the town was racked with typhus and cholera.

In those days — well into the Brontë era — hand-loom weaving was the mainstay of the local economy, and the upper floors of many of the houses lining the Main Street were both the home and workplace of weavers.

Above Haworth, the moors retain their grandeur: the wild, skyline setting at Top Withins may have inspired "Wuthering Heights" in Emily Brontë's novel. It is a popular destination for Brontë pilgrims today, reached in about an hour along a path starting at the Penistone Hill Country Park.

**Map,
page 296**

Wharfedale, an alluring mix of water, wood, crag and castle. **Bolton Abbey ❻**, 5 miles (8 km) northwest of Ilkley, dates to the 12th century. Its stunning location by the River Wharfe has long made it a major dales attraction.

West of Ilkley is the market town of **Skipton ❼**, the "gateway to the Dales", whose position on the Leeds–Liverpool Canal brought great prosperity during the Industrial Revolution. Many of the warehouses still stand, but so does the much older **Skipton Castle**, home of the powerful Clifford family from the 14th to 18th centuries (Mon–Sat and Sun pm). Skipton provides easy access to one of the great wonders of the Yorkshire Dales, namely **Malham Cove ❽**, an enormous limestone crag just north of the village of Malham. At the top of the cove is the largest area of limestone pavement in Britain.

Farther west still is the small market town of **Settle ❾**, an excellent point from which to begin a circular tour of the flat-topped **Ingleborough** hill, taking in the magnificent **Ribblehead Viaduct**, built in 1869–76 to carry the Settle-Carlisle Railway across Batty Moss. To the north, **Wensleydale** is broad and wooded, and seems serene until your eye catches the forbidding **Bolton Castle ❿** perched on a hillside (Mar–Nov: daily; tel: 01969-623 981). Tradition has it that the mortar was mixed with oxblood to strengthen the building. Wander through the stables area, into the open courtyard which was once the Great Hall, and you can readily imagine yourself transported back to 1568, when Mary, Queen of Scots was imprisoned here. Nearby are the impressive **Aysgarth Falls**.

At the bottom of the dale is the town of **Middleham ⓫**, famous for its race-horse stables and its **castle** (Apr–Oct: daily; Nov–Mar: Wed–Sun; tel: 01969-623 899), owned briefly by Richard III. Its remains include a 12th-century keep, 13th-century chapel, 14th-century gatehouse and two 14th-century chapels.

The foundations of the Ribblehead Viaduct are stabilised on thousands of sheep fleeces: one way to deal with uncertain terrain.

BELOW: the Ribble-head Viaduct.

King George VI summed up the significance of York's heritage: "The history of York," he said, "is the history of England." Part of its history is on display at Jorvik Viking Centre (above).

BELOW: York's Micklegate Bar.

The Romans set up a base in York in AD 71. Eight centuries later, the Vikings came, naming the settlement Jorvik. A routine archaeological dig in 1976 turned up a treasure chest of 15,000 artefacts, now the core of an inspired museum project, the **Jorvik Viking Centre B** (open daily). Queues, serenaded by buskers, form outside long before opening time. Visitors descend into a basement below a new shopping precinct and ride in electric buggies down a "time tunnel" into an authentically reconstructed 10th-century Viking village, complete with everyday sights, sounds and smells (often unpleasant ones, too). The buggies then pass through the actual excavation site.

Above ground again, you can wander through mazes of ancient alleyways, such as the **Shambles C**, the former butchers' quarter. Now antiques and souvenirs instead of carcasses are on display. Some alleys are so narrow that the overhanging upper storeys of buildings on opposite sides almost touch. You can walk on top of the city walls, in some parts wide enough for horses to pass – though it can take two hours to complete the circuit on foot. Medieval timber-framed buildings, such as **Merchant Adventurers' Hall D** (Mar–Nov: daily; Dec–Feb: Mon–Sat), abound. So do antiquarian bookshops. Further out is one of the North's top racecourses.

But it is the **Minster E**, a fusion of classical, Norman, Saxon and English influences, that dominates York. It seems to float above the city. It was built over a period of 250 years, as "an act of prayer by the most practical people in the world," and costs £3 a minute to maintain. Constantine the Great was declared emperor in this building, providing an improbable link between Yorkshire and the founding of Istanbul. Evidence of past centuries can be seen in a fascinating display in the Undercroft. And there is more history in the **Yorkshire**

GLORIOUS GLASS

As the masons worked and the Minster slowly took its present form, artistry of a different kind was flourishing in small studios all over York, and the city was becoming a centre of glass painting to rival anywhere in Europe. The whole history of English stained glass ranging from the 12th century to the present day can be seen in the Minster.

The Great East Window contains the world's largest area of medieval stained glass in a single window. It was completed in 1407 by Coventry glazier John Thornton, who received 4 shillings a week and £10 on completion. The window's theme is the beginning and the end of the world, using scenes from the Bible.

The West Window was painted in 1338 and has become known as the Heart of Yorkshire because of the heart shape in the ornate tracery of the window arch. The North Transept is dominated by the stunning Five Sisters' Window, the oldest complete window in the Minster, made of green and grey "grisaille" glass set in geometric patterns.

During World War I all 100,000 pieces of glass were taken out and buried for safety. Across in the South Transept is the Rose Window which narrowly escaped total destruction when lightning struck the Minster in 1984. The glass had to be dismantled and strengthened before being replaced.

Museum  (open daily) which has galleries depicting Roman, Anglo-Saxon and Viking life in the region.

For an insight into the 18th-century at its most magnificent, drive 15 miles (24 km) northeast from York on the A64, into the Howardian Hills, to **Castle Howard** ⓲ (Mar–Nov: daily; tel: 01653-648 444), a treasure-filled creation of architect Sir John Vanbrugh (1664–1726).

North York Moors

Further north still lie the North York Moors. Stretching all the way from the Vale of York to the East Coast, the Moors embrace the largest expanse of heather moorland in England and Wales.

The Moors can be approached either directly from York or from the A1. Just off the A1 is the thriving market town of **Thirsk** ⓳, now famous as the "Darrowby" of James Herriot's vet books, which have been translated into such successful television series as *All Creatures Great and Small*. Herriot's former **surgery** (open daily) is now a visitor centre devoted to the author.

Approaching the Moors from the west or the south, most visitors will arrive in **Helmsley**, whose quaint shops give it a distinctly "Cotswolds" feel. Nearby, tucked amid hanging woods and placid pastures deep in the Rye Valley, are the breathtaking ruins of **Rievaulx Abbey** ⓴ (open daily; tel: 01439-798228), an extensive Cistercian monastery founded in the 12th century.

Despite the predominant heather of the Moors, green fields are never far away. A network of dales penetrates the great dome of moorland. In some places they create dramatic natural features, such as the **Hole of Horcum** ㉑ above the Vale of Pickering; elsewhere they enfold villages and farmhouses built mainly of

Map, pages 296 & 300

Castle Howard was the opulent location for the television version of Evelyn Waugh's Brideshead Revisited.

BELOW:
Rievaulx Abbey.

TIP

A good souvenir from Whitby is a piece of jet jewellery, made in the town since Victorian days and still produced at the Victorian Jet Works.

ABOVE: Jet crafts-man in Whitby.
BELOW: Robin Hood's Bay.

warm, honey-coloured sandstone. The prettiest villages include **Hutton-le-Hole** ㉒ in Farndale, with its broad green, and nearby **Lastingham**, with its splendid Norman crypt. On the northern flanks, above Eskdale, are **Goathland** and **Beck Hole** ㉓, the former the setting for the TV series *Heartbeat*, the latter a delightful hamlet with an arc of cottages facing a green. Across it all, from Pickering to Grosmont, runs the steam-powered **Moors Railway**, while, for the more energetic, there is the **Lyke Wake Walk**, which traverses the Moors between Osmotherley and Robin Hood's Bay.

Coastal highlights

The Moors end at the east coast, where breaks in the precipitous cliffs provide space for pretty villages and also the occasional town. **Whitby** ㉔ is a pictur-esque fishing port with a jumble of pantiled cottages climbing from the harbour. On **East Cliff** are the 13th-century remains of **Whitby Abbey** (open daily) on which site a 7th-century monk wrote the *Song of Creation*, considered to mark the start of English literature. The Antarctic explorer Captain Cook (1728–79) lived in this former whaling port – a whale's jawbone still acts as an arch to remind people of the town's former trade. **Cook's house** in Grape Street is the focal point of a heritage trail tracing his life throughout the region (Apr–Nov: daily; Mar: weekends).

To the north of Whitby, steep roads lead down to **Runswick Bay**, a self-con-sciously pretty assortment of fishermen's cottages, and **Staithes**, where the young Cook was briefly and unhappily apprenticed to a grocer. To the south, seekers after solitude can divert from the coastal road to find **Ravenscar**, "the re-sort that never was"; it has fine walks, but never developed economically

beyond one rather imposing clifftop hotel. **Robin Hood's Bay**, close by, once offered sanctuary to the benign outlaw and was a haunt of smugglers.

Further south lies **Scarborough ㉕**, whose eclipse as a posh watering hole is exemplified by the fate of the **Grand Hotel**, among the handsomest in Europe when it opened in 1867 and now run by holiday-camp cheerleaders. The 12th-century **castle** is worth seeing (Easter–Nov: daily; Dec–Easter: Wed–Sun), and Anne Brontë – who, like so many invalids, came for the bracing air – is buried in the graveyard of **St Mary's Church**. The town also has an enviable theatrical reputation built around Alan Ayckbourn, the local-born playwright, who premiers all his plays at the **Stephen Joseph Theatre**.

Filey ㉖ offers unpretentious delights to day trippers, including amusement arcades, a splendid beach and **Filey Brig**, the breakwater at the northern end of the bay. Off the dramatic 400-ft (130-metre) cliff at nearby **Flamborough Head**, John Paul Jones won a sea battle with two English men-of-war in 1779.

To Northumbria

Heading north from Whitby now and leaving Yorkshire behind, the lively sandy-beached resort of **Redcar ㉗** is a playground for the decaying industrial centres of **Middlesbrough, Stockton- on-Tees** and **Darlington ㉘**. The region boomed in the 19th-century, as coal and iron were discovered and the railways pioneered an undreamed-of prosperity. George Stephenson's Locomotion No. 1 (1825) is displayed at Darlington's **Railway Museum** (open daily), near where it once ran on the world's first railway line, between Stockton and Darlington.

Sixteen miles (25 km) to the west, on the River Tees, is the the old market town of **Barnard Castle ㉙**. Here the château-like **Bowes Museum** has a superb collection of exhibits and paintings; artists include El Greco and Goya (open Mon–Sat and Sun pm).

Near **Staindrop**, on the A688 to the northeast, is the commanding nine-towered **Raby Castle ㉚**, set in a 250-acre (100-hectare) deer park (open May–June: Wed and Sun pm; July–Sept: Sun–Fri pm; tel: 01833-660 202) . To the northwest, off the B6277 near **Middleton in Teesdale ㉛**, is the impressive **High Force** waterfall, where the River Tees, bottlenecked, crashes down 70 ft (23 metres). Further on, set amidst the bleak moorland of the **Upper Tees**, the enormous Cow Green Reservoir feeds another impressive waterfall, **Cauldron Snout**.

Durham ㉜ is a university city maintaining a scholarly, almost medieval, air. Until 1836, the prince-bishops of Durham were granted complete sovereignty within their diocese, holding their own parliaments and minting their own coins. The mighty Romanesque **cathedral** is one of the finest in Europe, and its Chapel of the Nine Altars is the final resting place of St Cuthbert, the 'Fire of the North' who evangelised Northumbria from his abbey on Lindisfarne. At the other side of Palace Green, the splendid **castle** was the only northern stronghold never to fall to the marauding Scots (open Mar–Sept: closed am in term times).

Most American visitors head for **Washington ㉝** and the **Old Hall**, ancestral home of the USA's first president; a collection of family relics is on show (Mar–Nov: Sun–Wed; tel: 0191-416 5454).

Map, page 296

The traditional Staithes bonnets are still occasionally worn in the village – and sold as souvenirs.

BELOW: Durham is dominated by its cathedral and castle.

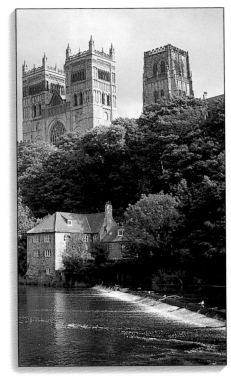

Dominating the area is one of Britain's workshops, **Newcastle upon Tyne** ❸❹. It is a sprawling shipbuilding city, celebrated for its resilient natives ("Geordies"), whose dialect borders on impenetrability, and for its potent brew, Newcastle Brown (pronounced *broon*) Ale. No town prospered more from the Industrial Revolution – its streets were the first in Europe to be lit by electricity. And despite the setbacks caused by the decline in the local coal and shipbuilding industries, Newcastle, with its famous railway bridge over the Tyne, remains an extremely vibrant place, and likes to remind visitors that it is the third home (after Stratford and London) of the Royal Shakespeare Company.

The strategic importance of the site of Newcastle was first recognised by the Romans who founded the city as a minor fort and bridge on **Hadrians's Wall**. The Roman fort of **Arbeia** (open Mon–Sat and Sun pm; Oct–Easter: closed Sun; tel: 0191-456 1369) has been excavated at nearby **South Shields**.

Fearing that such ancient attractions would be insufficient bait for modern tourists, the South Shields city fathers have created "Catherine Cookson Country"; one problem is that many of the slums she graphically describes in her novels have been pulled down. However, for a realistic and lively look at what life used to be like in the northeast, visit the **Beamish Open Air Museum** ❸❺, to the south of Newcastle near Consett, which features a working 1913 village made up of buildings and artefacts collected from the region (Apr–Oct: daily; Nov–Mar: closed Mon and Wed; tel: 01207-231 811).

Hadrian's Wall itself, 15 ft high and 7½ ft thick (5 metres by 2.5 metres), snakes westwards across the Border country for 73 miles (117 km). It has several easy points of access from the A69. Just above Hexham, **Chesters** ❸❻ is a beautiful site, occupied by a military bath-house and headquarters building (open

ABOVE: all aboard at Beamish. **BELOW:** walkers at Hadrian's Wall.

daily; tel: 01434-681 379). A few miles further west **Housesteads** (Vercovicium) is a well-preserved fort (open daily; tel: 01434-344 363) and nearby **Vindolanda** has been extensively excavated (open daily; tel: 01434-344 277).

Coastal strongholds

The fortified town of **Alnwick ③**, 34 miles (54 km) to the north of Newcastle, has one of Britain's best examples of a medieval fortress on an extremely large scale. The **castle** (open daily) radiates power and enabled the Percy family to exercise it over northeast England for 600 years. There are more fine fortresses along the coast, including the romantic ruins of **Dunstanburgh** and the giant keep of **Warkworth**, both nearby. But the most stunning of them all is **Bamburgh Castle ③**, which sits on a clifftop 16 miles (25 km) to the north (Mar–Oct: daily; tel: 01668-214 515). From here, on a clear day, you can see the **Farne Islands**, 4½ miles (7 km) offshore. Monks from Iona settled on **Lindisfarne ③** (also known as Holy Island) in the 7th century, turning it into a centre of scholarship renowned throughout Europe. As well as the old **priory** ruins, the island, which can be reached at low tide by a 3-mile (5-km) causeway, has a small fairy-like **castle** dating from 1550 (Apr–Oct: Sat–Thur; tel: 01289-389 244). Birdwatchers also flock to see the islands' breeding grounds.

On the border between England and Scotland is the old seaport of **Berwick upon Tweed ④**. Take a walk along the top of the well-preserved Elizabethan ramparts and you can gaze down into its twisting cobbled streets and out towards the salmon fisheries and shore-line. History suffuses the stone of Berwick, though because the stones had to be reassembled after each border war few really old buildings survive in this, the most northerly town in England. ❑

Map, page 296

TIP

From the harbour at Seahouses you can take an exciting boat trip to the Farne Islands in season. The islands are famous for their breeding colonies of seabirds and their large colony of grey seals, all of which are visible from the boat.

BELOW: Bamburgh Castle.

THE LAKE DISTRICT

Map, page 312

From the time of the first guidebook to the area, Thomas West's 1778 "Guide to the Lakes", its pleasures have remained those of the eye; the landscape is what matters most

The Lake District in northeast England covers a small area, measuring scarcely more than 30 miles (48 km) from north to south and 20 miles (32 km) east to west. But the poet William Wordsworth, who was born here at Cockermouth in 1770 and spent most of his life in the region, rightly remarked: "I do not know any tract of country in which, within so narrow a compass, may be found an equal variety in the influences of light and shadow upon the sublime or beautiful features of landscape." The landscape is indeed beautiful, with the varied treasures of soft hills and woodland, the lengthy panoramas of the great lakes, the unexpected discoveries of the smaller waters or tarns, the bare contours of the fells and high ground and the awe-inspiring power of the more remote mountains and mountain passes.

The Lake District is 250 miles (400 km) from London and 75 miles (120 km) north of Manchester and it is more frequently visited by day tourists and holiday-makers than any other region of outstanding natural beauty in the British Isles. Generally it has proven remarkably able to cope with the vast numbers of visitors, but traffic congestion can be a big problem in summer.

The two routes which were popularised by the first tourists in the 1760s and 1770s still carry the greatest share of summer traffic. One is from Penrith to Ambleside by the west shore of Ullswater (scene of Wordsworth's poem *The Daffodils*) and over the Kirkstone Pass, now the A592; the other is from Keswick to Windermere by the side of Thirlmere, Grasmere, Rydal Water and Windermere, now the A591.

Away from these it remains possible to find areas of great beauty. Here you can experience for a time the sense of aloneness with nature which the first visitors and the early 19th-century Romantic poets (Wordsworth and Samuel Taylor Coleridge) valued so highly.

Sheep and shopping

The central area of mountains was never much affected by industry or quarrying, and the 19th-century developments in shipbuilding, iron manufacturing, coal mining and lesser trades that once flourished by the Cumberland coast have now almost entirely disappeared. Sheep farming was the traditional way of life of the hill folk, and it continues today throughout the area covered by the Lake District National Park, often on farms owned and leased by the National Trust.

In the early 19th century, visitors began to walk the high paths over the fells, and after about 1860 they started to climb the more difficult rock faces. Climbers still congregate in **Great Langdale**, **Borrowdale** and **Wasdale** to tackle the central heights of the **Langdales, Scafell Crags**, **Great Gable**, **Steeple** and **Pillar**. There are hundreds of miles of paths to tempt the walker. Paths

PRECEDING PAGES: boating on Lake Windermere. **LEFT:** heading up the Kirkstone Pass. **BELOW:** excursion on Coniston Water.

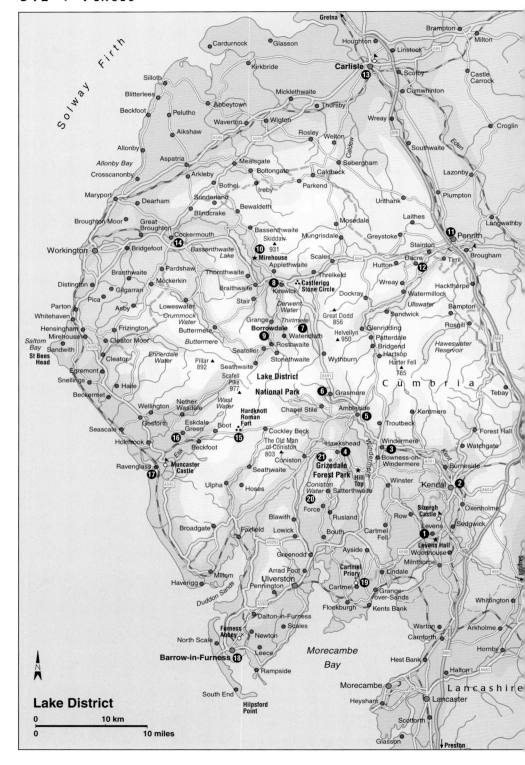

Solway Firth

Gretna
Brampton
Milton

Cardurnock
Glasson
Houghton
Linstock

Kirkbride
Carlisle **13**
Scotby
Castle Carrock

Silloth
Micklethwaite
Cumwhinton

Blitterlees
Abbeytown
Thursby
Wreay
Croglin

Beckfoot
Pelutho
Waverton
Wigton
Southwaite
Eden

Allonby
Aikshaw
Rosley
Welton
Caldew
Sebergham
Lazonby

Allonby Bay
Aspatria
Mealsgate
Boltongate
Caldbeck
Unthank
Plumpton

Crosscanonby
Arkleby
Bothel
Ireby
Parkend
Langwathby

Maryport
Dearham
Sunderland
Bewaldeth
Mosedale
Laithes
Penrith **11**

Broughton Moor
Great Broughton
Blindcrake
Bassenthwaite
Mungrisdale
Greystoke
Stainton
Brougham

Workington
Cockermouth **14**
Bridgefoot
Bassenthwaite Lake
Skiddaw 931 **10**
Mirehouse ★
Scales
Hutton
Dacre **12**
Tirril

Branthwaite
Pardshaw
Thornthwaite
Applethwaite
Threlkeld
Wreay
Hackthorpe

Distington
Mockerkin
Braithwaite
Keswick **8**
Castlerigg Stone Circle
Dockray
Watermillock
Bampton

Parton
Pica
Gilgarran
Asby
Stair
Derwent Water
Great Dodd 856
Sandwich
Rosgill

Whitehaven
Hensingham
Frizington
Loweswater
Crummock Water
Grange
Thirlmere
Borrowdale **7**
Helvellyn ▲ 950
Glenridding
Patterdale
Haweswater Reservoir

Mirehouse
Cleator Moor
Buttermere
Borrowdale **9**
Watendlath
Rosthwaite
Bridgend
Hartsop

Saltom Bay
Sandwith
St Bees Head
Cleator
Ennerdale Water
Pillar ▲ 892
Seatoller
Seathwaite
Stonethwaite
Wythburn
Harter Fell 765

Egremont
Snellings
Haile
Scafell Pike 977 ▲
Lake District
Grasmere
Cumbria
Tebay

Beckermet
Wellington
Nether Wasdale
Wast Water
National Park **6**
A6

Wellington
Eskdale Green
Boot **15**
Chapel Stile
Ambleside **5**
Kentmere
Forest Hall

Seascale
Gosforth
Hardknott Roman Fort
Cockley Beck
Windermere **3**
Bowness-on-Windermere
Watchgate

Holmrook
Beckfoot **16**
The Old Man of Coniston 803
Hawkshead
4
Burneside

Ravenglass
Muncaster Castle **17**
Coniston
Grizedale Forest Park **21**
Hill Top
Winster
Kendal **2**
Oxenholme

Ulpha
Seathwaite
Coniston Water
Satterthwaite
Sizergh Castle
Sedgwick

Hoses
Force **20**
Rusland
Row
Levens **1**
Levens Hall

Broadgate
Blawith
Bouth
Cartmel Fell
Ayside
Woodhouse
Milnthorpe

Foxfield
Lowick
Greenodd
Cartmel Priory **19**
Lindale
Whittington

Haverigg
Millom
Arrad Foot
Cartmel
Grange-over-Sands

Ulverston
Pennington
Flookburgh
Kents Bank

Duddon Sands
Dalton-in-Furness
Scales
Morecambe Bay
Warton
Arkholme

Furness Abbey
Newton
Leece
Carnforth
Hornby

North Scale
Barrow-in-Furness **18**
Hest Bank
Halton

Rampside
Morecambe
Lancashire

South End
Hilpsford Point
Heysham
Lancaster

Scotforth

Glasson
Preston

Lake District

0 ——— 10 km

0 ——— 10 miles

over the high fells must be tackled with respect for the region's notoriously rapid changes of weather, and with the proper equipment, but there are innumerable easy walks by the lakesides or along the streams which anyone can enjoy. Walking is the best way to witness the constant change of scene which is so characteristic of this small but endlessly varied district. In recent years the Lake District has developed a greater range of places of interest for visitors. Most of these are museums, preserving the history of the area, but they vary from permanent displays and houses to working mills and steam railways.

Approaching the Lake District from the south along the M6, a turn off at junction 36 leads to the town of **Levens ❶**. **Levens Hall**, a largely 16th-century house built around a 14th-century pele tower, with a famous topiary garden (open Apr–Sept: Sun–Thur; tel: 015395-60321), is little changed since its trees were first shaped in the 17th century. Nearby **Sizergh Castle** (open Apr–Oct: Sun–Thur, pm only; tel: 015395-60070) shows its origins as a medieval defensive structure even more clearly.

Fine historic buildings

Kendal ❷, a good centre for the Lakes, is a short distance north of Levens. It is, indeed, still a working town, not just a holiday centre, all the more fascinating for carrying on in the midst of fine 17th and 18th-century buildings. Among these are old coaching inns and a horn shop which sells locally manufactured items in this ancient material. The church is a fine, unusually broad Perpendicular building. Beside it stands **Abbot Hall** (open mid-Feb–Dec: daily), a mid-17th-century house which now displays a remarkable collection of furniture, china and paintings by local artists, in particular George Romney. There is also a room filled

**Map,
page 312**

Kendal, a town whose prosperity was based on wool, is now perhaps most famous for Kendal Mint Cake, a slabby, sweet confection which continues to be an essential part of many outdoor survival kits, whether in the Lake District or in the Himalayas.

BELOW LEFT: Herdwick sheep on Carrock Fell. **BELOW RIGHT:** pele tower at Levens Hall.

with watercolours by John Ruskin. Abbot Hall also houses the **Museum of Lakeland Life and Industry**, which has a room devoted to the *Swallows and Amazons* author Arthur Ransome (1884–1967).

Home of the Wordsworths

The A591 runs from Kendal to **Windermere ❸**. Below the town lies **Bowness**, with a pretty village centre unfortunately almost always too crowded for comfort. Mementoes from the age of steam (including the steam-launch *Dolly* of 1850, said to be the oldest mechanically powered boat in the world) are here at the **Windermere Steamboat Museum** (open Apr–Oct: daily). At Bowness, boats depart for **Belle Isle**, with the handsome late 18th-century circular house of the same name.

Also at Bowness is the car ferry to Far Sawrey and **Hill Top**, Beatrix Potter's house (open Apr–Nov: Sat–Wed; tel: 015394-36269), a fine example of a traditional Lakeland farmhouse.

In Main Street in nearby **Hawkshead ❹** is the **Beatrix Potter Gallery** (open Apr–Oct: Sun–Thur) in the former office of her husband, a solicitor. It has displays of many of the original drawings from her famous children's books.

William Wordsworth studied at the ancient **Grammar School** at Hawkshead, now a museum (open Apr–Oct: Mon–Sat, and Sun pm). Downstairs, it suggests little of the excellence of its teaching in the 1780s when the Wordsworth brothers studied there. But upstairs is a superb library with books dating back to the foundation of the school by Archbishop Sandys in Elizabeth I's reign. **St Michael's Church** preserves wall paintings of scriptural texts. From beneath its east window you can take in the view of this tiny, whitewashed town with its

ABOVE: Steamboat Museum, Bowness.
BELOW: Lake Windermere.

close-packed lanes and the occasional house still keeping the spinning gallery where the women would sit to work.

West of Hawkshead stands the medieval arched **Courthouse**, a relic of the times when the Cistercian monks from Cartmel ruled much of the southern part of the area. Further west, on the B5285, is **Tarn Hows**, considered by many to be the prettiest lake in the Lake District. Only a half-mile (800 metres) long, it was originally three smaller lakes but joined after the construction of a dam.

Whether you continue towards the head of Lake Windermere on this west side, or take the A591 northwest from Windermere, you will eventually reach **Ambleside ❺**, and just beyond it, Rydal Water. **Rydal Mount** (open Mar–Oct: daily; tel: 015394-33002) was home of the Wordsworths from 1813 until William died in 1850. The house contains portraits and family mementoes; the grounds are laid out in their original form and afford fine views.

Two miles (3 km) north lies **Grasmere ❻**. The southernmost part of the village, **Town End,** is where the poet and his sister Dorothy first settled in 1799. The white cottage is movingly simple in its furnishings, but it takes the display of manuscripts and portraits of the poet's family and friends in the nearby **Grasmere and Wordsworth Museum** (open mid-Feb–Dec: daily) to bring home the magnitude of the poetry which was written here and the importance which Wordsworth and Coleridge held in the cultural life of their day.

St Oswald's Church is a plain, roughly built structure with a remarkable and much-altered ancient timber roof. The Wordsworth family graves and that of Coleridge's son Hartley lie behind it. All about are the paths, streams and hills which Dorothy Wordworth described along with the daily life of **Dove Cottage** (included with a visit to the museum), in her 1800–02 *Journal*.

Map, page 312

TIP

Tarn Hows provides some of the most spellbinding views of the Lakeland fells. The best vantage point is the southern side of the lake, where the path takes to higher ground.

BELOW: the garden at the Wordsworth's Dove Cottage.

The 17-mile (28-km) journey to Keswick on the A591 passes **Thirlmere** ❼, a reservoir created out of two smaller lakes in 1890 to supply the water needs of Manchester. **Helvellyn**, the third highest mountain in England (3,118 ft/950 metres), rises steeply to the right. Close to Keswick you may turn off to **Castlerigg Stone Circle**, an ancient monument commanding tremendous views, which the early tourists associated with the Druids. Recent writers think the stones may have been intended as a giant calendar to show by its shadows the turn of the seasons for planting and reaping.

Pencils for poets

Keswick ❽, a Victorian town with an older centre, has been popular with visitors since the 1760s, when the poet Thomas Gray stayed there to explore its lake, **Derwent Water.** With fear and trembling, Gray ventured to the mouth of mountain-surrounded **Borrowdale** ❾, just past the southern end of the lake, which early visitors associated with the sublimity and terror of Salvator Rosa's paintings. Even today one might fear that the tottering pinnacles will detach themselves and fall upon one's head. A favourite excursion since Gray's time is the **Bowder Stone**, balanced on the side of the hill a little way up the valley. Another attraction is the waterfall at **Lodore**, near the head of Derwent Water.

ABOVE: Lodore Falls, Derwent Water.
BELOW: Castlerigg stone circle, near Keswick.

Borrowdale was famed among the early tourists for the "wad" or black lead mine which enabled the manufacture of pencils in Keswick, which is now home to the **Cumberland Pencil Museum** (open daily). Keswick's **Museum and Art Gallery** (open Easter–Oct: daily), in Fitz Park, has mementoes of Coleridge, Robert Southey and Hugh Walpole, who lived nearby, and whose "Rogue Herries" novels are set in and around the area.

Coleridge settled at **Greta Hall** on the outskirts of Keswick in 1800 and persuaded his brother-in-law Robert Southey, also a writer, to join him there. **Crossthwaite Church**, which stands about half-a-mile beyond Greta Hall, has memorials to Southey and members of his family. Thomas Gray described the view from outside the parsonage as one which, if it could be captured "in all the softness of its living colours, would fairly sell for a thousand pounds."

Northwards, the churchyard looks towards **Bassenthwaite Lake**, the eastern side of which is dominated by Skiddaw (3,054 ft/917 metres). Beneath the mountain lies **Mirehouse** ⓾, the 18th-century home of the Spedding family (open Apr–Nov: Sun and Wed pm only; also Fri in Aug; tel: 017687-72287).

A 15-mile (24-km) drive eastwards from Keswick on the A66 to the interesting old town of **Penrith** ⓫ can incorporate a visit to **Dacre** ⓬, a few miles before the town on the right. It has a largely Norman church, even earlier carvings and views of 14th-century **Dacre Castle**. Nearby is **Dalemain** (open Easter–mid Oct: Sun–Thur; tel: 017684-86450), an old house last altered in 1750 that offers fine interiors (including a Chinese drawing room with original mid-18th-century wallpaper), paintings and a pleasant garden. Dalemain lies just off the A592, which leads past **Ullswater** and over the Kirkstone Pass to Ambleside. Ullswater is the second-largest lake after Windermere. There are steamers on the lake from which one can enjoy magnificent views of Helvellyn and other surrounding mountains, and **Aira Force**, on the north shore beneath Gowbarrow Fell, is one of the most impressive waterfalls in the Lake District.

Brougham Castle, just southeast of Penrith, is a Norman castle built on the foundations of a Roman fort. The ruins here are impressive: the top gallery of the keep has fine views and is worth the effort of climbing.

Map, page 312

TIP

Just off the A6 south of Penrith is the Lowther Leisure and Wildlife Park, whose attractions are ideal for children. It also has the Lakeland Bird of Prey Centre which offers daily falconry displays.

ABOVE: Dalemain.
BELOW: Lakeland Bird of Prey Centre.

Carlisle **⓭**, just 21 miles (34 km) north of Penrith on the M6, also deserves an excursion. The **Castle** here obtained its unusual outline when its roof was strengthened to carry early cannons. The **Tullie House Museum and Art Gallery** (daily; Thur till 10pm, Sun from noon; tel: 01228-34781) houses an important collection of Roman materials and Pre-Raphaelite paintings.

In the other direction from Keswick, the A66 heads west for 15 miles (24 km) to **Cockermouth ⓮**. The **Wordsworth House** (open Apr–Oct: Mon–Fri, sometimes Sat) in Main Street is where William and Dorothy spent their earliest years. Cockermouth is an old-fashioned stone-built town stretching along a lengthy main street, very like the towns on the opposite side of the Scottish border.

Roman hairpins

Southwest Lakeland is rich in interest. One of the most dramatic sites of all is best approached on the Windermere-based "Mountain Goat" (tel: 015394-45161) mini-coach service by anyone lacking both an extremely agile car and nerves of steel. The road over the Wrynose and Hardknott passes, 10 miles (16 km) west of Ambleside, was improved by the Romans, but they probably intended their narrow road with its hairpin bends and sheer drops for pedestrians only. In summer, today's traffic conditions can make it somewhat hazardous. But the situation of **Hardknott Roman Fort ⓯** high above **Eskdale**, with its view of the highest peaks and the distant sea, is unforgettable.

ABOVE: farmhouse at Wrynose Pass.
BELOW: the Ravenglass to Eskdale Railway.

Eskdale's mines and quarries were the reason for the construction of the **Ravenglass and Eskdale Railway** (known locally as the "Ratty"), a narrow-gauge line which now delights summer tourists with its beautifully maintained miniature steam engines. The line runs for about 18 miles (28 km) through lush scenery. From **Eskdale Green ⓰** a road runs over Birker Fell to the **Duddon Valley**, still relatively unknown to visitors and an area of great natural beauty.

Ravenglass ⓱, on the coast, lies close to **Muncaster Water Mill** (open Apr–Oct: daily), a restored water-driven corn mill, in which the visitor can watch the production of stone-ground flour. Nearby is **Muncaster Castle** (open Apr–Nov: daily; closed Sat am; tel: 01229-717 614), home of the Pennington family since 1325, when a new tower was built on the foundations of a Roman watchtower commanding extensive views of the fells and Eskdale. Henry VI sought refuge here and is said to have given his drinking bowl, the "Luck of Muncaster", to his host, Sir John Pennington. The bowl is still in the house which, in the course of 18th and 19th-century alterations, has grown from a medieval tower into an attractive mansion.

Abbey lands

The southern tip of Lakeland was in medieval days the heart of the great Cistercian estate farmed by the monks of **Furness Abbey** (open Mar–Oct: daily). The abbey, on the northside of the shipbuilding town **Barrow-in-Furness ⓲**, was the second richest Cistercian establishment in England at the time of its suppression in 1537. Its buildings date from the 12th and 15th centuries and the impressive ruins in the Vale of the Deadly Nightshade lie in a setting of great loveliness.

Map, page 312

To the east is **Cartmel Priory** ⓫ (open daily exc during services; tel: 015395-32375), near the resort of Grange-over-Sands on a finger of land pointing down into Morecambe Bay. It was founded in 1188 by the Baron of Cartmel and it was saved from destruction at the time of Henry VIII's Dissolution of the Monasteries by the quick-wittedness of local people who claimed that it was, in fact, their parish church. The 15th-century tower is unusual; the upper part is set diagonally across the lower stage. Inside there is good medieval carving and old glass; the lovely east window also dates from the 15th century. The village setting is attractive.

Returning northward, the visitor approaches the foot of Windermere (from where the **Haverthwaite and Lakeside Steam Railway** runs in season) and, to the west, **Coniston Water** ⓴. Between the two lies **Grizedale Forest Park** ㉑, a large tract of land the Forestry Commission has imaginatively given over to nature trails, jolly modern sculptures and a 23-seat theatre. Coniston was made famous by the world water speed record attempts of Donald Campbell, who died in the last of them in 1967. Earlier, Coniston was famous for the residence of John Ruskin (1819–1900), the great Victorian art historian and writer on social and economic themes.

At **Brantwood** (open mid Mar–mid Nov: daily; rest of year: Wed–Sun; tel: 015394-41396), on the northeast shore of Coniston Water, many of Ruskin's own paintings are preserved, and the house remains much as he left it. The grounds, with their dramatic views of lake and fell, have recently been improved and developed. On the lake, the Victorian steam yacht *Gondola* operates once again, with all the elegance of a Tissot painting, after lying for nearly 40 years in shallow water close to the shore. ❑

ABOVE: sculpture in Grizedale Forest.
BELOW: the *Gondola* on Coniston Water.

Scotland

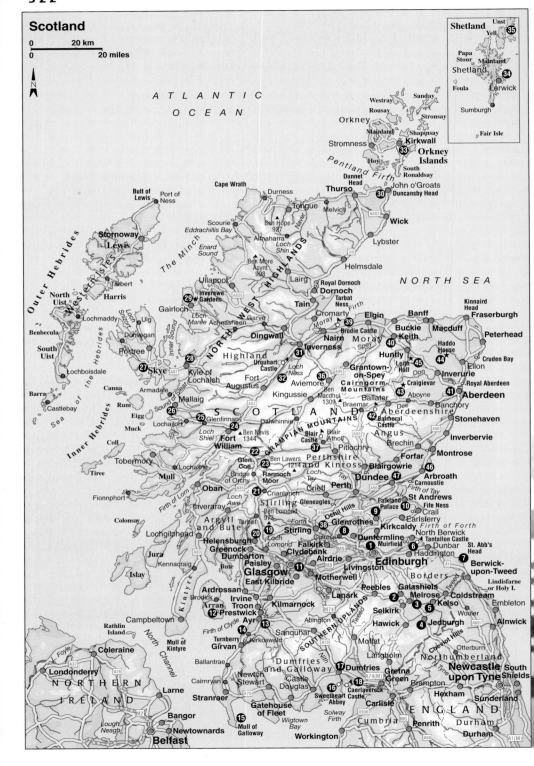

0 ___ 20 km
0 ___ 20 miles

N

ATLANTIC OCEAN

Shetland

Unst
Yell
35

Papa
Stour
Mainland
Shetland

34

Foula

Lerwick

Sumburgh

Fair Isle

Westray
Sanday
Rousay
Stronsay
Orkney
Mainland
Shapinsay

Orkney Islands

Stromness
Kirkwall
33

Hoy
South
Ronaldsay

Pentland Firth

Butt of Lewis
Port of Ness

Cape Wrath
Durness
Dunnet Head
John o'Groats
Duncansby Head
Thurso
30

Tongue
Melvich
Wick

Scourie
Eddrachillis Bay
Ben Hope 927
Altnaharra
Loch Shin
Naver
A882
A9
Lybster

Stornoway
Lewis

Enard Sound
Ben More Asynt 998
Lairg
Helmsdale

Outer Hebrides

Western Isles

Tarbert
Harris

Ullapool
Inverewe Gardens
29

NORTH WEST HIGHLANDS

Royal Dornoch
Dornoch
Tarbat Ness
NORTH SEA

North Uist
Lochmaddy
Uig

Gairloch
Loch Maree
Achnasheen
Garve
Dingwall

Tain
Cromarty
Moray Firth
Elgin
Banff
Kinnaird Head
Fraserburgh

Benbecula
Dunvegan
Portree

Inner Sound
Highland
Inverness
31
Brodie Castle
39
Nairn
Moray
Buckie
Keith
Macduff
Peterhead

South Uist
Lochboisdale
27
Skye
A87

28
Kyle of Lochalsh
Urquhart Castle
Loch Ness
32
36
Aviemore
Grantown-on-Spey
40
Huntly
Leith Hall
45
44
Cruden Bay
Ellon

Barra
Castlebay
Armadale
Fort Augustus
Kingussie
Ben Macdhui 1309
Cairngorm Mountains
Craigievar
43
Craigievar
41
Inverurie
Royal Aberdeen
Aberdeen

Canna
Sea of the Hebrides
Mallaig
Sound of Sleat
26
Glenfinnan
25
SCOTLAND
Ballater
Aboyne
Banchory
Stonehaven

Rum
Eigg
Muck
Lochailort
24
Loch Shiel
Ben Nevis 1344
Fort William
22
Braemar
42
Balmoral Castle
Aberdeenshire
Inverbervie

Coll
Tobermory
Lochaline
GRAMPIAN MOUNTAINS
Blair Castle
Blair Atholl
Pitlochry
Angus
Brechin
Montrose

Tiree
Mull
Glen Coe
23
Ben Lawers 1214
Rannoch Moor
Loch Tay
37
Perthshire and Kinross
Blairgowrie
46
Forfar
Arbroath

Fionnphort
Oban
21
Bridge of Orchy
Crianlarich
Crieff
Perth
47
Carnoustie

Colonsay
Inveraray
Loch Awe
Firth of Lorn
Stirling
Gleneagles
Falkland Palace
10
Dundee
Firth of Tay
St Andrews
Fife Ness
Crail

Lochgilphead
Argyll and Bute
Ben Lomond 973
Tarbet
38
Glenrothes
9
Earlsferry

Jura
Kennacraig
Bute
20
19
Stirling
Loch Lomond
8
Kirkcaldy
Firth of Forth
North Berwick
Tantallon Castle

Islay
Helensburgh
Greenock
Dumbarton
Paisley
11
Clydebank
Falkirk
Culross
Dunfermline
Muirfield
1
6
Edinburgh
Dunbar
Haddington
7

Glasgow
East Kilbride
Airdrie
Livingston
St. Abb's Head
Berwick-upon-Tweed

Ardrossan
Irvine
Troon
12
Prestwick
Kilmarnock
Motherwell
Lanark
Peebles
2
Galashiels
Melrose
3
Kelso
Coldstream
Lindisfarne or Holy I.
Embleton

Arran
Brodick
13
Ayr
Sanquhar
Abington
SOUTHERN UPLANDS
Selkirk
Hawick
4
Jedburgh
Wooler
Alnwick

Campbeltown
Rathlin Island
Coleraine
14
Turnberry
Girvan
Kirkoswald
Moffat
Langholm
Cheviot Hills
Northumberland
Otterburn

NORTHERN IRELAND
Larne
Ballantrae
Newton Stewart
Castle Douglas
17
Dumfries
Gretna Green
Brampton
Hexham
Sunderland

Londonderry
Stranraer
Dumfries and Galloway
16
18
Sweetheart Abbey
Caerlaverock Castle
Carlisle
ENGLAND

Bangor
Newtownards
15
Gatehouse of Fleet
Wigtown Bay
Solway Firth
Cumbria
Penrith
Durham

Belfast
Mull of Galloway
Workington
Durham

THE SCOTTISH LOWLANDS

Scotland is a place of endless variety: in the Lowlands there are hills and seascapes, impressive stately homes and historic Burns country, and the two vibrant cities of Edinburgh and Glasgow

Map, pages 322 & 324

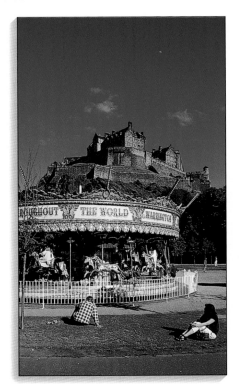

Scotland is a separate experience. The Scots themselves have a sense identity, of different values, and of their own history and traditions unp. alleled in Great Britain. Even though they relinquished their independence to England in 1707, they have maintained their own legal and educational systems, which are widely regarded as superior to those in England, and they still print their own design of bank notes – often the first clue to visitors that they are in a different part of Britain.

Occupying the north of Great Britain, two Roman emperors built walls across the country to keep in place the region's painted Celtic warriors, the Picts and Scots: Hadrian's Wall (*see pages 295 & 306*) and the Antonine Wall just south of the Glasgow/Edinburgh area. At 30,405 sq. miles (78,749 sq. km) Scotland makes up about one-third of Great Britain, yet its population is less than one-tenth, of which more than 30 percent live in or around the three most populous cities, Glasgow, Edinburgh and Aberdeen.

Aberdeen, on the northeast coast, boomed in the 1970s with the discovery of North Sea oil. Glasgow and Edinburgh, stimulating but quite different cities, lie only 45 miles (70 km) apart at opposite sides of the Lowlands, hidden from England by the rolling Southern Uplands and a breather before the dramatic hurdles of the Highlands. Both cities are about 380 miles (610 km) from London. Trains from London start from Euston and King's Cross, taking under five hours, and a "shuttle" air service from Heathrow airport is used by some people like a commuter train.

PRECEDING PAGES: on parade in Edinburgh. **BELOW:** Edinburgh Castle from Princes Street Gardens.

Scotland's capital city

Edinburgh ❶, on the south bank of the Firth (estuary) of Forth, did not become the capital of Scotland until the reign of David I (1124–53). Previously the capital had been further north at Scone, near Perth, where Scottish kings were crowned, seated on the Stone of Destiny (now returned from London's Westminster Abbey and sited in Edinburgh Castle) and latterly at Dunfermline just the other side of the Forth in Fife. There is evidence of an Iron-Age settlement on Arthur's Seat, the rocky outcrop behind the royal Palace of Holyroodhouse, and there was a Pictish stronghold here as early as the 5th century on the rock on which Edinburgh Castle stands.

Between the hills and the sea, Edinburgh has one of the most beautiful settings in the world. Whichever way you arrive – emerging from the tunnelled cavern of Waverley Station, driving in from the airport or motoring up from the English border through the rich farmlands and windswept golf courses of East Lothian – you end up in **Princes Street**, the heart of the city and one of the most dramatic thoroughfares in Europe.

Southward, across the gardens which were once the

Nor' Loch, rises the basalt ridge of rock on which medieval Edinburgh is built. The **Castle** (open daily) rides in the sky, often against a background of torn cloud, and the spires and turrets of the Old Town spike the skyline from the Castle battlements to the hidden Palace of Holyroodhouse below the green hill of Arthur's Seat.

In the Castle is Edinburgh's oldest building, the tiny **Queen Margaret's Chapel,** built for the saintly wife of King Malcolm Canmore by her son, David. The imposing **Great Hall** is still used for banquets and has one of the finest hammerbeam ceilings in Britain. You can also visit the tiny room where in 1566 Mary, Queen of Scots gave birth to James VI of Scotland (James I of England).

The Royal Mile

Four streets make up the **Royal Mile** that runs from the vast esplanade in front of the Castle (where the spectacular Tattoo is held during the Edinburgh Festival in August). It was the mainstream of Edinburgh life until the end of the 18th century and is still lively today. Along its descending route are some of the finest surviving examples of 16th and 17th-century houses in Britain, courtier's houses for the most part, leading to the Royal Palace of Holyroodhouse at the foot. Also, at the very top, is the **Scotch Whisky Heritage Centre** (open daily),which provides a thorough briefing on the national drink and a free dram at the end of the tour, and the nearby **Camera Obscura** (open daily), an extraordinary natural cinema providing live images of the surrounding city.

On the way down, there is much else to look out for: **Parliament House,** now the law courts; **Mowbray House,** dating from the 15th century and probably the oldest inhabited house in the city; the great crown-steepled **High Kirk of**

TIP

At Edinburgh Castle don't miss the display of the Scottish crown, sceptre and sword of state – the oldest royal regalia in Europe.

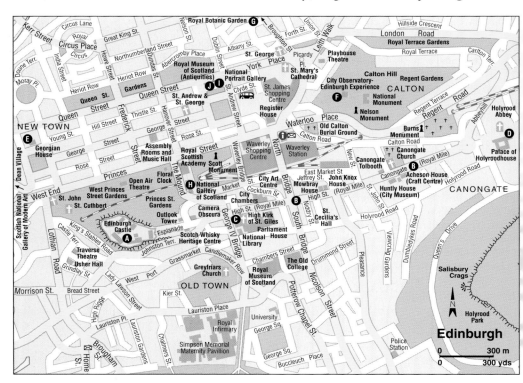

Edinburgh

see map opposite

St Giles ⓒ (open daily) with the magnificent **Thistle Chapel**; the **house of John Knox** (open Mon–Sat), the ruthless Protestant reformer who debated theology and the place of women in society with the young and spirited Mary, Queen of Scots, at Holyroodhouse; the 16th-century **Canongate Tolbooth** and the fine 17th-century **Canongate Kirk**.

At the bottom of the Royal Mile lies the **Palace of Holyroodhouse ⓓ** (open daily) the official residence of Her Majesty the Queen when she is in Scotland. Closely associated with Mary Queen of Scots, Holyroodhouse is a fascinating insight into grislier times. The state apartments have some fine French and Flemish tapestries and 18th-century furniture. Begun in 1498 by James IV, the palace was enlarged in the following century by James V and later by Charles II. The last of the Stuarts to live there was Bonnie Prince Charlie, when his troops occupied the city during the Jacobite Rebellion of 1745. Holyroodhouse returned to royal favour when George IV held a lévée there while visiting Scotland in 1822.

New Town classicism

New town is a graceful complex of streets, squares and crescents north of Princes Street, on the far side of the valley below the Castle. This is a splendid 18th-century example of town planning: the ordered, elegant Georgian facades are in marked contrast to the medieval chaos of the Old Town on the volcanic ridge. This intriguing architectural juxtaposition is matched by no other city in Europe. At **The Georgian House ⓔ**, 7 Charlotte Square, the National Trust for Scotland has reconstructed, in part, how the first residents of these houses must have lived.

To the east of the New Town, beyond St Mary's Cathedral, rises **Calton Hill**, another volcanic outcrop, with stunning views of the city and its surroundings.

Mary Queen of Scots lived at Holyroodhouse for six turbulent years: her Italian secretary, David Rizzio, was murdered in one of the rooms in March 1566 in a conspiracy led by her husband, Lord Darnley. Darnley himself died a few months later in a mysterious explosion at a house barely a mile away.

BELOW:
Holyroodhouse.

Crowning the hill is the **City Observatory**  with a Grecian-style dome; the adjacent **Edinburgh Experience** (open daily; Apr–Oct: closed Mon–Fri am) is an audio-visual, three-dimensional celebration of the city and well worth a visit. Calton Hill is also home to number of important monuments, including the **Nelson Monument** (open Mon–Sat), the **National Monument** and the **Burns Monument**. In the **Old Calton Burial Ground** lie many of the great names of Scotland's Enlightenment period.

To the west of the New Town lies **Dean Village**, a peaceful and picturesque haunt tucked away almost out of sight in the deep valley of the Water of Leith. From here, a walk along the lovingly restored Water of Leith Walkway is highly recommended, passing such sights as Thomas Telford's **Dean Bridge** and **St Bernard's Well**, a small, circular Roman temple. To the north is the world-famous **Royal Botanic Garden** (open daily; free).

It is tempting to linger in Edinburgh to explore all its museums and art galleries, including the **National Gallery of Scotland** in The Mound, the **Scottish National Portrait Gallery** and **Royal Museum of Scotland** in Queen Street, and the **Scottish National Gallery of Modern Art** to the west of Dean Village (all open Mon–Sat and Sun pm; free). In addition, there are numerous historic restaurants and pubs, as well as antiques shops and sporting facilities (28 golf courses within the city boundaries alone). And visitors in the last three weeks of August will have one of the world's greatest arts festivals for entertainment. As well as the main Edinburgh International Festival of music and drama, there are performances in sometimes obscure venues all across the city (and on the streets themselves) by numerous self-financing theatre groups, comedians and mime artists who are collectively known as the Festival Fringe.

ABOVE:
St Bernard's Well.
BELOW: the view
from Calton Hill.

South to the Borders

Beyond the Pentlands, the Moorfoots and the Lammermuir Hills, which ring Edinburgh to the south, lie the **Borders**. This is Scotland along the frontier with England, north of the Cheviot Hills and the Rivers Esk and Tweed, the first part of the land to encounter the Romans, the Angles and the English on their fruitless thrusts into the north. Today, it is gentle pastoral country with rolling green hills and bright clear streams where the industries are still farming, knitwear and tweed, and the passions are for trout and salmon fishing and rugby football, of which the Border towns are the great Scottish stronghold.

Sir Walter Scott (1771–1832) settled in a handsome house overlooking the River Tweed at **Abbotsford** (open late Mar–Oct: Mon–Sat and Sun pm; tel: 01896-752043) outside **Galashiels ❷**, 36 miles (44 km) south of Edinburgh on the A7. His family were Border people, and his romantic imagination was first stirred by the derring-do of his ancestors defending their land against England, the Auld Enemy. Abbotsford, still owned by one of Scott's descendants, is full of memorials of the author.

Historic reminders

Two miles (3 km) east of Abbotsford is the charming town of **Melrose ❸**, set beneath the triple mounds of the Eildon Hills, the haunt of the poet and seer Thomas the Rhymer (c1220–97) and the Queen of Elfland. On the easternmost of its breast-shaped summits is a Roman fort. From the highest hill is a breathtaking view of the Cheviots and the hills running westward towards Galloway. In the town itself lie the impressive ruins of the 12th-century **Melrose Abbey,** despite its final sacking by the English in 1544, still an architectural poem in

Map, page 322

Abbotsford's collection of historical relics, armour and weapons includes Rob Roy's gun, Montrose's sword and a quaich (drinking bowl) which belonged to Bonnie Prince Charlie.

BELOW: fly fishing in the Borders.

Floors Castle became well-known all over the world when it featured as Tarzan's ancestral home in the Hollywood film Greystoke.

BELOW LEFT: Jedburgh Abbey. **BELOW RIGHT:** golf at Gullane.

red sandstone. Melrose is an agreeable little town from which to take walks on the Eildon Hills, to fish or explore the Borders. There are fine medieval abbeys *(see pages 336–7)* nearby at **Dryburgh** 4 miles (6 km) beyond Melrose, where Scott is buried (open Mon–Sat and Sun pm; tel: 01835-822381); at **Kelso,** 10 miles (16 km) east on the A699 (open daily; free); and at **Jedburgh ❹** 8 miles (13 km) south of Dryburgh on the A68 (open Mon–Sat and Sun pm).

There are also several impressive stately homes, such as **Floors Castle,** the seat of the Duke of Roxburgh, just outside **Kelso ❺** (open Easter–Sept: daily; Oct: Sun and Wed; tel: 01573 223333). One of the Duke of Buccleuch's houses, **Bowhill,** is near Selkirk (open July: daily pm; garden open May–Sept: daily except Fri; tel: 01750-22204), and the Adam house of **Mellerstain** is on the A6089 Kelso to Gordon road (open May–Sept: Sun–Fri pm; tel: 01573-410225). All three have outstanding collections of paintings and furniture and Mellerstain has some of the finest Adam ceilings in Britain. At **Coldstream,** Scottish and English armies once forded the Tweed. The town lent its name to the Coldstream Guards raised for Cromwell's army and a crack regiment today.

The Firth of Forth

On the coast of the **Lothians** east of Edinburgh, the country is different once again, with wide lush farmland beyond the Lammermuir Hills and some of the finest golf courses in Britain – Muirfield, North Berwick, Longkniddry, Luffness, the three Gullane courses, Kilspindie and Dunbar.

There is good bird-watching just to the southwest, at **Aberlady Bay** with splendid dune-backed sweeps of sandy beach to stroll, and lots of castles to explore, like **Tantallon ❻** (open Apr–Sept: Mon–Sat and Sun pm; Oct–Mar:

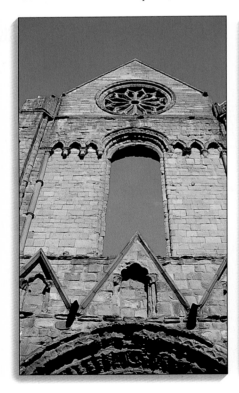

closed Thur am and Fri; tel: 01620-892727), an imposing ruin on a rocky head-land above the North Sea off the A198 between North Berwick and Dunbar. **Dirleton Castle** (open Mon–Sat and Sun pm; tel: 01620-850330) is on the same road between Gullane and North Berwick. Six miles (10 km) inland near **Haddington** is **Lennoxlove** (open May–Sept: Wed, Sat and Sun pm; tel: 01620-823720)**,** the seat of the Duke of Hamilton and Brandon, whose treasures include the death mask of Mary, Queen of Scots and the silver casket in which she kept her letters. Haddington, with its restored 17th and 18th-century houses, is worth a visit, and there is a signposted walk through the town. Just outside East Linton, 7 miles (11 km) east on the A1, is **Preston Mill** which dates from the 16th century and is the oldest mechanically working, water-driven meal mill in Scotland.

St Abb's Head ❼, above Eyemouth some 20 miles (32 km) southeast on the A1, is an impressive headland jutting into the North Sea with 300-ft (90-metre) cliffs, and a bird sanctuary. Colonies of kittiwakes, guillemots, shags, fulmars, herring gulls and razorbills nest here.

Across the wide, pewter-coloured estuary of the Firth of Forth lies **Fife**, or "the kingdom of Fife" as it is still so arrogantly known from its days of insistent independence. Coal mines and industry are ubiquitous here and, although the countryside is not dramatic in structure, it has some surprises. On its western fringes along the north bank of the Forth, upriver towards Stirling, lies the village of **Culross ❽**. This is an ancient royal burgh which traded in coal, salt and griddle pans for making scones. It has some of the best-preserved and most picturesque small-town buildings from the 16th and 17th centuries in Scotland.

To the east is **Dunfermline**, the ancient Scottish capital with a 12th-century Abbey (open Apr–Sept: Mon–Sat and Sun pm; Oct–Mar: closed Thur pm and

Map,
page 322

TIP

Offshore at St Abb's is a marine nature reserve with some of the best scuba-diving in Scotland. Divers must get a permit from the Ranger.

BELOW:
Lennoxlove House.

Today it hosts a famous golf course, but St Andrews was once the ecclesiastical capital of Scotland; it was here that the 16th-century Protestant visionary, John Knox, preached his first sermon.

BELOW: Glasgow's Buchanan Street shopping centre.

Fri; tel: 01383-739026) in which Scotland's liberator, King Robert the Bruce, was buried in 1329. Also in Dunfermline is the museum of the birthplace of Andrew Carnegie (1835–1918), the poor weaver's son who became America's greatest steel baron and one of the world's great philanthropists (open Mon–Sat and Sun pm; Nov–Mar: closed am). On the south coast of the Neuk of Fife, the easternmost promontory, are the picturesque fishing ports of **Earlsferry, St Monance, Pittenweem, Anstruther** and **Crail**.

Inland is **Falkland Palace** ❾ (open Mon–Sat and Sun pm; tel: 01337-578397), the hunting lodge of the Stuarts from James IV to Mary, Queen of Scots, where a "real" (or "royal") tennis court is still in use. Near **Cupar** is the elegant Edwardian house known as the **Hill of Tarvit** (open Easter and May–Sept: daily pm; Oct: Sat and Sun pm; tel: 01334-653127) with its fine collection of furniture, tapestries and paintings. But certainly the most famous town in Fife is **St Andrews** ❿. This is the home of golf, with its famous Old Course on which the game has been played for 800 years, and the **British Golf Museum** (open daily; Nov–Mar: closed Tues and Wed; tel: 01334-478880). It is also the site of one of the UK's oldest universities (founded in 1412) and the town has many fine buildings. Its ruined castle is on a rock looking out to sea.

Glasgow's miles better

Glasgow ⓫ straddles the River Clyde 14 miles (22 km) from the estuary. It grew rich on shipbuilding and heavy engineering and by the end of the 19th century was Britain's second largest city, with a population of more than a million. But the solid, working-class manufacturing base on which the city was founded was whipped from under it during the recession of the 1970s. Although unemploy-

A TALE OF TWO CITIES

The Scottish Lowlands is divided into west and east almost as rigorously by character as by geography. Easterners regard themselves as people of taste and refinement, appropriately reflected in the ordered glory of Georgian Edinburgh. They approved of the city's sobriquet "Athens of the North". Just 40 miles (64 km) away, the westerners of industrial Glasgow consider themselves warm-hearted, less pretentious and more realistic than the scions of the Scottish capital. Glasgow's ambience is closer to that of an American city than anyother metropolis in Britain ("If you've got it, flaunt it!").

Like most long-cherished generalities, such comparisons do contain a grain of truth. There is something austere in Edinburgh's beauty and this, at times, is reflected in the restrained nature of its citizens. Glaswegians, by contrast, are ebullient and demonstrative, with a black, sardonic humour nurtured by the hard times that arrived as the city's industrial base, which helped power the British Empire, weakened in the 20th century.

Culturally, Edinburgh flaunts its annual arts festival, the world's biggest. But Glaswegians point out that they don't need this annual binge – *their* culture is vibrant for 12 months of the year. There's truth in this too.

ment rose distressingly, and the population has declined to less than 700,000, an extraordinary renaissance has occurred and in 1990 Glasgow was named City of Culture by the European Community. The place once famous for its drunks and disturbances is now a firm fixture on the aesthete's Grand Tour.

Glasgow's culture is not all newly created. Its 12th-century **Cathedral** (open Mon–Sat and Sun pm) in the Old Town is the only Scottish medieval cathedral to escape the destruction of the Reformation. Just opposite, in Castle Street, is the three-storey **Provand's Lordship**, which dates from 1471 and is the city's oldest house. It is now a museum (open daily).

The **Tenement House Museum** at 145 Buccleuch Street (open Mar–Nov: daily) is a reminder that this kind of housing, in which 20 percent of the people still live, was the backbone of the city for a century or more. This was the home of Miss Agnes Toward from 1911 to 1965 and it is gas-lit, just as she left it.

Two streets away is Renfrew Street and the **Glasgow School of Art** which has a wing built by Glasgow's most influential architect, Charles Rennie Mackintosh (1868–1928), wellspring of the Glasgow Art Nouveau style. Past the 1930s **Glasgow Film Theatre** and the important contemporary **McLellan Galleries** (open Mon–Sat and Sun pm), is Sauchiehall Street and the **Willow Tearoom**, in an immaculate Mackintosh setting.

To the west of Sauchiehall Street is the University area in Kelvingrove Park where the superb **Art Gallery and Museum** (open daily; free) is located. Second only to London's Tate Gallery in numbers of visitors, it has an impressive collection of paintings, including works from the *fin-de-siècle* Glasgow Boys and the Scottish Colourists of the post-war years.

In 1983, the art world became rather excited by **The Burrell Gallery** where

Map, page 322

ABOVE: Glasgow's George Street.
BELOW: Art Gallery and Museum at Kelvingrove.

A Night with Robert Burns

Few English people know the day William Shakespeare was born (23 April), but every Scot is aware that 25 January is the birthday of the country's most celebrated poet, Robert Burns. Indeed, on that day it is surprising how many people around the world suddenly recall the few drops of Scottish blood they have lurking in their veins.

Babbity Bowster's, a pub and hotel in a Robert Adam house in Blackfriars Street, Glasgow, has a reputation for its Burns Nights. Throughout the year its upstairs restaurant serves Scottish fare such as cullen skink (smoked haddock and potato soup), stovies (potatos cooked with onion), Loch Etive mussels and hot goat's cheese on wholemeal toast.

On Burns Night it is equally traditional. Just after 7.30pm, a kilted piper pipes in the first course of haggis, bashed neaps and tatties.

(Haggis is made with sheep's or calf's offal, oatmeal, suet, onions and seasoning boiled in the skin of an animal's stomach, although the restaurant has a vegetarian alternative; bashed neaps are mashed turnips; tatties are potatoes). Next comes a main course of perhaps venison in port, or beef marinaded in whisky. A chocolate pudding may round off the meal. And all this, of course, is washed down with *usquebaugh*, the water of life. In this case the whisky will be single malt (unblended and the product of one distillery). Meanwhile, guests read poems from Burns's works, starting with *Address to the Haggis*, and the evening ends after midnight as everyone crosses arms, holds hands and sings a rousing, fond chorus of *Auld Lang Syne*.

This song was one of some 200 ballads Burns collected or re-cast for the Scots Musical Museum. "It has never been in print nor even in manuscript until I took it down from an old man singing," said Burns. (The current tune may have been added later, though.)

Burns, the "heaven-taught ploughman" was a well-educated farmer's son, born in 1759 in Alloway in Ayrshire, south of Glasgow. Needless to say, there is a Burns Heritage Trail there now, which takes in most of the two dozen museums, mausoleum, inns and houses associated with the 37 years of his life. He was 26 when *Poems, chiefly in the Scottish Dialect* was published with such success that all Edinburgh society fell at his feet.

Burns could write perfectly good English and the fact that some of the Scottish dialect he chose to write in was just as unintelligible to its audience then as it is to us now did not matter. It was Scottish, and something to be proud of, for this was the beginning of the Romantic Age which was stirring all Europe. Burns supported the French Revolution and his lines on liberty and justice have touched a chord in peoples in many nations. But most of all Burns is celebrated for his carousing, his love of drink and good company and his lack of domestic responsiblity.

No wonder women were, for so long, excluded from Burns Nights. Even today they are liable to be a minority of the 100,000 who belong to Burns clubs in more than 20 countries, from the Pacific Rim to Russia where the "Ploughman Poet", champion of the workers, is particularly revered. ❑

a bequest of the shipowner Sir William Burrell (1861–1958) finally came to rest (open daily; free). There are some good pieces among the eclectic collection, but the gallery itself, in Pollock Country Park in the southwest of the city, is part of the show. Also in the park is the 18th-century **Pollok House** (open May–Sept: daily; free), which has a strong Spanish collection including works by Goya, El Greco and Murillo.

Robert Burns country

It has been unkindly said that Glasgow is a great city to get out of; it is certainly an easy one. A motorway runs right through the centre of the city and across the River Clyde down through Renfrewshire past Glasgow's airport at Abbotsinch and into Ayrshire. This is the land of Scotland's greatest poet, Robert Burns, and of the seaside resorts of **Largs, Troon, Prestwick** and **Girvan**.

From Weymss Bay on this coast, there are ferries to the islands of **Bute** and **Great Cumbrae**. From Ardrossan there are ferries to **Arran ⑫**, Glasgow's favourite holiday playground isle. At 166 sq. miles (430 sq. km), this mountainous and dramatic island is the biggest in the Clyde estuary. **Brodick Castle** (open Easter–Oct: daily; gardens open all year; tel: 01770-302202), parts of which date from the 14th century and have associations with Robert the Bruce, is at the foot of the almost 3,000-ft (900-metre) Goatfell. A treasure house of pictures, porcelain, sporting prints and silver which belonged to the Hamilton family, it is now in the care of the National Trust of Scotland.

The Ayrshire coast opposite Arran has some of the finest golf courses in Scotland. Among them are three venues for the Open Championship: Royal Troon, Turnberry, and Prestwick, where it all began in 1860. To the south of Ardrossan

Map, page 322

ABOVE: Burns Cottage, South Alloway. **BELOW:** Pollok House Gardens

*Burns's bed at his
house in Dumfries.*

is **Ayr** itself, 35 miles (56 km) southwest of Glasgow, and on the edge of the town at **Alloway** is **Burns Cottage** (open Apr–Oct: daily; Nov–Mar: closed Sun; tel: 01292-441215), the "auld clay biggin" where the poet was born.

At **Kirkoswald** ⓮, 12 miles (20 km) south on the A77, is **Souter Johnnie's House**, the home of the "ancient, trusty, druthy crony" featured in Burns' great narrative poem, *Tam O'Shanter*, and now a museum (open Easter–Sept: daily; Oct: Sat and Sun; tel: 01655-760274).

On the coast next to Kirkoswald is the magnificent **Culzean Castle** (open Apr–Oct: daily; country park open daily; tel: 01655-760 269), one of the greatest achievements of the 18th-century Scots architect, Robert Adam. A suite on the top floor was given as a life tenure to General Eisenhower, a tribute from the Scottish people. Besides a fine collection of paintings, weapons, furniture and porcelain, there is a museum commemorating the US president's achievements.

Moving south

In the southwestern-most corner of Scotland lie Dumfries and Galloway, an area of pretty towns and villages along the **Solway Firth** and wild moorland country in the interior. This culminates in the hammerhead peninsula of the **Mull of Galloway** ⓯, an area of great beauty with sandy beaches to the east, steep cliffs to the west, and the hills known as the Rhinns of Galloway running down the middle. The northern inlet is **Loch Ryan**, famous for its oysters, at the head of which is **Stranraer**, the principal departure port from Scotland to Ireland.

The Firth narrows near Southerness, one of Scotland's many "unknown" great golf courses, and nearby **Kirkbean** was the birthplace of John Paul Jones, founder of the US navy. Five miles (8 km) north on the A710, towards Dumfries, lies an impressive ruin, the red sandstone **Sweetheart Abbey** ⓰ (open Mon–Sat and Sun pm; Oct–Mar: closed Thur pm) built by Devorgilla, great-great-granddaughter of David I. She was the wife of John Balliol, founder of Balliol College in Oxford (1263) and mother of "Toom Tabard" (Empty Coat), the other John Balliol, the puppet king appointed to rule Scotland by Edward I of England.

Dumfries ⓱, nearby on the River Nith, where you can see salmon fishermen up to their waists in water, is the largest town in southwest Scotland. Burns spent the last six years of his life in Dumfries, and the house where he died, in 1796, is now a museum – the **Burns House** (open Mon–Sat and Sun pm; Oct–Mar: closed Sun and Mon; tel: 01387-255297). There is also a fine statue to him in the High Street, and in the nearby **Globe Inn**, one of his favourite taverns, the chair he usually occupied is preserved. At the **Robert Burns Centre** in Mill Road, there are audio-visual displays, models and other exhibits illustrating the life and work of the poet.

On the shores of the Solway Firth, 8 miles (12 km) southeast of Dumfries off the B725, are the ruins of the moated triangular-shaped fortress, **Caerlaverock Castle** ⓲ (open Mon–Sat and Sun pm; tel: 01387-770244), one of the great Border strongholds. In the 17th century the Earl of Nithsdale built a classical mansion inside the ruins, creating one of the oddest architectural additions in Scotland. ❑

HISTORIC CASTLES AND ABBEYS

An Englishman's home may be his castle but for centuries and, in some instances even today, a Scotsman's castle has been his home

Dotted throughout the Scottish landscape are more than 2,000 castles, many in ruins but others in splendid condition. The latter, still occupied, do not fulfil the primary definition of "castle" – a fortified building – but rather meet the secondary definition: a large, magnificent house.

Either way, all are not merely part of Scottish history: they are its essence. Many carry grim and grisly tales. Thus, Hugh Macdonald was imprisoned in the bowels of Duntulum Castle and fed generous portions of salted beef, but he was denied anything – even whisky – to drink.

In 1746 Blair Castle was, on the occasion of the Jacobite uprising, the last castle in the British isles to be fired upon in anger. Today, the Duke of Atholl, the owner of Blair Castle, is the only British subject permitted to maintain a private army, the Atholl Highlanders. Prior to the siege, Bonnie Prince Charlie slept here (visitors might be excused for believing there are few castles in Scotland where the Bonnie Prince and Mary, Queen of Scots did not sleep).

You, too, can sleep in Scottish castles. Culzean (*above*), Skibo and Inverlochy are but a trio where accommodation is available. And, for those eager to become a laird, don the kilt and own a castle, several are invariably on the market.

◁ **STRONGHOLD**
In 1314 Robert the Bruce reaffirmed Scottish supremacy won at Bannockburn by reclaiming Stirling Castle from the English.

△ **RELIGIOUS RELICS**
The ruins of St Andrews Cathedral give some idea of the grandeur of ecclesiastical building: this was once the greatest church in Scotland.

◁ GUARDING THE GLEN

Urquhart Castle was built to guard the Great Glen. It played an important role in the Wars of Independence, being taken by Edward 1 and later held by Robert the Bruce. During the Jacobite troubles part of the castle was blown up to prevent it falling into "rebel" hands. Today, its walls are a strategic spot from which to sight the Loch Ness Monster.

▽ ROYAL RESIDENCE

Stirling Castle, once called "the key to Scotland" because of its strategic position between the Lowlands and Highlands, witnessed many bloody battles between the Scots and English. Later, it became a favourite residence of Stuart monarchs. Nowadays it is also the home of the regimental museum of the Argyll and Sutherland Highlanders.

SCOTTISH BORDER ABBEYS

Scotland, especially the Borders, is full of abbeys that now lie ruined but were once powerful institutions with impressive buildings. During the reign of David I (1124–53), who revitalized and transformed the Scottish church, more than 20 religious houses were founded. Outstanding among these is a quartet of Border abbeys – Dryburgh (Premonstratensian), Jedburgh (Augustinian), Kelso (Tironensian) and Melrose (Cistercian). All have evocative ruins, though perhaps it is Jedburgh (*above*) with tower and remarkable rose window still intact, which is Scotland's classic abbey.

It was not the Reformation (1560) that caused damage to these abbeys but rather the selfishness of pre-Reformation clergy, raids in the 14th–16th centuries by both English and Scots, the ravages of weather and activities of 19th-century restorers. The concern of the Reformation, spearheaded by firebrand John Knox, was to preserve, not to destroy, the churches they needed.

Monasteries continued to exist as landed corporations after the Reformation. Why upset a system that suited so many interests? After all, the Pope, at the King's request, had provided priories and abbeys for five of James V's bastards while they were still infants.

◁ BARONIAL SPLENDOUR

Dunrobin, the largest pile in the Highlands, is seat of the Dukes of Sutherland who once owned more land than anyone in Europe. Originally a fortified square keep, it was transformed into a castle and then in the 19th century into a French château with Scottish baronial overtones. The gardens are magnificent.

THE SCOTTISH HIGHLANDS

The Highlands of Scotland form one of the last great wildernesses of Europe – endless stretches of wild country, mountains, glens and moorlands probed by the long fingers of sea lochs

Map, page 322

The southern edge of the Highland line runs across the country diagona from the Mull of Kintyre, the long spit of land stretching southwards fr Argyll on the western edge of the Firth of Clyde, right up to a point south-west of Aberdeen near Stonehaven. More than half of Scotland lies to the north of this line, most of it mountainous, with just a few fertile glens where crops can be grown and cattle reared. The population is sparse in the northwest – in Sutherland it is as low as 6 people per sq. mile (2.4 people per sq. km), compared to the national average of 955 (369).

Off the west coast lie several hundred islands, and these have the highest density of the 80,000 Gaelic speakers left in Scotland. The southernmost group comprises Gigha, Islay, Jura and Colonsay. Farther north there are the large islands of Mull and Skye and the Inner Hebrides of Iona, Staffa, Tiree, Coll, Muck, Eigg, Rum and Canna; and the Outer Hebrides group of Lewis, Harris, North Uist, Benbecula, South Uist, Eriskay and Barra.

To the north of the Scottish mainland are the Orkney and Shetland groups. You can reach some of the Scottish offshore islands by air – there are services to Islay, Benbecula, Lewis, Orkney, Shetland and Fair Isle. Ferries link the other inhabited islands to the mainland.

There is so much to see in the Highlands, such an enormous variation in the scenery of mountain, moorland, loch and glen, that anyone could spend a lifetime exploring it – and many Scots from the cities and towns do just that on weekends.

The westerly A82 out of Glasgow leads almost immediately to the Highlands, turning north after Dumbarton, along the Bonnie Bonnie Banks of **Loch Lomond ⓳**, the largest freshwater lake in Britain, 23 miles (37 km) long and 5 miles (8 km) across at its widest point. Hills dominate the landscape. Across the loch is **Ben Lomond**, first of the "Munros", Scotland's 277 mountains which rise to more than 3,000 ft (900 metres) and offer a perennial challenge to climbers from all over the country.

Scenic rail route

The A82 continues up to Fort William, a journey which can also be made by the scenic West Highland Line railway. Leaving Glasgow, the railway follows the banks of the Clyde to **Helensburgh ⓴**, the small resort town where the television pioneer John Logie Baird was born in 1888. This is also where the Glasgow Modern Movement architect Charles Rennie Mackintosh built the finest extant example of his domestic style, **Hill House** (open Easter–Oct: daily pm; tel: 01436-673900).

The line follows the shores of Loch Long and Loch Lomond, through the narrow valley of Glen Falloch, between bronze, green and heather-purple hills, to

LEFT: a herd of reindeer. **BELOW:** Highland steer.

Crianlarich ㉑, where the line to Oban branches off. Crianlarich to the south and Fort William to the north are both good entry points for one of the most popular "corners" of the Scottish Highlands: **Glencoe** ㉒. This deep mountain valley stretches more than 7 miles (11 km) from Loch Leven to Rannoch Moor through magnificent scenery. The often mist-shrouded peaks of the Glen are favourites among experienced rock climbers, although even the most experienced have fatal accidents here, particularly in bad weather.

Moorland splendour

The West Highland Line train from Glasgow to Mallaig allows the best opportunity for witnessing the bleak splendour of **Rannoch Moor** ㉓, 60 sq. miles (155 sq. km) of peat bog, lochs and winding streams through which no road runs (one goes as far as Rannoch Station). Lying to the east of Glencoe, Rannoch is a great empty moor ringed by mountains, on which lie the two loneliest railway stations in Britain, Rannoch and Corrour, 1,365 ft (410 metres) above sea level. The moor's inhabitants are waterbirds, plovers, skylarks, eagles, herds of red deer and the succulent brown trout inhabiting peat-brown lakelets called lochans; three or four lonely households manage to exist on its surface.

At the northern edge of the moor, the line swings west again, past the deep cleft cut by the River Spean in Monessie Gorge, to Fort William at the head of Loch Linnhe and the foot of **Ben Nevis**, Britain's highest mountain, 4,406 ft (1,343 metres) and 24 miles (39 km) around. From here there are impressive views down the sea loch and over the mountain ranges of Ardgour and Moydart.

The Highland rail tour can be continued by changing to the train to Mallaig, a fishing port opposite the Isle of Skye. From Fort William, Ben Nevis is not much

TIP

The huge expanse of Rannoch Moor can be formidably bleak in winter, but in summer it's a botanist's delight. Plants include the Rannoch rush, a plant found nowhere else in Britain.

BELOW: Glencoe.

THE MASSACRE AT GLENCOE

Translated literally as the Valley of Weeping, the name of Glencoe is a haunting reminder of the violent massacre that occurred here in February 1692. By order of the English King William III, more than 200 troops loyal to the English Crown, and commanded by Robert Campbell of Glenlyon, turned on the MacDonald clan, who had been their hosts for 12 days. 38 Men, women and children were slaughtered as a punishment for the tardiness of the chief of the MacDonald clan in giving allegiance to the English king.

The Massacre of Glencoe created a great deal of bad blood between the MacDonalds and Campbells and inceased the clans' mistrust of central government – many Highlanders also interpreted the Jacobite Risings which took place 23 years later as revenge for Glencoe.

Reminders of the massacre are everywhere: there is a memorial to the MacDonalds near the old Invercoe Road, and the Signal Rock near the Clachaig Inn is said to be the place from which a signal was sent to the Campbells to go ahead with the massacre. An excellent exhibition in the Glencoe Visitors' Centre provides further details of this notorious episode. Even today few can escape the sense of gloom that pervades as they descend the main road between the dark, brooding mountains.

more than a stiff walk, but proper clothes and boots are essential because the weather on mountain tops in Scotland can be treacherous even in high summer. When conditions are clear, the climb really is worth the effort.

Map, page 322

The original fortification at **Fort William** ㉔ was constructed in the 17th century to keep out "savage clans" and sundry other undesirables. Nothing of the fort remains today: it was demolished in the late 19th century to make way for the railway, which led to rapid the expansion of the town and its environs. Nowadays, being such an important crossroads in the Scottish Highlands, Fort William throngs with tourists. And the area yields much to the more intrepid explorer apart from Ben Nevis. A bus trip, for example, up to **Loch Ness**, 30 miles (48 km) to the northeast may just result in a sighting of the famous monster. In the town itself, near the tourist information centre, is the excellent **West Highland Museum**, which has a number of Jacobite relics including a "secret portrait" of Bonnie Prince Charlie, plus one of the panelled rooms of the old fort (open Mon–Sat; tel: 01397-702169).

The train to Mallaig follows the A830 west through Bonnie Prince Charlie country, beginning with the stunning view from the viaduct at **Glenfinnan** ㉕ down Loch Shiel, and over the monument on the shore that marks the spot where the Young Pretender himself raised the Stuart standard. Here the clans gathered to begin the Jacobite Rebellion of 1745. It was in this country, too, that he hid with a price of £30,000 on his head after the defeat at Culloden.

Beyond Lochailort there is a view seawards over the bright water and rocky islets of **Loch nan Uamh**, where the Bonnie Prince landed in 1745 with only nine men and from where he left 14 months later, despite all the pleadings of the haunting Jacobite songs, never to return. The pebbly beaches of Loch nan

ABOVE: the Glenfinnan Memorial
BELOW: Glenfinnan.

Gaelic–English roadsign on Skye.

Uamh give way to the silver sands of Morar and Arisaig, shining like snow on the edge of the steel-blue sea. Inland are the mountains looking over the dark waters of **Loch Morar**, the deepest lake in Britain at over 1,000 ft (300 metres), which is reputed to house a monster no less mysterious than the more famous one in Loch Ness.

Over the sea

The busy fishing port of **Mallaig** 26 is one of the ferry departure points for the Isle of Skye (the principal crossing is over the bridge at Kyle of Lochalsh, further north). Near the railway station is **Marine World** (open Apr–Oct: daily; tel: 01687-462292), with fine displays of aquatic life.

From the fjord-like sea lochs of the west, across to the sheer Cuillin Mountains in the south, and to the craggy northern tip of the Trotternish Peninsula, **Skye** 27 epitomises Scotland's wild Celtic appeal. The 19th-century Clearances saw whole glens emptied of their ancient settlements; since then, the population of Skye has steadily decreased and it is now around 12,000. Tourism has replaced the crofters' farms as the major source of income and has produced something of a "pre-packaged" feel in some of the main centres. But a day's hike or cycle ride around the 50-mile (80-km) long island will still set you squarely in the wilderness.

The **Cuillin Mountains** are a 6-mile (10-km) arc of peaks, 15 of which exceed the 3,000 ft (900 metres) needed to make them Munros. If the summits seem forbidding, take the walk down Glen Sligachan into the heart of these mountains and through to the other side 8 miles (13 km) due south to the beach of Camasunary in Loch Scavaig. On the southern tip of Skye is **Armadale Cas-**

BELOW LEFT: a good catch. **BELOW RIGHT:** the Red Cuillins.

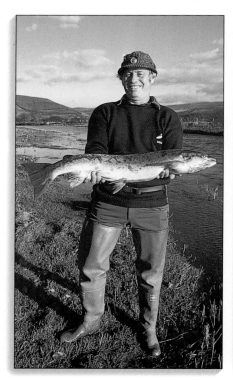

tle, now the site of the **Clan Donald Centre** (open Apr–Nov: daily; gardens year round; tel: 01471-844305). The main attraction of northwestern Skye is **Dunvegan Castle** (open mid-Mar–Oct: Mon–Sat; tel: 01470-521 206), which offers abundant insights into the clan spirit of Scotland in its paintings and relics from the Macleod clan.

On the west side of the Trotternish Peninsula, **Uig** is an attractive village that encircles a bay from where ferries depart for the outer isles. This northern arm of Skye has been less altered by tourism than any part of the island. Skye's easternmost town, **Kyleakin**, is where, upon payment of a toll, a bridge allows the islanders to reach the mainland at **Kyle of Lochalsh ㉓**, which is also the terminus of the second part of the West Highland Line from Inverness.

The train to Inverness, the capital of the Highlands, runs along the shores of **Loch Carron**, past the pretty village of **Plockton** on its islanded bay, with splendid views to the north of the mountains of Applecross and Wester Ross, then up Glen Carron through dramatic wild country, populated by little more than deer and eagles, wildcats and buzzards on its high tops and a few sheep and cattle among the narrow glens. As the train heads further east, so the ruggedness of the Highland landscape begins to fade. The change is first noticeable at **Garve**, where the landscape begins to melt into the civilisation of the rich farmland around the Moray Firth on the east coast. Inverness appears on the shoreline and beyond it the Monadliath mountains loom over Loch Ness.

An alternative route out from Kyle of Lochalsh is to head north by road on either the A890 through **Glen Carron** or the A896 via **Shieldaig**. Both roads intersect with the A832 which goes west down Glen Docherty to **Loch Maree**, one of the prettiest lochs in Scotland, and beyond to the extraordinary gardens at

Map, page 322

Dunvegan Castle claims to be the oldest continuously inhabited castle in Scotland; it has been the seat of the chiefs of Clan Macleod for more than 700 years.

BELOW: Plockton.

Britain's most northerly group of islands are the **Shetlands**, 48 miles (78 km) north of the Orkneys and nearer to the Arctic circle than to London. **Lerwick** ❸ is the archipelago's only town and there is a small airport on the main island served from most Scottish airports, a frequency maintained because of the Shetlands' significant oil installations. In recent years the discovery of oil in the North Sea left noticeably less room for tourism, though the oil boom has quietened down now and the Shetlands' antiquity once again attracts.

The tiny island of **Mousa**, off the east coast, is the site of the world's best-preserved Iron-Age *broch* tower, a fortress that is just about intact after more than 1,000 years of battering from Arctic storms. **Muness Castle** on **Unst** ❸, the most northerly of the dozen inhabited islands, and the ruins of **Scalloway Castle**, 6 miles (10 km) to the west of Lerwick, are also worth visiting.

At the southern tip of the mainland, next door to Sumburgh Airport, is **Jarlshof** (*see pages 32–33*), a remarkable "layer-cake" of an archaeological site (open Apr–Sept: Mon–Sat and Sun pm; tel: 01950-460112). Bronze Age dune dwellers, broch builders, Vikings and medieval inhabitants all left their marks.

South from Inverness

The A9 south from Inverness leads back towards Edinburgh and Glagow, through impressive scenery in the high glens of the **Grampians** with the massive summits of the Cairngorms towering over the ski and sports resort of **Aviemore** ❸. It also passes the pretty town of **Pitlochry**, a quaint hillside town that plays patient host to an endless stream of tourist-laden vehicles. The Pitlochry Festival Theatre, over the Aldour Bridge from town, runs from April to October and draws first-class performers from all over the world. Eight miles (13 km) north-

ABOVE: seeing the Highlands on wheels. **BELOW:** Shetland cottage.

west of Pitlochry is **Blair Castle** ③⑦ (open Apr–Oct: daily; tel: 01796-481207), dating from the 12th century and the seat of the Duke of Atholl, the last noble in Britain licensed to have a private army. **Perth,** generally considered the gateway to the Highlands (the first line of high hills rise over the horizon), has little of interest to the visitor.

A fitting endpiece to the southerly hike down the A9 is a visit to **Stirling** ③⑧. Equidistant from Edinburgh and Glasgow, this city still considers itself the rightful capital of Scotland. Stirling seems to have escaped the worst excesses of the Victorian Age; winding streets and medieval cobblestones are everywhere in evidence. **Stirling Castle** (open daily) seems to have grown out of the 150-ft (77-metre) crag on which it was built. It featured prominently in the Scottish wars of succession during the 13th and 14th centuries, passing back and forth between the English and the Scots until the Scots finally won it for keeps in 1342. The castle was the home of the Stuart kings between 1370 and 1603; it was they who shaped it into what it is today. Mary, Queen of Scots and James VI of Scotland (who became James I of England) also spent several years there.

A multi-screen presentation, at the **Royal Burgh of Stirling Visitor Centre** (open daily), traces the history of Stirling, bringing to life such events as the Battle of Bannockburn. The Centre also has an exhibition of life in Stirling during the 19th century. At the foot of the castle is the oldest part of Stirling, with a number of interesting buildings such as **Argyll's Lodging** and the **Guildhall**. Also worth visiting are two religious sites: the **Church of the Holy Rude** and the **Cambuskenneth Abbey.** The former is a 15th-century building with an unusual open timber roof and a five-sided apse in the choir. The 90-ft (28-metre) tower shows the scars of hostilities which may have occurred during the Jacobite Rebel-

**Map,
page 322**

Stirling has had to pay for its strategic position; the nearby battlefields of Stirling Bridge (1297), Bannock-burn (1314) and Sauchiburn (1488) are reminders of past struggles with the English.

BELOW: Stirling Castle

ling, valuable paintings and artefacts, and are in the care of the National Trust for Scotland (tel: 0131 226 5992).

North of Aberdeen, but still in the Grampian region (of which Aberdeen is the administrative capital), is **Haddo House** ❹ (house open Easter and May–Sept: daily; Oct: Sat and Sun; garden open daily; tel: 0131-226 5922), an 18th-century palatial mansion. It was designed by William Adam as the seat of the Earls of Aberdeen, one of whom – the 4th Earl – was Queen Victoria's prime minister from 1852–5, and it is full of treasures. Northwest of Aberdeen, off the A96, is **Leith Hall** ❺ (open May–Sept: daily from 1.30pm; Oct: Sat–Sun from 1.30pm; tel: 0131-226 5922), a handsome laird's house on a more modest scale.

North sea ports

The A92 coast road south of Aberdeen goes through the North Sea ports of **Montrose** and **Arbroath** ❻. At Arbroath are the ruins of a 12th-century **Abbey**, the scene of Scotland's noble Declaration of Independence in 1320.

Next comes **Dundee** ❼, the town of jam, jute and journalism (the three Js) looking across the estuary of the River Tay at the north coast of Fife. The three Js still play their part in the life of the city. D.C. Thomson produces local newspapers and weeklies that are read all over Scotland and the largest collection of children's comics in Britain. *The Discovery*, the ship Captain Scott took to the Antarctic in 1910, was built here and has now returned to find a final resting place (open daily). Also in the harbour is the HMS *Unicorn* (open Apr–Oct: daily; Jan–Mar: Mon–Fri), a frigate with 24 cannons which was launched in 1824. Dundee is one of the largest cities in Scotland; but with acres of docklands, industry and suburbs, it is also understandably one of the least visited.

And so across "the Silvery Tay", as the Bard of Dundee referred to it in so many of his poems, to Fife and an hour and a half's run back to Edinburgh. ❑

RIGHT: salmon fishermen.

INSIGHT GUIDES
Travel Tips

Insight Guides portray destinations in depth, providing the complete picture and the top photography

Insight Pocket Guides *focus on the best choices for places to see and things to do and include large fold-out maps*

Insight Compact Guides' *portability makes them the perfect books to carry with you for on-the-spot reference*

Three types of guide for all types of travel

INSIGHT GUIDES Different people need different kinds of information. Some want *background information* to help them prepare for the trip. Others seek *personal recommendations* from someone who knows the destination well. And others look for *compactly presented data* for on-the-spot reference. With three carefully designed series, Insight Guides offer readers the perfect choice. Insight Guides will turn your visit into an experience.

The world's largest collection of visual travel guides

CONTENTS

Getting Acquainted

The Place

Area England: 50,056 sq miles (129,645 sq km); Scotland: 29,794 sq miles (77,177 sq km); Wales: 7,967 sq miles (20,635 sq km).

Capital London.

Highest Mountain Ben Nevis (4,406 ft/1,343 metres).

Population England: 48.9 million; Scotland: 5.1 million; and Wales: 2.9 million.

Language English; 20 per cent of residents in Wales also speak Welsh; Gaelic in parts of Scotland.

Religion Protestant (Church of England): the monarch is the titular head of the church; the primate is the Archbishop of Canterbury.

Time Zone Greenwich Mean Time (GMT), 1 hour behind Continental European Time, 5 hours ahead of Eastern Seaboard Time. British Summer Time (+ one hour) runs from March to September.

Currency Pounds divided into 100 pence (as this book goes to press, £1 is approximately US$1.60). Scotland issues its own notes, which are not technically legal tender in England and Wales, though banks and some shops will accept them.

Weights and Measures Officially metric although imperial measurements are still widely used, notably for distances (miles) and beer in pubs (pints).

Electricity 240 volts, square, three-pin plugs; two-pin shaver plugs.

Direct Dialling country code: 44.

Climate

Temperate, generally mild and always unpredictable. It is unusual for any area in the British Isles to have a dry spell for more than two or three weeks, even in the summer months from June to September. However, it rains most frequently in the mountainous areas of north and west Britain where temperatures are also cooler than in the south.

In summer, the average maximum temperature in the South of England is in the 70s Fahrenheit (23–25°C), although over 80°F (27°C) is not unusual. In Scotland temperatures tend to stay within the mid-60s Fahrenheit (17–19°C). During the winter (November to February), the majority of Britain, with the exception of mountainous regions in the North, tends to be cold and damp rather than snowy.

For recorded weather information, tel: (0891) 500401.

Economy

Napoleon's statement that Britain is a nation of shopkeepers is still largely true. It is a trading country, with much of its economic wealth derived from the export of goods and services, particularly financial services. With 76 per cent of UK land farmland, cereal crops and vegetables are important both for the home and export market.

Although heavy industry is no longer a major earner, manufacturing remains crucial to the economy. Britain produces a wide range of goods, from food and drinks, to pharmaceuticals, textiles and machinery. Following devaluation of the pound against other European countries in the early-1990s, the British economy has gradually improved. The pinch of recession is still being felt by the public and business, but property sales have

Public Holidays

● **January** New Year's Day (1)
● **March/April** Good Friday, Easter Monday
● **May** May Day (first Monday), Spring Bank Holiday (last Monday)
● **August** Summer Bank Holiday (Last Monday)
● **December** Christmas Day (25), Boxing Day (26)

On British public holidays all banks are closed. Roads are usually a nightmare, especially during the summer bank holiday weekends, as people head for the coast, relatives or days out. On the Friday before a Monday off and on Christmas Eve, supermarkets can sell out of basics early in the day as people stock up in a frenzy for their long weekend.

improved and interest rates are lower than in the bust-and-boom 1980s. More new businesses are emerging and fewer failing, although unemployment is still high, particularly in areas of the country that have suffered the demise of long-existing industries such as mining. One encouraging aspect is that Britain is now attracting major investment (dominated by the car industry) from elsewhere, particularly the US and Japan.

Government

Britain is a constitutional monarchy with a parliamentary democracy. Although Queen Elizabeth II is head of state, she has no real power. Britain is governed centrally from Parliament at Westminster in London. Certain administrative differences exist for Scotland, and to a lesser extent for Wales, and legislation is currently under discussion for more power to be devolved to the Scottish and Welsh Assemblies. Parliament consists of two bodies, the House of Commons (consisting of 659 Members of Parliament or MPs) and the House of Lords (predominantly unelected hereditary or life peers). The Commons has supreme control of national policy, finance and legislation. The House of Lords is known as the Revising Chamber, which ratifies, fine-tunes and sometimes overturns Commons legislation.

Governments stay in power for a maximum term of five years. Voting is voluntary, and MPs are elected if they win the majority of votes in their constituency. The main two political parties are the Conservative Party (Tories), which dates back to the 18th century, and the Labour Party, which was formed at the end of the 19th century. Other opposition comes from the Liberal Democratic Party. There are also two nationalist parties, Plaid Cymru in Wales and the Scottish National Party.

The public can watch Parliament in session in the Public Galleries of the House of Commons and House of Lords. The Commons is in session 2.30–10pm Monday–Thursday, 9.30-noon Wednesday and 9.30am–3pm Friday. For information, tel 0171-219 4272 (Commons) or 0171-219 3107 (Lords). For tours of the Houses of Parliament, British residents should contact their MP.

Business Hours

Town centre shops generally open 9am–5.30pm Monday–Saturday, although smaller shops may close for lunch. Many small towns and villages have a half-day closing one day in the week and some shopping centres in towns and cities may have one evening of late-night shopping.

Supermarkets tend to be open 8.30am–8pm from Monday to Saturday and 10am–4pm on Sunday; some local corner shops and off-licences stay open until 10pm.

Offices usually operate 9am–5.30pm Monday–Friday with an hour for lunch.

British pubs are legally permitted to open between 11am and 11pm Monday–Saturday and noon–10.30pm on Sunday. However, some may close for periods during the day, and pubs can apply for a licence for extended opening hours for special events or nights such as New Year's Eve.

Planning the Trip

Clothing

Temperatures can fluctuate considerably from day to day so come prepared with suitable warm and wet-weather clothing whatever the season. Generally, short sleeves and a jacket are fine for summer but a warm coat and woollens are recommended for winter.

On the whole the British tend to dress casually and with a few exceptions formal dress is not essential for evening events, although a jacket and tie is required by smart hotels, restaurants and clubs.

The young are particularly style-conscious and as a consequence there is a strong presence of trendy street fashion in Britain's cities. At the other end of the scale, the British reputation for conservative and traditional clothing

Customs Regulations

If you enter the UK directly from another European Union (EU) country, you no longer need to exit Customs through a red or green channel – use the special EU blue channel, as you are not required to declare any goods you have brought in for personal use. However, if you bring in large amounts of goods such as alcohol, tobacco or perfume you may be asked to verify that they are not for resale.

Visitors entering the UK from non-EU countries should use the green Customs channel if they do not exceed these allowances for goods obtained outside the EU, or purchased duty-free in the EU, or on board ship or aircraft:

- **Tobacco** 200 cigarettes *or* 100 cigarillos *or* 50 cigars *or* 250g of tobacco
- **Alcohol** 2 litres still table wine *plus* 1 litre spirits (over 22 percent by volume) *or* 2 litres fortified wine, sparkling wine or other liqueurs
- **Perfume** 60 cc/ml of perfume *plus* 250 cc/ml of toilet water

- **Presents** £145 worth of gifts, souvenirs or other goods.

It is illegal to bring animals, certain drugs, firearms, obscene material and anything likely to threaten health or the environment without prior arrangement. Any amount of currency can be brought in.

For further information contact **HM Customs and Excise**, New Kings Beam House, 22 Upper Ground, London SE1 9PJ, tel: 0171-620 1313.

Station. From there trains run every 15 minutes to New Street station in the centre of the city, taking about 15 minutes. Intercity trains from New Street to London Euston run on the hour every hour and take about 80 minutes.

Scotland
Glasgow Airport (8 miles/ 13 km west of Glasgow) has coach services every 20 minutes to the centre of Glasgow, which take around 15 minutes. These also stop at Glasgow's two rail stations. **Prestwick Airport** is about 40 minutes south of Glasgow on the west coast of Scotland. The train from within the terminal takes 50 minutes to Glasgow's Central station. There are regular buses to Glasgow and Edinburgh. **Edinburgh Airport** (7 miles/ 12 km west of Edinburgh) is connected to Edinburgh city centre by the Airlink bus service which runs every 10 minutes and takes roughly 25 minutes.

Wales
Cardiff Airport (12 miles/19 km east) is used mainly by charter operators. There is a bus link to the city centre.

Channel Tunnel
By train
Eurostar provides regular passenger-only trains linking Britain with France and Brussels. Services run from London's Waterloo station to Paris Nord (3 hours) and Brussels Midi (2 hours 40 minutes), with some trains stopping in Ashford, Kent. Or there are trains from Glasgow, Manchester and Birmingham to the Continent.

Booking is not essential, but it is worth watching for offers on tickets bought in advance. For UK bookings, tel: 0345 303030. From the US, tel: 1-800-eurostar, or elsewhere tel: (44) 1233 617575.

Children's Fares

- **Airlines** Aged 2–12 about 10 per cent of adult fares, over 12 half to two-thirds.
- **Trains** Under 5s free on your knee, aged 5–15 half price most tickets.
- **Coaches** Under 5s free on your knee, 5 and upwards about half price.

By Car
"Le Shuttle" trains travel through the tunnel from Folkestone in Kent to Nord-Pas de Calais in France. Services are every hour in each direction from 7am to 11pm and every two hours through the night. Booking is not essential. Tel: 0990 353535.

Sea Transport
Sea services operate between 12 British ports and more than 20 Continental ones. The major ferries have full eating, sleeping and entertainment facilities. The shortest route to the Continent is to France from Dover to Calais, which takes about 90 minutes by ferry and half an hour by Hovercraft.

Brittany Ferries, UK tel: 0990 360360, sails to Portsmouth from St Malo (33-99 82 80 80) and Caen (33-33 22 38 98) in France; to Poole in Dorset from Cherbourg, France (33-33 32 22 38 98); and to Portsmouth or Plymouth, depending on the season, from Santander in Spain (34-42 214 5000).

Hoverspeed, UK tel: 0990 240241, runs a hovercraft service to Dover from Calais (33-21 46 12 14).

P&O European Ferries, UK tel: 0990 980980, sails to Dover from Calais (33-21 46 04 40), and to Portsmouth from Cherbourg (33-33 88 65 70) and Le Havre in France (33-35 19 78 50).

Sally Line, UK tel: (01843) 595522, sails to Ramsgate in Kent to Dunkirk in France

(33-28 26 70 70) and Ostend, Belgium (32-59 55 99 66).

Hoverspeed Seacat, UK tel: (01304) 240241, operates the fast hovercraft service to Folkestone from Boulogne, France (33-21 30 27 26).

Stena Line, UK tel: (01233) 6407047, sails to Dover from Calais (33-21 46 78 30); to Newhaven from Dieppe, France (33-50 63 90 03), and to Southampton from Cherbourg (33-33 20 43 38).

If you plan to bring a vehicle over by ferry it is advisable to book in advance, particularly during peak holiday periods. If travelling by night on a long journey it is also recommended that you book a sleeping cabin in advance.

From North America you could arrive on Cunard's *Queen Elizabeth II*, the world's only transatlantic superliner. Operating between April and December, she takes six nights to cross the Atlantic. For information in the UK, tel: (01703) 716500.

Special Facilities

Many Tourist Information Centres (TICs, *see page 359 for details*) have leaflets giving information on access and facilities for the disabled at places of interest.

Free holiday information for people with special needs, from the disabled and elderly to one-parent families, is available from Holiday Care Service, 2nd Floor, Imperial Buildings, Victoria Road, Horley RH6 7PZ, tel: (01293) 774535.

The Royal Association for Disability and Rehabilitation (RADAR), Unit 12, City Forum, 250 City Road, London EC1V 8AS, tel: 0171-250 3222, acts as an information service and can provide a free list of publications with travel details for the disabled.

Information Centres

There are over 800 Tourist Information Centres (TICS) throughout Britain, which provide free information and advice to visitors on local sights, activities and accommodation. Most are open office hours, which are extended to include weekends and evenings in high season or in areas where there is a high volume of visitors all year round. Some close in winter between October and March. TICS are generally well signposted and denoted by the distinctive italic i symbol (*i*).

For general information about the whole of the country, contact (by phone or fax only):
The English Tourist Board/ British Tourist Authority,
Thames Tower, Black's Road, London W6 9EL.
Tel: 0181-846 9000.
Fax: 0181-563 0302.

Alternatively, the following are information offices for the different regions of Britain which you can write to or telephone for information. They are administrative offices only and cannot be visited in person.
East of England Tourist Board
Toppesfield Hall,
Hadleigh, Suffolk IP7 5DN.

Tel: (01473) 822922.
Fax: (01473) 823063.
Heart of England Tourist Board:
Larkhill Road,
Worcester WR5 2EZ.
Tel: (01905) 763436
Fax: (01905) 763450.
London Tourist Board and Convention Bureau
6th Floor, Glen House, Stag Place, London SW1E 5LT.
Tel: 0171-932 2000.
Credit card reservations, tel: 0171-932 2020.
Fax: 0171-932 0222.
South East England Tourist Board
The Old Brew House,
Warwick Park,
Tunbridge Wells TN2 5TU.
Tel: (01892) 540766
Fax: (01892) 511008.
Southern Tourist Board
40 Chamberlayne Road,
Eastleigh SO50 5JH.
Tel: (01703) 620006
Fax: (01703) 620010.
West Country Tourist Board
60 St David's Hill,
Exeter EX4 4SY.
Tel: (01392) 425426
Fax: (01392) 420891.
Yorkshire Tourist Board
312 Tadcaster Road,
York YO2 2HF.
Tel: (01904) 707961.
Fax: (01904) 701414.

Tourist Board News

Visitorcall is a recorded information service (calls from the UK only). Phone 08939 123, followed by:
● Accommodation 435
● Attractions 480
● Exhibitions 403
● Guided tours and walks 431
● Museums 429
● Pubs, restaurants, teas 485
● Shopping 486
● West End productions 416

Northumbria Tourist Board:
Aykley Heads,
Durham DH1 5UX.
Tel: 0191-375 3000.
Fax: 0191-386 0899.
North West Tourist Board
Swan House, Swan Meadow Road, Wigan Pier,
Wigan WN3 5BB.
Tel: (01942) 821222
Fax: (01942) 820002.
Scottish Tourist Board
23 Ravelston Terrace,
Edinburgh EH4 3EU.
Tel: 0131-332 2433.
Fax: 0131-343 1513.
Wales Tourist Board
Brunel House, 2 Fitzalan Road, Cardiff CF2 1UY.
Tel: (01222) 499909.
Fax: (01222) 485031.

Tourist Information in London

● **Scottish Tourist Board**
19 Cockspur Street, London SW1Y 5BL.
Tel: 0171-930 8661.
Fax: 0171-930 1817.
● **Wales Information Bureau**
British Travel Centre, 12 Regent Street, London SW1Y 4PQ.
Tel: 0171-409 0969.
Fax: 0171-287 1761.
● **British Travel Centre**
12 Regent Street, Piccadilly Circus, London SW1Y 4PQ. Personal callers only. Represented here in addition to the British Tourist Authority are British Rail, American Express

and Room-Centre offering a booking service for rail, air and sea travel, sightseeing tours, theatre tickets and accommodation throughout Britain. There is also a currency exchange bureau. The centre is open: 9am–6.30pm Monday–Friday and 10am–4pm at weekends.
● **The London Visitor and Convention Bureau** (LVCB) provides general information and booking services for hotels, theatres, and sightseeing tours at the following centres: Victoria

Station, Liverpool Street tube station, Waterloo International terminal (arrivals hall), Heathrow terminals 1, 2, 3 (underground station concourse) and Selfridges (Oxford Street, W1).
● **London Regional Transport** (LRT) publishes a map and guide for visitors which is available from information centres at the following underground stations: Piccadilly Circus, Oxford Circus, Heathrow and at major train stations in the capital.
For further information, tel: 0171-222 1234.

Practical Tips

Lost Possessions

If you have lost your passport, you must get in touch as quickly as possible with your embassy.

For possessions lost on trains you must contact the station where the train on which you were travelling ended its journey. The same applies should you leave something on a coach.

For anything lost on public transport in London, contact the London Transport Lost Property Office, 200 Baker Street, NW1 5RZ, tel: 0171-486 2496) between 9.30am and 2pm Monday–Friday, or fill in an enquiry form, available from any London Underground station or bus garage. Leave at least two full working days after the loss before making a visit to the lost property office.

Tipping

Most hotels and restaurants automatically add a 10–15 per cent service charge to your meal bill. It's your right to deduct this amount if you are not happy with the service provided. Sometimes when service has been added, the final total on a credit card slip is still left blank, the implication being that a further tip is expected: don't pay it. You don't tip in pubs, cinemas, theatres or elevators, but it is customary to give hairdressers, sightseeing guides, railway porters and cab drivers an extra amount of around 10 per cent.

Media

Newspapers

With over 100 daily and Sunday newspapers published nationwide, there's no lack of choice in Britain. Although free from state control and censorship and financially independent of political parties, many nationals do have pronounced political leanings. Of the quality dailies *The Times* and *The Daily Telegraph* are on the right, *The Guardian* on the left and *The Independent* in the middle. On Sunday *The Observer* leans slightly left of centre, while the *Independent on Sunday* stands in the middle and the *Sunday Times* and *Sunday Telegraph* are both on the right.

The Financial Times is renowned for the clearest, most unbiased headlines in its general news pages, plus exhaustive financial coverage.

Radio Stations

- **Classic FM** 100.9 FM
  24-hour classical music unpompously presented.
- **Jazz FM** 102.2FM
  Jazz alone failed to provide big enough audiences, so the station was broadened to include soul and blues.
- **Kiss FM** 100FM
  24-hour dance.
- **1FM** 98.8FM
  Britain's most popular radio station, which broadcasts mainstream pop.
- **Radio 2** 89.2FM
  Easy-listening music and chat shows.
- **Radio 3** 91.3FM
  24-hour classical music, plus some drama.
- **Radio 4** 93.5FM
  News, current affairs, plays.
- **Radio Five Live** 909MW
  Rolling news and sport.
- **BBC World Service** 648kHz
  International news.

The tabloids, or smaller newspapers, are a less formal easy read. *The Sun, The Star* and *News of the World* (out on Sunday) are on the right and obsessed with the Royal family, soap operas and sex. *The Mirror, Sunday Mirror* and *Sunday People* are slightly left. The *Daily Mail* and *Mail on Sunday* are slightly more upmarket equivalents of the *Daily* and *Sunday Express*.

Scotland's own quality daily is *The Scotsman,* and the *Daily Record* is the most popular Scottish tabloid.

Wales has the *Western Mail* and the *Daily Post*.

Listing Magazines

To find out what's on in London, the long-established weekly *Time Out* (out on Wednesdays) is supreme. But the London-only *Evening Standard* includes a good free magazine, *Hot Tickets*, on Thursdays.

For details of events elsewhere, the quality daily newspapers have a limited listings section, but your best port of call is a Tourist Information Centre *(see page 359)*. Many local papers have a weekly section on Fridays with details of places to visit and things to do in their area.

Foreign Newspapers

These can usually be found in large newsagents and rail stations nationwide. Branches of John Menzies and W H Smith, in most towns, usually have a reasonable selection.

Television

Britain has a reputation for broadcasting some of the finest television in the world. There are five national terrestial channels: BBC1, BBC2, ITV, Channel 4 (C4) and Channel 5 (C5). Both the BBC (British Broadcasting Corporation) and ITV (Independent Television) have regional stations that broadcast

Emergencies

Only in an absolute emergency call **999** for fire, ambulance or police. In the case of a minor accident or illness, take a taxi to the nearest casualty department of a hospital. If you need the police, call Directory Enquiries on 192 and ask for the number of the nearest police station. They will also be able to give you the telephone number of your country's embassy or consulate.

local news and varying programme schedules in between links with the national networks based in London (see local newspapers for listings). The BBC is financed by compulsory annual television licences and therefore does not rely on advertising for funding. The independent channels, ITV, C4 and Channel 5, are funded entirely by commercials.

BBC1, ITV and C5 broadcast programmes aimed at mainstream audiences, while BBC2 and C4 cater more for arts, cultural and minority interests. However, the advent of cable and satellite channels has forced terrestial stations to fight for audiences with a higher incidence of programmes such as soap operas, game shows and situation comedies.

There are more than 60 cable and satellite channels on offer, ranging from sport and movies to cartoons and golden oldies. Pricier hotel rooms often offer a choice of cable stations, including CNN and NBC's Super Channel.

Postal Services

Post offices are open 9am–5.30pm Monday–Friday, and 9am–12.30 on Saturday. London's main post office is in Trafalgar Square, behind the church of St Martin-in-the-Fields, and it stays open until 8pm Monday–Saturday.

Stamps are sold at post offices, selected shops and newsagents, some supermarkets and from machines outside larger post offices. There is a two-tier service for mail within the UK: first class should reach its destination the next day, and second class will take a day longer. The rate to Europe for standard letters is the same as first-class post within Britain.

Mail can be forwarded to you at any post office in Britain if it is addressed c/o Poste Restante.

Telephones

It is often cheaper to use public phones rather than those in hotel rooms as hotels make high profits out of this service.

British Telecom (BT) is the main telephone operating company. Its public telephones are by far the most plentiful, though a number of other telephone companies, such as Mercury, also have kiosks. Some public phones take coins only, some plastic phone cards and/or credit cards, and some all three. Phone cards can be purchased from post offices and newsagents in varying amounts between £1 and £20.

The most expensive time to use the telephone is 8am–6pm weekdays, while the cheapest is after 6pm on weekdays and all weekend. Calls are charged according to distance, so a long-distance conversation on a weekday morning can eat up coins in a phone box .

Numbers beginning with the prefixes 0800, 0500, 0321 or 0645 are freephone lines. Those prefixed by 0345, 0645 or 0845 are charged at local rates irrespective of their distance. Those starting with 0891, 0839, 0640, 0660 and 0991 are very expensive.

Embassies

Most countries have diplomatic representation in London (a selection is given below), others can be found through the *Yellow Pages* or via telephone Directory Enquiries (192). Many also have consulates in Edinburgh and Cardiff.

Australia
Australia House, Strand, London WC2 4LA.
Tel: 0171-379 4334.

India
India House, Aldwych, London WC28 4NA
Tel: 0171-836 8484.

South Africa
South Africa House, Trafalgar Square, London WC2N 5DP.
Tel: 0171-930 4488.

United States: 24 Grosvenor Square, London W1A 1AF.
Tel: 0171-499 9000.

Medical Services

In a medical emergency, either call an ambulance (999) or make your way to the nearest Accident and Emergency department (in most large hospitals). Your hotel will give details. For emergency dental care go to the nearest hospital casualty ward. Otherwise, call Directory Enquiries (192) or consult the *Yellow Pages* telephone directory for the names and numbers of dentists near to where you are staying. See also *Planning The Trip – Health (page 356)*.

Useful Numbers

- **Emergencies** 999.
- **Operator**: (for difficulties in getting through) 100.
- **Directory Enquiries (UK)** 192.
- **International Directory Enquiries** 153.
- **International Operator** 155.
- **Telegrams** (now called telemessages) 190.

Getting Around

Driving

In Britain you should drive on the left-hand side of the road and observe speed limits. It is strictly illegal to drink and drive, and penalties for drink driving are severe. Drivers and passengers, in both front and back seats, must wear seat belts where fitted. Failure to do so can result in a fine. For further information on driving in Britain consult a copy of the *Highway Code*, widely available in bookshops.

If you are bringing your own car into Britain you will need a valid driving licence or International Driving Permit, plus insurance coverage, vehicle registration and a nationality sticker.

Parking

Road congestion is a problem in most town and city centres, and parking is often restricted. Never leave your car parked on a double yellow line, in a place marked for *permit holders only,* within a white zig-zag line close to a pedestrian crossing, or in a control zone. Also, don't park on a single yellow line when restrictions are in force, usually 8.30am to 6.30pm weekdays (consult signs on the curb). These are offences for which you can face a fine. Either use a meter or a car park (distinguished by a white P on a blue background).

Pay particular attention if leaving your car in central London. In many areas illegal parking may result in wheel clamping. This means your car is immobilised with a clamp until you pay to have it released – a process that can take several hours. Alternatively, your car may be towed away to a pound. Either way, retrieving your car will cost more than £100, plus the £30 parking fine. If you want to find out if your car has been towed away, phone 0171-747 4747.

Breakdown

The following motoring organisations operate 24-hour breakdown assistance. They have reciprocal arrangements with other national motoring clubs. All calls to these numbers are free.
AA 0800 887766.
Britannia Rescue 0800 591563.
Green Flag 0800 400600.
RAC 0800 828282.

Car Rental

To rent a car in Britain you must be over 21 years old (over 25 for some companies) and have held a valid full driving licence for more than one year. The cost of hiring a car will usually include insurance and unlimited mileage and road tax. It does not incorporate insurance cover for accidental damage to the interior of the car, wheels and tyres or insurance for other drivers without prior approval.

Some companies offer special weekend and holiday rates, so shop around. International companies (such as those listed opposite) are keen to encourage visitors to book in advance before they leave home and may offer holiday packages with discounts of as much as 40 per cent on advance bookings through travel agents or branches in your own country. Many rental firms provide child seats and luggage racks for a small charge.

Speed Limits

- Unless otherwise stated, **30 mph (50 kph)**.
- **60 mph (100 kph)** on normal roads away from built-up areas.
- **70 mph (112 kph)** on motorways and dual carriageways (divided highways).
- **Camping vans** or **cars towing a caravan** are restricted to 50 mph (80 kph) on normal roads and 60 mph (96 kph) on dual carriageways.

Driving in London

If you're staying only for a short time in the Greater London area, and are unfamiliar with the geography of the capital, don't hire a car. Central London is more than ever a nightmare to drive in, with its web of one-way streets, bad signposting and impatient drivers who will cut you up at the first hesitation. Taxi drivers in particular seem to regard hesitation as an invitation to pull into your lane.

Parking is also a major problem in congested central London. Meters are slightly cheaper than NCP car parks, but only allow parking for a maximum of two or four hours. If parking at a meter, do not leave your car a moment longer than your time allows or insert more money once your time has run out. For either of these infringements you can face a fine of around £30, and there are plenty of traffic wardens ready to give you a ticket. Most meter parking is free after 6.30pm each evening, after 1.30pm on Saturday and all day Sunday, but always check the details on the meter.

Avis 0990 900500.
Hertz 0990 996699.
Budget 0800 181181.
British Car Rental (01203)
716166.
Eurodollar Rent A Car
(01895) 233300.

Public Transport

Domestic Flights

From the major international
airports there are frequent
shuttle services to Britain's
many domestic airports. These
give quick and easy access to
many cities and offshore
islands. Airlines providing
domestic services are:
● **Air UK**, tel: 0181-745 7017.
● **British Airways** (the
country's largest airline),
Heathrow and Great Britain
flight information, tel: 0990
444000. Reservations, tel:
0345 222111.
● **British Midland Airways**, tel:
0345 554554.

For those who would like to
explore some of the less
accessible areas of Scotland in
a short time, British Airways
operates the Rover Ticket, which
entitles you to a maximum of 5
flights within Scotland and the
Shetlands over a period of three
months. Tickets must be booked
at least a week in advance.

Major Domestic Airports
Aberdeen
tel: (01224) 722331.
Bristol
tel: (01275) 474441.
East Midlands
tel: (01332) 852852.
Leeds-Bradford
tel: (0113) 250 9696.
Liverpool
tel: (0151) 486 8877.
Newcastle upon Tyne
tel: (0191) 286 0966.
Norwich
tel: (01603) 411923.
Southampton
tel: (01703) 629600.

Trains

The state train operator British
Rail no longer exists. It has been
replaced by 25 private operating
companies, which run trains in
regions round the country. This
means that the British train
system is in a period of flux.

There are many money-saving
deals available to travellers –
such as cheap-day returns – but
as the new companies become
established, saver tickets are
changing. It can also be difficult
to find out about offers, so if in
doubt ask again. Generally
tickets bought at least two
weeks in advance are vastly
cheaper than standard rates.
Some saver tickets are available
only if purchased abroad before
arriving.

For most journeys it is not
necessary to purchase tickets
until the day you travel, or to
make seat reservations, except
over the Christmas period when
InterCity trains are fully booked
well in advance.

Trains are divided into first
and second-class carriages, with
first-class accommodation up to
twice the price of second. It is
sometimes possible to upgrade
your ticket to first-class on
InterCity trains for a small extra
payment once you board.

On long distances overnight, it
may be worth having a sleeping
compartment. Available on
InterCity trains, these are basic
but comfortable sleeping
accommodation and must be
booked in advance.

In Scotland you can buy a
Freedom of Scotland Travelpass
entitling you to unlimited travel
within the Highlands and Islands
for specific periods on Scotrail

Penalty Fares

Ensure you have a ticket
before you board a train or
Tube. Anyone travelling
without a valid ticket is liable
to a heavy on-the-spot fine.

Train Enquiries

● **National Rail Enquiry
Service** For train times,
cancellations and advance
bookings by credit card
0345 484950 (24 hours
a day).
● **British Nationwide Train,
Bus & Coach Hotline**
For timetable information
0891 910910.
● **International Rail Enquiry
Service** For services from
Britain 0990 848848.

trains and most Caledonian
MacBrayne ferries to the islands
off the west coast. It also gives
20 per cent discount on P&O's
ferry services to Orkney.

For a really luxurious train
ride, take a trip on the famous
Royal Scotsman. For further
information contact
Abercrombie and Kent, tel:
0171-730 9600.

Coaches

National Express operates a
comprehensive network of coach
services throughout the country
with fast and comfortable
coaches running on long
journeys, equipped with
washrooms and stewards. Fares
are considerably cheaper than
the equivalent journey by train,
although you must book your seat
in advance. For enquiries and
bookings, tel: 0990 808080.

From April to November
National Express provides
scheduled day trips round the
country to cities of interest such
as Bath and Stratford-upon-Avon,
museums such as Madame
Tussaud's and the Natural
History Museum in London and
theme parks such as Alton
Towers (with entrance fees
included). **Green Line** (0181-668
7261) has some similar services.

Towns and rural communities
are generally well-served by
buses, often owned by private
companies.

Sightseeing Tours

- All British cities of historical interest have special double-decker buses that tour the sites. Some are open-topped so that, weather permitting, you can enjoy fresh air and uninterrupted camera angles. Many have a commentary in several languages.
- For guided tours of the capital, London Coaches (tel: 0181-877 1722) operates a hop-on, hop-off service so you take in the sites at your own pace over a 24-hour period.
- Golden Tours (tel 0171-233 7030) and Frames Rickards (tel: 0171-837 3111) offer sightseeing day trips from London to places like Oxford, Bath, Windsor and Canterbury, and include tour commentary from a Blue Badge Guide (considered to be the elite of tour guides) and, in some cases, lunch.

Taxis

Outside London and large cities and away from taxi ranks at stations, ports and airports you will usually have to telephone for a cab rather than expect to hail one in the street. By law cabs must be licensed and display charges on a meter. Add at least 10 per cent for a tip.

London "black cab" drivers are famous for their extensive knowledge of the city's streets. Minicabs (unlicensed taxis, which look like private cars) are not allowed to compete with black cabs on the street and have to be hired by telephone or from a kiosk. If hiring a minicab, agree to a fee beforehand and, unlike black cabs, don't expect them to know precise destinations.

If you have a complaint, make a note of the driver's licence number and contact the Carriage Office, tel: 0171-230 1631.

Travelling Around London

If you are staying in London for a while it is worth investing in an A-Z Map which gives detailed information of the capital's confusing complex of streets and post codes.

The Underground (also known as the Tube) is the quickest, but not always the easiest, way to get across London. Although it is one of the most comprehensive systems of its kind in the world, it is also the oldest. Apart from some central stations which have been revamped in recent years, many remain largely unchanged since the 1930s.

The Tube service starts at 5.30am and runs until around midnight. It gets packed in the rush hours (8–9.30am and 5–6.30pm). Make sure that you have a valid ticket while in the system as it is illegal to travel without one. Smoking is prohibited. Fares are based upon a zone system with a flat fare in the central zone. Tickets may be purchased from a ticket office or machine.

A ride on the Docklands Light Railway is an excellent way to

London Travel Passes

- **The Off-Peak One Day Travelcard** is a one-day pass that allows unlimited travel on the Tube, buses, Docklands Light Railway and services to stations in Greater London. It can be used after 9.30am on a weekday or all day on a Saturday, Sunday or bank holiday, but not on night buses, and is available from all Underground and some mainline stations.

- **Other Travelcards** are valid for a week or a month and can be used at any time of day. To buy a pass you will need to supply a passport-sized photograph.

see the modern re-development of London's old dock area. This fully automated system has two branches connecting up with the Underground network. It operates in the same way as the Tube, with similar fares.

London buses provide a comprehensive service throughout Greater London and have their route and number clearly displayed on the front. Unlike the Underground, buses carry on running hourly throughout the night, with services to most parts of London departing from Trafalgar Square. Smoking is prohibited on buses.

River Tours

Riverboats are an excellent way to see many major sights of London, whose history is intertwined with the river. During the summer these are plentiful, but there are limited winter services. Boats can be joined at the following piers: Richmond, Kew, Putney, Westminster, Charing Cross, London Bridge, the Tower of London and Greenwich.

Circular cruises between Hampton Court and Westminster Pier are available from:
Circular Cruises, HMS *President*, Victoria Embankment, London EC4Y 0HJ.
Tel: 0171-936 2033.
Fax: 0171-936 3383.

Scheduled daily services are run by:
George Wheeler Launches, Westminster Pier.
Tel: 0171-930 1616.
City Cruises (Westminster Tower Boat Trips), Westminster Pier.
Tel: 0171-237 5134.
Catamaran Cruisers, Charing Cross Pier.
Tel: 0171-839 3572.
Thames Passenger Services Federation (tel: 0171-930 2062) runs scheduled boats from Westminster Pier, plus evening and floodlit supper cruises.
Bateaux Cruises (tel: 0171-839 3572) runs luncheon cruises from Temple Pier.

Rover Tickets

Coach
National Express (tel: 0990 808080) offers a Tourist Trail Pass, which entitles you to unlimited travel on National Express coaches for specified periods.
Green Line (tel: 0181-668 7261) supplies a Diamond Rover ticket for unlimited travel for a day on Green Line coaches and buses.

Train
For UK residents there are several passes, including a Family, Senior Citizen's and Young Person's Railcard, which are valid for one year. They cost a fraction of a long-distance InterCity trip but allow you an unlimited number of journeys on off-peak trains. The BritRail ticket (available from European travel agents only) also gives you unlimited travel in Great Britain for specified periods.

Scottish Ferries
Ferry services between the 23 islands and the mainland of the northwest coast of Scotland have been monopolised by Caledonian MacBrayne. Its ferries cater largely for the needs of the islanders, delivering mail and groceries, so tourists should state in advance if they wish to disembark at a particular port.

The Island Hopscotch and Island Rover are two flexible tickets available to tourists. Ferries to Orkney and Shetland are operated by P&O. It is possible to make reservations on most services and they are strongly recommended for tourists wishing to take their cars. The ferry to the Isle of Skye has now been replaced by a new toll bridge from the Kyle of Lochalsh.

For details contact:
Caledonian MacBrayne
Tel: (01475) 650100.
P & O Scottish Ferries
Tel: (01224) 572615.

Waterways

Britain has over 2,000 miles (3,200 km) of rivers and canals, the latter a great legacy of the Industrial Revolution. There is a wide choice of boats and a large number of places from which to hire vessels. Possibilities include exploring Britain's many canals, from the Grand Union in the Midlands to the Caledonian Canal which stretches from coast to coast in Scotland, or taking a pleasure cruiser along major rivers such as the Thames, Avon or the Severn, or around the Norfolk Broads.

For information, contact:
British Waterways Board, The Toll House, Delemere Terrace, Little Venice, London W2 6ND, tel: 0171-286 6101.
Fax: 0171-286 7306.

The Inland Waterways Association is a voluntary body that has fought since 1946 for the restoration and maintenance of Britain's inland waterway network. It has saved many of Britain's waterways that would otherwise have disappeared. It is also concerned with other interests such as angling, nature conservation, walking and industrial architecture. Contact the Association at: 114 Regent's Park Road, London NW1 8UG. Tel: 0171-586 2510.

Steam Railways

Many steam rail lines have been restored by enthusiasts. Among the most notable are:
● **Bluebell Railway**
  Uckfield, E. Sussex TN22 3QL. Tel: (01825) 723777. Britain's most famous line.
● **Mid Hants Railway**
  Alresford, Hampshire SO24 9JG. Tel: (01962) 733810. Runs through beautiful country over steeply graded track.
● **Severn Valley Railway**
  Bewdley, Hereford & Worcs DY12 1BG. Tel: (01299) 403816. Spectacular views, plus over 25 trains.

● **Great Central Railway**
  Loughborough, Leics LE11 1RW. Tel: (01509) 230726. One of the most evocative restorations of the steam age.
● **Lakeside & Haverthwaite Railway**
  Nr Ulverston, Cumbria LA12 8AL. Tel: (015395) 31594. Steep ride, with connections to boats on the lake.
● **Ffestiniog Railway**
  Porthmadog LL49 9NF. Tel: (01766) 512340. Scenic ride through Snowdonia National Park. Narrow gauge.

● **North Yorkshire Moors Railway**
  Pickering. Tel: (01751) 472508. An 18-mile line through picturesque moorland, with an extensive collection of trains.
● **Isle of Man Railways**
  Douglas IM2 4NR (01624) 663637. Britain's largest network, with 15 miles (24 km) of track.
For a full listing, send a self-addressed envelope to Heritage Railways, 7 Robert Close, Potters Bar EN6 2DH.

Where to Stay

Choosing a Hotel

A variety of accommodation exists in Britain, from smart luxury hotels in stately homes and castles, to bed-and-breakfast (B&B) accommodation in private family homes or country farmhouses.

By international standards, hotels in Britain are expensive, so if you are holidaying on a tight budget you should consider staying in bed-and-breakfast accommodation. Alternatively there are plenty of youth hostels throughout the country, which take people of all ages (*see page 378 for details*). Wherever you go, always be sure to look at a room first before accepting it.

Not all hotels include breakfast in their rates and they are also likely to add a service charge of 10–15 per cent. However, all charges should be clearly displayed on the tariff.

It is advisable to book in advance, particularly at Christmas, Easter and throughout the summer, although during the rest of the year there is generally little difficulty in finding somewhere suitable to stay. You can book a room through a travel agent, directly with a hotel or via the Tourist Board.

Booking Services Tourist Information Centres *(see page 359)* displaying a Local Bed Booking Service sticker will book local accommodation (free or small fee) for personal callers, whereas those involved in the Book-A-Bed-Ahead scheme will reserve you somewhere suitable to stay in any area where there

is another TIC involved in the scheme. A small fee is required, the latter deducted from the hotel's bill. All TICs have free lists of local accommodation.

The British Travel Centre in Regent Street, London, provides an accommodation booking service for the whole of the country. You must visit the office in person to book and a small deposit may be required which should later be deducted from your hotel bill.

Hotel awards Great Britain has no national classification system for the facilities and quality of accommodation an establishment has to offer, several independent bodies run their own schemes.

The AA (Automobile Association) and RAC (Royal Automobile Club) provide a simple scheme awarding between one star (good, but basic) to five stars (luxury).

The English, Welsh and Scottish tourist boards award crowns, from one to five for facilities and services, and a separate measure of *Approved, Commended* and *Highly Commended* for ambience and quality.

A country inn with a mere 2 stars may prove to offer excellent and characterful accommodation, but lack facilities such as television and private bathrooms, while an impersonal concrete-block hotel with well-equipped shoe-boxes

University Lodgings

Many universities have accommodation to let during the long summer vacation. This can be an inexpensive option (not confined to students), particularly in the capital. Some offer full board. For further information, contact the university in the town of your destination (the local tourist office will advise).

for rooms may boast 4 stars.

A Michelin award is the accolade for which the most notable of hoteliers strive.

The **English Tourist Board** (0181-846 9000) produces a series of useful *Where To Stay* guides dealing with every type of accommodation in Britain, from farms to self-catering boating holidays. To be listed, an establishment first has to pay to be inspected and then pay to be included, so the leaflets are not exactly impartial. A series of books covering B&B and self-catering accommodation is also produced by the ETB. Contact local Tourist Information Offices or the BTA office in your own country for a list.

Stately homes Britain has many grand stately homes and castles which have been converted into country-house hotels. This growing trend in luxury accommodation has saved many splendid historic buildings from dereliction. Most provide an extremely high standard of traditional accommodation and service, often with superb restaurants, hence a selection appear in the *Where to Eat* section *(page 383)*.

Hotel Listings

Many hotels offer special weekend and low-season breaks between October and April. Details can be obtained from individual hotels, chains of hotels or from the English Tourist Board (tel: 0181-846 9000) which publishes a brochure, *Let's Go: Short Breaks in England,* giving details of reduced rates at hundreds of hotels nationwide.

The following suggestions are for hotels in places that will serve as good bases for exploring the regions covered in the guide's chapters. Unless otherwise stated, all the rooms in the hotels listed have private facilities.

London

The price of a hotel room in London is as high as the equivalent anywhere else in Europe. However, cost does not always mean quality, so look out for the LVCB membership sticker indicating that certain standards have been met and always try to view a room before accepting it. In the height of the summer season (April to September) it is advisable to book before you arrive as hotels fill up fast. The London Tourist Board provides a bed booking service through information centres or by telephone (credit cards only). Tel: 0171-932 2020.

The hotels listed below are located centrally and have been chosen either for their excellent positions or for providing welcoming English hospitality in characterful surroundings.

Many moderately priced hotels are small and don't have restaurant facilities, although they may provide room service. Some hotels offer babysitting and booking services for theatres and restaurants, while smarter establishments are fully geared up for the business traveller.

Numerous hotels, including the Ritz and the Savoy, offer special weekend rates depending on the season. These are well worth checking out and may include extra incentives such as guided tours and Champagne dinners.

Top Class

££££ Berkeley Hotel
Wilton Place, SW1X 7RL.
Tel: 0171-235 6000.
Fax: 0171-235 4330.
Many rate the Berkeley as the best in London. It's low key, seldom advertised, with a country house atmosphere. Not a business hotel. Swimming pool. Many English customers.

Price Guide

Prices quoted are for a double room including breakfast and VAT at high season.
££££ £180+
£££ £130–£180
££ £80–£130
£ under £80

££££ Claridge's
Brook Street, W1A 4ZX.
Tel: 0171-629 8860.
Fax: 0171-499 2210.
Has long had a reputation for dignity and graciousness.

££££ The Dorchester
Park Lane, W1A 2HJ.
Tel: 0171-629 8888.
Fax: 0171-409 0114.
One of the most expensive in London. Views over Hyde Park.

££££ Durley House
115 Sloane Square, SW1X 9PJ.
Tel: 0171-235 5537.
Fax: 0171-259 6977.
Seriously luxurious, with all mod cons and a Michelin award.

££££ The Four Seasons Hotel
Hamilton Place, Park Lane, W1A 1AZ.
Tel: 0171-499 0888.
Fax: 0171-493 6629.
A temple of modern opulence. Friendly staff.

££££ The Savoy
Strand, WC2R 0EU.
Tel: 0171-836 4343.
Fax: 0171-240 6040.
One of London's legends, with a solid reputation for comfort (its 600 rooms are excellent) and personal service (if a little over-formal). Conveniently central, but set back from the main road. Convenient for theatreland and Covent Garden.

Luxury

££££ Athenaeum Hotel
116 Piccadilly, W1V 0BJ.
Tel: 0171-499 3464.
Fax: 0171-493 1860.
Smart hotel (123 rooms) in the heart of smart London, close to shops and with views over Green Park. A very English hotel, full of character of the "gentleman's club" kind. Excellent service.

£££–££££ Blakes Hotel
33 Roland Gardens, SW7 3PF.
Tel: 0171-370 6701.
Fax: 0171-373 0442.
Very trendy and up-to-the-minute hotel popular with theatrical and media folk. Cosmopolitan, tolerant and laid-back in style. 52 rooms.

£££–££££ Brown's Hotel.
Albemarle Street, W1A 4SW.
Tel: 0171-493 6020.
Fax: 0171-493 9381.
A distinguished, very British, Victorian-style hotel. Smart Mayfair location. 116 rooms.

Hotel Chains

Hotels belonging to big chains such as Forte (now owned by Granada) and Hilton abound and tend to offer a reliable, if at times impersonal, standard of service. In addition there are a host of private hotels. The business traveller on an expense account is increasingly well catered for, in both urban and country areas, where there are many hotels offering large conference rooms and health and leisure facilities in addition to fax and secretarial services. The following organisations have hotels in most parts of the country:
Forte Tel: 0345 404040 in the UK, 1 (800) 225-5843 in the US.
Intercontinental Hotels & Resorts Tel: 0171-495 2500, fax: 0171-495 2769.
Hilton International Tel: 0800 8568003, fax: (01923) 218548.
Ibis Hotels Tel: 0181-759 4888, fax: 0181-564 7894.

London Hotels (continued)

£££–££££ Cadogan Hotel
Sloane Street, SW1X 9SG.
Tel: 0171-235 7141.
Fax: 0171-245 0994.
Another 19th-century style hotel, owned by the Thistle chain. 65 rooms. Interesting position between Knightsbridge and Chelsea. Lily Langtry lived in what's now the bar.

£££–££££ Capital Hotel
22-24 Basil Street, SW3 1AT.
Tel: 0171-589 5171.
Fax: 0171-225 0011.
Luxurious little hotel (56 rooms) in the heart of Knightsbridge. Restrained in style, with tasteful decor, and rooms in the Laura Ashley style. Friendly service. Restaurant has Michelin star.

£££–££££ Goring Hotel
15 Beeston Place, Grosvenor Gardens, SW1W 0JW.
Tel: 0171-396 9000.
Fax: 0171-834 4393.
Family-owned (the present manager, George Goring, is latest in a long line of Goring managers) delightfully traditional hotel near Buckingham Palace. Relaxed atmosphere. Home-made food, including the bread.

££££ The Halkin
5 Halkin Street, SW1X 7DJ.
Tel: 0171-3331000.
Fax: 0171-333 1100.
Top-class and ultra-modern. Every room has its own sitting room. Michelin rated.

Price Guide

Prices quoted are for a double room including breakfast and VAT at high season.
££££ £180+
£££ £130–£180
££ £80–£130
£ under £80

££££ Landmark London
222 Marylebone Road, NW1 61Q.
Tel: 0171-631 8000.
Fax: 0171-631 8080.
Opened in 1993, the modern eight-storey building with a glass domed atrium has good-sized rooms and all facilities.

££££ Pelham Hotel
15 Cromwell Place, SW7 2LA.
Tel: 0171-589 8288.
Fax: 0171-584 8444.
Elegant Victorian townhouse, with free use of garden and outdoor swimming pool.

££££ The Ritz
Piccadilly, W1V 9DG.
Tel: 0171-493 8181.
Fax: 0171-493 2687.
One of the most famous hotel names in the world. 130 rooms. Not quite what it was, despite refurbishment. Jackets and ties must be worn. Tea at the Ritz is reputedly one of the best.

£££–££££ Tower Thistle Hotel
St Katharine's Way, E1 9LD.
Tel: 0171-481 2575.
Fax: 0171-488 4106.
A big modern hotel situated on the fringes of docklands. It's more central than it sounds, and the locale is breathtaking, with Tower Bridge and the river. Handy for the City. A brisk five-minute walk to the nearest Tube station. 826 rooms, all with private bath. Meals.

££££ 22 Jermyn Street
22 Jermyn Street, SW1.
Tel: 0171-734 2353.
Fax: 0171-734 0750.
Right by Piccadilly, a peaceful townhouse excellent for business trips. Each room has two direct-dial phone lines and fax/modem link.

Moderate

£££ Academy Hotel
17-21 Gower Street, WC1 6HC.
Tel: 0171-631 4115
Fax: 0171-636 3442.
A small and welcoming Bloomsbury hotel. Licensed bar; evening meal available. 35 rooms, 5 with private bath.

£££ Basil Street Hotel
Basil Street, Knightsbridge, SW3 1AH.
Tel: 0171-581 3311.
Fax: 0171-581 3693.
Hotel with a tremendous reputation, and certainly lots of old-fashioned charm. For those who like a country house atmosphere. Rooms and service can vary with rates. Close to Harrods. 95 rooms, 82 with private bath.

££ Elizabeth Hotel
37 Eccleston Square, SW1V 1PB.

Reserving and Booking a Room

● When you book a hotel room, ensure that the price quoted is inclusive, and isn't going to be bumped up by a mysterious "travellers' charge" or other extras. Service is usually included in hotel bills.
● If you reserve in advance, you may be asked for a deposit. Reservations made, whether in writing or by phone, can be regarded as binding

contracts, and you could be prosecuted for failing to honour that contract by not turning up on the day.
● If you have reserved a room, the hotel will usually keep it for you until early evening, unless you let them know that you will be arriving later. Rooms must usually be vacated by midday on the day of departure.

● Make the most of your hotel. Many offer a wide range of services, from free information to booking theatre tickets.
● Most hotels offer extremely good rates if you stay for several nights, or opt for dinner, bed and breakfast. It can be worth your while to bargain, especially out of the peak season.

Tel: 0171-828 6812.
Fax: 0171-828 6814.
Friendly hotel set in an elegant period square, only two minutes' walk from Victoria station. 40 rooms, 22 with bath.

£££ The Rubens
39-41 Buckingham Palace Road, SW1W 0PS.
Tel: 0171-834 6600.
Fax: 0171-828 5401.
Traditional-style hotel with an added Regency Floor of 45 rooms. Smart location opposite the Royal Mews, and close to Victoria station. 188 rooms.

££ Tophams
26 Ebury Street, SW1W 1SD.
Tel: 0171-730 8147.
Fax: 0171-823 5966.
Old-style hotel with faded charm.

London Hotel Areas

Central isn't necessarily best. Prices are high and hotels less characterful than in areas a Tube ride from the West End.

- **SW1** Traditionally the hotel district.
- **Victoria** There are many delightfully old-fashioned hotels in Victoria, in most price brackets, and the streets close to Victoria station are full of terraced bed and breakfasts.
- **SW5** and **SW7** Around Kensington High Street, Earl's Court and Gloucester Road is a major centre for medium-range hotels.
- **West End** More expensive than elsewhere in London. Bloomsbury (WC1) is central yet has reasonable prices, its hotels having a dignity and providing personal touches that you won't find in the Oxford Street area.
- The best areas for moderately priced bed-and-breakfast accommodation are **Victoria, Knightsbridge, Earl's Court, Bayswater** and **Bloomsbury**.

Very popular and certainly one of the best-value places to stay in London. Welcoming and friendly atmosphere.

££ Wilbraham Hotel
1 Wilbraham Place, Sloane Street, SW1X 9AE.
Tel: 0171-730 8296.
Fax: 0171-730 6815.
Smart location between Knightsbridge and the King's Road, in a quiet street. The hotel is converted from three Victorian terraces. Old-fashioned. 52 rooms, 43 with bath. Exceptional value. No credit cards.

Inexpensive

££ Airways Hotel
29 St George's Drive, SW1V 4DG.
Tel: 0171-834 0205
Fax: 0171-932 0007.
Pleasant hotel close to Buckingham Place, Westminster Abbey, and Harrods. Friendly service. 32 rooms, 19 with bath.

££ Clearlake Hotel
19 Prince of Wales Terrace, W8 9PQ.
Tel: 0171-937 3274.
Fax: 0171-376 0604.
Comfortable bed and breakfast in a quiet location with views of Hyde Park. 17 rooms. Good value.

£ Curzon House Hotel
58 Courtfield Gardens, SW5 0NF.
Tel: 0171-373 6745.
Fax: 0171-835 1319.
Economical but comfortable small hotel which is close to Gloucester Road Underground station. 2 single, 2 twin, 2 doubles, 2 triples, 9 four-bedded, 2 five-bedded dormitories.

£ Garden Court Hotel
30-31 Kensington Gardens Square, W2 4BG.
Tel: 0171-229 2553.
Fax: 0171-727 2749.
Friendly bed and breakfast set in a traditional English garden square. 37 rooms, 12 with bath.

£ London House Hotel
81 Kensington Gardens Square, W2 4DJ.

Tel: 0171-727 0696
Fax: 0171-243 8626.
Cheap, friendly and comfortable hotel in a pleasant location, close to public transport. 73 rooms, 26 with bath.

££ Lonsdale Hotel
9-10 Bedford Place, WC1B 5JA.
Tel: 0171-636 1812
Fax: 0171-580 9902.
Established bed and breakfast hotel with real character in the heart of Bloomsbury. 34 rooms, 3 with private bath.

£ Hotel Strand Continental
143 Strand, WC2R 1JA.
Tel: 0171-836 4880
Fax: 0171-379 6105.
Despite the fancy name, one of the cheapest hotels in London, and one of the most central. Superb location. 22 rooms, none with private bath. No credit cards.

The Southeast

Alfriston

££ The George Inn
High Street.
Tel/fax: (01323) 870319.
Dating from the 15th-century, this pub and hotel is in the middle of a popular village. Has 4-poster beds, and the restaurant, where local fish is a speciality, has an inglenook fireplace.

Arundel

£££ Amberley Castle
nr Arundel.
Tel: (01798) 831992.
Fax: (01798) 831998.
Genuine 11th-century castle dripping with atmosphere. Opulently refurbished with antiques and the odd suit of armour. Individually decorated rooms, with spa pools in every bathroom. Excellent service. Recommended.

££ Dukes
65 High Street.
Tel: (01903) 883847.
No fax.
An elegant townhouse built in 1840. All rooms en-suite. Restaurant.

Southeast Hotels (continued)

££ Swan Hotel
27–29 High Street.
Tel: (01903) 882314.
Fax: (01903) 883759.
A listed building at the heart of a delightful village, very popular with tourists. Good restaurant.

Brighton
£££ The Old Ship Hotel
King's Road.
Tel: (01273) 329001.
Fax: (01273) 820718.
One of the oldest hotels in Brighton. Elegant, traditional but not too grand.
££ The New Madeira Hotel
Marine Parade.
Tel: (01273) 698331.
Fax: (01273) 606193.
Ask for a room at the front, with a bay window, to have a view of the bright lights of the pier. Weekend break special rates.
£ The Grapevine
30 North Road.
Tel: (01273) 681361,
No fax.
Good basic B&B and café in the middle of the bustling North Laine. No credit cards.

Canterbury
££ Falstaff
St Dunstan's Street,
Westgate.
Tel: (01227) 462138.
Fax: (01227) 463525.
Coaching inn, hard by the city walls and within easy reach of the cathedral and shops. 24 rooms.

Chichester
££ The Millstream Hotel and Restaurant
Bosham, nr Chichester.
Tel: (01243) 573234.
Fax: (01243) 573459.
Quiet country hotel near Bosham harbour with various rosettes and merits for its food and hospitality.
££ Suffolk House Hotel
3 East Row.
Tel: (01243) 778899.
Fax: (01243) 787282.

Price Guide

Prices quoted are for a double room including breakfast and VAT at high season.
££££ £180+
£££ £130–£180
££ £80–£130
£ under £80

Privately run hotel in a fine Georgian building with restaurant and small garden.

Midhurst
£££ Angel Hotel
North Street.
Tel: (01730) 812421.
Fax: (01730) 815928
Fine establishment dating back to 1420. The writer Hilaire Belloc called it "the most revered of all prime inns in England." Original features include Tudor bread ovens, a wig closet, fine Jacobean hall and 4-poster beds. 28 rooms.

New Romney
££ Romney Bay House
Coast Road, Littlestone, nr New Romney.
Tel: (01797) 364747.
Fax: (01797) 367156.
Right by the sea with stunning views over the Channel from the lounge, this is a gem. A quirky 1920s house, it was built by Portmeirion architect Sir Clough Williams-Ellis. Helmut and Jennifer Gorlich are excellent hosts and their two boxer dogs take guests for walks along the beach. The 10 rooms are splendidly and individually decorated. Good food, and excellent Sunday teas.

Rye
££ The Mermaid Inn
Mermaid Street.
Tel: (01797) 223065.
Fax: (01797) 225069.
Popular 15th-century inn in this ancient coastal port. Excellent restaurant. 28 rooms (15 with 4-poster beds).

The West Country

Barwick
Little Barwick House
Barwick, nr Yeovil.
Tel: (01935) 423902.
Fax: (01935) 420908.
Unpretentious Georgian dower house with gardens. Great place to escape to. Particularly noted for its hospitality.

Bath
££££ Priory Hotel
Weston Road.
Tel: (01225) 331922.
Fax: (01225) 448276.
Gothic-style 19th-century house west of Royal Victoria Park. Comfortable, individual and quiet.
££££ The Royal Crescent Hotel
15–16 The Royal Crescent.
Tel: (01225) 739955.
Fax: (01225) 339401.
The ultimate address in Bath, with a central location. Antiques, paintings, individually decorated rooms, a noted restaurant and secluded garden at the back. 45 rooms.
£££ Bath Spa Hotel
Sydney Road.
Tel: (01225) 444424.
Fax: (01225) 444006.
Near Sydney Gardens and set in its own extensive grounds. All comforts, including spa. Excellent restaurant.
£££ Francis Hotel
Queen Square.
Tel: (01225) 463411.
Fax: (01225) 319715.
Another famous address, this time on John Wood the Elder's square. 94 rooms.
£££ The Queensberry Hotel
Russel Street.
Tel: (01225) 447928.
Fax: (01225) 446065.
Small hotel occupying three Georgian houses knocked together. Comfortable and characterful, though some rooms are on the small side. The esteemed Olive Tree restaurant is in the basement.

££ Bloomfield House
46 Bloomfield Road.
Tel: (01225) 420105.
Fax: (01225) 481958.
Upmarket B&B in large 19th-century neoclassical house. Some rooms with 4-poster or half-tester beds. No smoking.

££ Holly Lodge
8 Upper Oldfield Park.
Tel: (01225) 424042.
Fax: (01225) 424042.
Large Victorian house on the south side of Bath. Emphasis on service and comfort. Excellent breakfasts. Frilly furnishings.

££ Somerset House Hotel and Restaurant
25 Bathwick Hill.
Tel: (01225) 466451.
Fax: (01225) 317188.
Attractive Georgian house, which is family-run and noted for its fine food. Dinner included.

££ Sydney Garden Hotel
Sydney Road.
Tel: (01225) 464818.
Fax: (01225) 445362.
Comfortable and pretty rooms.

£ Eagle House
Church Street, Bathford.
Tel/fax: (01225 859946).
B&B in a pretty conservation village just outside Bath. Friendly and homely but smart.

£ Holly Villa Guest House
14 Pulteney Gardens.
Tel: (01225) 310331.
No fax
Convenient Bathwick location. Attractive and comfortable. Some rooms en-suite. No smoking.

£ The Hollies
Hatfield Road.
Tel/fax: (01225) 313366.
Reasonably priced accommodation in Grade II listed

Victorian property. All rooms with own bath or shower rooms.

Bigbury-on-Sea
£££ Burgh Island Hotel
Tel: (01548) 810514.
Fax: (01548) 810243.
Unusual and characterful Art Deco hotel on an island first inhabited in AD 900 by monks, with access by sea tractor. Agatha Christie wrote two books here. 15 suites.

Box
££ Box House Hotel
London Road.
Tel: (01225) 744447.
Fax: (01225) 744333.
Attractive Georgian hotel conveniently located 4 miles (6 km) from Bath. Set back from the busy London Road. Swimming pool.

Gourmet Hotels

Broadway
£££ The Lygon Arms
High Street. Tel: (01386) 852255. Fax: (01386) 858611. Magnificent 16th-century coaching inn, with antique furnishings and log fires.

Chagford
££££ Gidleigh Park
Tel: (01647) 432367.
Fax: (01647) 432574.
Quintessentially English, a huge half-timbered, gabled house on the edge of Dartmoor, with babbling brook, all-year log fire and impeccable service.

Great Milton, nr Oxford
££££ Le Manoir aux Quat'Saisons
Church Road. Tel: (01844) 278881. Fax: (01844) 278847. Raymond Blanc's renowned restaurant and hotel with stunning gardens, including a Japanese tea garden. Luxurious rooms, all individually decorated and some even with own terrace. Recommended.

London
££££ The Connaught
Carlos Place, W1Y 6AL.
Tel: 0171-499 7070.
Fax: 0171-495 3262.
One of the best hotels in London. Discreet, immaculate service, superb decor.

Llyswen
£££ Llangoed Hall
Tel: (01874) 754525.
Fax: (01874) 754545.
17th-century manor house brimming with Laura Ashley fabrics (as it is owned by her widower). Excellent breakfasts.

New Milton
££££ Chewton Glen
Christchurch Road. Tel: (01425) 275341. Fax: (01425) 272310. One of England's best-known country house hotels occupying an elegant 18th-century mansion. The swimming pool is modelled on the bathhouses of ancient Rome, while the style of the rooms varies from country cottage to 4-poster antiquity.

Taplow
££££ Cliveden
Taplow, nr Maidenhead.
Tel: (01628) 668561.
Fax: (01628) 661837.
Majestic, historic hotel. Once the home of the Prince of Wales, several dukes and the Astors, it has 350 acres (140 hectares) of National Trust parkland. The height of luxury.

Ullapool
£££ The Altnaharrie Inn
Tel: (01854) 633230.
From the pretty fishing village of Ullapool it is worth the short boat ride or 4-mile (6-km) walk to sample some of the best cooking Scotland has to offer, from herb-and-hawthorn soup to cloudberry ice-cream.

Ullswater
££££ Sharrow Bay Hotel
Howton Road. Tel: (01768) 486301. Fax: (01768) 48634. This Italianate luxury hotel is set in formal gardens overlooking Ullswater.

West Country Hotels (continued)

Bradford-on-Avon
££ Bradford Old Windmill
Masons Lane.
Tel: (01225) 866842.
Converted windmill. No smoking.
££ Old Manor Hotel
Trowbridge Road, Widbrook.
Tel: (01225) 777393.
Fax: (01225) 765443.
16th-century manor farmhouse.
Restaurant.

Castle Combe
£££ Manor House
Castle Combe, nr Chippenham.
Tel: (01249) 782206.
Fax: (01249) 782159.
Old manor, some of which dates
back to the 14th century, with
clubby atmosphere. Best rooms
in the main house have beams,
exposed stone walls and quality
furnishings. Free use of golf
course for those with a
handicap certificate.

Dartmouth
££ The Royal Castle
11 The Quay.
Tel: (01803) 833033.
Fax: (01803) 835445.
This building on Dartmouth's
quayside was originally a 17th-
century coaching inn. Serves
good Devon cuisine and award-
winning breakfasts. 25 rooms
(some with river views).

Freshford
££ Homewood Park
Hinton Charterhouse, Freshford.
Tel: (01225) 723731.
Fax: (01225) 723820.
A few miles south of Bath, this
quintessentially English country
house hotel features outdoor
swimming pool, beautiful
gardens and a cosy bar. Some
bedrooms have Victorian free-
standing baths. 19 rooms.

Gillan
£ Tregildry
Gillan, Manaccan, nr Helston.

Tel: (01326) 231378.
Fax: (01326) 231561.
Small, friendly hotel with
stunning views over Gillan Bay.

Monkton Combe
£ The Manor House
Tel: (01225) 723128.
No fax.
Attractive 16th-century manor
offering very reasonably priced
accommodation. Breakfast
served until noon.

Penzance
£££ The Queen's Hotel
The Promenade,
Penzance, Cornwall.
Tel: (01736) 362371.
Fax: (01736) 350033.
Grand English seaside hotel with
wonderful views over Mounts
Bay to St Michael's Mount in the
distance. 71 rooms.
££ Abbey Hotel
Abbey Street.
Tel: (01736) 66906.
Fax: (01736) 351163.

Hotels with Sporting Facilities

Belton, nr Grantham
£££ Belton Woods Hotel
Tel: (01476) 593200.
Fax: (01476) 574547.
Two championship-standard 18-
hole golf courses. Gym, tennis
and jogging route.

Brockenhurst
£ Balmer Lawn Hotel
Lyndhurst Road. Tel: (01590)
623116. Fax: (01590) 623864.
Former hunting lodge with
superb views. Swimming pools,
tennis, squash, sauna and gym.

Colerne, nr Bath
£££ Lucknam Park
Tel: (01225) 742777.
Fax: (01225) 743536.
Luxurious manor with
equestrian centre and spa.

Grimston
££ Congham Hall
Tel: (01485) 600250.

Fax: (01485) 601191.
Pleasant country house hotel
with beautiful grounds. Cricket
pitch, pool and tennis court.

Keswick
££ Armathwaite Hall Hotel
Tel: (017687) 76551
Fax: (017687) 76220
Equestrian centre, gym, pool,
tennis, jogging tracks, bike trail,
canoeing, climbing and more.

Monkton Combe, nr Bath
**££££ Combe Grove Manor
Hotel & Country Club**
Brassknocker Hill. Tel: (01225)
834644. Fax:. (01255) 834961
Luxurious 18th-century house.
Pools, gym, tennis, golf driving
range, aerobics and dance.

Newport
££ Celtic Manor
The Coldra. Tel: (01633)
413000. Fax: (01633) 412910.

19th-century manor in 300
acres of grounds. Golf courses,
indoor pool, tennis, and more.

Pencoed
St Mary's Country Club
Tel: (01656) 861100.
Fax: (01656) 863400.
27-hole golf course, tennis
courts. Golfing breaks.

Woolacombe
Woolacombe Bay Hotel
Tel: (01271) 870388.
Fax: (01271) 870 613.
In 6 acres of grounds by the
sea. Pool, fitness classes,
squash, tennis, gym and bowls.

York
£££ Viking Moat House
North Street. Tel: (01904)
459988. Fax: (01904) 641793.
On the south bank of the river, a
smart multi-storey hotel with
sauna, solarium and gym.

Delightful period stuccoed building overlooking harbour from the heart of the old town. Bedrooms have been tastefully furnished with antiques and beautifully decorated. There is a small restaurant.

Saltford
£ Brunel's Tunnel House Hotel
High Street. Tel: (01225) 873873. Fax: (01225) 874875. Midway between Bath and Bristol. One-time home of Isambard Kingdom Brunel. Rooms individually furnished. Ensuite facilities.

Sandy Park
£ Mill End Hotel
Sandy Park.
Tel: (01647) 432282.
Fax: (01647) 433106.
Pretty old mill, complete with wheel in operation, in a peaceful setting on the River Teign, Dartmoor. Excellent for families, with good children's menu.

Ston Easton
£££ Ston Easton Park
Tel: (01761) 241631.
Fax: (01761) 241377.
Most notable for its gardens (which were designed by Humphrey Repton with grotto, bridges over the River Norr and an 18th-century ice house), this fine Palladian manor provides country house splendour and service at its finest. Some rooms with Chippendale 4-posters. No children under 7, except babes in arms.

Isles of Scilly

Bryher
££ Hell Bay Hotel
Tel: (01720) 422947.
Fax: (01720) 423004.
A fairly new hotel with beautiful gardens and fine views out to the sea.

St Martin's
£££ St Martin's Hotel
Tel: (01720) 422092.

Price Guide

Prices quoted are for a double room including breakfast and VAT at high season.
££££ £180+
£££ £130–£180
££ £80–£130
£ under £80

Fax: (01720) 422298.
Nestling in a sheltered cove, with its own beach and even its own yacht, this hotel has been landscaped to blend discreetly with its natural surroundings. The restaurant has a reputation for excellence.

St Mary's
£££ Tregarthen's Hotel
Tel: (01720) 422540.
Fax: (01720) 422089.
Established in 1840 by shipowner Captain Tregarthen. Views of sea and harbour from terraced garden.
££ Star Castle Hotel
Tel: (01720) 422317.
Fax: (01720) 422343.
Occupying the castle, with four acres of gardens and a tennis court, as well as a covered heated swimming pool.
£ Hotel Godolphin
Tel: (01720) 422316.
Fax: (01720) 422252.
On the edge of Hugh Town close to the beaches, this hotel has a long-standing reputation for good food and friendly service.

Tresco
£££ Island Hotel
Tel: (01720) 422883.
Fax: (01720) 423008.
Fine hotel with wonderful location in beautiful sub-tropical gardens near Old Grimsby. Closed November–March.
£ New Inn
Tel: (01720) 422844.
Fax: (01720) 423200.
A moderately priced inn near the waterfront at New Grimsby.

Hardy Country

Brockenhurst
£££ New Park Manor
Tel: (01590) 623467.
Fax: (01590) 622268.
This excellent country retreat was once the hunting lodge of Charles II and is set in 6 acres (2.4 hectares) of beautifully landscaped grounds in the heart of the New Forest. Facilities include excellent restaurant, stables, heated pool and tennis court. 25 rooms.
££ Careys Manor
Tel: (01590) 623551
Fax: (01590) 622799.
This fine Arts and Crafts mansion of 1888 will appeal to the active: mountain bikes are available, and there is a pool, gym, sauna and children's playground. Rooms in the garden wing have balconies overlooking the walled garden.
£ Whitley Ridge Hotel
Beaulieu Road.
Tel: (01590) 622354
Fax: (01590) 622856.
A friendly small hotel in a secluded Georgian house set amid parkland, with 13 rooms, views over woodland and fields. Log fires on cooler evenings.

Evershot
££ Summer Lodge
Tel: (01935) 83424.
Fax: (01935) 83005.
The house that played Highbury in the film *Emma*, this former Georgian dower house is set in mature gardens. Tastefully furnished and particularly noted for its excellent service and hospitality.

Lyme Regis
£££ The Alexandra
Pound Street.
Tel: (01297) 442010.
Fax: (01297) 442010.
Large 18th-century white house, former home of Countess Poulet, set in fine grounds overlooking the bay. Comfortable and welcoming. 26 rooms.

Hardy Country Hotels (continued)

Sparsholt
££ Lainston House Hotel
nr Winchester.
Tel: (01962) 863588.
Fax: (01962) 776672.
Beautiful country house in
extensive grounds with a good
restaurant. 38 rooms.

The Thames Valley

Aylesbury
££ Hartwell House
Oxford Road, nr Aylesbury.
Tel: (01296) 747444.
Fax: (01296) 747450.
Country house hotel set in 90
acres of grounds. Plush baroque-
style public rooms, bedrooms
furnished with antiques and
excellent leisure facilities. 45
rooms. No children under 8.

Henley-on-Thames
££ Red Lion
Hart Street.
Tel: (01491) 572161.
Fax: (01491) 410039.
Just right for the regatta, this
hotel overlooks the finishing
post on the River Thames. 26
comfortable rooms.

Windsor
£££ Oakley Court
Tel: (01628) 74141.

Fax: (01628) 37011.
A charming Victorian house with
spacious grounds leading down to
the River Thames. Convenient for
London. Lovely, mostly big, rooms.

Oxford to Stratford

Bibury
££ Bibury Court
Tel: (01285) 740337.
Fax: (01285) 740660.
This glorious Jacobean house
fulfils everyone's idea of the
perfect Cotswold manor. Rarely
does such a sense of history
come with so low a price tag.
££ The Swan
Tel: (01285) 740695.
Fax: (01285) 740473.
In a beautiful riverside setting in
its own private gardens, this hotel
features antique furnishings and
good service. 18 rooms.

Buckland
£££ Buckland Manor
Tel: (01386) 852626.
Fax: (01386) 853557.
13th-century manor in extensive
gardens. Michelin rated.

Cheltenham
££ On the Park
Evesham Road.
Tel: (01242) 518898.
Fax: (01242) 511526.
Pretty townhouse opposite

Self-Catering Agencies

Blakes Country Cottages
Tel: (01282) 445555.
Fax: (01282) 841399.
Over 2,000 cottages sleeping
2–8 people in pleasant areas
and villages.
Cornish Traditional Cottages
Tel: (01208) 821666.
Fax: (01208) 821766.
About 400 cottages in Cornwall
sleeping 2–12.
English Country Cottages
Tel: 0990 851155.
Fax: 0990 851150.
Wide variety of about 3,000
country properties including

oast houses, barns, castles
and manor houses sleeping
2–22 people.
Forest Holidays
Tel: 0131-314 6100.
Fax: 0131-334 0849.
Truly rustic, 5 or 6-berth cabins
or cottages owned by the
Forestry Commission, in
Yorkshire, Cornwall and
Scotland.
Service Suites
Tel: 0171-730 5766.
Fax: 0171-730 1261.
Serviced London flats and
apartments for short lets.

Romantic Breaks

Many hotels have 4-poster
beds and offer special
packages for those seeking a
romantic weekend. From
champagne, chocolates and
flowers awaiting in your room,
to a candlelit dinner, to
balloon flights, hotels will
arrange just about anything
you ask for.
 Book well in advance for
Valentine's Day (14 February),
though, Britain's day for
lovers. Partners are expected
to show their appreciation for
each other with a romantic
meal and red roses. Many
people also send a
Valentine's Day card to each
other, also a legitimate way
for shy admirers to declare
their interest in someone
anonymously.

Pittville Park with tasteful,
individually decorated bedrooms
and luxurious bathrooms. No
children under 8.
££ The Greenway
Shurdington, nr Cheltenham.
Tel: (01242) 862352.
Fax: (01242) 862780. Peaceful
Elizabethan mansion covered in
Virginia creeper, where personal
service by owner David White is
immaculate and very much in
evidence. Most bathrooms have
natural light.

Lower Slaughter
££££ Lower Slaughter Manor
Lower Slaughter, nr Bourton-on-
the-Water. Tel: (01451) 820456.
Fax: (01451) 822150.
Luxurious Georgian manor in its
grounds, with grand pannelled
library and galleried landing, and
meticulous service (including
windscreen polish on
departure). Stay in the manor
itself or adjoining coach house,
both equally magnificent with
antiques, chintzy fabrics and
bathrooms with his and hers
washbasins. Superb breakfast.

Oxford

££££ Old Parsonage Hotel,
1 Banbury Road.
Tel: (01865) 310210.
Fax: (01865) 311262.
A fine hotel in the renovated old parsonage at the top of St Giles, with 30 luxuriously appointed en-suite bedrooms. The Parsonage Bar restaurant is open all day to hotel guests and non-residents.

££££ Randolph Hotel
Beaumont Street.
Tel: (01865) 247481.
Fax: (01865) 791678.
Grand Victorian hotel in central Oxford offering traditional service with all the trimmings. 109 rooms.

£££ Bath Place Hotel
4–5 Bath Place.
Tel: (01865) 791812.
Fax: (01865) 791834.
Family-run hotel in the heart of Oxford occupying a group of restored 17th-century cottages. Excellent restaurant. 12 rooms.

£££ Cotswold Lodge Hotel
66a Banbury Road.
Tel: (01865) 512121.
Fax: (01865) 512490.
Beautiful Victorian building, situated in a quiet conservation area, only a few minutes' walk from the city centre. 50 rooms.

£££ Eastgate Hotel
23 Merton Street.
Tel: (01865) 248244.
Fax: (01865) 701681.
Traditional hotel in central location, adjacent to the site of Oxford's old East Gate and opposite the Examination Schools. Restaurant and bar.

££ The Galaxie Hotel
180 Banbury Road,
Summertown.
Tel: (01865) 515688.
Fax: (01865) 556824.
Friendly family-run hotel near the shopping and leisure facilities of the Summertown residential district.

£ Cotswold House
363 Banbury Road.
Tel/fax: (01865) 310558.
Commended B&B. No smoking.

£ Norham Guest House
16 Norham Road.
Tel: (01865) 515352.
Fax: (01865) 793162.
Situated in a traditional Victorian residence in a quiet part of north Oxford, close to University Parks and within 15 minutes' walk of the city centre. All rooms have en-suite facilities. There are several good restaurants nearby.

Stow-on-the-Wold

££ The Grapevine
Sheep Street.
Tel: (01451) 830344.
Fax: (01451) 832278.
Immaculately maintained hotel within an old stone building providing a good base from which to tour the Cotswolds. Guests are well catered for in this welcoming hotel, named after the old vine that grows in its conservatory restaurant. 23 rooms.

Stratford-upon-Avon

£££ The Shakespeare
Chapel Street. Tel: (01789) 294771. Fax: (01789) 415411. This 17th-century half-timbered building is the best hotel in town and one of Stratford's most famous and beautiful buildings. Centrally located with large open fires and a good restaurant. 63 rooms.

£ Caterham House
58-9 Rother Street.
Tel: (01789) 267309.
Fax: (01789) 414836.
Georgian house popular with theatre-goers (pre-theatre dinner by arrangement). Quirky but special.

Tetbury

££ The Snooty Fox
Market Place.
Tel: (01666) 502436.
Fax: (01666) 503479.
Old Cotswold stone coaching inn on the square of this historic market town. Interior features oak panelling, log fires and is furnished with antiques. Fine restaurant. 12 rooms.

£ Tavern House
Willesley.
Tel: (01666) 880444.
Fax: (01666) 880254.
Upmarket B&B in former coaching inn near Westonbirt Arboretum.

Upper Slaughter

£££ Lords of the Manor
Upper Slaughter,
nr Bourton-on-the-Water.
Tel: (01451) 820243.
Fax: (01451) 820696.
A 16th-century former rectory with Victorian additions, set in rolling Cotswold countryside. Many of the rooms have views of parkland and the lake. A baronial atmosphere with chintzy fabrics, Oriental rugs, antiques and family portraits.

Weston on the Green

£££ Weston Manor
Tel: (01869) 350621.
Fax: (01869) 350901.
16th-century manor house set in beautiful gardens. Excellent cuisine in the Baronial Hall.

Cambridge & E. Anglia

Aldbury, nr Tring

£££ Stocks Hotel & Country Club
Stocks Road.
Tel: (01442) 851341.
Fax: (01442) 851253.
An elegant 18th-century manor house, set in its own grounds in the peaceful countryside just outside the pretty village of Aldbury. 18 rooms.

East Anglia Hotels (continued)

Burnham Market
££ The Hoste Arms
The Green.
Tel: (01328) 738777.
Fax: (01328) 730103.
Characterful inn on the green of
the village where Nelson was
born. Restaurant. Live jazz.

Cambridge
£££ Cambridge Garden House
Granta Place, Mill Lane.
Tel: (01223) 259988.
Fax: (01223) 316605.
Modern Moat House by river,
with own punts and rowing
boats. Convenient central
location.
£ Arundel House Hotel
53 Chesterton Road.
Tel: (01223) 367701.
Fax: (01223) 367721.
Privately owned terraced hotel
overlooking the River Cam near
the centre of the university town.
No room service. 105 rooms (79
with private baths).
£ Quy Mill
Newmarket Road, Stow-cum-Quy,
nr Cambridge.
Tel: (01223) 293383.
Fax: (01223) 293770.
Within a taxi ride of Cambridge
city centre, a 19th-century
watermill in 11 acres with
fishing. 23 rooms.

Ely
£ Lamb Hotel
2 Lynn Road.
Tel: (01353) 663574.
Fax: (01353) 662023.
Former coaching house in city
centre.

Hintlesham, nr Ipswich
££ Hintlesham Hall
Tel: (01473) 652268.
Fax: (01473) 652463.
Stylish hotel with magnificent
Georgian facade and 175 acres
(70 hectares) of rolling parkland.
Luxury rooms with en-suite
bathrooms, plus library, garden
room and cosy parlour to retreat
to. 33 rooms.

Stepping Back in History

For a taste of Britain past, it is
possible to stay in a number
of restored old buildings, from
medieval castle or lighthouse.
Many such properties have
been beautifully restored and
are maintained by The
Landmark Trust and The
National Trust.

    The Landmark Trust is a
private charity, set up in 1965
to rescue small historic
buildings. It now has over 200
properties of architectural or
historical note available to let.
Ranging from castles and
Gothic temples to water
towers, lighthouses, forts
and follies, all have been
restored and furnished in
keeping with the original
character of the building.

Lavenham
££ The Angel
Market Place.
Tel: (01787) 247388.
Fax: (01787) 248344.
Historic inn dating back to 1420
overlooking the market place of
this old wool market town. The
recommended restaurant offers
a regularly changing menu using
fresh local ingredients. 8 rooms.

Morston, nr Holt
££ Morston Hall
Tel: (01263) 741041.
Fax: (01263) 740419.
Flint manor on the Norfolk coast.
Good food.

Wells-next-the-Sea
££ Crown Hotel
The Buttlands.
Tel: (01328) 710209.
Fax: (01328) 711432.
A fine old coaching inn in a
picturesque port on the north
Norfolk coast. It has a popular
bar and restaurant.

Detailed information on each
property is given in a
handbook available by post.
The price of the handbook is
refunded against bookings.
Tel: (01628) 825925.
    **The National Trust and
National Trust for Scotland**
have more than 200 cottages
and smaller houses of
historical interest to let, from
a romantic cabin hideaway for
two overlooking a Cornish
cove to an apartment in York
with clear views of the
Minster. For members only.
For details write to: The
National Trust, 36 Queen
Anne's Gate, London SW1H
9AS; The National Trust for
Scotland, 5 Charlotte Square,
Edinburgh EH2 4DU.

The Lake District

Alston
£ Lowbyer Manor
Tel: (01434) 381230.
Fax: (01434) 382937.
Characterful 17th-century manor
house with exposed beams and
inglenook fireplaces, once
owned by the Earl of
Derwentwater. Situated on the
Pennine Way, it provides
excellent hospitality and a
good base from which to explore
the Lake District, Northumbria
and North Yorkshire. 8 rooms.

Ambleside
££ Rothay Manor
Rothay Bridge.
Tel: (01539) 433605.
Fax: (01539) 433607.
Quintessential English country
house hotel with gardens. Warm
and friendly.
££ Wateredge Hotel
Borrans Road, Waterhead.
Tel: (01539) 432332.
Fax: (01539) 431878.
Family-run hotel with views over
Lake Windermere from most
rooms. No children under 7.

Cartmel, nr Grange-over-Sands
£ Aynsome Manor
Tel: (01539) 36653.
Fax: (01539) 536016.
16th-century house in a
picturesque lakeland village, off
the tourist track.

Clappersgate, nr Ambleside
**££ Nanny Brow Country
House Hotel**
Tel: (015394) 32036.
Fax: (015394) 32450.
One of the best hotels in the
Lakes, this Edwardian house is
peacefully situated in lovely
grounds, with stunning views.
18 rooms.

Keswick District
£££ Stakis Keswick Lodore
Lodore Falls, Borrowdale.
Tel: (01768) 777285.
Fax: (01768) 777343.
Luxury hotel in 40 acres with
excellent facilities. Some rooms
overlook Derwent Water.

Price Guide

Prices quoted are for a double
room including breakfast and
VAT at high season.
££££ £180+
£££ £130–£180
££ £80–£130
£ under £80

££ The Mill
Mungrisdale.
Tel: (01768) 779659.
Fax: (01768) 779155.
Former mill cottage. Good food.
££ Pheasant Inn
Bassenthwaite Lake, nr
Cockermouth
Tel: (01768) 776234.
Fax: (01768) 776002.
This heavily beamed inn lies in a
beautifully peaceful setting in
the Lake District.
£ Aaron Lodge
Tel: (01768) 772399.
Stationmaster's house, 5
minutes from town centre.
£ The Anchorage
Ambleside Road.
Tel: (01768) 772813.

Near lake and park. Good views.
No smoking. Open February–
November only.
£ The Cottage in the Wood
Whinlatter Pass.
Tel: (01768) 778409.
Former coaching house.

Ullswater District
£ Barco House
Patterdale.
Tel: (01768) 482474.
Near lake.
£ Waterside House
Watermillock.
Tel: (017684) 86038.
Fax: (017684) 86132.
18th-century house on lake
shore. Open from April to
October only.

Merseyside/Shropshire

Chester
££ Queen Hotel
City Road.
Tel: (01244) 350100.
Fax: (01244) 318483.
Very handy for the station, this
smart hotel has a small
restaurant and garden.
90 rooms.

Chaddesley Corbett
££ Brockencoate Hall
Chaddesley Corbett,
nr Kidderminster.
Tel: (01562) 777876.
Fax: (01562) 777872.
Stylish hotel set in 70 acres with
large bathrooms and
conservatory lounge.

Kings Norton
££ The Mill House
180 Lifford Lane.
Tel: 0121-459 5800.
Fax: 0121-411 2202.
15 minutes from Birmingham,
this newcomer has already won
awards (including Michelin) for
its quality and service. Its 9
rooms are individually designed
with features like original
paintings, *trompe l'oeils* and
stained glass windows. Indoor
swimming pool.

Liverpool
£££ The Britannia Adelphi Hotel
Ranelagh Place.
Tel: 0151-709 7200
Fax: 0151-708 8326.
Large and impressive, this is
Liverpool's premier hotel and its
grand classical stone facade
provides a major landmark next
to Lime Street station. 390
rooms, plus health club
facilities.

Shrewsbury
£££ The Lion
Wyle Cop.
Tel: (01743) 353107.
Fax: (01743) 352744.
Attractive, heavily beamed 18th-
century coaching inn located in
the centre of this historic
medieval town. 59 rooms.

Yorkshire & Northeast

Belford
£ The Blue Bell Hotel
Market Square.
Tel: (01668) 213543.
Fax: (01668) 213787.
Lovely hotel within a picturesque
17th-century coaching inn on the
east coast close to Holy Island.
Interior is well-furnished in
period style. Lovely garden.
15 rooms.

Bolton Abbey
**£££ Devonshire Arms Country
House Hotel**
Tel: (01756) 710441.
Fax: (01756) 710564.
On the Bolton Abbey Estate in
Wharfedale. Open fires, lounges
furnished with antiques and
portraits from Chatsworth, home
of the Duke and Duchess of
Devonshire. 41 rooms.

Burnsall
£ Red Lion
Tel: (01756) 720204.
Fax: (01756) 720292
Village inn on banks of River
Wharfe. Fresh fish, game and
local produce.

*Yorkshire & Northeast Hotels
(continued)*

Harrogate
£ The Albany
Tel: (01423) 565890.
Small hotel overlooking the
Valley Gardens.

Helmsley
£££ Black Swan Hotel
Market Place.
Tel: (01439) 770466.
Fax: (01439) 770174.
Extremely comfortable Forte
Heritage hotel in the centre of
this town at the foot of the North
York Moors. 44 rooms.

Hexham, Priestpopple
££ County Hotel
Tel: (01434) 602030.
Fax: (01434) 603202.
Excellent hospitality in a market
town. Handy for exploring the
Pennines, Hadrian's Wall and
Southern Scotland. 12 rooms.

Wensleydale
££ The Wheatsheaf
Carperby.
Tel: (01969) 663216.
Fax: (01969) 663019.
Where the real-life James Herriot
and his wife spent their
honeymoon.

York
£££ Dean Court
Duncombe Place.
Tel: (01904) 625082.
Fax: (01904) 620305.
Comfortable, traditional hotel
close to the Minster and in its
own traffic-free zone. 40 rooms.
£££ Middlethorpe Hall
Bishopthorpe.
Tel: (01904) 641241.
Fax: (01904) 641241.
A 17th-century house which has
been turned into an elegant
country hotel and is run with
style and grace. 30 rooms.
££ Elmbank
The Mount. Tel: (01904)

610653. Fax: (01904) 627139.
A city hotel with a country-house
atmosphere.
££ Jarvis Abbey Park
The Mount.
Tel: (01904) 658301.
Fax: (01904) 621224.
A former Georgian townhouse
converted into a comfortable 85-
bedroom hotel within five
minutes' walk of the city walls.
£ Ashcroft
Bishopthorpe Road.
Tel: (01904) 659286.
Fax: (01904) 640107.
Once a Victorian mansion, this
hotel is set in more than two
acres of wooded grounds sloping
down to the River Ouse.
£ Hudson's Hotel
Bootham.
Tel: (01904) 621267.
Fax: (01904) 654719.
Four minutes from the Minster,
this skilful conversion of two
Victorian houses has a rooftop
garden with superb views over
the city.
£ Savages
St Peter's Grove.
Tel: (01904) 610818.
Fax: (01904) 627729.
Victorian gentleman's townhouse
turned into a comfortable family
hotel within easy walking
distance of the city centre.

Youth Hostels

There are over 200 youth
hostels in Britain ranging from
town houses to beach chalets
which are graded *simple,
standard* and *superior*.
Facilities are very basic, but
the accommodation is
extremely cheap, usually
comprising shared dormitories
of bunk beds.
   Everyone is expected to do
their fair share of the daily
chores, so youth hostels are
only for those who don't mind
mucking-in, communal living
and a shortage of creature
comforts. The maximum length
of stay in each hostel is three
nights. You must be a national
or international member to stay
at a hostel, although anyone of
any age can join the association, overseas or in the UK.
Youth Hostel Association
(YHA), 8 St Stephen's Hill,
St Albans AL1 2DY.
Tel: (01727) 855215.

Scottish Youth Hostels
Association (SYHA)
7 Glebe Crescent, Stirling .
Tel: (01786) 451181.
YHA Shop
14 Southampton Street,
London WC2E 7HY.
Tel: 0171-836 8541.

London Hostels
Earl's Court
38 Bolton Gardens, SW5 0AQ.
Tel: 0171-373 7083.
111 beds.
Hampstead
4 Wellgarth Road, NW11 7HR.
Tel: 0181-458 7196.
200 beds.
Holborn
36–8 Carter Lane, EC4V 5AB.
Tel: 0171-236 4965.
Nearly 200 beds.
Kensington
Holland House,
Holland Walk, W8 7QU.
Tel: 0171-937 0748.
201 beds.

Peak District and East Midlands

Ashford in the Water
**£££ Riverside Country House
Hotel**
Tel: (01629) 814275.
Fax: (01629) 812873.
Small 18th-century country
house on the Wye with
4-poster beds, log fires and
antiques. 15 rooms.

Bakewell
££ Milford House Hotel
Mill Street.
Tel: (01629) 812130.
Fax: (01629).
Peaceful Georgian hotel in its
own grounds; family-run with
traditional English cooking.

Buxton
££ Old Hall Hotel
The Square.
Tel: (01298) 22841.
Fax: (01298) 72437
A landmark in Buxton since the 16th century, this dignified hotel is located on the town square overlooking the Pavilion Gardens with the Opera House close at hand. 37 rooms.

Dovedale
£££ Izaak Walton Hotel
Tel: (01335) 350555.
Fax: (01335) 350539.
One of the Peak's most stylish and famous hotels, named after the author of *The Compleat Angler* who often fished in the area. Right in the jaws of Dove Dale beneath Thorpe Cloud. 32 rooms.

Hassop
££ Hassop Hall Hotel
Tel: (01629) 640488.
Fax: (01629) 640577.
One of the Peak's most elegant venues. Classical Georgian house formerly owned by the Eyre family, set in spacious parkland 2 miles from Bakewell. 13 rooms.

Hathersage
££ George Hotel
Main Road.
Tel: (01433) 650436.
Fax: (01433) 650099.
Former 16th-century coaching inn with a lovely garden and a fine restaurant.
££ Millstone Inn
Sheffield Road.
Tel: (01433) 650258.
Fax: (01433) 651664.
Above the village with fine views down the Hope Valley to Kinder Scout.

Matlock
££ Riber Hall Hotel
Tel: (01629) 582795.
Fax: (01629) 580475.
Tudor mansion high above the town with wonderful views from mullioned windows. 11 rooms.

Price Guide

Prices quoted are for a double room including breakfast and VAT at high season.
££££ £180+
£££ £130–£180
££ £80–£130
£ under £80

Matlock Bath
££ Temple Hotel.
Tel: (01629) 583911.
Fax: (01629) 580581.
On a hilltop with splendid views, this hotel is owned by Austrians who feature their national dishes on the menu. 14 rooms.

Rowsley
££ East Lodge Country House Hotel
Tel: (01629) 734474.
Fax: (01629) 733949.
Pretty, tastefully furnished country house in 10 acres (12 hectares) of its own grounds, just off the A6. The restaurant has a fine reputation.
£££ Peacock Hotel
Tel: (01629) 733518.
Fax: (01629) 732671.
Fine old listed hotel named after the peacock emblem of the Manners family which stands guard over the entrance. Famous in the world of angling for fine fishing in the nearby River Wye.

Stapleford, nr Melton Mowbray
£££ Stapleford Park
Tel: (01572) 787522.
Fax: (01572) 787651.
Sumptuously appointed 17th-century country house hotel with 500 acres (200 hectares) designed by "Capability" Brown. The deluxe rooms were designed by eminent names, including Nina Campbell, David Hicks and Crabtree & Evelyn. 42 rooms.

Wye Valley & S. Wales

Brecon
££ Peterstone Court
Llanhamlach, Brecon.
Tel: (01874) 665387.

Fax: (01874) 665376.
Comfortable 18th-century manor in the middle of the National Park. 21 rooms.

Crickhowell
££ Gliffaes
Tel: (01874) 730371.
Fax: (01874) 730463.
Italianate mansion overlooking the River Usk set in 29 acres. Good base for walking, with fishing rights to two stretches of the river. Elegant and spacious, but not overly formal.

Hereford
£££ The Castle Pool Hotel
Castle Street.
Tel/fax: (01432) 356321.
This grand house was the former home of the Bishop of Hereford. Today it provides an excellent base in the centre of Hereford, a short walk from the cathedral. Particularly renowned for its restaurant. 26 rooms.

Llangammarch Wells
£££ The Lake Country House
Tel: (01591) 620202.
Fax: (01591) 620457.
Edwardian mansion set in grounds that slope down to the lake. Wonderful views from bedrooms with canopied or four-poster beds.

Swansea
££ Fairyhill Country House
Tel: (01792) 390139.
Fax: (01792) 391358.
12 miles (20 km) west of Swansea, close to the breathtaking beaches of the Gower Peninsular, is this 18th-century country house peacefully situated within 24 acres (10 hectares) of parkland. Down to earth and friendly, with one of the best restaurants in the area. 11 rooms.
£ Norton House
Mumbles, nr Swansea.
Tel: (01792) 404891.
Fax: (01792) 403210.
Elegant Georgian ex-mariner's house with sea views.

South Wales Hotels (continued)

Welshpool
££ Golfa Hall Hotel
Tel: (01938) 553399.
Fax: (01938) 554777.
Pretty whitewashed country hotel with beautiful grounds overlooking a wooded valley west of Welshpool. Local produce is served in the restaurant. 12 rooms.

North Wales

Anglesey
££ Ye Olde Bull's Head
Castle Street, Beaumaris.
Tel: (01248) 810329.
Fax: (01248) 811294.
Historic coaching inn at the centre of Beaumaris whose distinguished guests have included Charles Dickens. Comfortable Laura Ashley-style bedrooms, fine restaurant and old-world charm. 10 rooms.

££ Tre-Ysgawen Hall
Capel Coch, nr Llangefni.
Tel: (01248) 750750.
Fax: (01248) 750035.
Five miles (8 km) north of Llangefni, this Victorian stone mansion has a magnificent galleried hall and oak staircase. Renovated with style over recent years.

Betwys-y-Coed
££ Tan-y-Foel Country House
Capel Garmon
nr Betwys-y-Coed.
Tel: (01690) 710507.
Fax: (01690) 710681.
Good for touring, yet off the beaten track, this award-winning stone manor country hotel is a great place to get away from it all. Stunning views. Good food. No children under 7.

Llandrillo, nr Corwen
£££ Tyddyn Llan Country House
Tel: (01490) 440264.
Fax: (01490) 440414.
Excellent base for walking, this grey stone Georgian house in the Vale of Edeyrnion has 4

miles (6 km) of fishing on the River Dee. Rooms elegantly furnished with antiques and period furniture. Great views. Large gardens.

Llandudno
£££ Bodysgallen Hall
Tel: (01492) 584466.
Fax: (01492) 582519.
Stunning sandstone manor house with superb gardens and woodland walks. Country-house feel with antiques and friezes. Spa. No children under 8.

££ St Tudno Hotel
The Promenade.
Tel: (01492) 874411.
Fax: (01492) 860407.
Small 21-room seaside hotel run by husband and wife. Very friendly. Great for families.

£ Empire Hotel
Church Walks.
Tel: (01492) 860555.
Fax: (01492) 860791.
The third generation of the Maitland family run this elegant Victorian hotel. Quality fittings and marble bathrooms, all with whirlpool baths.

Llansanffraid Glan Conwy
£££ The Old Rectory
Llanrwst Road.
Tel: (01492) 580611.
Fax: (01492) 584555.
Justly awarded Michelin commendation for both cuisine and accommodation, this Georgian hotel has some of the finest views from Conwy Castle to Snowdonia and is well-loved for its informal atmosphere. A no-choice menu is served at a communal long mahogany table unless diners request something more private, after which there is cards or chess in the drawing room.

Eglwysfach, nr Machynlleth
££–£££ Ynyshir Hall
Tel: (01654) 781209.
Fax: (01654) 781366.
Small, eccentric country house hotel with 8 bedrooms. Dating back to the 1500s, it was one of

Queen Victoria's hunting lodges but now has an exuberant Mediterranean feel with public rooms painted in terracottas and deep blues and the huge, boldly coloured paintings of the owner, artist Rob Reen, on most walls. Warm service and very good food. Nature reserve on the doorstep.

Portmeirion
£££–££££ Hotel Portmeirion.
Tel: (01766) 770228.
Fax: (01766) 771331.
This eccentric hotel is central to architect Sir Clough Williams-Ellis's model fantasy village on the coast above Tremadog Bay. The interior has been decorated on exotic themes and each of the 14 rooms has its own character. Twenty further rooms in other village buildings are also available.

Talsarnau, nr Harlech
££ Maes-y-Neuadd
Tel: (01766) 780200.
Fax: (01766) 780211
Excellent views, bar with inglenook fireplace and a friendly welcome are just some of the charms of this Michelin-rated hotel, some of which dates back to the 15th century. Rooms are variable, the best with 4-posters.

Scottish Lowlands

Edinburgh
££££ Howard Hotel
32–36 Great King Street.
Tel: 0131-557 3500.
Fax: 0131-5576515.
Quiet, luxuriously decorated hotel in the New Town. First-class restaurant. 15 rooms.

££££ Sheraton Edinburgh Hotel
1 Festival Square.
Tel: 0131-229 9131.
Fax: 0131-228 4510.
Although it has very modern facilities, this luxury hotel manages to retain some of its Scottish old-world atmosphere. 261 rooms.

£££ Prestonfield House Hotel
Priestfield Road.
Tel: 0131-668 3346.
Fax: 0131-668 3976.
Old-world charm in 17th-century mansion located under Salisbury Crags. 31 rooms.

£ 24 Northumberland Street
24 Northumberland Street.
Tel: 0131-556 8140.
Fax: 0131-556 4423.
Upmarket B&B in Grade I listed Georgian house.

Glasgow

££–£££ One Devonshire Gardens
1 Devonshire Gardens.
Tel: 0141-339 2001.
Fax: 0141-337 1663.
Head and shoulders better than any other Glasgow hotel, this is luxury at its best. An altogether civilised place to stay, with immaculate service. The bedrooms are plush, and contain all modern facilities, including CD players. But do remember to ask for a quieter room at the rear of the building.

££ Malmaison
278 West George Street.
Tel: 0141-221 6400.
Fax: 0141-221 6411.
Smart hotel with decor inspired by the Paris Malmaison. Owned by Ken McCulloch of One Devonshire Gardens, so good atmosphere and service are guaranteed. Brasserie.

£ Babbity Bowster
16-18 Blackfriars Street.
Tel: 0141-552 5055.
Fax: 0141-552 7774.
Named after an 18th-century wedding dance, this is a popular hotel with trendy café/bar serving good food. Simple rooms with no TV.

£ Sherbrooke Castle
11 Sherbrooke Avenue.
Tel: 0141-427 4227.
Fax: 0141-427 5685.
Grand 19th-century baronial castle surrounded by its own grounds in a quiet residential area 3 miles (5 km) from the city centre. Well located for Pollock Country Park and the Burrell Collection. 25 rooms.

Peebles

££ Cringletie House Hotel
Tel: (01721) 730233.
Fax: (01721) 730244.
Wonderfully located within a 28-acre estate, this turreted baronial mansion house has outstanding cuisine and a great atmosphere. 13 rooms.

Auchterarder

££££ Gleneagles Hotel
Tel: (01764) 662231.
Fax: (01764) 662022.
Famous for its golfing and sports facilities, Gleneagles is a magnificent hotel on a massive scale set in 830 acres of rolling countryside. Expect to see more than a few famous faces. 234 rooms.

Banchory

£ Tor-Na-Coille Hotel
Inchmarlo Road.
Tel: (01330) 822242.
Fax: (01330) 824012.
Imposing old country house with a recommended restaurant.

Beasdale, by Arisaig

££££ Arisaig House
Tel: (01687) 450622.
Fax: (01687) 450626.
One of the most distinguished hotels in the West Highlands, superbly furnished and fitted. 14 rooms.

Bridge of Marnoch, nr Huntly

££ The Old Manse of Marnoch,
Tel/fax: (01466) 780873.
Peaceful early 19th-century house, decorated in rich colours, with stunning gardens. Great breakfasts, with figs, Afghan apricots, venison sausages, kedgeree, porridge and more.

Vegetarian Hotels

The following are hotels recommended by Britain's Vegetarian Society, tel: 0161-928 0793.

West Country
£££ Waterloo House Hotel
Lynton. Tel: (01598) 753391.
19th-century lodging house.

Southeast
Coombe Lodge
Wotton-under-Edge.
Tel: (01453) 845057.

Georgian country house hotel. 3 double rooms.

East Anglia
Sprowston Manor Hotel
Norwich. Tel: (01603) 410871.
Four-star hotel in 10 acres (4 hectares) of park.

Lake District
Lancrigg Vegetarian Country House Hotel
Easdale, Grasmere.
Tel: (01539) 435317.

Set in 30 acres (12 hectares). Stylish rooms.

Yorkshire
Wentworth House
Whitby. Tel: (01947) 602433.
4-storey Victorian house, 5 minutes from the beach.

Scotland
Tigh Na Mara
Loch Broom, nr Ullapool.
Tel: (01854) 655282.
Guesthouse on shore of loch.

Scottish Highlands Hotels (continued)

Bunchrew
£££ Bunchrew House
Tel: (01463) 234917.
Fax: (01463) 710620.
Live like a lord at this 17th-century baronial turreted mansion where guests are given freedom of the estate for salmon fishing, golf and sailing. Traditional Scottish cuisine is served in the restaurant which overlooks the sea. A great retreat. 6 suites.

Dunkeld
££££ Kinnaird
Kinnaird Estate, on the B898 just off the A9. Tel: (01796) 482440. Fax: (01796) 482289. Overlooking the River Tye, with landscaped gardens, this is a luxurious 18th-century country house hotel but manages to retain some of the intimacy of a private home. Individually decorated rooms feature sofas and gas log fires.

Fort William
££££ Inverlochy Castle
Torlundy. Tel: (01397) 702177.
Fax: (01397) 702953.
Majestic 1863 castle set in 500 acres of grounds at the foot of Ben Nevis. Everything is on a grand scale, from the frescoed Great Hall and crystal chandeliers to individually decorated bedrooms with marbelled bathrooms, and service is exemplary.
£ The Lodge on the Loch
Creag Dhu, Onich.
Tel: (01855) 821237.
Fax: (01855) 821463.
In a stunning location perched on the edge of Loch Linnhe, this hotel provides a good base from which to explore the Western Highlands. Fine Scottish fare and warm hospitality. 18 rooms.

Glenlivet
£ Minmore House
Tel: (01807) 590378.

The British Breakfast

A century ago breakfast was a great British institution among the better off. Lords and ladies of the manor would sit down to a full meal, from a lavish fry-up to kedgeree, kidneys or kippers. Today, few Britons normally eat such a hearty affair, but for many it is usually an indulgent start to the day on holiday.

Most traditional is fried egg, bacon, sausage and grilled tomato. Or you may be offered a choice of eggs, poached, scrambled or boiled. This is followed by rounds of toast, with marmalade, jam or honey, washed down with tea or coffee. For those who can't face anything on quite such a grand scale, most hotels and bed and breakfasts also offer a Continental breakfast, and large hotels follow the European tradition of cold meats and cheeses with bread rolls and crispbreads.

Fax: (01807) 590472.
Victorian guesthouse offering views over wonderful scenery. Excellent teas included in price.

Inverness
££ Dunain Park
Tel: (01463) 230512.
Fax: (01463) 224532.
Georgian mansion with gardens and woodland, overlooking the River Ness and Caledonian Canal. Stunning views. Swimming pool. Traditional country house feel with congenial service. Over 200 malt whiskies.

Inns and Pubs

Inns are a great British institution that have become an increasingly popular choice of accommodation in recent years. Not only are they cheaper and smaller than hotels but they may also offer charm, character and the opportunity of integrating with the local community, to which they are central.

Unique to Great Britain, the inn has a long history dating back to Roman times. Consequently there are many historic taverns, particularly in rural towns and villages. Many are by road sides where travelling pilgrims may have rested in the Middle Ages or stage coaches stopped in the days of highwaymen. Often they retain an old-world character with welcoming open fires, low beams and a warm ambience (combined, of course, with modern comforts). Ask local people for recommendations, as many of the best pubs are off the tourist track.

Staying at an inn or pub may not always be such a cosy experience, however, especially in urban areas where you are likely to find pubs with an institutional feel. Standards vary from basic to sophisticated, with food facilities ranging from bar snacks to quality restaurants.

CAMRA, the Campaign for Real Ale, publishes a book listing the best pub accommodation. Contact CAMRA at 230 Hatfield Road, St Albans AL1 4LW. Tel: (01727) 86720. Fax: (01727) 867670.

B&Bs and Guesthouses

These are generally private homes with a few rooms available for rent. As with all types of accommodation, standards will vary, but you can usually expect friendly hospitality, which will include a hearty English breakfast of eggs and bacon, and helpful advice on where to visit and eat in the area. Distinguished by a B&B sign placed outside, they are most abundant on the edge of towns and in prime tourist areas.

B&Bs tend to be exceptional value and it is always advisable to book in advance during the peak seasons. B&B accommodation is also available in many farmhouses, which provide the opportunity of rural accommodation with an insight into British farm life. Contact local tourist offices for lists of recommended accommodation.

Somewhere between a hotel and a B&B in terms of size, price and facilities, guesthouses are generally small and friendly, family-run businesses. Breakfast is usually included.

Companies that specialise in B&Bs include:

Bed and Breakfast Nationwide Tel: (01255) 831235. Fax: (01255) 831437.

The London Bed & Breakfast Agency Tel: 0171-586 2768. Fax: 0171-586 6567.

The AA publishes an annual guide to over 3,000 good bed and breakfasts, available from most good bookshops.

Where to Eat

To many, the thought of British food conjures up a picture of unappetising stodgy fare that rests heavily on the stomach, leaving taste buds asleep. However, times (and tastes) have changed.

A generation of talented modern British chefs has injected new life into traditional recipes, combining them with French and international influences, to produce lighter, more delicately flavoured meals

The Sandwich

For a quick, light snack, nothing beats the sandwich. This British stalwart, the most popular lunch among office workers, was the brainchild of the fourth Earl of Sandwich. An infamous gambler, he had such a good hand one night in 1762 that he could not bear to be parted from the gaming table. So he asked his manservant to rustle up a hunk of beef between two slices of bread, and so the sandwich was born.

Today, just about anything is found between two slices of bread, although Oscar Wilde considered the cucumber sandwich to be "the aristocrat of the tea-table". Even the smallest town has several bars selling take-away sandwiches, or you can enjoy a more leisurely sandwich at a tearoom *(see page 387 for some of the best)*. Marks & Spencer's range is also recommended.

using the finest ingredients grown on British soil.

Meat Although beef is the nation's most traditional meat, game is now a favourite among restaurateurs, with duck, pheasant, partridge, grouse, venison and, increasingly, boar appearing on the best menus. Welsh lamb is especially prized for its succulence and flavour, and traditionally served with mint sauce.

Seafood As Britain is an island, seafood plays a major part in the daily diet. Salmon from the lochs and rivers of Scotland is internationally renowned, as is the seafood from its shores. Fish such as haddock, cod and plaice is most common on the English dinner plate, while oysters are a delicacy, eaten only during months with an *r* in them. Some of the best oysters come from North Farm, East Mersea in Colchester where tours of the oystery are given on the first Friday of each month.

Fruit and vegetables British farmers are justifiably proud of their labours, entering their produce in the many county shows that are held throughout the country during summer. From Kent in particular, known as the garden of England, come some of the finest fruit and vegetables, best bought from small farm shops.

Sunday lunch is a solid British tradition, bringing families together each week for a meal of roast meat and vegetables. Traditional weekly feasts are roast beef and Yorkshire pudding with horseradish sauce, and roast pork with stuffing and apple sauce. Many pubs serve hearty, good-value roasts.

Pies are very much a British staple. Among the nation's favourite savouries are steak and kidney, pork and game. Cornish pasties, a mix of lamb, potato and vegetables in a pastry packet, are well worth sampling in Cornwall. Apple pie is probably the best-loved of sweet pies, but custard pie, lemon meringue and, at Christmas, mince pies are regulars on dessert lists.

Sausages, another British tradition, are enjoying a resurgence in popularity. As well as old favourites, such as Cumberland, black pudding (best in the North), and Scotland's ever-loved haggis, interesting new variants are being invented by the top chefs.

Pub grub International fast food chains proliferate in every town centre. Some of the better chains are Pizza Express, Pasta & Pizza and Pizza Piazza. But for a quick and inexpensive bite to eat it is far more enjoyable and relaxing to go to a cosy café or pub serving homemade fare. A typical pub bar snack menu will offer wholesome food such as soups, steak-and-kidney and pork pies, lasagne, quiche, filled rolls and the ever-popular "ploughman's lunch" of bread, cheese, pickle and salad.

Pre-theatre menues If you have booked tickets for a night at the theatre, many restaurants (especially in London's West End) will serve two courses before you see your show, saving a more leisurely dessert and coffee for your return later.

Taste of Scotland In Scotland, the Taste of Scotland scheme promotes hotels and restaurants that offer quality traditional cooking using the best local ingredients. Look out for the blue-and-white stockpot symbol. An up-to-date guide to establishments is available from Taste of Scotland, 33 Melville Street, Edinburgh EH3 7JF. Tel: 0131-220 1900.

The following list is a selection of some of Britain's finest restaurants. Many are within country-house hotels. A much fuller list of the capital's top restaurants can be found in the *Insight Guide: London*.

London

Top Notch
£££ Chez Nico
90 Park Lane, W1.
Tel: 0171-409 1290.
A passionate perfectionist, Nico Ladenis serves classic French cuisine which has earned him three Michelin stars. Closed at weekends.
££££ La Tante Claire
65 Royal Hospital Road, SW3.
Tel: 0171-352 6045.
Three Michelin stars have been awarded to this chic, exclusive

Chinatown

Many of London's best Chinese restaurants are in Chinatown, which centres around Gerrard Street. Paved over and made into something of a theme park with pagoda telephone boxes and oriental-style arches, this lively area is crammed with restaurants serving mainly Cantonese cuisine. If you are baffled by the choice, those well-patronised by the Chinese themselves are generally a good bet. Three of Chinatown's best-loved are:
££ Chuen Cheng Ku
17 Wardour Street, W1.
Tel: 0171-437 1398.
Huge and functional, but with the reputation for serving some of the best dim sum in town (until 6pm)
££ Fung Shing
15 Lisle Street, WC2.
Tel: 0171-437 1539.
Has long been regarded as one of the best restaurants in Chinatown and is consequently always packed.
£ Wong Kei
41 Wardour Street, W1.
Tel: 0171-437 8408.
Regulars aren't deterred by the rude service for which this restaurant is famed. Three floors serving good-value Cantonese food. Cash only.

little restaurant. Imaginative modern French cooking. Recommended for those who don't flinch at spending £16 on a starter.
£££ Le Gavroche
43 Upper Brook Street, W1.
Tel: 0171-408 0881.
Having confidently been one of England's top restaurants for many years, its high standards never waver. Two Michelin stars. Set lunch is best value.
££££ Restaurant Marco Pierre White
66 Knightsbridge, SW1.
Tel: 0171-259 5380.
Marco Pierre White may not be a particularly modest chef but he certainly is inventive. Fish especially fine. Three Michelin stars.
£££ The Ritz
Louis XVI Restaurant, Piccadilly, WI.
Tel: 0171-493 8181.
Elegant Edwardian restaurant decorated in Louis XVI style. Sumptuous and refined dining. The best of English cuisine accompanied by the gentle strains of a string quartet and a magnificent view over Green Park. Formal dress.

Traditional
£££ The English House
3 Milner Street, SW3.
Tel: 0171-584 3002.
Quaint chintzy English dining room within a pretty Chelsea town house. A touch frilly but the food has flair.
£££ Simpsons-in-the-Strand
100 Strand WC2.
Tel: 0171-836 9112.
The Grand Divan Tavern is an Edwardian dining room renowned for serving the best roast beef in London. Staunchly traditional. Informal dress not acceptable.
£££ Wilson's
236 Blythe Road, W14.
Tel: 0171-603 7267.
Has justly earned a reputation for serving one of the best Sunday lunches in town.

££ Tate Gallery Restaurant
The Tate Gallery, Millbank, SW1.
Tel: 0171-887 8877.
This fine lunch restaurant has beautiful decor, including a mural by Rex Whistler. Renowned wine list.

Trendy
£££ Aubergine
11 Park Walk, SW10.
Tel: 0171-352 3449.
Mediterranean-style dishes from one of London's premier new chefs, Gordon Ramsay.

££ Criterion Brasserie
224 Piccadilly, W1.
Tel: 0171-930 0488.
Worth a visit for the grand, Moorish decor alone, Marco Pierre White's latest venture, fast gaining a reputation for innovative sophistication.

££ Joe Allen
13 Exeter Street, WC2.
Tel: 0171-836 0651.
One of London's best-loved American restaurants, noted as much for post-theatre actor spotting as for its lively atmosphere and cuisine.

£££ Langan's Brasserie
Stratton Street, W1.
Tel: 0171-491 8822.
Langan's large reputation for attracting celebrities often overshadows the food.

££ Hard Rock Café
150 Old Park Lane, W1
Tel: 0171-629 0382.
A shrine to rock music. Great hamburgers, long queues, high decibel level, good fun.

£££ The Ivy
1 West Street, W1.
Tel: 0171-836 4751.
High-quality decor, gallery-worthy art and good food.

£££ Kensington Place
205 Kensington Church Street, W8.
Tel: 0171-727 3184.
Informal, bustling, New York-style restaurant. Modernist decor and adventurous food.

£££ Maison Novelli
29 Clerkenwell Green, EC1.
Tel: 0171-251 6606.

Price Guide

Prices are per person for a three-course meal with half a bottle of house wine:
££££ £100+
£££ £50–100
££ £20–50
£ under £20

Jean-Christophe Novelli makes an artform out of fine modern-European dishes in this intimate brasserie. Currently one of the capital's trendiest.

££ Mezzo
100 Wardour Street, W1.
Tel: 0171-314 4000.
Three restaurants and café run by Terence Conran. Bright, modern, good value.

££ Quaglino's
16 Bury St, SW1.
Tel: 0171-930 6767.
The buzz of 1930s London, with a wide menu.

££ Zinc Bar and Grill
21 Heddon Street, W1.
Tel: 0171-255 8899.
Conran's latest venture, complete with 12-metre zinc bar, majoring on grills, salads and crustacea.

Continental
£££ Alastair Little (French)
49 Frith Street, W1.
Tel: 0171-734 5183.
The chef-owner is something of a celebrity for his inventive approach to food on a basic French mode. Delicious, fresh, nouvelle-style cooking. Very trendy. Rather stark retro-1980s decor.

££ Le Caprice (French)
Arlington House, Arlington Street, SW1.
Tel: 0171-629 2239.
Black and white café-style restaurant that is a fashionable place to graze and be seen. Pianist in the evenings. Excellent New York-style Sunday brunch.

££ Interlude (French)
5 Charlotte Street, W1.

Tel: 0171-637 0222.
Romantic little restaurant offering sophisticated French cooking of a calibre unmatched by most of its close neighbours.

£££ Orso (Italian)
27 Wellington Street, WC2.
Tel: 0171-240 5269.
Basement Italian restaurant fashionable with theatre and media crowd.

£££ The River Café (Italian)
Thames Wharf, Rainville Road, W6. Tel: 0171-381 8824.
By the Thames near Hammersmith, designed by the controversial architect Richard Rogers and run by his wife. Delightful northern Italian food and riverside tables. Book weeks in advance.

££ Soho Soho
11-13 Frith Street, W1.
Tel: 0171-580 8788.
Popular restaurant and bar serving Provençal food.

Other Nationalities
£££ Bombay Brasserie
(Indian)
Bailey's Hotel, Courtfield Close, SW7.
Tel: 0171-370 4040.
The stylish decor harks back to the days of the Raj. The interesting menu is well thought-out, with dishes from many regions. The lunch-time buffet is good value.

£££ Blue Elephant (Thai)
4-6 Fulham Broadway, SW6.
Tel: 0171-385 6595.
A tropical jungle in the middle of Fulham. Excellent food and charming service from waitresses in traditional costume.

Restaurant Call

Restaurant Services supplies up-to-date, impartial information on London's restaurants and a free booking service.
● Tel: 0181-888 8080.

London Restaurants (cont.)

£ Brilliant (Indian)
72-4 Western Road,
Southall, Greater London.
Tel: 0181-574 1928.
One of the best Indian
restaurants in the country.
££ Chiang Mai (Thai)
48 Frith Street, W1.
Tel: 0171-437 7444.
Modelled on a traditional stilt
house, with an extensive menu
of good northern Thai cuisine.
£££ Chutney Mary (Indian)
535 King's Road, SW10.
Tel: 0171-351 3113.
Booking is essential for this
popular restaurant which serves
a variety of dishes from all over
India. Expensive.
£££ Nobu (Japanese)
19 Old Park Lane, W1.
Tel: 0171-447 4747.
New York's hottest restaurant
has come to London, with
celebrated Japanese chef
Nobuyuki Matsuhisa bringing a
blend of South America and
California to modern Japanese
cuisine, in this 4-star hotel.
££ Rebato's (Spanish)
169 South Lambeth Road, SW8.
Tel: 0171-735 6388
Restaurant worth a detour.
Authentic tapas.
£££ The Red Fort (Indian)
77 Dean Street, W1.
Tel: 0171-437 2410.
Renowned Soho restaurant that
offers good Mogul cooking in
luxurious surroundings.
££ Yoshina (Japanese)
Basement, Japan Centre, 66
Brewer Street, W1.
Tel: 0171-287 6622.
Sit at this bar and try some of
the cheapest Japanese food in
the capital.

Modern European
£ Odette's
130 Regent's Park Road, NW1.
Tel: 0171-586 5486.
Busy and cheerful local offering
good-value 3-course lunch.
££ L'Odéon
65 Regent Street, W1.

Price Guide

Prices are per person for a
three-course meal with half a
bottle of house wine:
££££ £100+
£££ £50–100
££ £20–50
£ under £20

Tel: 0171-287 1400.
Superb globe-trotting menu from
innovative Raymond Blanc-
trained chef Bruno Loubet.
£££ Oxo Tower
Bankside SE1.
Tel: 0171-803 3888.
Brasserie and restaurant run by
Harvey Nichols. Main attraction
is the stunning river view.
Expensive.
£££ Les Saveurs
37a Curzon Street, W1.
Tel: 0171-491 8919.
Elegant basement restaurant in
the heart of Mayfair regarded as
one of London's finest new
modern British offerings.
££ Turner's
87-9 Walton Street, SW3.
Tel: 0171-584 6711.
Excellent value for money and
charming ambience for top-
quality food from bluff
Yorkshireman Brian Turner.

The Southeast

Amberley, nr Arundel
££ Amberley Castle
On the B2139 between
Storrington and Bury Hill.
Tel: (01798) 831992.
Evocatively restored 12th-
century castle, complete with
battlements. Take a stroll round
the picture-postcard village, then
dine in splendour in the Queen's
Room Restaurant with a
splendid 16th-century mural.
Classic cuisine cooked and
served with panache.

Brighton
££ The Sussex Arts Club
7 Ship Street.
Tel: (01273) 727371.

Serves British food in the clubby
atmosphere of a Georgian
building. Reserve.
£ Terre à Terre
71 East Street.
Tel: (01273) 729051.
Bustling café offering a brilliantly
innovative vegetarian menu and
organic wine.
£ Food for Friends in the Lanes
42 Market Square.
Tel: (01273) 202310.
A vegetarian favourite.

Chilgrove, nr Chichester
££ White Horse Inn
Tel: (01243) 535219.
Country pub and restaurant with
a long-standing reputation.
Al fresco meals in summer.
After-theatre meals.

Frant, nr Tunbridge Wells
££ Bassetts Restaurant
37 High Street.
Tel: (01892) 750635.
Good-quality Provençal cooking
in a plush front room
atmosphere, on the high street
of a pretty village.

East Grinstead
£££ Gravetye Manor
Vowels Lane.
Tel: (01342) 810567.
An Elizabethan manor house,
beautifully decorated with wood-
panelled rooms and surrounded
by fine gardens, this is somewhere special. Equally pleasing
is the excellent traditional and
modern British cooking.

Hastings
££ Röser's
64 Eversfield Place,
St Leonard's.
Tel: (01424) 712218.
Unpretentious seafront
restaurant offering simple food
superbly prepared by Gerald
Röser (an excellent home curer
who also has a passion for
mushrooms). Good wine list.

Jevinton
££ The Hungry Monk
High Street.

Tel: (01323) 482178.
In the Cuckmere Valley, this restaurant retains its quirky rustic character. Fixed-price menu with excellent desserts and cheeseboard, and plenty of local produce.

Midhurst
££ Maxine's
Red Lion Street.
Tel: (01732) 0816271.
In a half-timbered house next to the Swan Inn, Maxine's is an established restaurant that has won accolades without being too pricey. Robert de Jager is the chef, and his wife Marti runs the front of house. Closed on Mondays.

Rye
££ Landgate Bistro
5–6 Landgate.
Tel: (01797) 222829.
Up-and-coming chef Toni Ferguson-Lees has a local following for her blend of British and Mediterranean styles. Her speciality is seafood, although that is just part of an extensive repertoire at this popular bistro.

Tunbridge Wells
££ Chi
26 London Road.
Tel: (01892) 513888.
Upmarket Chinese, the best for miles. Pleasant decor.
££ The Hare
Langton Road, Langton Green, nr Tunbridge Wells.
Tel: (01892) 862419.
Meals from the blackboard are served in a drawing room-cum-library atmosphere. Large portions of upmarket food, with excellent desserts. Booking is essential.
££–£££ Thackeray's House
85 London Road.
Tel: (01892) 511921.
In this pretty former home of the 19th-century novelist, chef-patron Bruce Wass serves excellent Anglo-French country cooking which consistently picks up awards. A wine bar in the

Tearooms

Many foreigners are amused at the British habit of taking afternoon tea – that is, until they try a cream tea for themselves. This consists of scones, jam and cream (clotted cream in Devon and Cornwall) with a pot of tea.

Several of London's hotels, including the Ritz, Waldorf and Dorchester, are favourite haunts for afternoon tea. Listed here are tearooms around the country for which it is worth making a detour. All have won awards from the Tea Council:

The Southeast
Pavilion Tea Rooms
Royal Parade,
Eastbourne. Tel: (01323) 410374.
Shepherds Tea Rooms
35 Little London, Chichester.
Tel: (01243) 774761.

Oxford to Stratford
Bo-Peep Tea Rooms and Restaurant
Riverside,
Bourton-on-the-Water.
Tel: (01451) 822005.
The Marshmallow
High Street,
Moreton-in-Marsh.
Tel: (01608) 651536.

Cambridge and East Anglia
Margaret's Tea Rooms
Chestnut Farmhouse, The Street, Baconsthorpe, nr Holt.
Tel: (01263 577614).
The Cake Table Tearoom
5 Fishmarket Street, Thaxted.
Tel: (01371) 831206.
The Tea & Coffee House
6–7 Market Place, Hitchin.
Tel: (01462) 433631.

The Lake District
Sharrow Bay Country House Hotel
Lake Ullswater, Howtown.
Tel: (017684) 86301.

The West Country
The Canary
3 Queen Street, Bath.
Tel: (01225) 424846.
Carpenter's Kitchen
The Harbour,
Boscastle.
Tel: (01840) 250595.
The Commodore Hotel
Marine Parade, Instow.
Tel: (01271 860347).
Greys Dining Room
96 High Street, Totnes.
Tel: (01803) 866369.
The Parlour
112 East Street,
South Molton.
Tel: (01769) 574144.
The Bridge Tea Rooms
24A Bridge Street,
Bradford-on-Avon.
Tel: (01225) 865537.
The Tea Shoppe and Restaurant
3 High Street, Dunster.
Tel: (01643) 821304.

Yorkshire and the Northeast
Bettys Café Tea Rooms
6-8 St Helen's Square, York.
Tel: (01904) 627050.
Other branches: Harrogate, Ilkley and Northallerton.
Crathorne Hall Hotel
Crathorne, nr Yarm.
Tel: (01642) 700398.

Peak District and E. Midlands
Olde School Tearoom
Carburton, nr Worksop.
Tel: (01909) 483517.

Wales
St Tudno Hotel
Promenade, Llandudno.
Tel: (01492) 874411.

Scotland
The Caledonian Hotel
Princes Street
Edinburgh.
Tel: 0131-459 9988.
Kind Kyttock's Kitchen
Cross Wynd, Falkland
Tel: (01337) 857477.

Southeast restaurants (cont.)

basement offers less expensive, but equally good bistro meals.

Uckfield
££ La Scalata
Hook Hall, 250 High Street.
Tel: (01825) 766844.
Stylish regional and northern Italian food at modest prices.

The West Country

Barwick, nr Yeovil
££ Little Barwick House
Tel: (01935) 423902.
Peaceful Georgian dower house with six rooms for B&B and a great selection of seasonal dishes with top-quality produce.

Bath
£££ The Hole in the Wall
16 George Street.
Tel: (01225) 425242).
A long-established restaurant which has been revived to great acclaim. Highly imaginative haute cuisine.
££ Lettonie
35 Kelston Road.
Tel: (01225) 446676
A popular haunt, Lettonie is special. Innovative food is presented with painstaking aplombe.
££ The Moon and Sixpence
61 Broad Street.
Tel: (01225) 460962.
Modern British food, plus some foreign imports. Old favourites are given an imaginative twist. Attractive setting.
£££ The Olive Tree
Queensbury Hotel, Russel Street. Tel: (01225) 447928.
'Foodie' favourite. Modern British cooking with French, Italian and Moroccan influences.
£££ The Royal Crescent Hotel
Royal Crescent.
Tel: (01225) 739955.
Within the walled gardens of the hotel. Fine food, elegant surroundings.
£ Sally Lunn's
4 North Parade Passage.

Price Guide

Prices are per person for a three-course meal with half a bottle of house wine:
££££ £100+
£££ £50–100
££ £20–50
£ under £20

Tel: (01225) 461634.
Excellent option for a lunchtime snack, overly expensive at night.

Bristol
££ Markwick's
43 Corn Street.
Tel: 0117-926 2658.
Elegant little restaurant with an excellent reputation for its flavoursome, trend-setting Anglo-Provençal cooking.

Chagford
££ 22 Mill Street.
Tel: (01647) 432244.
Ex-sous chef at Gidleigh Park Duncan Walker serves food in the Gidleigh tradition but at affordable prices.

Colerne
££–£££ Lucknam Park.
Tel: (01225) 742777.
Sophisticated classic British cuisine with a serious wine list at seriously expensive prices in the spacious, chandelier-lit dining room of this Georgian manor.

Dartmouth
£££ The Carved Angel
2 South Embankment.
Tel: (01803) 832465.
Well-established restaurant serving accomplished modern British and European cuisine based on good local produce, in a picturesque setting overlooking Dartmouth harbour and the Dart estuary.

Drewsteignton
£–££ Hunts Tor
Tel: (01647) 281228.
A no-choice menu lovingly prepared with home-grown

organic produce in a tiny dining room (seating eight). No children under 10.

Hunstrete, nr Chelwood
££–£££ Hunstrete House
Tel: (01761) 490490.
Opulent surroundings and refined cuisine in a Georgian mansion that is set in 92 acres of deer park.

Mousehole
££ The Lobster Pot Hotel
South Cliff.
Tel: (01736) 731251.
Seafood as it comes ashore, eaten as you watch the changing light on St Michael's Mount.

New Polzeath
££ Cornish Cottage Hotel
Tel: (01208) 862213.
Stunning location by the coastal path overlooking Polzeath beach. Trained by the renowned Marco Pierre White, Tim Rogers is yet another master in the modern British mode.

Padstow
£££ The Seafood Restaurant
Riverside.
Tel: (01841) 532485.
One of the best seafood restaurants in Britain. Situated on the quay at Padstow to guarantee freshest ingredients, its dining room is an informal conservatory. The infectiously enthusiastic chef Rick Stein shows his passion for fish with simple dishes cooked with minimum fuss. Booking essential
££ St Petroc's Bistro
4 New Street.
Tel: (01841) 532700.
Sample the cutting edge of Rick Stein's fish cooking at a fraction of the price of The Seafood Restaurant nearby. And you won't have to book months ahead, either.

Plymouth
££ Chez Nous
13 Frankfurt Gate.

Tel: (01752) 266793.
Seriously good French bistro with great selection of inexpensive wines.

St Ives
£ Alfresco Café-Bar
Wharf Road.
Tel: (01736) 793737.
Trendy harbourside bar offering excellent Mediterranean menu at lunch and stylish, mainly fish dinners.

Taunton
£££ Castle Hotel
Castle Green.
Tel: (01823) 272671.
Stylish, classic British cuisine, first-class service, imposing setting.

Virginstow, nr Launceston
££ Percy's at Coombeshead
Tel: (01409) 211236.
Small farmhouse hotel with restaurant that prides itself on flavoursome food prepared with ingredients grown a stone's throw away.

Hardy Country

Beaulieu
£££ Montagu Arms Hotel
Palace Lane.
Tel: (01590) 612324.
Hotel and restaurant serving excellent English food. An ideal base for exploring the New Forest.

Brockenhurst
£££ Le Poussin
The Courtyard, 49–55 Brookley Road. Tel: (01590) 623063.
First-rate French haute-cuisine of self-taught chef Alex Aitkin, who skilfully incorporates organic local ingredients. Nicely located in a picturesque New Forest village not far from the coast.

Hythe
££ Boathouse Brasserie
29 Shamrock Way, Hythe Marina Village. Tel: (01703) 845594.
Talented chef Ian McAndrew's

British Cheeses

One of Britain's less well-known culinary delights is its cheeses. As well as the more traditional hard cheeses (most notably Cheddar, Cheshire, Double Gloucester, Lancashire, Red Leicester and Wensleydale), there are numerous soft, tangy goat's and sheep's cheeses. Soft varieties like Caerphilly, Sussex Slipcote and Wealden (a tangy cheese flavoured with herbs or black pepper and sold within three days of being made) are growing in popularity. But undoubtedly, the king of British cheeses is Stilton.

Hotels given Egon Ronay awards for their particularly fine cheeseboards include: L'Ortolan in Shinfield, Harveys

waterside restaurant is strong on fish. Excellent-value 2-course set lunch.

Hordle, nr Lymington
££ Gordelton Mill Hotel
Silver Street
Tel: (01590) 682219.
The extensive menu and superb French cuisine of the Provence Restaurant make this ivy-clad mill-cum-hotel a popular venue for local diners. Huge wine list with a full range of good choices.

Stuckton
££ The Three Lions
Stuckton Road.
Tel: (01425) 652489.
Michael Womersley cooks like a dream. Food admirably straightforward, technically consummate and deliciously flavoured.

Winchester
££ Hotel du Vin & Bistro
14 Southgate Street.
Tel: (01962) 841414.
A wine lover's heaven, complete with an attractive menu of top-notch modern British food.

Restaurant in Bristol, Poppies in Brimfield and The Lygon Arms in Broadway.

To see cheese manufactured in the traditional way, visit Viscount Chewton's Cheese Dairy at Priory Farm, Chewton Mendip in Somerset.

For under £15 you can sample as many as you like out of a superb selection of about 40 cheeses at La Fromagerie, 30 Highbury Park, London N5 2AA (tel: 0171-359 7440).

There are many specialist cheese shops around the country. Neal's Yard Dairy, 17 Short Gardens, London WC2 is a favourite London source. And Paxton & Whitfield has branches in London, Bath, Solihull and Stratford.

The Thames Valley

Bray
£££ The Waterside Inn
Ferry Road.
Tel: (01628) 620691.
In an idyllic spot overlooking the Thames, this is one of England's most exceptional restaurants. The genius of Michel Roux has received great acclaim and several Michelin stars over the years.
££–£££ The Fat Duck
1 High Street.
Tel: (01628) 580333.
From the bare wooden tables to the short menu and no-nonsense presentation, rising star Heston Blumenthal makes simplicity an artform. But painstaking work goes into every dish – and it shows in the flavour. His unique brand of modern British cookery has earned him the respect of many established top chefs.

Epsom Downs
£ Le Raj
211 Firtree Road.
Tel: (01737) 371064.

Thames Valley (continued)

Stylish Bangladeshi cuisine with an excellent reputation.

Goring
££ The Leatherne Bottle
Tel: (01491) 872667.
A characterful old riverside inn where the food is excellent and imaginatively produced with great care using the finest fresh ingredients.

St Albans
£ The Waffle House
Kinsbury Watermill,
St Michael's Street.
Tel: (01727) 853502.
The excellent waffles range from bestselling ham and mushroom, to ratatouille, to pecan nut with butterscotch sauce. Inexpensive and great for families, this popular café does get crowded in summer, particularly at lunchtime.

Shinfield
£££ L'Ortolan
The Old Vicarage,
Church Lane.
Tel: (01734) 883783.
Stunning flavours, innovative Anglo-French cuisine and food that's a feast to the eye as well as the tastebuds are guaranteed at this well-respected restaurant. Excellent cheeseboard, too *(see page 389)*.

Oxford to Stratford

Bibury
££ The Swan
Tel: (01285) 740695.
In a stunning location by the bridge over the River Coln, this charming stone hotel puts a stylish Mediterranean twist on modern British dishes.

Birmingham
£ St Paul's Bar and Restaurant
50–54 St Paul's Square,
Hockley.
Tel: 0121-605 1001.
Trendy wine bar.

Cheltenham
£££ Le Champignon Sauvage
24-26 Suffolk Road.
Tel: (01242) 573449.
Wild mushrooms might well be incorporated in the dishes offered on the interesting menu at this restaurant. The food has a touch of class, and chef David Everitt-Matthias has won awards for his meat and desserts.

Chipping Campden
£ Red Lion
High Street.
Tel: (01386) 840760.
At the opposite end of the High Street from the church, this popular old beamed coaching inn, with its numerous quiet niches, welcomes children and serves everything from a full meat and two veg lunch to bar snacks such as the excellent pork and leek sausages in French bread.

Price Guide

Prices are per person for a three-course meal with half a bottle of house wine:
££££ £100+
£££ £50–100
££ £20–50
£ under £20

Kington
££ Penrhos Court
Tel: (01544) 230720.
In a refurbished farm Daphne Lambert proves that healthy eating can be gastronomic, with most ingredients organic (including many wines) and salt rarely used.

Malvern Wells
££–£££ Croque-en-Bouche
221 Wells Road.
Tel: (01684) 565612.
Open just Thursday to Saturday most of the year, or four nights in summer, this is a foodies' delight. Marion and Robin Jones grow their own vegetables, salad leaves and around 80 herbs, and Marion's use of them is

masterly. The wine list of over 1,500 bins is unparalleled.

Nailsworth
££ William's Bistro
3 Fountain Street.
Tel: (01453) 835507.
Excellent light food from this deli-cum-restaurant.

Old Minster Lovell
££ Lovells at Windrush Farm
Tel: (01993) 779802.
Dining is taken seriously at this former gentleman farmer's house and booking is essential. Dinner is seven courses with no choice, taken at a leisurely pace, and the balance and finesse of Marcus Ashenford's cooking ensures that this is no marathon. Recommended.

Olton
££ Rajnagar International
256 Lyndan Road, Olton,
Solihull. Tel: 0121-742 8140.
Said to be the best Bangladeshi restaurant in the country with pleasant decor and service and authentic food, especially fish.

Oxford
££ Browns
5-11 Woodstock Road.
Tel: (01865) 511995.
This well-established restaurant offers breakfast, light lunches and three-course meals in a relaxed atmosphere. Open 11am-11.30pm. Bookings are only taken for parties of eight or more, and only Monday to Thursday, so expect queues at busy times. Children welcome.
££ Chiang Mai Kitchen
130a High Street.
Tel: (01865) 202233.
Top-quality Thai cuisine at very reasonable prices in one of the finest 17th-century houses in the city, Kemp Hall.
££ Gee's Brasserie
61a Banbury Road.
Tel: (01865) 558346.
Well-established restaurant in the Raymond Blanc tradition in a beautiful, airy conservatory.

££ Le Petit Blanc
71-2 Walton Street.
Tel: (01865) 510999.
Raymond Blanc's latest venture
in Oxford. Light but traditional
French dishes in an airy
atmosphere – open all day,
including for breakfast. Decor by
Terence Conran.

**£££ Ma Cuisine Restaurant
Français**
21 Cowley Road.
Tel: (01865) 201316.
Top-quality French cuisine in an
intimate front-room atmosphere.
Excellent wine list.

£ The Polash
25 Park End (opposite the
railway station).
Tel: (01865) 250244.
Tandoori restaurant specialising
in the cuisine of Madras.

Paulerspury, nr Northampton
££ Vine House
100 High Street.
Tel: (01327) 811267.
Old stone farmhouse with some
fine modern English dishes.

Thame
£ The Old Trout
29–30 Lower High Street.
Tel: 01844 212146.
Brasserie-style restaurant,
particularly good on fish.

Upper Slaughter
££–£££ Lords of the Manor
Upper Slaughter,
nr Bourton-on-the-Water.
Tel: (01451) 820243.
Quintessentially English former
rectory in 8 acres (3 hectares) of
parkland with lake, a haven of
good taste and beautifully
presented modern dishes, rich
in flavour.

Winchcombe
££ Wesley House
High Street.
Tel: (01242) 602366.
There's lots of atmosphere in
this heavily beamed 15th-
century former merchant's
house, which serves a stylish
selection of modern European
dishes from the blackboard.

Cambridge & E. Anglia

Cambridge
££ Three Horseshoes
High Street,
Madingley, nr Cambridge.
Tel: (01954) 210221.
Thatched inn in pretty village two
miles (3 km) from Cambridge.
Reasonably priced modern
Mediterranean food and wine.

£££ Midsummer House
Midsummer Common.
Tel: (01233) 369299.
Walled Victorian house on the
banks of the River Cam. Elegant
modern European cuisine in
stylish surroundings.

Ely
£ Steeplegate
16-18 High Street.
Tel: (01353) 664731.
Home-cooked cakes, scones
and fresh cream teas in
picturesque building backing
onto the cathedral.

Heacham
£ Norfolk Lavender
Caley Mill, nr Heacham.
Tel: (01485) 571965.
Cream teas are a speciality in
this old miller's tearooms-cum
restaurant in the middle of
stunning lavender/herb gardens.
Book for Sunday lunch by
the open fire from October
to April.

Hintlesham, nr Ipswich
£££ Hintlesham Hall
Tel: (01473) 652268.
Two restaurants in an opulent
classical country-house hotel
in the peaceful Suffolk
countryside serving high-quality
British food.

Holt
££ Yetman's
37 Norwich Road.
Tel: (01263) 713320.
Quirky and stylish, the daily
menu centres on finest local
produce including organic meat,
freshly caught fish and
biodynamically grown veg.

King's Lynn
££ Rococo
11 Saturday Market Place.
Tel: (01553) 771483.
Light food imaginatively styled,
with fish and vegetarian dishes a
speciality. Lunch especially good
value.

Melbourn
££–£££ The Pink Geranium
Station Road.
Tel: (01763) 260215.

Favourite Desserts

When dining out in Britain, it is
as well to save a corner for
dessert. Traditional British
puddings are not for the faint-
stomached, however, with large
helpings of home-baked apple
pie and fruit crumble, treacle
tart, bread and butter pudding
and sherry trifle on the
dessert menus of most pub
restaurants. They are usually
served with lashings of custard
or cream too.

But the recent trend is for
sweets that are altogether
daintier and more intricate. Old
favourites such as summer
pudding, ice cream and
meringues are given interesting
new twists by the top chefs,
with their appearance almost
as important, it seems, as their
taste. Restaurants that have
won the coveted Egon Ronay
award for excellent desserts
include: The Old Vicarage in
Ridgeway, Le Champignon
Sauvage in Cheltenham,
The Castle in Taunton and
L'Ortolan in Shinfield.

Cambridge & E. Anglia (cont.)

Highly sophisticated French cooking from Steven Saunders (of the BBC programme, *Ready, Steady Cook*) in a 15th-century thatched cottage.

Nayland
££ Martha's Vineyard
18 High Street.
Tel: (01206) 262888.
The American chef here believes in baking bread and making fresh pasta daily – a real treat.

Norwich
££ Adlard's
79 Upper St Giles.
Tel: (01603) 633522.
Cosy, welcoming restaurant with classic decor, serving modern British food with a French twist. Chef-patron David Adlard's dedication to fresh seasonal produce is apparent in all dishes. Good-value lunches.

Stanton
£–££ Leaping Hare Café
Wyken Vineyards.
Tel: (01359) 250287.
Elegant café-restaurant at one of Britain's best vineyards. Californian-style cooking.

Sudbury
£ Red Onion Bistro
57 Ballingdon Street.
Tel: (01787) 376777.
Bustling bistro. Excellent value.

Swaffam
££ Strattons
Stratton House, 4 Ash Close.
Tel: (01760) 723845.
Family-run hotel with a passion for East Anglian ingredients, from flour to cockles, and excellent home-grown organic herbs and vegetables.

The Lake District

Ambleside
£ The Glass House Café Restaurant
Rydal Rd. Tel: (015394) 32137.

A 16th-century woollen mill, behind the famous Bridge House. Mediterranean and modern British food for the discriminating. Teas served during the day.

Bowness-on-Windermere
££ Linthwaite House
Crook Road.
Tel: (01539) 488600.
English country house cooking with superb views over lake.
££ Porthole Eating House
3 Ash Street.
Tel: (01539) 442793.
A taste of the Mediterranean in an informal but intimate surroundings.

Crosthwaite, nr Kendal
£ Punch Bowl Inn
Tel: (01539) 568237.
Stephen Doherty, former chef at Le Gavroche, provides upmarket French-style pub grub at very reasonable prices. 3-course set menu for just over £10.

Eskdale
£ The Woolpack Inn
Tel: (019467) 23230.
Well-known hostelry in western Lake District. Good food with a selection of real ale.

Keswick
££ Swinside Lodge
Newlands.

Tel: (01768) 772948.
Fantastic views from a fine Victorian lodge serving a 5-course set menu. Unlicensed.

Leck, nr Cowan Bridge
££ Cobwebs
Tel: (01524) 272141.
Just south of Kirby Lonsdale, a remote Victorian house offering hearty 4-course, no-choice dinners. Overnight accommo-dation possible.

Ullswater
£ Dalemain
Tel: (017684) 86450.
Historic house, home of the Hazells for 300 years. Bar lunches and home-made teas in medieval hall. Open 11.15am–5pm weekdays.

Windermere
£££ Miller Howe
Tel: (015394) 42536.
John Tovey's well-known restaurant, for gourmets who like immaculate service.

Merseyside/Shropshire

Altrincham
£ Juniper
21 The Downs.
Tel: 0161-929 4008.
Seriously good food in a bistro-style setting.

Baltis in Birmingham – and London

A pleasant legacy of Britain's colonial past is its wealth of Indian restaurants. In London good areas for cheap Indian food are Brick Lane and Southall. Drummond Street, near Euston station, has good vegetarian Indian restaurants.
   Birmingham is home of the balti. Its finest, according to aficionados, are:
£ Adil
148 Stoney Lane, Sparkbrook.
Tel: 0121-449 0335.

£ Royal Naim
417-9 Stratford Road.
Tel: 0121-766 7849.
If you want to sample award-winning cuisine in a trendy café atmosphere, head for:
£ Shimla Pinks
214 Broad Street.
Tel: 0121-633 0366.
   Leicester, too, has some of Britain's finest Indians along its "Golden Mile". The local council publishes a Taste of Asia leaflet with a list, tel: 0116-254 7799.

Chester
££ Arkle Restaurant
Chester Grosvenor Hotel, Eastgate Street.
Tel: (01244) 324024.
Named after the famous steeplechaser, this is a thoroughbred of restaurants in a grand hotel on the city's main street. The food is traditional British excellently presented, including one of the best bread boards in the country, but the wine list is overly expensive.

Langho
££–£££ Northcote Manor.
Northcote Road.
Tel: (01254) 240555.
Victorian country-house hotel with superb views of the Ribble Valley offering extensive menus of stylish traditional dishes.

Longridge, nr Preston
££–£££ Paul Heathcote's Restaurant
Tel: (01722) 784969.
The Northwest's best restaurant, in a converted row of three early-1800s cottages. Paul Heathcote puts an individual stamp on modern British cuisine while flying the flag for Lancashire with black pudding and excellent potato dishes. Recommended for the brave: the 10-course Signature Menu.

Ludlow
££ Merchant House
Lower Corve Street.
Tel: (01584) 875438.
Imaginative cooking with top-quality ingredients and a no-nonsense approach are the hallmarks of popular chef Shaun Hill. Booking is recommended as the small dining room of this medieval half-timbered ex-merchant house seats 20.

Ramsbottom, nr Bury
£ Village Restaurant
Tel: (01706) 825070.
Despite the pew seating and brasserie style, this informal

Price Guide

Prices are per person for a three-course meal with half a bottle of house wine:
££££ £100+
£££ £50–100
££ £20–50
£ under £20

bistro (drawing heavily on the deli in the basement, which specialises in organic and free-range produce) serves upmarket food at great prices (like lunch for £5).

Waterhouses
££–£££ Old Beams
Leek Road.
Tel: (01538) 308254.
Oak beams, open fires and Windsor chairs are the homely setting for French-style food of a consistently high standard.

Yorkshire/Northeast

Bilbrough
£££ Bilbrough Manor
Tel: (01937) 834002.
Traditional English cuisine and good hospitality at this homely Edwardian country house hotel. Set in 100 acres of grounds just outside York.

Bolton Abbey
£££ Devonshire Arms Country House Hotel
Tel: (01756) 710441.
The Burlington Restaurant, named after the 18th-century patron of the arts Lord Burlington, is furnished with antiques and portraits from Chatsworth, home of the Duke and Duchess of Devonshire. Elegant on a grand scale with classic dishes given a tasteful modern touch.

Burnsall
££ Red Lion
Tel: (01756) 7200204.
A 17th-century country village inn on the banks of the Wharfe, between Bolton Abbey and

Grassington. Specialities are fish, game and local produce.

Durham
£ Bistro 21
Aykley Heads House, Aykley Heads.
Tel: 0191-384 4354.
Robust Anglo-French cooking in a 16th-century farmhouse. Don't be put off by its site, on a business park.

Grassington
£ Paul & Cheryl's Licensed Restaurant
Tel: (01756) 752417.
Bistro-style atmosphere, with light lunches and à la carte in the evening.

Heaton, nr Bradford
££ Restaurant Nineteen
North Park Road.
Tel: (01274) 492559.
Stylishly decorated Victorian townhouse restaurant with bed and breakfast accommodation. Classic dishes, superbly prepared from a fixed-price three-course menu.

Hetton
££ Angel Inn
Tel: (01756) 730263.
Off the beaten track, but with long queues for the popular bar meals. A fixed-price restaurant offers an extensive menu with excellently priced food and wine.

Helmsley
££ Crown Hotel
Market Square.
Tel: (01439) 770297.
Comfortable former posting house offering a wide choice of country-style dishes.

Huddersfield
£ Café Pacific
3 Viaduct Street.
Tel: (01484) 559055. The highly individual, pan-global style of chef Scott Hessel is very popular in this slate-floored restaurant under a railway viaduct.

Northeast restaurants (cont.)

Ilkley
££ Box Tree
37 Church Street.
Tel: (01943) 608484.
Intimate restaurant with a cottagey feel serving a blend of classic French and modern British dishes without frills.

Malham
££ The Buck Inn
Tel: (01729) 830317.
Overlooking the village green. Home-cooked traditional fare in the bar. A la carte meals served in the restaurant.

Moulton
££ Black Bull Inn
Tel: (01325) 377289.
Whitewashed inn particularly popular for its fish bar (no reservations). A la carte menu in the Brighton Belle, a 1932 Pullman carriage, and Conservatory.

Northallerton
£££ McCoy's
The Cleveland Tontine, Staddlebridge.
Tel: (01609) 82671.
English eccentricity at its best. Lavish period surroundings, laid-back atmosphere and some of the most interesting food Britain has to offer. Open for evening meals only.

West Witton
£ The Wensleydale Heifer
Tel: (01969) 622322.
Beside the A684 between Leyburn and Aysgarth, a 17th-century inn. Home cooking.

Winteringham
££–£££ Winteringham Fields
Tel: (01724) 733096.
A gem of a hotel just south of the Humber Bridge with beams, panelling and open fireplaces. Expect surprises on the extensive menu ranging from game to gravadlax to goat. The Swiss chef, Germain Schwab, takes huge pride in his ingredients, mainly from excellent local suppliers, including many home-grown organic vegetables.

Whitby
££ The Magpie Café
Pier Road.
Tel: (01947) 602058.
Legendary habourside restaurant in merchant's house that became the Pilotage. Though most famed for its superb Whitby fish and chips, it satisfies most other tastes with equal aplomb. Children's menu.

York
££ Melton's
7 Scarcroft Road.
Tel: (01904) 634341.
Unassuming, child-friendly restaurant serving a mix of conventional and exotic English dishes. Good vegetarian selection especially on Tuesday and Thursday. Special price reductions for customers prepared to leave by 7.45pm, and the maximum mark-up on wines is only £10.
£ Mulberry Hall
Stonegate.
Tel: (01904) 620736.
Up above the porcelain shop light lunches and teas are served in very civilised surroundings. Views from the windows of York's best shopping street.

Peak District and East Midlands

Ashford in the Water
££ Riverside Country House Hotel
Fennel Street.
Tel: (01629) 814275.
In a beautiful position overlooking the River Wye, the gourmet conservatory restaurant of this secluded Georgian house offers high-class English cuisine.

Baslow
£££ Fischer's Baslow Hall,
Calver Road.
Tel: (01246) 583259.
Outstanding restaurant serving top-quality traditional British

British Beer

The British are renowned for beer drinking and, with over 400 breweries in the country, each producing several beers (from bitter, stout and pale ale to lager and real ale), they certainly have more than enough to choose from.

Fans of real ale, led by the Campaign for Real Ale (CAMRA), have promoted a greater appreciation of this traditional brew, which undergoes a second natural fermentation in the cask and is served without gas pressure. Many local breweries now produce their own real ale, and quirky brews are not uncommon (from an ale flavoured with whisky to seasonal beers named after the 12 signs of the zodiac).

However, three-quarters of the beer market is dominated by multi-national brewing companies, and weak, fizzy lagers have been winning an increasing share of the market.

One of the biggest beer producers, Bass, has a museum at its brewery in Burton-on-Trent (open 10am–5pm all year). Conducted tours can also be arranged. Tel: (01283) 511000.

To see a smaller, more traditional local brewery at work, you can visit the Theakston Brewery Visitor Centre in Ripon, open 10.30am–4pm all year. Tel: (01765) 689544.

cuisine in a well-renovated, turn-of-the-century hotel. The in-house brasserie, Café Max, is a great way to sample Max Fischer's five-star food cheaply.

Dovedale, nr Ashbourne
££ Izaak Walton Hotel
Tel: (01335) 350555.
The dining room of this 17th-century former farmhouse overlooking Dovedale in the Peak District Park is Regency style and specialises in English and French dishes.

Hambleton
££–£££ Hambleton Hall,
Hambleton, nr Oakham.
Tel: (01572) 756991.
Elegant dining room serving modern British cuisine in a fine country house hotel set in delightful countryside.

Hassop
££ Hassop Hall Hotel
Tel: (01629) 640488.
This is one of the finest hotel restaurants in the Peak District, set in parkland at the heart of the Peak District National Park, and booking for meals is essential. Extensive menu.

Hathersage
££ The George Hotel
Main Road.
Tel: (01433) 650436.
The Charlotte Restaurant serves traditional and Continental dishes. The George Bar offers delicious home-made pies.

Leicester
£ Café Bruxelles
90-92 High Street.
Tel: 0116-224 3013.
Trendy bar food, plus over 30 Belgian beers.

Ridgeway, nr Sheffield
££ Old Vicarage
Tel: 0114-247 5814.
Large Victorian house in gardens with a country house feel. A fixed-price menu of outstanding pedigree.

Rowsley
££ Peacock Hotel
Tel: (01629) 733518.
Favoured by anglers fishing the River Wye, the Peacock also has a fine restaurant offering a lunchtime buffet.

Wye Valley & S. Wales

Abergavenny
£££ The Walnut Tree
Tel: (01873) 852797.
Hospitable whitewashed country inn offering an excellent menu with an Italian emphasis.

Cardiff
££ Gilby's
Oldport Road,
Culverhouse Cross.
Tel: (01222) 670800.
Stylish restaurant with particularly fine fish. Good-value Businessman's Menu.

Price Guide

Prices are per person for a three-course meal with half a bottle of house wine:
££££ £100+
£££ £50–100
££ £20–50
£ under £20

Llanwrtyd Wells
££ Carlton House
Dolycoed Road.
Tel: (01591) 610248.
Small Edwardian house hotel offering a well-priced 4-course "epicurean" menu and good-value, reasonable wine list. Self-taught chef Mary Ann Gilchrist puts flavour at the top of the agenda.

Rosebush
££ Tate's at Tafarn Newydd
Tel: (01437) 532542.
Rustic, globe-trotting menu in a remote pub at the foot of the pass through the highest part of the Preseli Hills.

The Toast

When British friends drink together, you'll almost certainly witness them raise or clink their glasses and say "Cheers" (or, less formally, "Bottoms up"). It's also traditional to make a "toast", wishing your drinking companions good health and the best of luck. As midnight strikes on New Year's Eve, people toast the New Year (usually with a glass of Champagne), and at weddings a toast is always drunk to the newlyweds.

Swansea
££ L'Amuse
2 Woodville Road, Mumbles.
Tel: (01792) 3666006.
Quirky French-style restaurant. Kate Cole's *pièce de résistance* are complimentary *amuse gueules* – tasty morsels to "entertain the mouth" between courses.

££ Number One Wind Street
1 Wind Street.
Tel: (01792) 456996.
Rustic French cooking with a heavy Welsh bias. Bistro atmosphere.

£ The High Tide Café
61 Newton Road, Mumbles.
Tel: (01792) 363462.
Innovative café with a young clientele. Organic products are used wherever possible.

Whitebrook
££ The Crown at Whitebrook
Tel: (01600) 860254.
The cottagey dining room in this restaurant-with-rooms has a relaxed atmosphere under Roger Bates, while his wife Sandra cooks stylish Gallic dishes behind the scenes.

North Wales

Colwyn Bay
££ Café Nicoise
124 Abergele Road.
Tel: (01492) 53155.
A French-style café where you can enjoy Welsh lamb cooked to perfection. Other local fresh ingredients are also used as much as possible.

Eglwysfach, nr Machynlleth
££ Ynyshir Hall
Tel: (01654) 781209.
Fine modern British cooking from up-and-coming chef Chris Colmer, with extensive use of superb local ingredients such as Cardigan Bay seafood, wild salmon, venison and game and Welsh farmhouse cheeses.

Llansanffraid Glan
££ Old Rectory
Llanrwst Road.
Tel: (01492) 580611.
Small hotel in an 18th-century rectory with excellent views across the Conwy Estuary. A husband and wife team offer friendly service and a stylish and inexpensive set dinner using the finest Welsh produce.

Llanberis
££ Y Bistro
45 High Street.
Tel: (01286) 871278.
A cosy bistro with a dedication to all things Welsh, with local lamb always on the menu.

Pwllheli
£££ Plas Bodegroes
Nefyn Road.
Tel: (01758) 612363.
Stylish, award-winning restaurant with an excellent reputation for fine Welsh food.

Trefriw
£–££ Chandler's Brasserie
Tel: (01492) 640991.
Well-priced, elegant brasserie with open fire and separate vegetarian menu.

Scottish Lowlands

Anstruther
££ Cellar
24 East Green.
Tel: (01333) 310378.
Stone walls, peat fires in winter and sewing machine tables. Fish is a speciality.

Edinburgh
££ The Atrium
10 Cambridge Street.
Tel: 0131-228 8882.
Overtly modern restaurant, complete with railway sleeper tables and iron sculptures within the atrium of a building that also houses a theatre.

Glasgow
££–£££ One Devonshire Gardens
Tel: 0141-339 2001.
Glasgow's finest restaurant in a hotel of distinction. The quality

Price Guide

Prices are per person for a three-course meal with half a bottle of house wine:
££££ £100+
£££ £50–100
££ £20–50
£ under £20

of the fixed-price French menu and ornate decor make a meal here an occasion.
££ Yes
22 West Nile Street.
Tel: 0141-221 8044.
Smart modern brasserie with modern art on every wall. Stylish contemporary cuisine.

Gullane
££ Greywalls
Muirfield.
Tel: (01620) 842144.
Country house hotel serving well-priced Anglo-French food.
££ La Potinière
Main Street.
Tel: (01620) 843214.
Traditional Scottish meets rustic French. Well-established, excellently priced with exemplary standards.

Linlithgow
£££ The Champany Inn
Tel: (01506) 834532.
Famous for serving some of the best steaks in Britain, which are cut from prime Highland Aberdeen Angus cattle.

Wine, Cider and Scotch Whisky

Wine: Though not famous for its wine, southern England does produce some of its own. Most of the wines are white, and are made from German grape varieties, especially modern hybrids like Müller-Thurgau. In Kent, Lamberhurst, England's largest winery, has a shop and conducts tours by appointment. Tel: (01892) 890844.
  Cider: Devon, Somerset,

Hereford and Dorset are known for cider and scrumpy. Made from apples, these brews were undoubtedly brought across from France by the conquesting Normans in the 11th century. You can visit the Cider Museum and King Offa Distillery in Hereford, Sheppy's Cider and Rural Life Museum near Taunton, or Perry Cider Mills in Illminster (tel: 01460 52681).

Whisky is the spirit of Scotland, where over 100 distilleries produce their own distinctive single malts, the aristocrats of whiskies. Follow the whisky trail through the Spey Valley where half of Scotland's distilleries are concentrated. Many are keen to show visitors the secrets behind the making of whisky, usually followed by a tasting.

Turnberry
££–£££ Turnberry Hotel
Tel: (01655) 331000.
The Turnberry Restaurant of this
golfers' hotel (with two
championship courses) has
superb sea views, plus refined
British cuisine.

Scottish Highlands

Aberfeldy
££ Farleyer House
Tel: (01887) 820332.
Menzies Restaurant in this 18th-
century dower house is
traditional, with local seafood
and game a speciality.

Aberfoyle
££ Braeval
Aberfoyle, Stirling.
Tel: (01877) 382711.
First-class modern British food,
prepared with the tasteful
simplicity that has become the
hallmark of TV chef Nick Nairn
(of *Wild Harvest* fame).

Ballater
££ Green Inn
9 Victoria Road.
Tel: (01339) 755701.
Serious Scottish food
overlooking the village green.

Cupar
£££ Ostlers Close
25 Bonnygate.
Tel: (01334) 655574.
The appearance of this modest
restaurant belies its excellent
menu, incorporating the best
local produce available.

Dunkeld
££ Kinnaird
Kinnaird Estate.
Tel: (01796) 482440.
Grand Victorian hunting lodge in
beautiful landscaped gardens
where first-rate ingredients are
used to excellent effect in
creative modern dishes.

Fort William
£££–££££ Inverlochy Castle
Torlundy.

Tel: (01397) 702177.
Expect full pomp and ceremony
at this Scottish castle located at
the base of Ben Nevis where
modern British food is prepared
from the freshest ingredients.

Kingussie
££ The Cross
Tweed Mill Brae, Ardbroilach
Road.
Tel: (01540) 661166.
Cosy atmosphere with rough
stone walls and beams. Scottish
fare cooked with pride.

Loch Lomond
££–£££ Cameron House Hotel
Georgian Room.
Tel: (01389) 7555565.
Lochside hotel offering rich Euro-
classical dishes.

Orkney
££ The Creel
Front Road, St Margaret's Hope.
Tel: (01856) 831311.
Friendly Orkney fish restaurant.

Port Appin
££ Airds Hotel
Tel: (01631) 730236.
Whitewashed inn with dining
room overlooking Loch Linnhe.
First-class country-house cuisine
from a wide-ranging menu,
including excellent local fish.

£–££ Pierhouse
Tel: (01631) 730302.
Lochside fish and chip
restaurant. Seafood as it should
be, fresh from the quay.

St Andrews
££ Peat Inn
Peat Inn, nr St Andrews.
Tel: (01334) 840206.
David and Patricia Wilson have
dedicated 25 years to the dishes
that Scotland does best.
Unassuming but with an
excellent reputation.

Sites

There are two main organisations
that look after Britain's old
buildings, gardens and countryside. The Heritage organisations,
which are government-funded, run
key historic sites while the
National Trust, a popular charity,
maintains stately homes and
areas of coast and countryside.

English Heritage has more
than 400 properties, including
Stonehenge and Dover Castle.
Annual membership entitles you
to free entry to all these sites,
plus discounts off concerts held
at them during the summer. Also
available is an Overseas Visitor
Pass, which lasts for two weeks.
For further information contact:
English Heritage, Key Sign
House, 429 Oxford Street,
London W1R 2HD. Tel: 0171-
973 3000. Fax: 0171-973
3429.

Historic Scotland maintains
more than 300 properties
including Glasgow Cathedral and
Edinburgh Castle. Annual
membership again allows free
access to all these. Further
information from: Historic
Scotland, Longmore House,
Salisbury Place, Edinburgh EH9
1SH. Tel: 0131-668 8800. Fax:
0131-668 8888.

Cadw (Welsh Heritage) has
more than 100 properties, from
prehistoric sites to castles such
as Caernarfon, Conway and
Beaumaris and Tintern Abbey.
For information: Cadw, The
Welsh Office, Cathays Park,
Cardiff CF1 3NQ. Tel: (01222)
500200. Fax: (01222) 826375.

The National Trust was
founded in 1895 as an

independent charity for the conservation of places of historic interest and natural beauty in England and Northern Ireland. It has over 250 properties open to the public, from large country houses and abbeys to lighthouses and industrial monuments. It also maintains over 150 gardens and protects 244,000 hectares of countryside, including 565 miles of shoreline and woodland. The majority of its funding comes from its members.

Membership entitles you to free entry to properties and a copy of *The National Trust Handbook*. The annual fee can easily be recouped by a family taking a two-week holiday of leisurely sightseeing. Further information from: The National Trust, 36 Queen Anne's Gate, London SW1H 9AS. Tel: 0171-222 9251. Fax: 0171-222 5097.

The National Trust For Scotland is a separate body with over 100 properties covering 100,000 acres (40,500 hectares). Sites in its care include castles, battlefields, islands, countryside and the birthplaces of several famous Scots. For further information: The National Trust For Scotland, 5 Charlotte Square, Edinburgh EH2 4DU. Tel: 0131-226 5922. Fax: 0131-243 9501.

All these heritage groups have reciprocal arrangements, generally giving members half-price entry for the first year, and free access to sites thereafter. The NT also has reciprocal arrangements with trusts overseas, including Australia, India, New Zealand, Jamaica, Malaysia, Malta, Ireland and the Netherlands.

Visitors can also purchase a **Great Britain Heritage Pass** which allows unlimited access to over 500 stately homes, castles, historic houses and abbeys in the UK. It is a definite bargain

Private Gardens

Under the National Gardens Scheme (tel: 01483 211535), the gardens of Britain's many horticultural enthusiasts are open to the public. For a small entrance fee visitors can explore nearly 3,500 gardens from early-February to the end of September. *The Gardens of England & Wales, Open for Charity*, is a book listing all the gardens open each year (from larger bookshops).

for the history-minded visitor. It is available from certain overseas offices of the BTA, and can be purchased on arrival from London's British Travel Centres at ports, airports and selected TICS.

National Parks

Brecon Beacons The Beacons (in south Wales) are a series of red sandstone mountains, many over 1,000 ft (300 metres) high. Also woodland, lakes, waterfalls, caves, farmland and the valley of the River Usk.

Dartmoor Dartmoor ponies roam freely across this expanse of moorland in Devon with exposed granite *tors*, heath and peaty bogs. Highest point is High Willhays (2,038 ft/620 metres). Harsh home of Dartmoor prison and setting for *the* Sherlock Holmes mystery *The Hound of the Baskervilles.*

Exmoor Straddling the border between Somerset and Devon, with heathery moorland and breathtaking coastline. Home to Exmoor ponies, sheep, red deer and cattle.

Lake District Stunningly beautiful countryside in Cumbria: 16 lakes are interspersed with high fells, the highest being Scafell Pike (3210 ft/980 metres). A haven for fishing, boating, climbing and swimming.

Northumberland 398 sq miles (1,030 sq km) in England's far

northeast, stretching north to the Cheviots at the Scottish border and westwards to Cumbria. Characterised by rugged stretches of moorland, it includes some of the most spectacular coastline in the whole of Britain and encompasses Hadrian's Wall.

North York Moors A coastline of rugged cliffs, expanses of low moorland, deep valleys and heathered uplands, this national park covers 553 sq miles (1,430 sq km), including the 100-mile (160-km) long Cleveland Way.

Peak District This well-preserved area of natural beauty situated at the tip of the Pennines between Sheffield, Derby and Manchester, was England's first designated national park. It is characterised by high, wild and bleak moors and low, gentle limestone countryside with dramatic wooded valleys and rivers.

Pembrokeshire Coast Remote and ragged coastal park which takes up most of the coast of Pembrokeshire, southwest Wales. There is a coastal path stretching 180 miles (290 km), from Amroth beach to Teifi near Cardigan.

Snowdonia A large and diverse area of stunning beauty covering 838 sq miles (2,170 sq km) in the northwest of Wales. Encompassing forests, lakes and torrential streams, it is most admired for its craggy high peaks, with Mount Snowdon itself the highest south of the Scottish border. Excellent mountaineering, walking, pony trekking, canoeing, fishing and sailing.

Yorkshire Dales This wild expanse of great natural beauty covers 680 sq miles (1,760 sq km) in the Pennine Hills, featuring deep dales, waterfalls, caves and quarries.

Literary Pilgrimages

Ayrshire: Robert Burns
(1759–96). Scotland's literary hero. The original copy of his *Auld Lang Syne* resides in the museum next door to the small white cottage where Burns was born in Alloway, near Ayr. During the last years of his short life, he lived in a small house in a back street of Dumfries which is now a museum. The Bachelor's Club in Tarbolton, a 17th-century thatched cottage where Burns and his friends formed a literary club in 1780, is now run by the National Trust for Scotland.

Dorset: Thomas Hardy
(1840–1928). Hardy was born in Higher Bockhampton where he wrote *Far From the Madding Crowd* and *Under The Greenwood Tree*. He later lived in Dorchester where he studied to be an architect, building his own house at Max Gate on the Wareham Road in the late-19th century. The Dorset County Museum in Dorchester (tel: 01305 262753) has a memorial collection devoted to Hardy. Hardy used The King's Arms, 30 High Street, Dorchester, an 18th-century coaching inn as a setting in the *Mayor of Caster-bridge*. He also wrote *Return of the Native* and *Tess of the d'Urbervilles* there.

Hampshire: Jane Austen
(1775–1817). The daughter of a Hampshire clergyman, she grew up in the village of Steventon. Between 1800 and 1817 she lived with her mother and sister in Chawton, Hampshire, where she wrote *Mansfield Park*, *Emma* and *Persuasion*. Now a museum (tel: 01420 83262), the house contains personal effects, letters and manuscripts. She also spent time in Bath and Lyme Regis, where she wrote much of *Persuasion* from Bay Cottage on The Parade. She is buried in Winchester Cathedral.

Kent: Charles Dickens
(1812–70). Most of his life was spent in Kent and London. The house where he grew up is at No 11 Ordnance Terrace, Chatham, Kent. Between 1837 and 1839 he lived with his wife and son at 48 Doughty Street, London WC1, now owned by the Dickens Fellowship and housing a wide range of personal belongings, manuscripts and books (tel: 0171-405 2127). In 1856 Dickens moved to Gad's Hill Place near Rochester (now a girls' school), where he died. Dickens was fond of the seaside town of Broadstairs and went there to live in Bleak House to write part of *David Copperfield*. He also spent time in the Royal Albion Hotel there.

The Lake District: William Wordsworth (1770–1850). In Main Street, Cockermouth, Cumbria, you can visit the house where Wordsworth was born in 1770, which contains some of his personal belongings (tel: 01900 924805). Dove Cottage, now a museum, can be found in Town End, Grasmere, Cumbria where he lived with his sister Dorothy during the most creative years of his life (tel: 015394 35003).

Nottingham: D. H. Lawrence
(1885–1930). The son of a Nottinghamshire miner, Lawrence grew up in a tiny house in Victoria Street, Eastwood, which has been

Top Tourist Attractions

London
Greater London's top 10 visitor attractions, according to the London Tourist Board's latest figures, are:
- British Museum (6 million)
- National Gallery (5 million)
- Madame Tussaud's (2.7 million)
- Tower of London (2.5 million)
- Tate Gallery (2 million)
- Chessington World of Adventures, Surrey (1.7 million)
- Natural History Museum (1.6 million)
- Science Museum (1.5 million)
- Victoria & Albert Museum (1.3 million)
- St Paul's Cathedral (1 million)

The National Trust
The 10 most visited NT properties are:
- Fountains Abbey & Studley Royal, Yorkshire
- Wakehurst Place, Sussex
- Stourhead Garden, Wiltshire
- Polesden Lacey, Surrey
- St Michael's Mount, Cornwall
- Sissinghurst Gardens, Kent
- Bodiam Castle, East Sussex
- Quarry Bank Mill, Cheshire
- Corfe Castle, Dorset
- Bodnant Garden, Conwy

Stately Homes
According to the Historic Houses Association (2 Chester Street, London SW1), Britain's most visited stately homes are:
- Windsor Castle
- Warwick Castle
- Hampton Court Palace
- Leeds Castle
- Blenheim Palace
- Chatsworth House
- Buckingham Palace

Theme/Leisure Parks
Top of the country's attractions include:
- Alton Towers, Staffordshire
- Blackpool Pleasure Beach, Lancashire
- Chessington World of Adventures, Surrey
- Funland and Laserbowl, London
- Lego Land, Windsor
- Palace Pier, Brighton
- Strathclyde Country Park
- Thorpe Park, Surrey

Blackpool Pleasure Beach has been Britain's most popular tourist attraction for many years. The British Museum, which doubled its visitors in the 1980s, is second.

restored to give an insight into his working-class childhood (the Lawrence Birthplace Museum, tel: 01773 763312). Nearby at 28 Garden Road is *Sons and Lovers* Cottage where the Lawrence family lived between 1887 and 1891.

South Wales: Dylan Thomas (1914–53). Thomas was born in the industrial town of Swansea in Wales, growing up in 5 Cwmdonkin Drive in the Uplands district. Follow the Dylan Thomas Uplands Trail and visit the boat house where he lived and worked in Laugharne (tel: 01994 427420).

Warwickshire: William Shakespeare (1564–1616). Stratford-upon-Avon is synonymous with Britain's greatest playwright. The Shakespeare Birthplace Trust (tel: 01789 204016) administers the following Tudor properties which have Shakespeare associations (an inclusive admission ticket is available): Shakespeare's Birthplace, Henley Street; Anne Hathaway's Cottage, Shottery, where Shakespeare's wife grew up; Hall's Croft, Old Town; New Place/Nash's House, Chapel Street; Mary Arden's House and the Shakespeare Countryside Museum, Wilmcote, the house where Shakespeare's mother grew up (and now a museum of rural life).

Yorkshire: The Brontë Sisters: Anne (1820–49), **Charlotte** (1816–55), **Emily** (1818–48). All were born in Thornton, West Yorkshire, although their family home was at the Parsonage in Haworth, West Yorkshire. Now a museum run by the Brontë Society, it has been restored to the way it was when this famous literary family lived here (1820–61) and contains some of their furniture, manuscripts and personal belongings (tel: 01535 642323).

Culture

Theatre

Britain's rich dramatic tradition is reflected in the excellent quality and range of its theatre. Although London is naturally the centre, most towns and cities have at least one theatre that hosts productions from their own theatre company or from touring companies that might include the Royal Shakespeare Company (RSC) and the National Theatre (NT).

Around half of London's theatres – totalling over 100, including fringe and suburban – are in the West End, centred around Shaftesbury Avenue and Covent Garden.

Tickets West End shows are popular so good tickets can be hard to obtain. If you cannot book a seat through the theatre box office, try Ticketmaster, 48 Leicester Square, WC2 (tel: 0171-344 4000; fax: 0171-915 0411) and First Call (tel: 0171-420 0000).

The Globe Theatre

Completed in June 1997, The Globe Theatre (tel: 0171-401 9919) is a reconstruction of Shakespeare's original Elizabethan theatre. It hosts a season of plays by the Bard, attempting to recreate the atmosphere of the original 16th-century performances. The Globe Exhibition (tel: 0171-928 6406) tells the story of Elizabethan theatre and the reconstruction of the Globe. Open 10am–5pm daily.

Avoid ticket touts unless you're prepared to pay several times a ticket's face value for a sold-out show. The SWET Ticket Booth at Leicester Square has unsold tickets available at half price on the day, from noon for matinées and from 2pm for evening performances. Be prepared to pay cash only and for long queues. Some theatres, such as the National, keep back some tickets to sell at the box office from 10am on the day.

Fringe For fringe theatre there is usually no problem in buying a ticket on the door. Consult the listings in London's weekly *Time Out* magazine or quality newspapers for what's on in the West End and at London's many fringe theatres.

Open-air plays On a summer's evening Shakespeare's plays are performed (weather permitting) at the open-air theatre in Regent's Park. Check London tourist offices for listings.

Barbican Arts Centre, Barbican, Silk Street, London EC2Y 8DS. Box office tel: 0171-638 8891. Fax: 0171-382 7270. Purpose-built concrete arts complex containing the Barbican Theatre, Concert Hall and The Pit which are well thought-out and comfortable with good acoustics, although somewhat sterile. Tube: Barbican.

National Theatre South Bank, London SE1 Tel: 0171-928 2033. Fax: 0171-620 1197. A wide range of modern and classical plays can be seen at three repertory theatres housed within this massive concrete structure on the banks of the Thames: the Olivier, the Lyttelton and the Cottesloe. Tube: Waterloo.

Royal Court Theatre Sloane Square, SW1. Tel: 0171-565 5000. Home to the English Stage Company, which produces plays by contemporary playwrights. Tube: Sloane Square.

Glyndebourne

For classical music lovers Glyndebourne is a highlight. Off the beaten track in Kent, it is not the most obvious site for a major international opera festival. But ever since an ex-Eton schoolmaster inherited a mansion there and built an opera house, it has attracted top artists from around the world and become a major event. Performances are in the evening ((bring your own Champagne and hampers) from May until October. Tel: (01273) 812321.

The Royal Shakespeare Theatre, Stratford-upon-Avon. Box office tel: (01789) 295623. 24-hour booking information, tel: (01789) 269191. The world-famous Royal Shakespeare Company (RSC) performs a repertoire of plays by the Bard at the Royal Shake-speare Theatre, while works by his contemporaries are staged across the river at the Swan Theatre (an Elizabethan-style playhouse). Nearby, at The Other Place, modern productions are performed. The RSC season at Stratford runs from March to September. The company also tours for a certain period of the year at the Barbican Centre in London.

It is always advisable to book tickets in advance, either from the box office or through commercial ticket agents in major cities. On weekdays, visitors can tour behind the scenes and see RSC costumes, props and paintings.

Classical Music

Many British cities have their own professional orchestras and promote seasons of concerts. These include the Royal Liverpool Philharmonic, The Hallé in Manchester and the City

of Birmingham Symphony Orchestra. In London there are the London Philharmonic and, at the Barbican Arts Centre, the London Symphony Orchestra.

In the summer the Scottish National Orchestra (SNO) presents a short Promenade season in Glasgow, while in London the BBC sponsors the Henry Wood Promenade Concerts (usually known as the Proms) at the Royal Albert Hall. The BBC also funds several of its own orchestras, the BBC Symphony and the BBC Scottish Symphony Orchestra.

Chamber music has considerable support in Britain and there are several professional string and chamber orchestras such as the English Chamber Orchestra and The Academy of Ancient Music.

London Venues
Barbican Hall
Silk Street, London EC2 (tel: 0171-588 8211) is home to the London Symphony Orchestra and the English Chamber Orchestra.
Royal Festival Hall
South Bank, London SE1 (tel: 0171-960 4242) is the capital's premier classical music venue. Also within the South Bank arts complex are the Queen Elizabeth Hall where chamber concerts and solos are performed, and the small Purcell Room.
Wigmore Hall
36 Wigmore Street, London W1 (tel: 0171-935 2141) is an intimate hall renowned for its lunchtime and Sunday chamber recitals.
Royal Albert Hall
Kensington Gore, London SW7 (tel: 0171-589 8212) comes alive in summer for the Proms.

Major venues outside London that attract world-class performers include:
St David's Hall, The Hayes, Cardiff (tel: 01222 878444)
Theatre Royal, 282 Hope Street, Glasgow (tel: 0141-332 9000).

Open-air concerts In summer, open-air evening concerts are performed at the Kenwood Lakeside Theatre, Hampstead Lane, NW3 (tel: 0171-973 3427).

Opera

The Royal Opera and the English National Opera perform regular seasons in London.

Royal Opera House The Royal Opera resides at the Royal Opera House in Covent Garden, London WC2. This is a magnificent theatre with a worldwide reputation for lavish performances in their original language. Dress is generally formal and tickets very expensive. The Opera House is closed for refurbishment and rescheduled to open in December 1999, but the Royal Ballet and Royal Opera are still touring the country.

London Coliseum Not far away in St Martin's Lane, WC2, this elegant Edwardian theatre is where the English National Opera (ENO) puts on less traditional performances in English. Tel: 0171-632 8300

Sadler's Wells In late-1998 London's Sadler's Wells Opera Company is scheduled to transfer from its temporary base at the Peacock Theatre, WC2 back to its home in Islington. The new-look Sadler's Wells Theatre will host a wide selection of dance and opera from top international artists. Tel: 0171-314 8800.

Welsh National Opera The Welsh are renowned for their fine voices. Most districts of Wales have a choir of some sort and there are more than 100 male voice choirs. The Welsh National Opera has an excellent reputation worldwide and performs regular seasons at the New Theatre in Cardiff (tel: 01222 878889) and at the Grand Theatre in Swansea (tel: 01792 475715).

Scottish Opera Scotland, too, has its own opera company, based at the Theatre Royal in Glasgow (0141-332 9000). It tours Scotland and the north of England, performing several short seasons in Edinburgh throughout the year.

Opera North Regional opera companies include Opera North, which is based in Leeds and tours the north of England.

Buxton In Buxton, Derbyshire, the Opera House hosts a major opera festival from July to early-August (tel: 01298 72190).

Ballet and Dance

As with opera, the major venues for ballet are the Royal Opera House (currently closed until December 1999) and the London Coliseum, home to the Royal Ballet and the Royal Festival Ballet respectively.

Birmingham Royal Ballet is based at the Hippodrome and tours nationwide. Tel: 0121-622 2555.

Northern Ballet Company Based at the Dance House in Manchester, the company tours throughout England (tel: 0161-237 9753).

Wales Leading ballet companies perform at the New Theatre in Cardiff (tel: 01222 878889) and the Grand Theatre in Swansea (tel: 01792 475715).

The Scottish Ballet tours Scotland and the UK. Tel: 0141-331 2931.

Jazz

There are many pubs and clubs that host live jazz, most notably in Camden, London; Bracknell, Berkshire; and Edinburgh. Ronnie Scott's (tel: 0171-439 0747) in the heart of London's Soho is Britain's best-known jazz venue, with a great atmosphere and top international artists.

Diary of Events

For details of events in the different regions of Britain, contact local tourist boards.

January
Burns Night (25 January) The birthday of Scotland's most famous poet, Robert Burns (1759–1796), celebrated with great festivity by the Scots.
London International Boat Show Earl's Court.

February
Chinese New Year Colourful celebrations in London and Manchester Chinatowns.
Crufts Dog Show Earl's Court, London. Pedigree dogs compete for the world's most coveted canine prize.
Shrove Tuesday "Pancake Day",

when the nation gorges on pancakes, originally the prelude to a fast until Easter.

March
Ideal Home Exhibition Earl's Court, London.
London Book Fair
Sheffield Chamber Music Festival

April
April Fool's Day (1 April) The day when people play practical jokes (at least until noon). Most national newspapers include a spoof story or two (which can be hard to separate from the absurdity of the real news).
Harrogate Spring Flower Show
Queen's Birthday (21 April) Her real birthday (as opposed to the official birthday in June) is celebrated with a gun salute in Hyde Park and at the Tower of London.
Royal Shakespeare Theatre in Stratford-upon-Avon opens the new season.

May
Bath International Festival Choral and chamber music.
Brighton Arts Festival
Chelsea Flower Show Major horticultural show in the grounds of the Royal Hospital, Chelsea, London.
Glyndebourne Festival Opera season opens.

Arts Festivals Around Britain

There are hundreds of arts festivals for music, dance, theatre and literature held throughout Britain each year.

Edinburgh The most famous of Britain's arts festivals (actually two simultaneous festivals, the official one and the "fringe"), this takes place for about 3 to 4 weeks in August and September. The city also hosts jazz, folk and film and TV festivals at other times during the year. Tel: 0131-473 2001.

Glasgow hosts the Mayfest in May as well as holding its own jazz and folk festivals.

Wales The Royal National Eisteddfod of Wales dates back to 1176 and is the most important of the hundreds of *eisteddfodau* which take place in Wales annually. It is a festival devoted to music and literature in the Welsh language and is held for a week in August in a different venue each year.

The Llangollen International

Eisteddfod, which takes place in the picturesque town of Llangollen in north Wales each July, was established after World War II to bring nations together in a festival of song, dance and music.

Countrywide Other notable arts festivals are held at Chichester, Brighton, Buxton, Malvern, Salisbury, Harrogate and York. Music festivals are at Aldeburgh, Cheltenham, Newbury, Stratford and Bath.

Mayfest, Glasgow
Newbury Spring Festival
Nottingham Festival
Perth Festival of Arts

June
Aldeburgh Festival of Arts & Music
Beating Retreat in Horse Guards Parade, Whitehall, London. Military bands.
Biggin Hill International Air Fair Biggin Hill, Kent.
Bournemouth Music Festival
Dickens Festival Rochester, Kent
Glastonbury Pilgrimage Abbey Ruins, Glastonbury, Somerset.
Grosvenor House Antiques Fair Grosvenor House Hotel, Park Lane, London.
Royal Academy of Arts Summer Exhibition Burlington House, Piccadilly, London. Large exhibition of work by professional and amateur artists running until August. All works for sale.
Royal Highland Show Ingliston, Newbridge, Edinburgh.
Trooping the Colour Horse Guards Parade, Whitehall, London. The Queen's official birthday celebrations.

July
Birmingham International Jazz Festival
Cambridge Festival
Cheltenham International Festival of Music
Llangollen International Musical Eisteddfod
Royal Agricultural Show, Stoneleigh Park, Warwickshire.
Royal Tournament: Earl's Court, London. Military displays.
Proms Classical concerts at the Royal Albert Hall, London.

August
Edinburgh International Festival
Edinburgh Military Tattoo Edinburgh Castle.
Great British Beer Festival Venues vary.
Notting Hill Carnival (bank holiday weekend) Ladbroke

Grove, London. Colourful West Indian street carnival with exciting costumes, live steel bands, reggae music and hundreds of thousands of revellers.
Royal National Eisteddfod of Wales

September
Cardiff Festival
Farnborough Air Show Every two years.
Salisbury Festival

October
Birmingham International Film and TV Festival
Cheltenham Festival of Literature
Motor Show Earl's Court, London. Every two years.
National Gaelic Mod Strathclyde, Scotland.
Norwich Jazz Festival
Stratford Mop Fair Stratford-upon-Avon.
Swansea Music Festival

November
Cardiff Festival of Music
Christmas Lights Switched on in Oxford and Regent Streets, London.
Guy Fawkes Day (5th) Firework celebrations to commemorate the failure of Guy Fawkes to blow up the Houses of Parliament in 1605.
London Film Festival: South Bank, London SE1.
London to Brighton Veteran Car Run (1st Sunday) Hundreds of veteran cars and their proud owners start from Hyde Park and limp to Brighton.
Lord Mayor's Show Grand procession from the Guildhall in The City, London.
Military International Tattoo NEC, Birmingham.
State Opening of Parliament: House of Lords, Westminster, London.

December
Hogmanay New Year's Eve revels in Scotland.

Shopping

What to Buy

If you are looking for something typically British to take back home, you will not have to look very far.

Cloth and wool Probably Britain's most famous speciality, top-quality wools and clothes worth seeking out include the wonderful hand-knitted woollens from the Scottish islands of Shetland, Arran and Fair Isle, and the Guernsey and Jersey sweaters of the Channel Islands. There is fine Harris Tweed cloth from Lewis. You can even have a kilt made in your own clan tartan. The scenic Ochil Hills north of Edinburgh have a long tradition of woollen production where visitors can "do" The Scottish Mill Trail.

Another important centre for the cloth and wool industry is Bradford through which 90 per cent of the wool trade passed in the 19th century. The area's many mill shops are a bargain-hunter's paradise where lengths of fabric, fine yarns and fleeces from the Yorkshire Dales can be bought. Some mills give guided tours. The British Wool Centre in Clayton has a historic display and items on sale from the British Wool Collection. Wales, too, has many mills that produce colourful tapestry cloth in striking traditional Celtic designs.

Shoes and lace Nottingham is the traditional manufacturing centre for these. At the Lace Hall, High Pavement, you can watch lace being made, learn about its history and, of course, buy gifts.

Groceries

The small, friendly neighbourhood baker, butcher and greengrocer have generally fallen victim to large supermarkets. Stores such as Tesco and Sainsbury occupy huge out-of-town sites and dominate the British groceries market.

However, hundreds of family-run food companies still produce local specialities worth sampling, from Scotland's haggis to farmhouse cheeses.

Some of Britain's finest consumables (including hams, sausages, preserves, biscuits and cakes) are sold at delicatessens, farm shops and smokeries nationwide, the most renowned of which are Scotland's producers of smoked salmon and trout. Some of these supply their produce for export, so if you develop a taste for smoked salmon you can continue to enjoy it when you return home.

Cakes, fudge and home-made toffees are to be found in most tourist spots, and a few make gifts that travel well. Some regional specialities to look out for include: chocolates filled with Scotch whisky, Bakewell tarts, Eccles cakes, Kendal mint cake and Kentish cobnuts in chocolate.

For good-quality groceries, Marks & Spencer's food departments, in most large towns, are a safe bet (if a bit pricey) especially for pre-cooked meals. For Britain's food at its finest, your first port of call should undoubtedly be Fortnum & Mason, Piccadilly, London W1, an Aladdin's cave of mouthwatering goodies. Harrods has a renowned Food Hall as well, with spectacular displays of cheeses, wonderful breads and fresh seafood.

Suits The flagship of Britain's bespoke tailoring industry is Savile Row in London where gentlemen come from all over the world to have their suits crafted. Other outlets for traditional British attire are Burberry's (for raincoats), Aquascutum, Austin Reed and Jaeger which have branches in Piccadilly in London and in many department stores in cities nationwide.

Fashion Britain has a thriving fashion market, with its heart in London. Its top designers (including Caroline Charles, Jasper Conran, Katharine Hamnett, Bruce Oldfield, Paul Smith and Vivienne Westwood) are the height of haute couture and world famous. Many top international designers can also be found in London's Knightsbridge and Mayfair, and to a lesser extent in department stores nationwide. For quality everyday clothing Marks & Spencer's stores have a longstanding reputation.

China and porcelain Top-price china, glass and silver items can be found in Regent Street and Mayfair in London at exclusive shops such as Waterford, Wedgwood, Thomas Goode, Aspreys and Garrards. Stoke-on-Trent (in "the Potteries", Staffordshire) is the home of the great china and porcelain houses, including Wedgwood, Minton, Royal Doulton, Spode, Coalport and Royal Stafford. All these have visitor centres where you can often pick up some real bargains. You can also visit Portmeirion in North Wales, the Caithness Glass factory at Wick in Scotland and Dartington Crystal at Great Torrington in Devon.

Jewellery The centre for British jewellery production is in Hockley, Birmingham, an industry that developed here in the 18th century along with other forms of metal working such as brass founding and gun smithing. Today more than 200 jewellery manufacturers and 50 silversmiths are based here.

Perfumes English flower perfumes make a delightful gift. The most exclusive of these come from Floris in Jermyn Street, and Penhaligons in Wellington Street, London. The Cotswold Perfumery in the picturesque village of Bourton-on-the-Water, Gloucestershire, makes its own perfumes.

Antiques If you are coming to Britain to look for antiques it is worth getting in touch with the London and Provincial Antique Dealers' Association (LAPADA), 535 King's Road, London, SW10, tel: 0171-823 3511. It runs an up-to-date computer information service on the antiques situation throughout the country. A number of antique fairs are held nationwide throughout the year and many towns such as Bath, Harrogate and Brighton have antique centres and markets.

Consumables British delights that are easy to take home include Twinings or Jacksons tea, Scotch whisky and shortbread and numerous brands of chocolate. Benticks is famous for its after-dinner mints, Thornton's produces fine confectionery made from fresh ingredients while, on a more popular level, Cadbury's is a national favourite.

Britain is particularly proud of its conserves, jams, honeys, pickles and mustards (not least the famous anchovy spread, Gentleman's Relish). Local delicatessens and farm shops nationwide are often worth exploring for edible gifts.

Crafts Almost every town has a street market once a week where cheap clothes and domestic ware can be bought and there may also be a good presence of local craft. There are many workshops in rural areas of Britain where potters, woodturners, leatherworkers, candlemakers and other craftsmen can be seen producing their wares. A free map of these can be obtained from the Crafts Council, 44a Pentonville Road, London N1, tel: 0171-930 4811.

Books University towns are the best source of books. Blackwells in Oxford and the many branches of Heffers in Cambridge are equally good for publications in English and most prominent foreign languages. Waterstones branches nationwide are popular, and Foyles in London has several crammed floors. Serious book lovers should head for Hay-on-Wye, which has over 25 second-hand bookshops.

Gifts Some of the best places to seek out tasteful presents to take home are museum gift shops (especially the one at London's British Museum) and National Trust shops. Naturally British, 13 New Row, London WC2 supplies a wide selection of British goods in natural materials.

Export Procedures

VAT (value added tax) is a standard sales tax of 17.5 per cent that is added to virtually all goods except food and books. It is generally included in the price marked on the item. Most large department stores and smaller gift shops operate a scheme to refund this tax to visitors, but often require that more than a minimum amount (usually £50) is spent. To get a refund you need to fill in a form from the store, have it stamped by Customs when you leave the country and then post it back to the store or hand it in to a cash refund booth at the airport. Provided you leave the country with the goods within three weeks of purchase you will be refunded the tax less an administration fee.

Sport

Tickets

Tickets for major sporting events can be purchased from commercial agents such as Ticketmaster (tel: 0171-344 4000) and First Call (tel: 0171-420 0000).

Spectator Sports

Football

Also called soccer, this is the country's most popular spectator and participant sport. The professional season runs from August until May. England and Scotland have separate football associations (FAs), with four divisions in England (top of which is the Premier League) and three in Scotland.

Most Premier League matches can be watched only on satellite TV. The climax of the season is the English FA Cup played at Wembley in London and the Scottish FA Cup at Hampden Park in Glasgow. Wembley also

plays host to many international games. League matches usually start at 3pm on Saturday or Sunday and 7pm midweek.

For details of Premier League fixtures, tel: 0171-976 7886. For other England matches, tel: (01253) 729 421. For Scottish fixtures: 0141-332 6372.

Rugby

Rugby is said to have been invented when one of the pupils of Rugby public school picked up the ball and ran in a game of football early in the 19th century. It is certainly a national institution today, with two types (Union, played in Scotland, Wales and predominantly the South of England) and League (the northern game).

The Rugby Union season runs from September to May, with matches played at Twickenham, Murrayfield and Cardiff Arms Park. One of the highlights of the season is the Five Nations Championship, a knock-out between England, Ireland, Scotland, Wales and France.

Rugby League, formerly for amateurs only, is now professional and several players have defected from Union. Played in summer, it culminates in the Super League final at Old Trafford in September.

For details of Rugby Union fixtures, tel: 0181-892 8161.

Wimbledon Tennis Championship

The Wimbledon fortnight is one of Britain's best-loved sporting highlights, attracting nearly 400,000 spectators in person and millions of television viewers worldwide. It takes place in June/July on the immaculate grass courts at the All England Club in Wimbledon, southwest London.

Most tickets are allocated by postal ballot (send a self-addressed envelope to The All England Lawn Tennis Club, PO

Box 98, Wimbledon, London SW19 5AE by the end of the previous year). For details, tel: 0181-944 1066. But a few tickets are kept back for some courts if you are prepared to camp out the night before, and spare seats are always to be had late-afternoon for some entertaining doubles matches. Expect to pay more than 10p per strawberry if you are desperate enough to want strawberries and cream.

For Rugby League, tel: 0113-232 9111.

Cricket

Quintessentially British, cricket can be seen on village greens up and down the country throughout the summer. Usually a light-hearted performance, it is played by very amateurish amateurs, with a visit to the pub a ritual at the close of play.

Britain's professional teams compete in a national championship, with 3 and 4-day matches taking place all summer. But one of the most entertaining ways to be initiated into the intricacies of the game is to go along to a pacier, less serious one-day match.

On an international level, every season England plays a 5-day Test Match against touring teams from Australia, India, New Zealand, Pakistan, Sri Lanka or the West Indies. These take place at half a dozen grounds in Britain including Lords and the Oval in London, Edgbaston in the Midlands and Headingly in Leeds. Tickets are sought-after and sell well in advance.

The Marylebone Cricket Club (MCC), based at Lords cricket ground in St John's Wood, north London, is the governing body of the world game. Tel: 0171-289 1611.

Equestrian Sports

Horse racing is a major British industry and takes two forms, flat racing and steeplechasing or hurdle racing.

Flat racing takes place between March and early November. The most important races are the Derby and Oaks at Epsom, the St Leger at Doncaster and the 1,000 and 2,000 Guineas held at Newmarket. The Royal Ascot meeting is quite a spectacle and a major social event where race-goers dress up in their finest regalia in the presence of the Queen.

Steeplechasing and hurdle

The Sporting Calendar

March
Football Coca Cola Cup Final, Wembley, London.
Racing Cheltenham Gold Cup, Cheltenham, Gloucestershire.
University Boat Race Oxford and Cambridge, on the Thames between Putney and Mortlake, London.

April
Horse Racing: Grand National Race Meeting, Aintree, Liverpool.
London Marathon, Greenwich Park, London.
Rugby Union County Championship Final, Twickenham. Five Nations Cup.

May
Cycling The Milk Race, from Westminster Bridge, London.
Football FA Cup Final, Wembley.
Golf Benson & Hedges International Open, Oxfordshire.
Horse Trials Badminton, Avon.
Horse Racing 1,000 and 2,000 Guineas Stakes, Newmarket, Suffolk.
Horse Show Royal Windsor, Home Park, Windsor.
Polo Queen's Cup.
Rugby League Silk Cut Challenge Cup Final.
Snooker World Championships.

June
Cycling London to Brighton cycle ride.
Horse Racing Royal Ascot, Ascot, Berkshire.
Horse Racing The Derby, Epsom, Surrey.
Horse Racing The Oaks, Epsom, Surrey.
Tennis Stella Artois Tournament, Queen's Club, London.
Tennis Wimbledon Lawn Tennis Championships,

All England Lawn Tennis & Croquet Club. The world's most famous tennis tournament, held in a southwest London suburb.

July
Show Jumping Royal International Horse Show, Hickstead.
Motor Racing British Grand Prix, Silverstone, Northamptonshire.
Rowing Henley Royal Regatta Week, Henley-on-Thames.

August
Highland Games Dunoon, Perth & Aboyne, Scotland.
Horse Racing Glorious Goodwood
Polo Cheltenham Cup
Sailing Cowes Week Regatta, Isle of Wight.

September
Braemar Royal Highland Games, Balmoral, Scotland.
Cricket Nat West Trophy final, Lord's Grounds, London.
British Superbike Championship Silverstone and Donnington.
Show Jumping Horse of the Year Show, Wembley Arena, London.

October
Golf Dunhill Cup Final, St Andrew's, Fife.
Golf: World Matchplay, Wentworth, Surrey.
Show Jumping Horse of the Year Show, Wembley Arena, London.

November
Lombard RAC Car Rally, Harrogate, North Yorkshire.
RAC London–Brighton Vintage Car Run.

December
Olympia International Show Jumping, Olympia, London.

racing take place between September and early June. The National Hunt Festival meeting at Cheltenham in March is the most important event where the highlight is the Gold Cup. The most famous steeplechase, watched avidly and gambled on by millions in Britain, is the Grand National held at Aintree in Liverpool.

Show jumping is the equestrian sport every young rider aspires to. Major events are the Royal International Horse Show at the NEC in Birmingham, the Horse of the Year Show at Wembley, London, and the Olympia International Show Jumping Championships in London.

Polo matches take place at Windsor Great Park or Cowdray Park, Midhurst, West Sussex on summer weekends. The governing body is the Hurlingham Polo Association (tel: 01869 350044).

Horse Trials are held in spring and autumn nationwide. The major 3-day events (cross-country, show jumping and dressage) are held at Badminton, Windsor, Bramham, Burghley and Chatsworth.

The main equestrian body in Britain is The British Horse Society which governs the Pony Club and Riding Club. It also runs the British Equestrian Centre at Stoneleigh in Warwickshire, where it is based. For further information, tel: (01926) 707700.

Athletics

Athletics are governed by the Amateur Athletics Association (AAA), with the main national sports centre for athletics at Crystal Palace, south London (tel: 0181-778 0131).

Highland Games are held in Scotland between August and September when they coincide with the annual gatherings of clans. Activities include tossing the caber and throwing the

hammer as well as dancing and piping competitions. The best known games are at Braemar, near Balmoral, in September; these are sometimes attended by the Royal Family. There are also gatherings at Aboyne, Argyllshire and Cowal.

Golf

Without question, the most important national golfing event is the Open Championship which takes place every July. Other prestigious tournaments include the the Ryder Cup for professionals and the Walker Cup for amateurs.

For information on dates and venues of tournaments contact the Professional Golfer's Association (PGA), Apollo House, The Belfry, Sutton Coldfield, tel: (01675) 470333.

Motor Racing

The heart of motor racing worldwide, Britain has produced a number of World Champions, from Mike Hawthorn and James Hunt to Nigel Mansell and Damon Hill. The British Grand Prix, held at Silverstone in July, is the highlight of the British motor racing calendar. But Britain's race tracks (most notably Brands Hatch and Donnington) also host a range of race meetings, from touring cars to Formula Ford. Rallying is also very popular.

Details of races from the Royal Automobile Club (RAC), tel: (01753) 681736.

Participant Sport

Most towns have a sports centre and swimming pool. There are also plenty of facilities for golf and tennis, or for the more outward bound, climbing, sailing and windsurfing.

For information on public sports and leisure facilities in each area you can contact the local council's leisure services department. Alternatively, get in

touch with the English Sports Council, 16 Upper Woburn Place, London WC1H 0QP (tel: 0171-273 1500).

The British Sports Association for the Disabled was founded in 1961 to encourage and provide opportunities for people with disabilities. For further information, contact the Council at 13 Brunswick Place, London N1 (tel: 0171-383 7277).

Horse Riding

If you want to go out for a hack in the countryside, there are plenty of public riding stables in rural areas. However, most stables do not let riders out unaccompanied. Pony trekking is particularly popular on Dartmoor, Exmoor, in the New Forest and in Wales.

For further information, contact The British Horse Society, Stoneleigh Deer Park, Kenilworth CV8 2XZ (tel: 01926 707700).

Golf

There are hundreds of courses around the country that welcome visitors. Wales alone has over 100. So does Scotland, where even the most famous are open to the public. St Andrew's, however, is so much in demand that games are subject to a lottery. Courses close to London are generally heavily booked.

Watersports

Britain offers plenty of opportunities to those interested in sailing, particularly on the south coast and around Pembrokeshire, southwest Wales, but also on the lakes and lochs of the north of England and Scotland. There are excellent facilities for canoeing, windsurfing, jet skiing and boating too on Britain's many inland waters.

There are National Water Sports Centres at Great Cumbrae Isle, Firth of Clyde, Scotland and Holme Pierrepont, Nottinghamshire.

Further Reading

Good Companions

Artist's London by David Piper, Fascinating images of London over the ages.

Cider with Rosie by Laurie Lee. Memories of an idyllic youth in Gloucestershire.

A Concise History of Scotland by Fitzroy MacLean.

The Concise Pepys by Samuel Pepys. Read a first-hand account of the Great Fire of London and find out about daily life in 17th-century England.

Four Scottish Journeys by Andrew Eames.

A Guide through the District of the Lakes by William Wordsworth. Lyrical descriptions of the poet's beloved Lake District.

A History of Modern Wales by David Williams.

Hound of the Baskervilles by Sir Arthur Conan Doyle. Sherlock Holmes explores the mystery on the moors.

How Green was my Valley by Richard Llewellyn. Story of a Welsh mining community.

Jamaica Inn by Daphne du Maurier. A tale of Cornish "wreckers", who loot shipwrecks.

A Journey to the Western Isles by Dr Samuel Johnson and **James Boswell's Journal of a Tour to the Hebrides**. Two accounts of the same trip made in the 18th century by the great lexicographer and his biographer.

London: A Concise History by Geoffrey Trease. Good illustrated history.

Lorna Doone by R.D. Blackmore. The story of a tragic heroine and her lawless family brings Exmoor landscapes to life.

The Mabinogion by Gywn Jones and Thomas Jones (translators). Eleven medieval stories from Wales.

Mary, Queen of Scots by Antonia Fraser.

Mrs Dalloway by Virginia Woolf. A day-in-the-life of an Edwardian matron in London.

Oliver Twist by Charles Dickens. The classic tale of Victorian pickpockets in London's East End.

On the Black Hill by Bruce Chatwin.

The Oxford Companion to the Literature of Wales by Meic Stephens.

Pride and Prejudice by Jane Austen.

The Prime of Miss Jean Brodie by Muriel Spark. The story of a strong-willed Edinburgh schoolmistress in the 1930s.

A Shropshire Lad by A.E. Housman. Poems on the themes of Shropshire country life, and the life of a soldier.

Spectacle of Empire by James Morris. Popular history of the British Empire and its decline.

Tilly by Catherine Cookson. Set in Durham, the story of a girl born into a poor family in Victorian times.

Tour Through the Whole Island of Great Britain by Daniel Defoe.

Under Milkwood by Dylan Thomas.

Vanishing Cornwall by Daphne du Maurier. A perceptive view of the changing face of Cornwall.

Waverley by Sir Walter Scott. A gripping tale of the Highland clans at the time of the Jacobite rising of 1745.

Westward Ho! by Charles Kingsley. Heroic tale of West Country seafarers.

The Woodlanders by Thomas Hardy. Rural life and high emotions in the Wessex countryside.

Wuthering Heights by Emily Brontë. Passion and repression on the brooding Yorkshire Moors.

Other Insight Guides

Three types of Insight Guide are designed to meet the needs of every traveller.

The 190-title **Insight Guides** series includes books on *London, Scotland, Wales, Oxford, Glasgow, Edinburgh* and *The Channel Islands.*

The 110-title **Insight Pocket Guides** series offers personal recommendations and a full-size map; titles include *South-East England, London* and *Scotland.*

The 97-title **Insight Compact Guides** series provides the ideal portable, fully illustrated guidebook to specific areas. Twenty titles cover every tourist area in the UK, from Cornwall to the Scottish Highlands.

ART & PHOTO CREDITS

INSIGHT GUIDE
GREAT BRITAIN

Maps **Lovell Johns**
Cartographic Editor **Zoë Goodwin**
Production **Mohammed Dar**
Design Consultant **Klaus Geisler**
Picture Research **Hilary Genin**

Index

The Insight Approach

The book you are holding is part of the world's largest range of guidebooks. Its purpose is to help you have the most valuable travel experience possible, and we try to achieve this by providing not only information about countries, regions and cities but also genuine insight into their history, culture, institutions and people.

Since the first Insight Guide – to Bali – was published in 1970, the series has been dedicated to the proposition that, with insight into a country's people and culture, visitors can both enhance their own experience and be accepted more easily by their hosts. Now, in a world where ethnic hostilities and nationalist conflicts are all too common, such attempts to increase understanding between peoples are more important than ever.

Insight Guides:
Essentials for understanding
Because a nation's past holds the key to its present, each Insight Guide kicks off with lively history chapters. These are followed by magazine-style essays on culture and daily life. This essential background information gives readers the necessary context for using the main Places section, with its comprehensive run-down on things worth seeing and doing.

Finally, a listings section contains all the information you'll need on travel, hotels, restaurants and opening times.

As far as possible, we rely on local writers and specialists to ensure that information is authoritative. The pictures, for which Insight Guides have become so celebrated, are just as important. Our photojournalistic approach aims not only to illustrate a destination but also to communicate visually and directly to readers life as it is lived by the locals. The series has grown to almost 200 titles.

Compact Guides:
The "great little guides"
As invaluable as such background information is, it isn't always fun to carry an Insight Guide through a crowded souk or up a church tower. Could we, readers asked, distil the key reference material into a slim volume for on-the-spot use?

Our response was to design Compact Guides as an entirely new series, with original text carefully cross-referenced to detailed maps and more than 200 photographs. In essence, they're miniature encyclopedias, concise and comprehensive, displaying reliable and up-to-date information in an accessible way. There are almost 100 titles.

Pocket Guides:
A local host in book form
However wide-ranging the information in a book, human beings still value the personal touch. Our editors are often asked the same questions. Where do *you* go to eat? What do *you* think is the best beach? What would *you* recommend if I have only three days? We invited our local correspondents to act as "substitute hosts" by revealing their preferred walks and trips, listing the restaurants they go to and structuring a visit into a series of timed itineraries.

The result: our Pocket Guides, complete with full-size fold-out maps. These 100-plus titles help readers plan a trip precisely, particularly if their time is short.

Exploring with Insight:
A valuable travel experience
In conjunction with co-publishers all over the world, we print in up to 10 languages, from German to Chinese, from Danish to Russian. But our aim remains simple: to enhance your travel experience by combining our expertise in guidebook publishing with the on-the-spot knowledge of our correspondents.

66 I was first drawn to the
Insight Guides by the
excellent "Nepal" volume.
I can think of no book
which so effectively
captures the essence of
a country. Out of these
pages leaped the Nepal
I know – the captivating
charm of a people and
their culture. I've since
discovered and enjoyed
the entire Insight Guide
series. Each volume deals
with a country in the
same sensitive depth,
which is nowhere more
evident than in the
superb photography. 99

Sir Edmund Hillary

The World of Insight Guides

400 books in three complementary series cover every major destination in every continent.

Insight Guides

Alaska
Alsace
Amazon Wildlife
American Southwest
Amsterdam
Argentina
Atlanta
Athens
Australia
Austria
Bahamas
Bali
Baltic States
Bangkok
Barbados
Barcelona
Bay of Naples
Beijing
Belgium
Belize
Berlin
Bermuda
Boston
Brazil
Brittany
Brussels
Budapest
Buenos Aires
Burgundy
Burma (Myanmar)
Cairo
Calcutta
California
Canada
Caribbean
Catalonia
Channel Islands
Chicago
Chile
China
Cologne
Continental Europe
Corsica
Costa Rica
Crete
Crossing America
Cuba
Cyprus
Czech & Slovak Republics
Delhi, Jaipur, Agra
Denmark
Dresden
Dublin
Düsseldorf
East African Wildlife
East Asia
Eastern Europe
Ecuador
Edinburgh
Egypt
Finland
Florence
Florida
France
Frankfurt
French Riviera
Gambia & Senegal
Germany
Glasgow

Gran Canaria
Grèat Barrier Reef
Great Britain
Greece
Greek Islands
Hamburg
Hawaii
Hong Kong
Hungary
Iceland
India
India's Western Himalaya
Indian Wildlife
Indonesia
Ireland
Israel
Istanbul
Italy
Jamaica
Japan
Java
Jerusalem
Jordan
Kathmandu
Kenya
Korea
Lisbon
Loire Valley
London
Los Angeles
Madeira
Madrid
Malaysia
Mallorca & Ibiza
Malta
Marine Life in the South
  China Sea
Melbourne
Mexico
Mexico City
Miami
Montreal
Morocco
Moscow
Munich
Namibia
Native America
Nepal
Netherlands
New England
New Orleans
New York City
New York State
New Zealand
Nile
Normandy
Northern California
Northern Spain
Norway
Oman & the UAE
Oxford
Old South
Pacific Northwest
Pakistan
Paris
Peru
Philadelphia
Philippines
Poland
Portugal
Prague

Provence
Puerto Rico
Rajasthan
Rhine
Rio de Janeiro
Rockies
Rome
Russia
St Petersburg
San Francisco
Sardinia
Scotland
Seattle
Sicily
Singapore
South Africa
South America
South Asia
South India
South Tyrol
Southeast Asia
Southeast Asia Wildlife
Southern California
Southern Spain
Spain
Sri Lanka
Sweden
Switzerland
Sydney
Taiwan
Tenerife
Texas
Thailand
Tokyo
Trinidad & Tobago
Tunisia
Turkey
Turkish Coast
Tuscany
Umbria
US National Parks East
US National Parks West
Vancouver
Venezuela
Venice
Vienna
Vietnam
Wales
Washington DC
Waterways of Europe
Wild West
Yemen

Insight Pocket Guides

Aegean Islands★
Algarve★
Alsace
Amsterdam★
Athens★
Atlanta★
Bahamas★
Baja Peninsula★
Bali★
Bali Bird Walks
Bangkok★
Barbados★
Barcelona★
Bavaria★
Beijing★
Berlin★

Bermuda★
Bhutan★
Boston★
British Columbia★
Brittany★
Brussels★
Budapest &
  Surroundings★
Canton★
Chiang Mai★
Chicago★
Corsica★
Costa Blanca★
Costa Brava★
Costa del Sol/Marbella★
Costa Rica★
Côte d'Azur★
Crete★
Denmark
Fiji★
Florence★
Florida★
Florida Keys★
Gran Canaria★
Hawaii★
Hong Kong★
Hungary
Ibiza★
Ireland★
Ireland's Southwest★
Israel★
Istanbul★
Jakarta★
Jamaica★
Kathmandu Bikes &
  Hikes★
Kuala Lumpur★
Lisbon★
Loire Valley★
London★
Macau★
Madrid★
Malacca
Maldives
Mallorca★
Malta★
Mexico City★
Miami★
Milan★
Montreal★
Morocco★
Moscow
Munich★
Nepal★
New Delhi
New Orleans★
New York City★
New Zealand★
Northern California★
Oslo/Bergen★
Paris★
Penang★
Phuket★
Prague★
Provence★
Puerto Rico★
Quebec★
Rhodes★
Rome★
Sabah★

St Petersburg★
San Francisco★
Sardinia
Scotland★
Seville★
Seychelles★
Sicily★
Sikkim
Singapore★
Southeast England
Southern California★
Southern Spain★
Sri Lanka★
Sydney★
Tenerife★
Thailand★
Tibet★
Toronto★
Tunisia★
Turkish Coast★
Tuscany★
Venice★
Vienna★
Vietnam★
Yogyakarta
Yucatan Peninsula★

**★ = Insight Pocket Guides
with Pull out Maps**

Insight Compact Guides

Algarve
Amsterdam
Bahamas
Bali
Bangkok
Barbados
Barcelona
Beijing
Belgium
Berlin
Brittany
Brussels
Budapest
Burgundy
Copenhagen
Costa Brava
Costa Rica
Crete
Cyprus
Czech Republic
Denmark
Dominican Republic
Dublin
Egypt
Finland
Florence
Gran Canaria
Greece
Holland
Hong Kong
Ireland
Israel
Italian Lakes
Italian Riviera
Jamaica
Jerusalem
Lisbon
Madeira
Mallorca
Malta

Milan
Moscow
Munich
Normandy
Norway
Paris
Poland
Portugal
Prague
Provence
Rhodes
Rome
Salzburg
St Petersburg
Singapore
Switzerland
Sydney
Tenerife
Thailand
Turkey
Turkish Coast
Tuscany

UK regional titles:
Bath & Surroundings
Cambridge & East
  Anglia
Cornwall
Cotswolds
Devon & Exmoor
Edinburgh
Lake District
London
New Forest
North York Moors
Northumbria
Oxford
Peak District
Scotland
Scottish Highlands
Shakespeare Country
Snowdonia
South Downs
York
Yorkshire Dales

USA regional titles:
Boston
Cape Cod
Chicago
Florida
Florida Keys
Hawaii: Maui
Hawaii: Oahu
Las Vegas
Los Angeles
Martha's Vineyard &
  Nantucket
New York
San Francisco
Washington D.C.
Venice
Vienna
West of Ireland